교원임용시험 전공영어 대비 [제1판]

NEW Build Up

박현수 영어교육론

Ⅳ-1 문제은행 [기입형]

Guideline for Pre-service Teachers

박현수 편저

박문각

Preface

"많은 것을 읽는 것이 아니라, 올바르게 선택된 것을 반복해서 읽는 것이 중요하다."
—Arthur Schopenhauer(1788~1860)

임용시험을 준비하는 여정은 마라톤과도 같습니다. 호흡과 페이스 조절이 절대적으로 요구되며, 때로는 혼란스럽고 조급해지고, 내가 제대로 가고 있는지조차 확신이 서지 않는 순간들이 반복될 것입니다. 그리고 끝이 보이지 않는 그 순간순간이 여러분을 시험할지도 모릅니다.

특히 영어교육론처럼 방대한 내용과 깊이를 요구하는 영역에서는 '어디까지 해야 하나'보다 '무엇에 집중해야 하는가'라는 질문이 끝없이 따라붙습니다. 이럴 때야말로, 쇼펜하우어의 말처럼, "많은 것을 읽는 것"보다 **"올바르게 선택된 것을 반복해서 읽는 것"**이 중요해집니다. 공부가 버겁게 느껴질 때마다 쇼펜하우어의 말을 떠올려 보시기 바랍니다.

이 책 『Build-up IV』는 그 고민 앞에 서 있는 여러분에게 작은 나침반이 되어 주고자 기획되었습니다. '문제은행'이라는 형식을 따르고 있지만 단순히 문제를 푸는 책이 아닌, 영어교육론의 핵심 개념을 반복적으로 학습하고, 기출과 출제 경향을 분석하며, 여러분 자신의 약점을 파악하고 전략적으로 2026년 중등 임용 영어교육론 실전에 대비할 수 있는 기반을 마련하는 데 목적을 두었습니다.

모든 것을 다 하려고 하면, 결국 아무것도 제대로 할 수 없습니다. 슬럼프가 찾아올 때는 방향을 새로 잡아야 한다는 신호일 수 있습니다. **'선택과 집중'**을 통해 지금 나에게 꼭 필요한 것, 시험장에서 요구되는 사고력과 응용력, 그리고 미래의 교실에서 필요한 교사로서의 역량을 스스로 판단하고 갈고 닦을 수 있도록 『Build-up IV』가 실질적인 길잡이가 되어 주기를 바랍니다. 그리고 이 책이 여러분의 꿈을 단순한 이상이 아닌 현실 속 성취로 바꾸는 데 기여할 수 있기를 진심으로 바랍니다.

이번 『New Build-up IV』(제1판)은 2023~2024년 전국 모의고사와 9~10월 실전 모의고사, 11월 최종 모의고사를 기반으로 구성했으며, 기출분석에서 익힌 전략이 실전형 문항에 자연스럽게 연결될 수 있도록 Main Topic & Sub-topic 구조로 정리했습니다. 또한 두 권의 분권 체제로 구성하여 Part 1(기입형)에서는 **핵심 개념의 반복을 통한 기입형 전략 훈련**을, Part 2(서술형)에서는 **정보 선택력, 감점 회피 전략, 명확한 채점을 위한 답안 구성 능력**을 집중적으로 훈련할 수 있도록 설계했습니다.

이 책이 나오기까지 함께 고민하고 편집 구성을 도와주신 **유다현 선생님**께 깊은 감사를 전합니다. 또한, 우리 보석 같은 조교들—**인서, 수진과 상은, 준현 미카엘, 승희**—여러분과 함께하는 시간 덕분에 연구실이 더욱 밝고 단단해졌습니다.

한결같은 지원을 아끼지 않으시는 **유희태 선생님**, 그리고 여러분의 영원한 멘토, **앤드류 채 선생님**께도 깊이 감사드립니다. 마지막으로, 이 책의 출간을 위해 시간을 다투며 애써주신 **변수경 편집위원**께도 진심 어린 감사를 전합니다.

2025년 8월, 여러분의 열정과 투지를 기대하며

임용시험을 준비하는 시간은 수많은 조각을 하나하나 맞춰가는 퍼즐과도 같습니다. 처음엔 어디에 어떤 조각이 들어가는지조차 막막하지만, 어느 순간부터는 자신만의 흐름과 방향이 생기고, 비로소 전체 그림이 조금씩 모습을 드러내기 시작합니다. 그리고 그 과정 하나하나가 결국 교사로서의 역량과 태도를 만들어가는 중요한 여정이 됩니다.

그동안 수험생으로서 살아온 여러분의 하루하루는 결코 가볍지 않았을 것입니다. 반복되는 루틴 속에서도 방향을 잃지 않으려 애쓰고, 불안한 마음을 달래며 스스로 다잡는 일이 쉽지 않다는 걸 잘 알고 있습니다. 저는 앞으로의 강의에서 단지 정보를 전달하는 사람을 넘어, 여러분이 걸어가는 이 길에 함께 고민하고, 함께 버텨주는 사람이고 싶습니다.

여러분이 이미 충분히 잘하고 있다는 것을, 지금 이 순간에도 조금씩 자신의 퍼즐을 완성해가고 있다는 것을 기억해 주세요. 이 책이 여러분의 준비에 든든한 조각이 되기를, 그리고 강의 속에서 그 퍼즐을 함께 맞춰갈 수 있기를 진심으로 바랍니다.

끝으로, 늘 따뜻한 조언과 신뢰로 이 길을 이끌어 주신 박현수 교수님께 진심으로 감사드립니다. 또한, 저의 처음을 함께 하며 든든한 힘이 되어 주는 조교들, 인서, 상은, 수진, 준현, 승희에게도 진심으로 감사의 마음을 전합니다.

2025년 8월
유다현

Guide

2025학년도 기출분석 및 2026학년도 대비 영어교육론 시험 전략

2025학년도 중등 임용시험의 영어교육론은 총 23문항 중 2024학년 기출 문항수(11문항)보다 한 문항 적은 10문항이 출제되어 총 80점 중 36점을 차지하였다. 여전히 교사 시험답게 영어교육론의 출제 비중이 50%에 달하는 것을 확인할 수 있다. 이것은 중등 임용시험의 정체성에 따라 영어교사의 필수 자질인 how to teach에 대한 자필평가의 중요성을 반영한 것으로 판단된다. 2025학년도 중등 임용시험은 전년도에 비해 비교적 난이도가 중/중하로 구성된 문항들이 출제되었으며, data-based item과 knowledge-based item이 기입형과 서술형에 고르게 출제되었다. 우선, 2025학년도 중등 임용 출제 방향을 살펴보면 첫째, 2022년 개정 교육과정의 주요 학습 개념인 Project-based learning과 digital literacy가 반영된 것을 확인할 수 있다. 둘째, 학생 중심 교실 수업을 계획할 수 있는 교사의 자질에 대한 평가로서 material adaptation, lesson objectives 및 modified lesson의 방식과 특징들이 출제되었다. 셋째, 학생 측면에서는 중간언어 형태의 특징과 reading strategies 등의 유무에 초점을 두어 출제되었으며, 마지막으로 언어학습의 최종 목표가 목표 문화의 수용이라는 측면에서 매년 문화지도가 출제되는 경향이 있는데 이번에도 역시 문화지도에 대한 내용이 출제되었다.

A형 기입형 문항

기입형 3, 4번은 예년보다는 평이한 개념이자 반복적으로 출제된 term인 'modifying'과 'inter-rater reliability'를 묻는 문항이 출제되었다. 이때 3번의 경우, term 도출 방식은 Original Material을 토대로 Adapted Material에 어떤 변화가 있는지 살펴보고, 해당 변화를 설명한 term을 data에서 고르는 방식으로 출제되었다. 4번의 term인 'inter-rater reliability'는 두 선생님의 대화 내용과 Mr. Lee의 Teaching Journal로 유추하여 찾을 수 있으며, comments에 나온 definition으로 해당 term을 확정할 수 있다. 다만, 4번은 data에서 찾아 쓰는 data-matching 방식으로 term을 도출했던 3번과 달리 example이나 situation, definition을 보고 해당 개념을 정확히 도출하는 knowledge-based 방식의 문항이다.

A형 서술형 문항

- 8번(data-based item)은 〈A〉에 학생들의 중간언어 발전 단계에 대한 L2 학생들의 다양한 변이적인 중간언어 형태에 관련된 설명과 예시를 data로 주고, 〈B〉에서 제공한 학생 대화와 matching하는 문항이다.
- 9번(data-based item)은 말하기 평가 원리에 관한 문항으로, 〈A〉에서 4개의 평가 원리를 제시하고 〈B〉에서 Mr. Jeong이 Item 1과 2에서 평가한 사례를 보고 matching하는 문항이다.
- 11번(knowledge-based item)은 〈A〉에서 각각 듣기/읽기와 말하기/쓰기에 대한 수업 목표를 제시하고, 〈B〉의 Teaching Procedure에서 제시되는 활동과의 관계를 파악하는 문항이다.
- 12번(data-based item)은 〈A〉에서 다양한 Reading Strategies에 대한 category를 제시하고 〈B〉에서 학생들의 읽기에 대한 문제점을 제공하여, 이를 해결할 수 있는 Reading Strategies를 고르는 문항이다.

B형 서술형 문항

- 6번(data-based item)은 〈A〉에 2022년 개정 교육과정의 핵심 교수 방법 중 하나인 Project-based learning에 대한 학습 단계가 제시되었고, 〈B〉에 실제 일정 기간(1st Week~6th Week)의 교실 수업 단계가 제시되어 두 단계 간의 mismatching을 묻는 문항이다.
- 7번(knowledge-based item)은 〈A〉에 제시된 초임교사와 주임교사 간 대화로 효율적인 수업을 위한 수업 계획 수정(modified lesson)에 관련된 문항으로, intensive listening을 이해하고 creative writing에 대한 개념을 묻는 문항이다.
- 10번(data-based item)은 다년간 중등 임용시험에서 주요 토픽으로 다루고 있는 문화학습 관련 문항이다. 〈A〉에서 문화학습 과정인 noticing, comparing, reflecting, interacting의 개념들과 두 학생의 문화학습 단계를 보여주는 발화 간 matching을 묻고 있고, 〈B〉에서는 두 학생의 대화로 알 수 있는 문화학습 과정을 규명하는 문항이다.
- 11번 문항(knowledge-based item)은 〈A〉에 how to use digital tools에 대한 원리를 제시하고, 〈B〉에서 8차 시간 수업 중 원리 mismatching에 대한 것을 고르는 문항이다. 이 문항은 discovery learning과 drill 간의 차이와 individualized feedback의 이해 여부를 묻는 문항이다.

2026학년도 대비 중등 임용 영어교육론의 방향

A형과 B형의 문항 유형에서 살펴봤듯이, 2025년 기출의 가장 큰 특징은 실제 교실 수업에서 교사의 자질과 학생들의 주도적 학습을 위한 교실 계획 및 언어학습의 궁극적인 목적인 목표 문화학습으로 꼽을 수 있다. 중등 임용시험에서 영어교육론의 난이도는 문학과 영어학 등 다른 영역에 비하면 중간 정도의 익숙한 문항들이 출제되고 있으나, 다른 내용학의 어려움에 대한 득점 손실을 만회할 수 있도록 영어교육론의 감점을 최소화하는 전략을 2026년 대비 중등 임용의 핵심 전략으로 삼아야 할 것이다. 이 목표를 성취하기 위해서는 영어교육론의 개념을 폭넓게 이해하고, 실전 문항의 data-processing / direction analysis/ correct answer에 대한 연습을 상반기부터 진행해야 한다.

Contents

Chapter 01 Second Language Acquisition ⋯ 10

Chapter 02 Classroom Context ⋯ 58

Chapter 03 Receptive Skills ⋯ 100

Chapter 04 Productive Skills ⋯ 136

Chapter 05 Vocabulary & Grammar ··· 178

Chapter 06 Assessment ··· 210

정답 및 모범 답안 ··· 240

NEW
Build Up

Chapter 01

Second Language Acquisition

Chapter 01 — Second Language Acquisition

01 Read the passage and follow the directions.

Ms. Park : Ms. Kim. I've been thinking about how the (1) _____ hypothesis might affect middle school students in terms of English language acquisition. Have you considered this?

Ms. Kim : Yes, it says that there's an optimal period for language acquisition. Am I right?

Ms. Park : You're right. According to this hypothesis, young learners at the age of less than 11 can acquire a new language more quickly and much better than adolescent learners.

Ms. Kim : If so, how can we help our students learn English more effectively? As you said, they are no longer in their (1) _____ for language acquisition.

Ms. Park : That's the point I am still thinking of. Most of the reference books mention that this hypothesis enables younger students to achieve perfect native-like pronunciation only. But, as you know, to have a good command of English means mastering lots of things beyond just the pronunciation.

Ms. Kim : So, are there any teaching strategies for our students?

Ms. Park : In my opinion, our students in adolescence can pay attention to the subject much easier than young children. So, they can easily acquire more complicated and abstract concepts.

Ms. Kim : That's right! You mean, we should prepare some classroom techniques and activities, which can stimulate and activate our students' cognitive structure.

Ms. Park : Exactly! However, while comparing themselves to others, they often feel insecure and consequently develop (2) _____ to protect their self-identity. This can function as unseen barriers that encircle and protect a delicate self-image.

Ms. Kim : Hmm, we need to create a warm classroom atmosphere and more interesting and relevant lessons for our students, don't we?

Ms. Park : Yes. By doing so, we can lower their (2) _____, the feeling of embarrassment or worry that prevents our students from saying or doing what they want. Plus, please do not forget to carefully consider their unique learning styles and paces.

Ms. Kim : Absolutely, Ms. Park. I will.

Fill in each blank with the ONE or TWO most appropriate word(s).

Your Answer   (1) _____
                 (2) _____

02 Read the conversation and follow the directions.

> *One English teacher and her students just read an article about Artificial Intelligence.*
>
> T : Okay, we've gathered quite a bit of information about Artificial Intelligence (AI), haven't we? Minwoo, what are your thoughts on AI technology?
> Minwoo : AI can greatly simplify our lives in many ways. I believe it's beneficial for us!
> T : Excellent, and what about you, Leah?
> Leah : I see AI as a potential threat. It might replace certain jobs soon, which could lead to job loss for many people.
> T : Indeed, that is a possibility. Now, let's discuss the pros and cons of AI technology in groups.
> Inyoung : Sorry? Pros? Cons?
> T : Yes, I'm asking you to discuss the positive and negative points of AI technology. Understand?
> Inyoung : Oh, yes! I got it now.
> T : I'll give you 10 minutes. Ready? Go!

Complete the comment by filling in the blank with the TWO most appropriate words.

> When students communicate with the teacher in English, they often face challenges that necessitate adjustments in the teacher's speech to facilitate comprehension. This requires significant effort from both parties. In the conversation, when Inyoung seeks clarification, the teacher effectively rephrases "pros and cons" to "positive and negative points," simplifying the language to ensure understanding. Such modification is crucial in providing what is known as _____. This adjustment ensures that the input is clearer and more understandable by using simpler vocabulary and concepts.

Your Answer _____

03 Read the conversation and follow the directions.

> *Below is an excerpt from a conversation between Ms. Kim and the students who are talking about plastic use in our daily lives.*
>
> *(T shows photographs of various food items wrapped in plastic packaging.)*
>
> T : Do you know what they are?
> S1 : They are bananas, kiwis, and bread.
> T : Right! Look at the packaging. They are wrapped by …?
> S1 : Plastic vinyl.
> T : Correct! These photographs were taken in a local supermarket. People from our neighborhood started a recent campaign that encouraged customers to stop buying anything in plastic packaging for one week! Plastic vinyl is a representative example we have to reduce in daily life. What are the other examples of plastic in our lives?
> S2 : Plastic bottles!
> S3 : Plastic straws!
> T : Correct! Then, I will show you other photographs. *(T shows two photographs of eggs, one is wrapped in cardboard and the other is in plastic.)* One is the free-range eggs and the other is not. Yes, Young-ji?
> S4 : Say that again, please? Free… what?
> T : Free-ran-ge. Free-ran-ge which means the hens move around the field freely, not growing up in cages.
> S4 : So the hens grow up in grass freely!
> T : Exactly! The hens which grow up freely make healthier eggs than others! Do you get it?
> S4 : Yes, thank you, Ms. Kim.

Guideline for Pre-service Teachers

Complete the comments by filling in each blank with the TWO most appropriate words.

> In the conversation above, when Young-ji does not understand the word 'free-range', Ms. Kim provides a brief explanation to help her understand the word considering her language proficiency. In the process of meaning negotiation, such language input that the student can understand is called (1) _____. Based on this, Young-ji can clearly understand the meaning of 'free-range'. Then, Ms. Kim adds one more fact that free-range hens are healthy and then uses a/an (2) _____ saying "Do you get it?" to make sure that the student understands the concept of 'free-range eggs'.

Your Answer (1) _____

(2) _____

04 Read the passage in <A> and a teacher's note in <B>, and follow the directions.

A

Michael Long proposed a/an (1) _____ approach that the learner must be aware of the meaning and use of the language features before the form is brought to their attention. This occurs when a learner has a communication problem, and so is likely to understand the meaning or function of the new form. These are the conditions most researchers would consider optimal for learning. In this regard, they suggest one best way to teach problematic grammar forms within a communicative framework, which is a/an (2) _____ activity. It aims to focus learners' attention quite explicitly on the form of the grammar structure while stimulating meaningful L2 communication and creating a purposeful context for language use.

B

Teacher's Note

After reading an article about effective pedagogical ways to teach grammar forms, I designed the following task aimed at directing learners' attention to some specific linguistic form when they process both the input (listening to a script) and the output.

Lead-in (2-5 minutes): To set lesson context and engage student

T tells Ss that they'll do dictation and explains how it is going to happen.

Exposure (3-5 minutes): To provide a model of production expected in coming tasks

- T writes on the board the sentence: 'What time do you have breakfast?' and highlights 'what' 'do' 'have' in the sentence.
- Then T asks Ss whether these words help reconstruct the question or not.
- T asks about the remaining ones 'time', 'breakfast' and tells Ss that these are helpful because these are the keywords.

Guideline for Pre-service Teachers

Receptive Task(s) (8-10 minutes): Provide students with a grammar dictation activity

- T asks Ss to put pens down and listen carefully.
- T reads the 1st time and Ss listen only. Then T gives Ss 2 minutes to write key-words. T reads one more time and Ss listen only. Then T gives Ss 2 minutes for them to add to their notes.
- At this stage, Ss work individually and they should not consult with their peers.

Productive Task(s) (13-18 minutes): To provide an opportunity to practice target productive skills

- T puts Ss in pairs and asks them to look at their notes and try to build up the text. The pair will have one strong and one weak students.
- T then asks in each pair to join another pair and form a group of four and compare their texts, discuss and make improvements to their final versions.

Feedback and Error Correction (3-5 minutes): To provide feedback on students' production

T hands out copies of the original text and asks Ss to read both and compare content and accuracy.

Controlled Practice (4-6 minutes): To check whether students included all relevant information as in the original text

T asks Ss some questions about the information in the original text to see whether Ss have included all relevant information.

Language Focus (4-6 minutes): Clarify grammar and revise the indefinite article

T asks Ss to underline the indefinite articles in the original text and compare it to the ones in their versions. T then quickly explains how the indefinite article works and clarifies any mistakes Ss might have made in their texts.

T=teacher, Ss=students

Based on the information in \<A\> and \<B\>, fill in each blank in \<A\> with the ONE most appropriate term. Write the answers in order.

Your Answer (1) _____
              (2) _____

05 Read the interaction between two friends below, and follow the directions.

> *Below is part of the conversation between two high school students.*
>
> John : Hey, what's up?
> Lisa : Not much. How about you?
> John : I'm good.
> Lisa : That's good to hear. So, would you like to go to the movie theater with me this evening?
> John : I'd love to! Do you know what is playing?
> Lisa : Yeah, 'Furiosa'. I heard it is really popular with young people right now.
> John : Sounds cool! What is the movie about?
> Lisa : I am still thinking about the history exam we will have next week.
> John : What?

Complete the comments on the interaction above by filling in the blank with TWO words.

> Conversation relies on a process known as conversational turn-taking. Essentially, one person's remark (the first turn) prompts a response (the second turn), forming a pair that keeps the conversation going. When the second turn is relevant to the first, the interaction flows smoothly. However, if the response is irrelevant in context, the conversation fails to continue. These paired exchanges are called _____, and they often form familiar patterns like greeting followed by a greeting, question followed by an answer, or suggestion followed by acceptance. In the last part of the interaction above, Lisa's utterance, "I am still thinking about the history exam we will have next week." is an inappropriate reply to John's question, "What is the movie about?" because her response doesn't address the movie, 'Furiosa', and thus disrupts the flow of the conversation.

Your Answer _____

Guideline for Pre-service Teachers

06 Read the passage, and follow the directions.

Min-ji and Eun-hye, two middle school students, are having a casual conversation sitting on a bench in Han river park.

Min-ji : Look! There is a little cute dog!
Eun-hye : It's so lovely!
Min-ji : I love dogs. I want to have one in my family! Do you have one?
Eun-hye : Unfortunately, no. My sister has an allergy to cats and dogs.
Min-ji : Hmm... I am not sure if I have an allergy or not. I want to find it out! Eun-hye, can you go to a pet cafe with me today?
Eun-hye : Hmm... I have my swimming class at 8 o'clock but it's only 4 now.
Min-ji : Yeah~! Let's go then!

Complete the comments by filling in the blanks with appropriate words.

The conversation above has good cohesion in that there is continuity between one part of the conversation and another based on (1) _____ (TWO words). For example, 'a little cute dog' from the first utterance is replaced or substituted by the pronouns 'it' and 'one' in the conversation. Sometimes, a conversation can be united without any connectors if another important qualification of discourse is met. In the conversation, you can see that the overall meaning is united in terms of functions (i.e., suggestion → acceptance) and creates (2) _____ (ONE word) of the conversation.

Your Answer (1) _____
(2) _____

18

07 Read the passage and follow the directions.

> *Below is a letter written by Teo, 3rd grader student in a middle school.*

Dear teacher,

I am writing this in the **intermission** between classes to tell you of my **extolment** for your class. Your group work **rouses a deep sense of admiration and joy** within me. I enjoy **every step of the work** in your class. It **comes without speaking** that your class is the best. I don't know how to **give vent to my feelings**. You help me with the **difficultness** of English. I know other **guys** and I **suggest them** to take your class. I'm **so much happy** to be student of a **sagely teacher** such as you and getting your **advices**. Your help is beyond **valuability**.

Bye for now,
Teo

Guideline for Pre-service Teachers

Complete the comments by filling in the blank with the ONE most appropriate word.

> According to Teo's letter, it appears that he knows enough about the words to communicate, but there are gaps in his word knowledge. For example, to know a word means to know a considerable amount about its meaning; Teo uses the word *intermission* ("a short period of time between the parts of a play, film, concert, etc.") to apply to the *break* between classes. He knows the literal meaning of *give vent to his feelings* but misses the subtle distinction that *vent* is usually used with *negative feelings*. In addition, to know a word or phrase means to know its collocations. For example, although *every step of the way* is a recognizable collocation, *every step of the work* is not. While we understand the meaning of *It comes without speaking*, we are accustomed to the formulaic expression *It goes without saying*. Knowing a word also means knowing its grammatical function (e.g., *suggest* is a transitive verb, *advice* is an uncountable noun) and its word parts (e.g., *difficulty* rather than *difficultness*, and *value* rather than *valuability*). Finally, knowing a word means to know its _____, or level of formality. *Extolment* is a noun (meaning "enthusiastic praise and admiration"), but it is very inappropriate in that it might not be suitable for a student's letter to his teacher. It is more suitable for the field of marketing and advertising or professional achievements. Teo also uses several other very formal terms (*rouses a deep sense of admiration and joy*) along with some very informal ones (*guys; Bye for now*).

Your Answer _____

08 Read the passage and follow the directions.

> Below is part of the lesson procedure that Ms. Kim, an English teacher in a middle school, prepares for her 2nd grade students.

Teacher : Good morning, everyone! Today, we're going to dive into an exciting exploration of a key part of how we communicate—the idea of _____. This interesting concept is all about how we change the way we talk based on the situation we're in. Can anyone remember a time when we spoke differently to a friend than we did to a parent or teacher?

Student 1 : When I chat with my friends, I often use casual language and jokes, but when I'm speaking with my teacher, I make sure to be respectful and use formal language.

Teacher : Excellent example! The way you change your language in different situations is based on three key elements of _____: Field, Tenor, and Mode. Let's delve deeper into these!

1. Field

Teacher : Let's start with 'Field'. Picture yourself on a soccer field. What would you talk about? Most likely, it would be about soccer, right? In the same way, 'Field' refers to the topic or the 'what' in our conversation. When two people communicate, they engage within a certain field, meaning they discuss a specific subject or topic.

2. Tenor

Teacher : Next, how about tenor? Picture this: when you chat with a buddy, your conversation is likely light and informal. But when you converse with your principal, your language might shift to be more formal and polite. 'Tenor' reflects our relationships and roles in a conversation. It's about 'who' we are talking to and 'how' we relate to them. Different relationships, such as *friend-friend, student-teacher, or customer-salesperson*, require diverse tones and manners of speaking.

> **Guideline for Pre-service Teachers**

> 3. Mode
>
> Teacher : Lastly, let's talk about the 'Mode' of communication. This refers to 'how' we communicate—is it spoken or written? Is it formal or informal? An informal mode could be texting your friend using abbreviations and emojis. In contrast, a formal written mode could be writing a cover letter for a job application, carefully crafted and free of any internet slang.
>
> **Activity Procedure**
>
> Teacher : Shortly, we'll break into groups, and I'll give you different scenarios. Your task will be to identify the field, tenor, and mode used in each context. Remember, understanding and effectively using _____ allows us to smoothly navigate through various social and professional situations!

Fill in the blanks with the ONE most appropriate word in common.

Your Answer _____

09 Read the passage and follow the directions.

Ms. Park's Writing Class

1. Topic Development
   - Students read materials and case studies about extreme exploration.
   - Students engage in discussion about reading materials.
   - Students choose a topic after consulting with peers and the teacher.

2. Outline Creation
   - Students create a tentative plan for their writing.
   - Teacher provides feedback on the plan.

3. First Draft Composition
   - Students independently write a first draft.
   - Students meet with the teacher to discuss the first draft.

4. Final Draft Completion
   - Students independently revise the first draft into a final draft.
   - Students perform a final proofreading before submission.

Complete the comments by filling in the blanks with the ONE most appropriate word.

The writing procedure outlined above demonstrates how the teacher provides _____ to help students complete a writing task that they might not be able to accomplish in one go. In this specific instance, students in Ms. Park's class are not immediately given the daunting task of writing a lengthy paper. Instead, she provides step-by-step support at various stages to guide students through the process of writing the final paper. This method gradually enables students to independently complete the paper, a task that they might have found overwhelming at an earlier stage.

Your Answer _____

10 Read the teacher's journal and follow the directions.

Teacher's Journal

Learning a second language (L2) often entails the development of a new identity. This process, central to cultural learning, is commonly referred to as _____ which involves an individual adopting, acquiring, and adjusting to a new culture. This adaptation is crucial for successful language acquisition, emphasizing how deeply intertwined language learning is with cultural integration.

By understanding the cultural context inherent in a language, students do more than merely learn to communicate; they gain insights into its practical use in everyday interactions. This approach moves learners beyond simple memorization of vocabulary to actively applying language skills in real-life scenarios. Such an immersive method not only enriches the educational experience but also deeply connects learners with the cultural practices, traditions, and values of native speakers. Thus, language learning becomes a dynamic, all-encompassing journey that is integrally linked to cultural adaptation, underscoring the importance of cultural understanding in mastering a second language.

John Schumann's model reinforces this perspective by linking the success in acquiring a second language directly to the process of _____. It explains that success in second language acquisition is determined by the extent to which learners can orient themselves to the target language culture.

Based on this perspective, I employ a variety of culture-teaching activities in my English class. For instance, Culture Island creates immersive environments that simulate aspects of the target culture by displaying posters, maps, objects, and pictures of people, of the target culture. Also, Artifact Study involves students in hands-on exploration of cultural items. These interactive experiences enable students to simultaneously navigate the language and its cultural underpinnings, enhancing their overall learning journey.

While engaging in various cultural activities for my lessons, I realize once again that integrating culture into language education not only enhances the learning experience but also significantly improves language proficiency.

Fill in the blanks with the ONE most appropriate word. Use the SAME word for the blanks.

Your Answer _____

11 Read the passage and follow the directions.

> **Interview Questions for Speaking Test**
>
> 1. How frequently do you engage in social interactions with native English speakers?
> 2. Do you actively seek opportunities to interact with native English speakers?
> 3. What challenges do you encounter when conversing with native speakers?
> 4. How would you describe the sense of community in your surroundings?
> 5. Are there any shared values you recognize between your culture and American culture?
> 6. When you use English, how comfortable do you feel? Rate it from 1 to 10. (1: extremely uncomfortable, 10: totally comfortable)

Complete Ms. Yoo's reflection by filling in the blank with most appropriate TWO words.

Ms. Yoo's Reflection

During the final exam, I presented the interview questions above to some students who had resided in the U.S.A. for a year. The purpose was to assess both their speaking proficiency and the level of acculturation they had achieved. Referring to the Acculturation Model, second language learning involves not only acquiring a new language but also adopting a second identity by embracing the culture, values, and behavioral patterns of the target community. These questions examine the _____ which refers to the cognitive and affective proximity of two cultures that come into contact within an individual. Besides, some of the questions focus on examining the psychological distance, the level of comfort that individual learners experience with their target language learning task. Therefore, a learner's success in second language acquisition relies on their ability to reduce both factors effectively.

Your Answer _____

12 Read the part of a lesson procedure and follow the directions.

	Lesson Procedure
Stage 1 (Demonstrate)	• T puts colorful but different-sized rods on the front table. • T picks two different sized rods up and shows them to Ss. • T says 'longer' lifting up the longer rod higher. • T says 'shorter' lifting up the shorter rod higher. • T repeats the action with two different rods and sees if Ss tries to say the words. 　　　　　* Target Words: longer, shorter, bigger, smaller
Stage 2 (Make a sentence)	• T writes 'is' and 'than' on the board. • T tries not to say anything but waits for Ss' utterance while lifting up the two rods. • T remains silent when Ss make a mistake to give them time to self-correct. • T points the words on the board if necessary. • T encourages Ss to make a sentence while looking at the two different rods with T's gestures. 　e.g. 'Blue is longer than Red.' 　　　'Red is shorter than Yellow.'

T=teacher, Ss=students

Complete the comments by filling in the blank with the TWO most appropriate words.

　The teacher designs this lesson based on ＿＿＿＿ which emphasizes learner autonomy and active participation as an innovative method. In this method, the teacher's silence is the most important tool to encourage students to accelerate their learning. Using silence and gesture appropriately the teacher gets students' attention, elicits responses from them, and encourages them to correct their own errors. Also, according to this method, learning is facilitated if the learner discovers or creates what is to be learned by accompanying physical objects such as different sizes of rods as shown in the above lesson procedure.

Your Answer ＿＿＿＿＿＿＿＿＿＿＿＿＿＿

13 Read the lesson procedure and Minji's learning log. Then, follow the directions.

Lesson Procedure
- Your Favorite Field Trip -

1. Students share stories about their school trip to Busan.
2. The teacher transcribes students' words on the board in an organized way to create the text.
3. The class reads the story aloud and discusses it. The teacher asks if the students want to make any corrections or additions to the story. Then, the teacher marks the suggested changes, and makes further suggestions if needed.
4. The final story can be read in a choral or echo style, or both. Students can also read in small groups or pairs, and then individually.
5. This text can be used for various literacy activities, such as creating illustrations or comprehension questions.

Minji's Learning Log

Today's English class focused on reading. Initially, my teacher invited us to share our stories about school trips. My classmates talked about their visits to Seoul Land, Yongsan Family Park, Hyundai Art Gallery, and other places. Our favorite was the trip to Busan. As we shared our experiences, Ms. Kim noted our stories on the board. After discussing our Busan trip, she displayed what she had written. She introduced new vocabulary like 'ride a train,' 'go on a trip,' 'sunrise,' 'the south,' and 'seafood.' Today's class was uniquely engaging compared to typical reading classes, which sometimes seemed irrelevant and dull. Creating a text from our own experiences was particularly exciting and motivating. I also appreciated how the activity integrated multiple skills—listening, speaking, reading, and writing—making it a more effective learning experience.

Guideline for Pre-service Teachers

Fill in each blank with the most appropriate words.

> Today's reading lesson exemplifies the Language Experience Approach (LEA), which uses students' own experiences, vocabulary, and language patterns to create texts for reading instruction. The LEA, actually, supports the (1) _____ (TWO words) education by engaging students holistically and treating language as a natural and meaningful communication tool. It enriches learning by promoting integrated skills, such as reading and writing, as well as communication skills through sharing personal experiences. Additionally, by creating their own materials and actively participating in the learning process, this approach significantly boosts students' (2) _____ (ONE word) motivation unlike typical reading lessons. Students are more engaged because they see the relevance of their own lives in their learning materials. Finally, this approach is excellent for creating reading texts for beginning-level ESL students with limited vocabulary and structures in English, as well as for those reading for the first time.

Your Answer (1) _____

(2) _____

14 Read the passage and follow the directions.

Lesson Procedure

1. Introduction

   Teacher (T) encourages students (Ss) to answer connection questions to elicit what they know about the topic ('How to Take Good Notes') and set expectations for the lesson.

   Connection Questions:
   - What do I already know about this topic?
   - How does this topic relate to something I already know?
   - What questions do I already have about this topic?

2. Development

   After activating Ss' schemata, T instructs them on how to organize their notes using a two-column method to balance comprehension and retention. T emphasizes being selective in what to note down to avoid clutter and focus on key points.

   2-1. Note Template

Learning Insights - 'ah-ha' moments, questions about the material, personal reflections	Classroom Notes -factual notes on lecture or presentation content
• •	• •

3. Closing

   Towards the end of class, T may provide prompts on the board to guide Ss in summarizing their notes and reflections.
   (1) What were the most important ideas from today's class?
   (2) What did I find most interesting in class today?

Guideline for Pre-service Teachers

Fill in each blank with the ONE most appropriate word from the passage.

> **Comments on the Learning Goal of Taking Good Notes**
>
> 1. Clarity and Structure: The lesson plan is well-structured, providing clear steps for students to follow.
> 2. Engagement: The inclusion of connection questions at the beginning engages students' (1) _____ and involves them right from the start.
> 3. Practical Application: The two-column note-taking method allows students to separate their insights and factual notes, aiding both comprehension and retention.
> 4. Reflection: The closing activity encourages students to reflect on what they have learned.
> 5. Supportive (2) _____: These, provided throughout the lesson, guide students in their note-taking and summarization, ensuring they remain focused on important aspects of the lesson.

Your Answer   (1) _____

(2) _____

15 Read the lesson procedure and follow the directions.

Lesson Procedure

Topic: Restaurants & Food

Part 1:
The teacher introduces two web pages of restaurants in New York.

T: Before reading the web page, think of the kind of information you are likely to find. Answer YES or NO to the following statements. Share your answers with your partner.

- ____ You usually leave 10 to 15% of the total bill as a tip for the waiter/waitress.
- ____ Lunch and dinner take place from 2:00 to 4:00 p.m. and 9:00 to 11:00 p.m. respectively.
- ____ Very frequently people say grace before they begin to eat.
- ____ You need not make reservations to dine at a restaurant on weekends.
- ____ Men usually sit down at the table before women do.
- ____ People ask for permission before leaving the table.
- ____ The host serves himself first and then he serves his guests.
- ____ It is considered polite to leave the table before everyone else is done.
- ____ Desserts are never eaten.
- ____ The most important meal is lunch.

Part 2: Worksheet
T provides the worksheet below.

[Worksheet]
   ※ Choose one of the websites provided below.
      http://www.menumart.com/thegreenhouse/
      http://www.menumart.com/waterhouse/

Guideline for Pre-service Teachers

※ Fill this out with the information you have found on the page.
    (1) Name of the restaurant _____
    (2) Postal address _____
    (3) Telephone number _____
    (4) E-mail address _____
    (5) Schedule _____

※ Fill this out with what you plan to eat.

Lunch
1. Appetizer _____
2. Soup _____
3. Pasta _____
4. Fish _____
5. Meat _____
6. Dessert _____

Dinner
1. Appetizer _____
2. Soup _____
3. Pasta _____
4. Fish _____
5. Meat _____
6. Dessert _____

※ Write a list of the differences you can find when comparing American and Korean restaurants (e.g. opening hours, prices, or kind of food). You will compare your list with the rest of the class later on.

Part 3:

T: In the next class, you guys in groups will make one dish bringing all the ingredients. So for the homework, choose one dish you want to make with your group members. To learn new recipes, visit the following page (https://www.allrecipes.com/) and go to the "most popular recipes" section. Read it carefully and look up any words you may not know. Then, log into our class blog and discuss with your group in the chatroom to choose one recipe. I cannot wait to see who's the best cook in our class.

T=teacher

Fill in the blank with the TWO most appropriate words.

The lesson procedure shows an example of _____ in that the teacher integrates a teacher-led in-class learning experience with a self-directed/self-regulated online learning at home. Simply put, in class, she introduces the topic and encourages students to surf a web page related to the food culture in English-speaking countries. Then, after class, she asks them to have a discussion in the online chatroom of the class blog.

Your Answer

16 Read the passage and follow the directions.

Lesson Procedure

Step 1. Introduction and Context Setting
- **Teacher's Note**: Begin by introducing the recent cancellation of the volunteering club's event due to drought, emphasizing the unexpected nature of such events and their broader implications.
- **Discussion Starter**: Use the context as a springboard, asking students how they think such events might impact their community and personal lives, thereby setting the stage for deeper investigation.

Step 2. Question Formulation
- **Engagement Activity**: Show a short video on the effects of drought on ecosystems.
- **Question Formulation**: Encourage students to generate a wide range of questions. Facilitate a brainstorming session that helps them think broadly and deeply about the impacts of drought.
- What are the ecological effects of a drought on a local lake ecosystem? (environmental impact)
- How do water shortages from droughts affect daily living in communities? (social impact)
- What are the economic consequences of drought on local businesses, like car washes or swimming pools? (economic impact)

Step 3. Research and Investigation
- **Group Work**: Let students in groups choose their own questions from the brainstorming session to guide their research, emphasizing that they may explore any aspect related to drought that interests them.
- **Data Collection**: Provide resources and support as students independently seek information from diverse sources, encouraging them to look beyond immediate answers and understand underlying causes and global patterns.

Step 4. Analysis and Hypothesis
As students gather information, guide them to formulate initial hypotheses based on their understanding of the data. For example, they might hypothesize about the effects of drought on local ecosystems or the social impacts of water scarcity.

Step 5. Analysis and Refinement of Hypotheses
- Group Analysis: Students analyze their collected data to test the validity of their initial hypotheses. They should consider if the data support or contradict their predictions.
- Discussion: Facilitate a discussion where each group presents their findings and hypotheses. Encourage peer feedback aimed at challenging and refining these hypotheses.

Step 6. Synthesis and Conceptual Understanding
- Synthesis: Students synthesize the findings from their research and the feedback on their hypotheses into a comprehensive understanding of the topic.
- Creative Output: Students create presentations that outline their initial questions, hypotheses, the data gathered, and the conclusions drawn from their analyses.

Step 7. Conclusion and Reflection
- Class Discussion: Reflect on the learning process, and the outcomes of their investigation. Think about the impact of drought on local ecosystems, and the importance of community involvement in environmental conservation.
- Written Reflection: Students write a reflection on what they learned and how they can apply this knowledge in future community service.

Guideline for Pre-service Teachers

Fill in the blank with the ONE most appropriate word.

The lesson plan begins by examining the cancellation of a local event due to drought, setting the stage for students to explore its extensive impacts. A brief video serves as a catalyst, prompting students to generate their own questions about the ecological, social, and economic effects of drought. This leads to group-based, student-driven research. Students then engage deeply with the data, formulating hypotheses about the drought's impacts. This process is enhanced by rigorous peer discussions that refine these hypotheses, promoting a collaborative learning environment. The lesson concludes by synthesizing their findings into presentations, providing a platform for students to articulate their comprehensive understanding. Discussions about the learning process and its broader implications allow students to reflect on how this exploration has shaped their perspectives and how they might apply this knowledge to future community service. This approach not only broadens students' understanding of drought but also cultivates essential analytical skills, embodying the dynamic and student-centered nature of _____ learning.

Your Answer _____

17 Read the passage and follow the directions.

　　Through classroom observation, Ms. Park, an English teacher at a middle school, had thought that every student responds differently to the same learning stimuli. That is, if some students are better at some things than others, she believed, it would indicate that there are differences in the ways individual brains work. If different intelligences predominate in different people, she thought that the same learning task might not be appropriate for all of her students. Accordingly, she decided to implement a unique teaching approach by organizing one of the first-grade classrooms into seven learning centers. Each school day, students engage with the day's lesson in seven different ways, fostering a well-rounded and immersive learning experience. Here are some specific examples of the activities at each center:

1. Personal Work Center: Students explore the current area of study through research, reflection, and individual projects, encouraging independent exploration.
2. Working Together Center: Cooperative learning skills are developed as students collaboratively solve problems, answer questions, create learning games, and engage in group discussions on the day's topic.
3. Music Center: Students express their understanding of the subject matter by composing and singing songs, making their own instruments, and incorporating rhythmical learning techniques.
4. Art Center: Through various art media, manipulatives, puzzles, charts, and pictures, students explore the subject area, fostering creativity and visual understanding.
5. Building Center: Bringing learning to life, students construct models, enact events through dramatization, and dance, all related to the content of the day's subject matter.
6. Reading Center: Traditional modes of reading, writing, and learning are emphasized here. Students analyze and organize information in written form, enhancing their literacy skills.
7. Math & Science Center: This center offers hands-on experiences with math games, manipulatives, mathematical concepts, science experiments, deductive reasoning, and problem-solving.

Guideline for Pre-service Teachers

Following their activities at the centers, a dedicated time is set aside for both groups and individual students to share their work. Throughout the rest of the day, students engage in independent projects, applying the diverse skills developed at the centers in either individual or small group settings. This approach greatly influences their ability to make informative, entertaining, and multimodal presentations of their studies.

Complete the comments by filling in the blank with TWO words.

After attending Ms. Park's class, Joohye and Sarah uploaded their feedback on their unique learning experience on the class blog as below:

1. Joohye (participated in 'Working Together Center'): I enjoyed collaborating with my classmates at the Working Together Center. It was great to see different ideas come together and help each other understand things better. I felt like we were a team, and I learned a lot from my classmates.
2. Sarah (experienced the 'Reading Center,'): The Reading Center was an amazing experience! It allowed me to read about the topic and then write about it. It made me think more deeply about what we're studying. Also, discussing our thoughts with friends was cool because we got to share different viewpoints. It's like reading and talking came together to help me understand things even more.

In essence, Ms. Park effectively applies _____ theory into her classroom learning to provide different students with diverse methods to grasp and present their understanding.

Your Answer _____

18 Read the conversation and follow the directions.

> *Ms. Lee, a new teacher, and Ms. Park, a head teacher, are discussing their students' pronunciation.*

Ms. Lee : Ms. Park. I have been listening to our students' English pronunciation and I noticed that they have a strong Korean accent.

Ms. Park : I agree with you. Their accent might be understandable to us, but it could cause communication problems with native English speakers.

Ms. Lee : Exactly. Some English sounds are tricky for Koreans to pronounce. For example, the "b" and "v" sounds. When I was a beginner, I used to confuse them and say "berry" instead of "very". And the "r" and "l" sounds are another common challenge for us.

Ms. Park : That's true. I had the same issues when I was learning English. And you know, the intonation and the rhythm of Korean sometimes influence the way our students speak English. Instead of stressing the important words as they should do in English, they pronounce everything with the same tone.

Ms. Lee : That's a good observation. Since we have experienced the same difficulties, we can probably provide them with specific feedback and practice. Maybe we can do more pronunciation drills or play recordings to show them the differences.

Ms. Park : You're right! Maybe we can also share our own stories of how we improved our pronunciation.

Ms. Lee : Great idea. Let's help them to communicate more clearly and confidently!

Guideline for Pre-service Teachers

Fill in the blank with the ONE most appropriate word.

In the dialogue, two English teachers, Ms. Lee and Ms. Park, discuss the strong Korean accents of their students when speaking English. They identify this as a case of _____, that the feature of one's native language affect how they use a second language. Both teachers mention common pronunciation challenges that Korean learners face, such as distinguishing between the "b", "v", "r", and "l" sounds and adapting to the intonation and rhythm of English.

Your Answer _____

19 Read the teaching log in <A> and concordancers in <B>, and follow the directions.

A

Ms. Kim's Teaching Log

In order to minimize the students' lexical errors in writing, dialog, and exams, I designed my lessons based on the lexical approach. I believed that mechanically memorizing many words itself does not guarantee the right use of the words, so I wanted them to learn words in context and the relation among words. After several English lessons, I realized that many of my students used unacceptable combinations of words such as "look a novel" or "eat medicine," influenced by their native language, in particular Korean meaning system. Hence, I decide to introduce a specific type of concordancer in class to help the students to use words properly.

B

Concordancer 1		
Isle of Man investors to	get	payout.
took the piss out of it to	get	through.
I tried to	get	the trade unions into a form.
Right,	get	on with it.
So high you can't	get	over it.
She must	get	the bike before the car returned.
If you can't	get	a replacement, lift the gutter.

Results when searched for "get". The length of sentences were edited.

Concordancer 2		
Count	%	Word
97	0.4612%	take
91	0.4333%	you
78	0.3984%	other
77	0.3395%	make
68	0.2709%	choice
60	0.2459%	our
55	0.2201%	great
49	0.2134%	time

Results when searched for words (e.g., take, you, other...) with news articles.

Complete the following comments by filling in the blanks in appropriate words.

According to Ms. Kim's teaching log, she wanted students to focus on some words to co-occur in English. Of two types Concordancer 1 is more appropriate for her students. That is, it provides (1) _____ (ONE word) of the word 'get' so that students can figure out which words can go together with 'get'. Besides, with this activity students can develop their awareness to the proper use of words in given context as well as refrain from using some unacceptable word combinations such as "look a novel" or "eat medicine," which are caused by (2) _____ (ONE word) of Korean language.

Your Answer (1) _____
(2) _____

20 Read the passage and follow the directions.

Ms. Kim's Teaching Note

Today I participated in a teacher's seminar talking about common phenomenons of students found in early cognitive development. Before attending the seminar, I was deeply worried about the frequent errors from my low intermediate-level students. For example, in the first step of learning, they seemed to use the target rule correctly. However, in the next step, even after learning some grammar rules clearly and practicing repeatedly, they show incorrect usage of the rule by especially overgeneralizing them. Thus, I really wanted to know what was wrong with my grammar lessons. Thanks to the seminar, I realized that I need to wait until my students have recovered from the regression rather than considering it as a problem. Below is part of the article I have read from the teacher's seminar.

The _____ course of development

Michael Long perhaps says it best when speaking of the trajectory of a language learner's progress: "Progress is not linear; backsliding is common, giving rise to so-called _____ behavior observed in first and second language acquisition". _____ behavior or a "_____ course of development" as Ellis refers to it, describes situations in L2 acquisition when a learner's proficiency suddenly but temporarily drops off only to return once again to their usual level. According to Ellis, "It is clear that this occurs because learners reorganize their existing knowledge to accommodate new knowledge". The reorganization of prior knowledge is often referred to as restructuring. Language instructors whose students regress upon learning about and attempting to practice a new linguistic form should understand that their students are actually advancing, even when, early on, they already seemed to have "acquired" the form. In second language acquisition and teaching, patience is indeed a virtue. Below is the graph showing the _____ course of development.

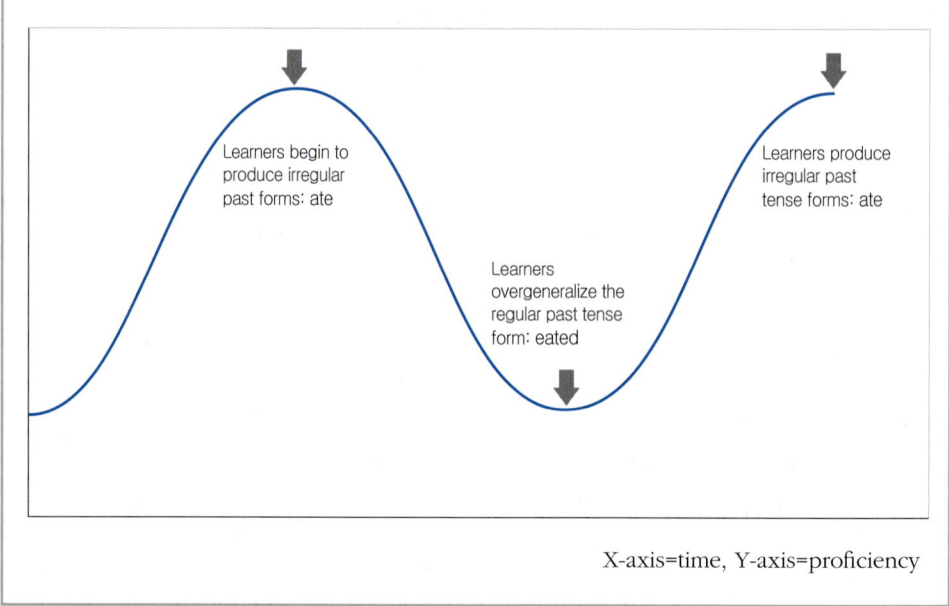

X-axis=time, Y-axis=proficiency

Fill in the blanks with the ONE most appropriate word in common.

Your Answer _____

21 Read the conversation and follow the directions.

> T1: Lately, I've observed a concerning pattern in my speaking classes.
> T2: Oh? What's happening?
> T1: A number of my students persistently make the same grammatical errors.
> T2: That's quite interesting. Do they have difficulty correcting the mistakes?
> T1: They grasp the corrections when we go over them, but the errors persistently recur. I'm concerned that these mistakes are becoming ingrained.
> T2: I've encountered something similar. It seems as if these errors are becoming embedded in their language habits.
> T1: Exactly. For example, they frequently mix up "he goes" with "he go", or misuse "much" for "many". It appears these mistakes have become entrenched.
> T2: I've seen comparable issues, like saying "I have went there" instead of "I have been there".
> T1: And it's not limited to grammar or vocabulary—pronunciation errors are common too, like mixing up the vowel sounds in "sheet" and "ship".
> T2: Indeed, it's baffling. These mistakes seem deeply ingrained rather than mere lapses.
> T1: Perhaps a direct approach is needed, with lessons specifically designed to address these errors. What are your thoughts?
> T2: I agree. A focused strategy might be crucial in breaking these persistent patterns.
> T1: We're dealing with what's known as the _____ phenomenon in their interlanguage, where errors solidify into permanent features rather than occasional slips.
> T2: Acknowledging that is an important first step. Let's explore more strategies to correct these deeply rooted errors.

Fill in the blank with the ONE most appropriate word.

Your Answer

Guideline for Pre-service Teachers

22 Read the conversation and follow the directions.

> *Two English teachers, Ms. Choi and Mr. Kim, are discussing their students' speaking performance. Ms. Choi teaches advanced level students whereas Mr. Kim, low-intermediate level students.*

T1 : Ms. Choi, how was your speaking class? Did your students actively participate?

T2 : Yes, they seem to really enjoy speaking activities! How about your students?

T1 : They, too, like speaking activities the most although they make a lot of errors.

T2 : Oh yeah? So, how do you usually handle errors when they occur?

T1 : I normally make note of the crucial errors that have occurred during the activity and later explain them to the whole class. I just want students to maintain the communicative flow without interruptions.

T2 : That's right! I thought the same. However, I do notice some minor slips when my students say something during the activity.

T1 : Can you give me some examples of the errors?

T2 : Some students tend to omit the '-s' in the third person singular form of verbs. For instance, they say "as she say," "what he mention," "what Minji experience," and so on.

T1 : Even advanced students make such mistakes while speaking!

T2 : Yes, that's true. Actually, I didn't correct such errors, thinking my students made just simple mistakes. But, I realized that I was wrong.

T1 : Yeah, these errors would continuously occur.

T2: Exactly. The incorrect form seems to have been permanently incorporated into their speaking competence. So, starting from the next speaking activity, I will make sure to remind my students not to omit the third person singular '-s'. For those who continue to make mistakes, also, I will explicitly correct the errors to prevent _____.

T1: That's a great idea. With your help, they'll be able to correct the errors quickly since they are intelligent students.

T2: I'm glad you think so.

T=teacher

Fill in the blank with the ONE most appropriate word.

Guideline for Pre-service Teachers

23 Read the dialogue and follow the directions.

> Ms. Park : Hi, Ms. Yoo! How are you doing?
> Ms. Yoo : I'm doing well, thank you. How about you?
> Ms. Park : I'm good too, thanks for asking. I wanted to talk to you about how we can manage our grammar-based classes more engaging and effective.
> Ms. Yoo : Sure, what's on your mind?
> Ms. Park : How about giving students an opportunity to use the target forms in communicative situation?
> Ms. Yoo : Can you give some examples?
> Ms. Park : Sure! In class, for example, suppose the auxiliary verb "will" is taught as the target form. We can ask questions that relate to their personal experiences, such as "Where do you plan to travel next?" or "Any plans for the weekend?" This way, they get to personalize the future tense while talking about their personal plans.
> Ms. Yoo : Very nice!! So, students have the chance for _____ of the form 'will'.
> Ms. Park : That's the point! Making it more personal might just be the key. Students have an opportunity to express their own preference, feelings and opinions using the target form.
> Ms. Yoo : I see what you mean. That would definitely make our grammar lessons more engaging and effective.
> Ms. Park : Exactly! And it would also help us build rapport with our learners and create a genuine connection with them.

Fill in the blank with the ONE most appropriate word.

Your Answer _____

24 Read the following CALL material in <A> and its comments. Answer the question.

---- **A** ----

Not all CALL materials provide clear feedback for learners, but teachers can find CALL software for grammar that does. Teachers can look for software that provides grammar assessment and feedback about correctness both before and after instruction. Take a look at the grammar section below. It begins with two assessments: Diagnosing Your Grammar Errors and Grammar test. This shows the learner the results for the grammar test. Color is used to show correctness—blue for correct, red for incorrect, and green for corrected. By clicking on "Feedback" at the bottom right on the screen, the learner is informed of the type of mistakes made, and directed to go to the textbook or grammar software program for more work in the problem areas—in this case, articles, the passive, and count/noncount nouns.

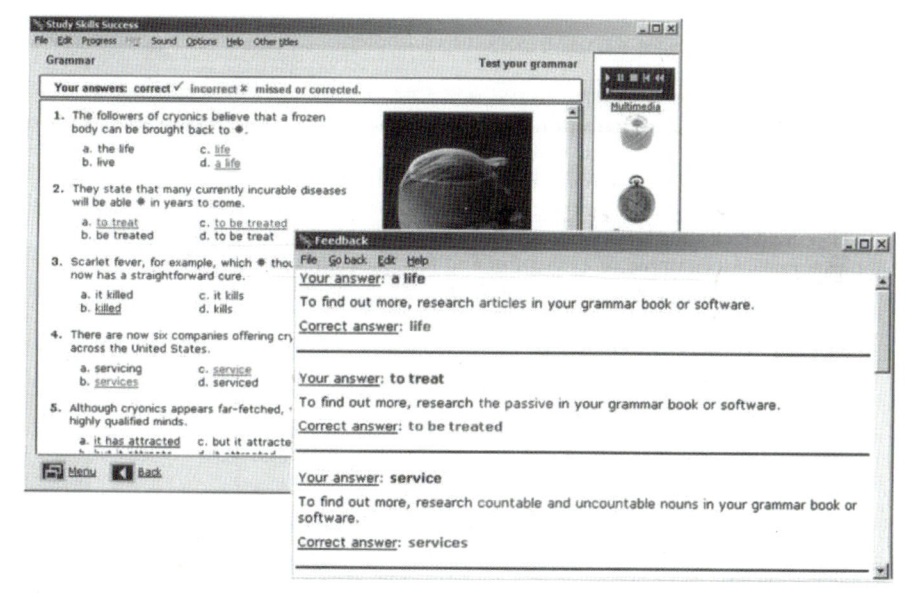

Guideline for Pre-service Teachers

Complete the comments on the diagnostic grammar test in <A> by filling in the blank with THREE words.

B

   Most researchers argue that explicit feedback for learners about why their responses were correct or incorrect produced the best results for grammar learning, compared to feedback that simply pointed out the location of learners' errors. That is when they receive explicit feedback on their performance, they have the opportunity to _____ between their knowledge and correct grammar.

Your Answer _____

25 Read the conversation below, and follow the directions.

> *In a class, a teacher and students are talking about their favorite movies.*
>
> Jin : My favorite movie is "Titanic" because I love Leonardo DiCaprio who is impossibly handsome. I watched its 3-D version, too.
> Hoyoung : Hmm . . . But that's too old one. I recently have watched a movie titled "The detective" which was released last week. I could not help sobbing because of Christopher's acting. He is a new talent but his acting is super.
> T : <u>'Talent' is a wrong word. You need to say, 'Christopher is a new actor.'</u>
> Hoyoung : Okay. Christopher is a new actor.
> T : Good. Go ahead.
> Hoyoung : Anyway . . . After watching it, I go back home and search the reviews of the movie, which were high praise overall.
> T : <u>Oh, you went back home and searched the reviews?</u>
> Hoyoung : Yes. I search them on the Internet at that day.
>
> T=teacher

Fill in each blank with ONE word.

> The conversation above demonstrates how the teacher provides Hoyoung with feedback fundamental to second language acquisition. Two types of feedback were used. First, in the first underlined feedback the teacher provides the (1) _____ evidence of the target language to inform the learner of the incorrectness of his utterance. On the other hand, the teacher's second underlined feedback is the (2) _____ evidence of the target language which exposes the learner to the well-formed target language.

Your Answer   (1) _____
                  (2) _____

26 Read the passages and follow the directions.

A

T	: Joo-hyun, what did you do for summer vacation?
Joo-hyun	: Well, I visit my cousin's house in Yang-yang.
T	: You visit?
Joo-hyun	: Oh, I visited my cousin's house.
T	: Oh yeah? What did you do there?
Joo-hyun	: I go surfing.
T	: You go?
Joo-hyun	: Ah! I went surfing!
T	: Great! That must be a lot of fun.
Joo-hyun	: Yes, it is fun.
T	: It is?
Joo-hyun	: Oh my, okay. It was fun!

B

T	: Eun-ji, you did a good job! You get grade 'A' in your writing test.
Eun-ji	: Oh, don't say that.
T	: Sorry?
Eun-ji	: I mean, I did my best and . . . I think 'A' is undeserved.
T	: Oh, I get it. You tried to show modesty. That's the way the Koreans say. In American culture, you just show your appreciation.
Eun-ji	: Oh, I see! Thank you for giving me a good grade.
T	: It sounds better! Well, I evaluated the test based on objective criteria. So, you deserve 'A'.

T=teacher

Referring to <A> and <B>, fill in each blank with a suitable term.

In the conversation <A>, the teacher uses (1) _____ (ONE word) that prompts the student to self-correct. On the other hand, in the conversation <B>, the teacher uses a clarification request which gives signals to the student that there is an error in her utterance and invites the student to reformulate it. Through giving feedback on the errors, the teacher pushes his students, Joo-hyun and Eun-ji, to use the grammatically and sociolinguistically correct utterances, which is called (2) _____ (TWO words).

Your Answer (1) _____

(2) _____

NEW Build Up

Chapter 02

Classroom Context

Chapter 02 Classroom Context

01 Read the conversation between two teachers and follow the directions.

> *Two teachers are selecting a new reading material for the beginner and intermediate level students. The following is part of their conversation.*
>
> T1: So, did you check the two texts? I went with Text A.
> T2: Text A? May I ask you why?
> T1: I think that the picture coming with Text A makes the text more attractive.
> T2: I agree! Text A contains a realistic photo to grab our students' attention and make them want to read it more.
> T1: That's it. So, you do pick Text A, don't you?
> T2: Well, actually no. I think Text B is better for my students than Text A.
> T1: Hmm... could you clarify your point a bit more?
> T2: Well, I mean, considering its vocabulary difficulty and sentence length, Text A is too demanding for my students.
> T1: That's true, but I think that Text A has more realistic language use.
> T2: You may be right. Authentic language can motivate students but not so effective for low-level students.
> T1: I see. Then, what should we choose? Text A or B?
> T2: Well, in my opinion, Text B is more appropriate and less difficult. Besides, with more elaborated expressions in Text B, students can comprehend the text more easily.
> T1: You're right! Then, let's choose Text B and add a more authentic visual.
> T2: That will be nice! Okay, what's next? Reading activities?
>
> (ellipsis)
>
> T=teacher

Identify the pedagogical criterion for selection of reading text that the two teachers focused on.

Your Answer _____

Guideline for Pre-service Teachers

02 Review the lesson procedure and follow the directions.

Below is an overview of a new teaching model for the upcoming semester designed by a middle school English teacher, Ms. Yoo.

Day 1	T presents a whole group lesson to review foundational skills, introduce the overarching questions of the unit, and preview the unit's timeline and milestones.
Day 2-8	Students work independently in the online curriculum. Students who have questions put a red plastic cup on their desks to let the teacher know they need help.
	Based on students' questions and real-time data, the teacher works with students one-on-one, in a small group, or teaches a mini-lesson to the whole class.
	Once a week, the teacher dedicates a class period to a learning game, class discussion, project, or some activity related to the unit of study.
	Twice a week, students write their feeling and reflections about the class and send an email to the teacher. Then, the teacher responds to each student's email with her feedback and personal reactions.
Day 9	The teacher facilitates a study session to review for the unit test.
Day 10	Every student completes the unit test in their online curriculum during the class period.
...	...

Fill in the blanks with the most appropriate words.

> The lesson presented above utilizes (1) _____ (ONE word) learning involving both online curriculums and in-person components such as one-on-one, or a small group lesson. The online learning goes with a written interaction between the teacher and an individual student. Also, twice a week, they regularly exchange e-mails about their ideas, feelings, or reflections about the class, which are called electronic (2) _____ (TWO words).

Your Answer   (1) _____

(2) _____

Guideline for Pre-service Teachers

03 Read the passages and follow the directions.

Mr. Park's Lesson Plan

Step 1. T plays a record of a conversation between two students talking about a history class assignment.

Step 2. After listening to the conversation, Ss do some tasks for comprehension check. (True or False statements and comprehension check-up questions.)

Step 3. Then, T provides Ss with a handout to complete. Ss write down functional expressions excerpted from the text for each blank.

Asking for Advice	Advice 1	Advice 2
• What should I do? • _____ • _____	• How about ~? • _____ • _____	• You could ~. • _____ • _____

Step 4. Ss in pairs engage in problem/advice conversations using the key phrases within a contextualized framework. T lets Ss create the role-play dialogue themselves in pairs.

[Example of Conversations]

A: I need help with __(a problem)__. What should I do?
B: How about __(a solution)__?
...

Referring to the lesson plan above, fill in each blank with the ONE most appropriate word from the passage above.

> The above lesson involves students listening to an authentic conversation to help students understand how language is used in context. Additionally, it emphasizes teaching language through specific communicative functions, such as asking for and giving advice, which is the key aspect of the (1) _____ syllabus. Finally, engaging students in role-play activities that mirror real-life situations, it allows them to practice and apply the language in a/an (2) _____ way. This kind of practice ensures that students not only learn the language but also understand how to use it effectively within a given context.

Your Answer (1) _____

(2) _____

04 Read the classroom technique in <A> and follow the directions.

A

Referring to a story she has just read aloud to students, Ms. Park has a conversation with her students in an English lesson.

Ms. Park : Did you enjoy it? Wow, you guys did it! All right! So, then, let's talk and write about the story altogether! Who goes first? Oh, yes, Jinhee?
Jinhee : I didn't like this story.
Ms. Park : You didn't? Why? Why didn't you like it?
Jinhee : I didn't like when Maria keep the ring. It didn't belong to her.
Ms. Park : Do the rest of you feel the same way? Did you not like it when Maria kept the ring? *(Five students raise their hands.)* How do some of the rest of you feel?
Jun-ho : It's okay.
Ms. Park : What's okay?
Jun-ho : To keep the ring. It was her mother's ring.
Jinhee : But her mother gave it to the neighbor.
Ms. Park : How many of you agree with Jun-ho that it was all right to keep the ring? *(Three students raise their hands.)* Okay, what should we write?
Jun-ho : Write "Some of us want Maria keep the ring. It belonged to her mother."
Ms. Park : Some of us wanted Maria to keep the ring? *(She looks at Jun-ho as she begins to write. Jun-ho nods. She writes "Some of us wanted Maria to keep the ring. It belonged to her mother.")*

Complete the commentary in <B> about this classroom technique in <A> by filling in each blank with ONE word.

B

As shown in <A> the writing continues as Ms. Park guides the students, bringing out their ideas and helping them to express their own thoughts. She, in a sense, becomes a coauthor, as well as a/an (1) _____ who asks questions, clarifies meaning and makes a few contributions of his or her own. Moreover, she is providing language upon which the students can scaffold. Note also that indirect corrections are made through modeling. For example, she chooses a/an (2) _____ as a feedback type saying "Some of us wanted Maria to keep the ring?"

Your Answer (1) _____

(2) _____

Guideline for Pre-service Teachers

05 Read the passage and identify the type of academic scheduling that the teachers are talking about.

Head Teacher : Let's start the meeting now. Today's agenda is the new scheduling system. If anybody has any opinion about this, please speak up.

Teacher A : Well. I think that this new system is very effective. Since each class is scheduled for a longer period of time than normal, I can let my students practice enough of the new forms they learn on the day. For example, for the first 50 minutes, I lead the lesson based on necessary interaction with my students and for the second 50 minutes, my students do a group activity the entire time. I help them whenever they need me. My students seem to be satisfied with this new system.

Head Teacher : Thank you for your sharing, Mr. Moon. Any other opinions?

Teacher B : I agree with Mr. Moon's opinion. Because I have 100 minutes for one class, I can spend enough time offering background knowledge using a video clip or a short article related to the topic for the day. It enables my students to understand the lesson much easier with more fun.

Teacher C : Might I add, this new system allows us to place students into different classes based on their English level. So I can plan the lessons with the right level of content for my students. Furthermore, I have more time to communicate with my students. For instance, before applying this new scheduling system, I could not talk with them one by one due to the time constraint. But now I interact with each student very often. Also, feedback from my students shows that they are highly satisfied.

Head Teacher : What great opinions from all of you. Through this new system, I believe that all students can have more recess. Also this system offers more concentrated experiences of subjects. Even after this meeting, if you have any further opinion on this system, please feel free to come to my office and talk to me. Now I'd like to finish this meeting.

Your Answer

06 Read the teacher's log and follow the directions.

> **Ms. Yoo's Teaching Log**
>
> I am currently teaching middle school students who have low-intermediate proficiency level. To facilitate their communication skills, I often provide various speaking activities in class. While they perform the activities, I walk around the classroom and observe their performance. Since the goal of the lesson is to improve speaking fluency, I do not interrupt their communication even when I find some grammatical errors. However, I have recently noticed that many of my students are making errors when using the past tense. To address this issue, I prepared a simple speaking exercise to help them practice the past tense. On using the target grammar, I encouraged them to answer meaningfully in communicative context rather than repeating only one correct answer. Here is an example of the practice I prepared today:
>
> T : Good morning, class. Last weekend I went to a restaurant and I ate salmon. Minji, what did you do last weekend?
> S1: I went to park and I play soccer.
> T : Minji, you play soccer or you played soccer?
> S1: Oh...eh...I played soccer.
> T : Good, Jiho, did you go to the park last weekend?
> S2: I went to a movie.
> T : Great, and what did you do, Eunju?
>
> (ellipsis)
>
> This way, my students engaged in a form-focused communicative practice where they could repeatedly use the past tense while talking about their own information. After practicing this exercise several times, I noticed that my students were using the past tense patterns more correctly than before.
>
> T=teacher, S=student

Fill in the blank with the ONE most appropriate word.

> In the teaching log above, Ms. Yoo uses a communicative _____ in which the students are encouraged to repeatedly practicing the past tense while providing their own information. This exercise is designed to force students to use the past tense and their own information simultaneously as seen in S1's and S2's answers.

Your Answer _____

07 Read the conversation between two English teachers and follow the directions.

Ms. Lee : Hi, Mr. Choi. I'm struggling to help my students improve their reading skills. They're mostly field dependent learners.
Mr. Choi : Hi, Ms. Lee. So, you mean, they are good at finding the main ideas but miss specific details?
Ms. Lee : Exactly, that's right.
Mr. Choi : I understand. Then, it's important to enhance their skills in locating details.
Ms. Lee : Right, but they usually get overwhelmed when narrowing their focus.
Mr. Choi : Then, I'd like to recommend starting with a structured activity that combines both their strengths and areas for improvement. For example, ask them to find the main idea first, and then guide them to find specific details in groups.
Ms. Lee : That approach might work. How would I structure such an activity?
Mr. Choi : Begin with individual work to identify the main idea. Then, have them engage in group discussions to locate specific details more effectively.
Ms. Lee : So, group work could help them stay focused. Do you think visual aids would be helpful?
Mr. Choi : Absolutely. _____, which are pedagogical tools that use visuals such as tables, Venn diagrams, and semantic maps, are excellent resources. Additionally, they make abstract relationships between concepts more concrete, aiding students in understanding and organizing complex information from the text.
Ms. Lee : That sounds great. I'll create some visual aids to help them improve their understanding of detailed concepts from the text.
Mr. Choi : Sounds like a solid plan.

Ms. Lee : Thanks, Mr. Choi. I'm optimistic this will help them balance their reading approach.
Mr. Choi : You're welcome! Let me know how it goes.
Ms. Lee : Will do. Thanks again for your support!

Fill in the blank with the TWO most appropriate words.

Your Answer _____

Guideline for Pre-service Teachers

08 Read the conversation and follow the directions.

> Mr. Kim : Hi, Ms. Jung. I'm about to start teaching "To Kill a Mockingbird" to my third-grade students and I'm a bit worried about how to introduce the historical and cultural context.
> Ms. Jung : Hello, Mr. Kim, it's great to hear you're tackling such a significant novel. What exactly are your concerns?
> Mr. Kim : Well, this novel requires some understanding of specific historical contexts and knowledge. So, I want to make sure my students have a solid understanding of the background before we dive into the novel.
> Ms. Jung : I understand. Have you thought about using a/an _____?
> Mr. Kim : I haven't yet, but that sounds like it could be effective. Could you explain a bit more about how I might implement that?
> Ms. Jung : Sure! You could provide a brief overview of the historical period using graphic organizers like a flow chart or semantic maps before reading. Also, showing a short documentary clip about the era might also help them visualize and connect with the time period and setting of "To Kill a Mockingbird."
> Mr. Kim : That's a great idea. This way, I can lead students to preview what they are going to read. Specifically, visuals could help make the historical context more concrete for them. Do you have any specific resources in mind?
> Ms. Jung : I can email you some links to documentaries and visual resources that I've used before. They should give you a good starting point.
> Mr. Kim : That would be fantastic, thank you! I appreciate your help.
> Ms. Jung : You're welcome, Mr. Kim! Just let me know how it goes, and feel free to reach out if you have any more questions.

Fill in the blank with the TWO most appropriate words.

Your Answer _____

09 Read the passages and follow the directions.

A

Below is part of a listening lesson procedure with the topic of 'Climate change and its impact'.

Lesson Procedure

1. Introduction
   • Begin with a brief discussion on climate change to activate prior knowledge.
   • Divide the class into three groups (A, B, and C).

2. Listening Phase
   • Each group, in turns, listens to a different audio segment in a separate space at the corner of the classroom.
   • Each group takes notes on key points and important details from their segment on the worksheet.

3. Group Discussion
   After listening, each group discusses their segment's content to ensure a clear understanding.

4. _____ Phase
   • Regroup students so that each new group contains at least one member from each original group (A, B, and C).
   • Students take turns sharing information from their original segments with their new group members.
   • Each student listens, asks questions, and takes notes on the other segments.

5. Task Completion
   Students, in their new groups, answer the comprehension questions in the handouts by integrating information from all three segments.

6. Whole-class Check and Feedback
   • Review the answers to the comprehension questions.
   • Encourage students to reflect on what they learned about climate change and the listening process.
   • Provide feedback on their listening and collaboration skills.

B
Teacher's Note

Today, I prepared a/an _____ listening activity for my 2nd-grade middle school students. The aim of this lesson is to enhance students' listening, speaking, and comprehension skills through a collaborative and integrated approach. In this activity, students can improve their listening skills by focusing on isolated audio segments, their speaking skills through group discussions, and their comprehension skills by synthesizing information from what they listen to.

Fill in the blanks in <A> and <B> with the ONE most appropriate word in common.

Your Answer _____

10 Read the passage and follow the directions.

> Mr. Lee, an English teacher in a middle school, is having a conversation with his students in the classroom.
>
> T : Hi, everyone.
> Ss : Hello, Mr. Lee.
> T : Did you have a great weekend? (a) What did you guys do on this weekend? Yes, Kyumin?
> Kyumin : I went to....... Hackwon.... math.. Hackwon..
> T : Oh! You went to Math Academy. (b) What did you do there?
> Kyumin : I studied and studied. It was not fun. Then, Mr. Lee, what did you do on this weekend?
> T : I went to an Italian restaurant. Minsu, (c) what did I just say?
> Minsu : Yesterday, you went to... somewhere.
> T : To where? Any volunteer?
> Sungjin : You went to an Italian restaurant.
> T : Great! Sungjin, (d) what did you do yesterday?

Fill in each blank with TWO words.

> In the classroom conversation above, all the questions posed by the teacher begin with "what". However, questions (a), (b), and (d) are (1) _____ that do not have a pre-determined answer and ask about students' activity that the teacher cannot predict. On the other hand, question (c) is a/an (2) _____ which has a given answer and asks if the student understands the previous utterance. If the goal is to manage a communication-oriented language classroom, the former questions will be more useful as they elicit both content and language from students. Furthermore, as the proficiency level of the students increases, teachers can venture into (1) _____. These types of questions stimulate real, lengthy, and more complicated responses from students compared to the other types of questions.

Guideline for Pre-service Teachers

Your Answer   (1) _____

(2) _____

11 Read the conversation and follow the directions.

> When Ms. Park walked into the classroom, she noticed Joohee's excitement. Joohee was chatting enthusiastically with her classmates and had a big grin on her face. Curious about what had happened, Ms. Park decided to ask.
>
> Ms. Park : Joohee, you look really thrilled today! What has gotten you so excited?
> Joohee : (*Grinning even wider*) Ms. Park, I win the first prize in the English speech contest last weekend!
> Ms. Park : (*Changing intonation*) WIN?
> Joohee : Oh, I won the first prize in the English speech contest!
> Ms. Park : Haha, that's correct! Anyway, congratulations, Joohee! I'm so proud of your achievement.

Complete the comments by filling in each blank with ONE or TWO word(s).

> In the classroom dialogue above, the first question of the teacher, 'What has gotten you so excited?' is a/an (1) _____ which is to require real information from the student. That is, the teacher wanted to know the real reason why the student has looked so excited. When Joohee responds to her teacher, however, she makes an error by using the simple present tense, 'I win' instead of the past tense, 'I won'. Accordingly, in order to make a proper correction verbally, the teacher gives the feedback, (2) _____ by highlighting the ill-formed part of Joohee's utterance with a change in intonation. Then, Joohee responds to the teacher's feedback and repairs her utterance correctly.

Your Answer (1) _____

(2) _____

Guideline for Pre-service Teachers

12 Read the passages and follow the directions.

> *Below is an excerpt from a conversation between a teacher and students in a middle school English classroom.*
>
> T : Happy new year, everyone! It's great to see you again. Did you all set your New Year's resolution? How about Jimin? (1) Do you have a New Year's resolution?
> S1 : Hmm, this year, I will do a diet.
> T : Diet? You will start a diet?
> S1 : Yes, I am have to.
> T : (2) AM HAVE? Should we need both verbs?
> S1 : Oops, I have to.
> T : (3) That's correct! Then, how about Minsu? (4) What's your goal for this year?
> S2 : I ... I play [fleɪ] ... game.
> T : (5) Huh?
> S2 : (6) I will play [pleɪ] tennis game.
> T : (7) Do you play tennis? How long have you been playing tennis?
> S2 : For 5 years.
> T : (8) Wow, you must be really good at tennis!
>
> T=teacher, S=student

As seen in the conversation above, a language teacher uses questioning usually to get students to actively engage in the classroom talk. Through effective questioning techniques, he or she can elicit responses from reluctant speakers or even prevent communication breakdowns. These questioning techniques consist of different teacher questions depending on the situation. In the classroom talk above, the teacher used three types of questions as the conversation went on. The one type in (1), (4) and (7) encourages students' higher-order thinking skills and authentic use during the conversation. Such type is called (1) _____ which require information unknown to the teacher. That's why the teacher shows a genuine reaction in (8) to the student's response following this question. On the other hand, another type in (2) leads the teacher to check and test students' ongoing learning as an important tool in the classroom. For the student's response to the second type, thereby, he or she provides evaluation as seen in (3). Finally, the other type in (5) is used for meaning negotiation because the teacher does not understand the student's previous utterance on account of wrong pronunciation. Thanks to this question in (5), he or she invites the student to reformulate their utterance as seen in (6), resulting in solving communication breakdown. The final question type is called a/an (2) _____.

Complete the comments on the conversation above by filling in each blank with TWO words.

Your Answer (1) _____

(2) _____

2. Classroom Context

Guideline for Pre-service Teachers

13 Read the passage and follow the directions.

> *Two English teachers are discussing a crucial skill they plan to teach their students in the upcoming semester.*
>
> Ms. Park : Ms. Yoo. I've been thinking about how we can better prepare our students for the digital world.
> Ms. Yoo : Oh, you mean like teaching them _____ skill?
> Ms. Park : Exactly! Such skill is more than just knowing how to use a computer. Also, it is about being able to find and create content and solve problems using technology.
> Ms. Yoo : I see. But how do we incorporate that into our English lessons?
> Ms. Park : Well, we could start by using technology to make our lessons more interactive. For example, we could use online resources to supplement our textbooks or use digital tools to create engaging assignments.
> Ms. Yoo : That sounds like a great idea! But, we also need to make sure our students are safe online.
> Ms. Park : Absolutely. Part of _____ is understanding the risks and knowing how to protect oneself online. So, we are going to teach online safety as part of our lessons.
> Ms. Yoo : I agree. And I think it's important for them to understand that this skill is not just for school, but for their future careers as well.
> Ms. Park : Yes, that's a good point! Let's start planning on how we can integrate the crucial skill into our curriculum.

Fill in the blanks with the TWO words in common.

Your Answer _____

14 Read the conversation and follow the directions.

> Below is part of the conversation between a Native English teacher and a Korean English teacher.

Martin (Native Teacher): Hi, Mr. Kim. I need to talk to you about something that happened in class today.
Mr. Kim (Korean Teacher): Sure, what's going on?
Martin : Seojin didn't submit his homework again and stayed silent when I asked him about it. I thought he was ignoring me, and it frustrated me.
Mr. Kim : In Korean culture, students may stay silent out of respect or guilt, especially when they feel they've done something wrong. Silence can show humility rather than disrespect.
Martin : I didn't realize that. I got angry and told him that he had to stay after school until his homework was done.
Mr. Kim : That sounds like a cross-cultural misunderstanding. You could teach students about British classroom expectations using a/an _____.
Martin : What's that?
Mr. Kim : It's where you present students with a scenario showing a cross-cultural misunderstanding, and then they complete the worksheet by choosing the right explanation from several options. You can guide a discussion afterward.
Martin : So I create a scenario and prepare a worksheet to help guide the discussion.
Mr. Kim : Exactly, it'll help highlight cultural differences and improve understanding in the classroom.
Martin : That makes sense. I'll give it a try.
Mr. Kim : I'll help you prepare materials. Let's work together to raise awareness of these cultural differences.
Martin : Thanks a lot for your help.

Fill in the blank with the TWO most appropriate words.

Your Answer _____

15 Read the passage and follow the directions.

> *Ms. Park, a teacher at a middle school, intends to assess one of the learning styles of her students using the survey questions provided below.*

Survey Questions	Score
1. While reading something in English, I become impatient when I don't fully grasp the meaning.	5 4 3 2 1
2. It bothers me when I can't comprehend what my teacher is saying in English.	5 4 3 2 1
3. When I write in English, I feel frustrated if I struggle to express my ideas accurately.	5 4 3 2 1
4. It can be frustrating not to have a perfect understanding of certain English grammar rules.	5 4 3 2 1
5. I feel uneasy about my English pronunciation not being entirely accurate.	5 4 3 2 1
6. It makes me uncomfortable when I can't convey my thoughts clearly in English.	5 4 3 2 1

Complete the comments by filling in the blank with the TWO most appropriate words.

> In second language learning, learners often encounter a considerable amount of seemingly contradictory information: new words that deviate from their native language, rules that not only differ but also contain certain "exceptions," and sometimes an entirely distinct cultural system compared to their own native culture. However, Ms. Park believes that successful language learners should be patient with these uncertainties occurring in the second language learning situation. Therefore, through the survey questions mentioned above, she plans to measure her students' level of _____. According to her, students who has optimal level of this learning style can be willing to take risks and open to change as well as perform well in new complex situations, leading to successful language learners.

Your Answer _____

Guideline for Pre-service Teachers

16 Read the two students' comments below, and follow the directions.

> *Below are reflections from second-year middle school students, Jihoon and Haeun, discussing their recent experiences in their speaking and reading classes:*
>
> ### Jihoon's Reflection
>
> In today's activity, I was paired with Haemi. It was a challenging experience during our collaboration due to our contrasting learning styles. Haemi tends to speak rapidly and often makes mistakes, while I prefer to take my time to ensure accuracy in my responses. Anyway, during the pair work, Haemi kept telling me to hurry up but that's just not my style. For future activities, I hope I can work with someone who's more like me—slow and steady.
>
> ### Haeun's Reflection
>
> In today's reading class, our teacher shared some cool reading strategies that successful language learners use. She talked about how to spot the main idea, dig out specific details, and guess words we don't know. I started off trying to find the main idea in the text, which was a piece of cake for me. But as the class went on, I had a hard time picking up on the specific details. Like, when the teacher asked, "When did Emma leave for the birthday party?", I was totally lost. So, I guess I need to practice more on catching those little details to get better at reading.

Complete the comments by filling in the blanks with the ONE most appropriate word.

> The two students, Jihoon and Haeun, exhibit distinct learning styles during classroom activities. Jihoon identifies himself as a/an _____ learner, characterized by his tendency to articulate his thoughts slowly and meticulously. On the other hand, Haeun demonstrates traits of a/an _____ learner in her approach to reading comprehension. She is good at grasping the overall message of a story but struggles with understanding specific elements within the narrative. She acknowledges this challenge and recognizes the need for additional practice to enhance her reading skills.

Your Answer   (1) _____

(2) _____

Guideline for Pre-service Teachers

17 Read the two students' conversation, and follow the directions.

Below is the conversation between first-year middle school students. They are talking about their recent experience in speaking and reading classes, respectively.

Hyo-min : Hey, Jin-su. How was your speaking lesson?
Jin-su　 : It was okay except my speaking partner, Yoonha.
Hyo-min : Yoonha? Why? What was the problem?
Jin-su　 : Well, she spent too much time thinking! To top it off, she talks slow!
Hyo-min : Oh . . . Did you ask her to speak a little faster?
Jin-su　 : Of course, I did. However, she kept hesitating before speaking. She didn't try to guess anything. Totally different from me! I don't care about making mistakes! Also, I prefer to answer something immediately, but she needs much time to answer my questions.
Hyo-min : That's not good. That lessons sounds so tough!
Jin-su　 : It was actually tough! What about you? How was your reading lesson?
Hyo-min : Today, we were asked to find the main idea of a text while reading it. It was okay because I am good at it.
Jin-su　 : That's nice! I am not good at it, though. What's your secret?
Hyo-min : Well, I usually read a text as a whole. At the same time, I use my background knowledge to imagine the story as a big picture.
Jin-su　 : Sounds cool. I should try. Then, was it all good?
Hyo-min : Actually, I had one problem. Remembering details from a text was so difficult. It's not really my style. For example, in a table completion activity, I got so many wrong answers. I just could not remember the exact words and expressions.
Jin-su　 : Well, don't worry. Keep practice! You definitely can!
Hyo-min : You think so? Thank you. That encourages me a lot.

Complete the comments by filling in each blank with the appropriate term.

According to the conversation above, Jin-su is a/an (1) _____ (ONE word) learner given that he responds immediately without thinking enough and does not care much about making mistakes. As for Hyo-min, she is a field dependent learner who processes the text holistically. Also, she is good at grasping the overall message of a reading text using her prior knowledge. In other words, she prefers to use (2) _____ processing (ONE word) by activating her world knowledge to facilitate the comprehension of the text.

Your Answer (1) _____

(2) _____

18 Read the passage and follow the directions.

Ms. Yoo's Teaching Reflection

  Today, I conducted a lesson for our middle school's intermediate-level 2nd graders, who have been studying English for six years. Despite their experience, comprehending a five-paragraph passage remains a challenge for them. To address this, I used a new technique to model how skilled readers approach a text. I prepared a reading material about holidays around the world. In today's lesson, I had a plan to make them not just read the text but deeply engage in the text. To achieve this, I guided the students through a series of reflective questions. I read a paragraph aloud and paused at key sections to articulate my thoughts and strategies for understanding the text. During these pauses, I demonstrated how to apply the following questions by verbalizing my thinking and responses:

1. Do I understand what I just read?
2. What do I think will happen next?
3. What were the most important points in this reading?

  After demonstrating the use of these questions, I encouraged the students to employ the same technique. As they read each paragraph, they were to pause, reflect, and verbally answer these questions themselves, thereby actively engaging with and processing the text. Moreover, at the end of each paragraph, there was a reflective exercise students needed to complete statements such as "So far, I've learned...", "I think ... will happen next", "I was confused by...", and "I think the most important part was...". While completing these statements, they engaged in the text actively through synthesizing, inferencing, clarifying, and identifying some ideas.
  Once they put the technique into practice, the students engaged in group discussions to share their personal experiences. They compared and contrasted the impact of the technique, reflecting on its effectiveness before and after its implementation. Finally, I wrapped up the day's lesson, offering additional guidance to enhance their reading comprehension skills.

Fill in the blank with the ONE most appropriate word.

According to teaching reflection above, Ms. Yoo uses a special technique to teach effective reading strategies commonly employed by skilled readers. With this _____ technique, she verbalizes her own reading process to show how to utilize effective reading strategies. The purpose of using this technique is to help students monitor their comprehension and improve their reading skills.

Your Answer _____

19 Read the passage and follow the directions.

> **Teacher's Note**
>
> After having several times of reading lessons, my students were accustomed to using reading strategies such as skimming, scanning, and reading for details. Thus, at this time, I'd like to help them to examine their own way to read and learn best. Until now, I gave directions on which strategies they need to use to read a text properly. However, from the next lesson, I will train them to choose some reading strategies by themselves. In other words, they need to plan, monitor, and evaluate their reading process on their own. By controlling their own reading, I believe, they can be active learners who learn more deeply. Thus, I will prepare lessons including the following strategies.
>
> - Identifying what you already know.
> - Monitoring and clarifying your comprehension. (Think-aloud)
> - Summarizing the text.
> - Visualizing the meaning from the text.
> - Writing a reading journal.

Complete the comments on the Teacher's Note above by filling in the blank with ONE word.

> For reading lessons, the teacher tries to teach various kinds of _____ strategies to help students understand the way they learn.

Your Answer _____

20 Read the passage and follow the directions.

> *Below is an excerpt from a conversation between a teacher and her students during one speaking lesson.*

Ms. Kang : Ji-hoon, what do you want to be when you grow up?
Ji-hoon : I want to be... a fixologist!
Ms. Kang : A fixologist? That's a cool word! But do you mean something like an engineer?
Ji-hoon : Oh, yes. An engineer! I made up 'fixologist'. I thought it sounded interesting.
Ms. Kang : I like it! It's very creative, Ji-hoon. Using your creativity like that can be very helpful in many jobs, including engineering. Now, Min-seo, how about you? What do you dream of becoming?
Min-seo : I want to be a weathercaster.
Ms. Kang : A weathercaster? Wow! That sounds really exciting. What steps are you taking to get there?
Min-seo : Well, I practice by mimicking my favorite weathercaster. Sometimes I even try describing the weather in English. Like, "Dark clouds are stuck in the sky today."
Ms. Kang : That's a vivid description! In English, you might say, "It's overcast with dark clouds." It's a more typical way to express that the sky is covered with dark clouds.
Min-seo : It's overcast? Got it, thank you, Ms. Kang!

Guideline for Pre-service Teachers

Referring to the conversation, fill in each blank with the suitable communication strategy in TWO words.

> In the conversation above, the students employ different communication strategies to avoid communication breakdown. First, Ji-hoon employs (1) _____ by creating the term 'fixologist' instead of using the word 'engineer.' He creatively adds the suffix '-ologist' to the root 'fix,' inventing a non-existent word in the target language (L2). This demonstrates his attempt to communicate his thoughts despite vocabulary gaps. As for Min-seo, she uses (2) _____ in her description of the weather. Her phrase "Dark clouds are stuck in the sky today" is a direct translation of conceptual and lexical elements from her first language (L1) to English, intended to convey what is typically described in English as 'it's overcast with dark clouds.'

Your Answer (1) _____

(2) _____

21 Read the passage and follow the directions.

Mr. Kim prepares a speaking activity to help students communicate only using their own knowledge and skills even when they don't know exact words.

Speed Game: What I am

1. Students make a pair.
2. Student A checks the given word. (Student B cannot see the word.)
3. Student A explains the word using definitions, descriptions, or examples.
4. Student B guesses the word and says it out loud.
5. For 3 minutes, the pair with the most correct answers wins the game.

[Example] Word: bedside table

Student A : Well it... uhm ... how would you say, it's a piece of furniture which is just near your bed, er... where ... a bedlamp is staying on it and where I can put my books, for example, my jewelry and all my things.
Student B : Hmm... bedside table?
Student A : Correct! The next word! You use this when...
　　　　　　　　　　　(ellipsis)

Guideline for Pre-service Teachers

Complete the comments by filling in each blank with ONE word.

> The activity demonstrated above aims to increase students' (1) _____ competence as a significant part of 'communicative competence' as defined by Canale and Swain (1980). Through it, students are expected to practice a/an (2) _____ strategy by describing, exemplifying, or defining the given word. Thus, with this strategy, they will not hesitate or get blocked anymore when they don't know exact words. In short, they can reduce the possibility of communication breakdown by making up for their insufficient language ability.

Your Answer   (1) _____

(2) _____

22 Read the passage and follow the directions.

Ms. Jo's Teaching Log

Today, I prepared a writing activity whose topic was 'Do you agree or disagree with the death penalty.' In this activity, different levels of students were expected to collaboratively work together. For example, they exchanged their own opinion about the death penalty. Then, they chose a side between agreement or disagreement in groups and wrote a paragraph about their group decision on the death penalty. To be specific, during the group writing, high level students provided low level students with language supports if needed. So, all groups could complete the writing activity successfully without any group members left behind. Then, after listening to each group's presentation, students voted for the best paragraph, which they had known from the beginning of the activity. Consequently, these two points seemed to motivate them to achieve the desired outcome. The following is an excerpt from the conversation between students on the way to a group outcome.

S1 : Okay. Let's win the first prize!
S2 : Yeah! Let's do it. How can we start the paragraph then?
S3 : We completely disagrees with the death penalty.
S2 : Disagrees?
S1 : I guess *We completely disagree* is right.
S3 : Good.
S1 : Okay, then 'We completely disagree with the death penalty. There is three reasons . . .'
S2 : Wait, it should be a plural form. There are.
S1 : Oh, yes. You're right.

S=student

Guideline for Pre-service Teachers

Referring to the passage above, fill in each blank with an appropriate term.

According to Ms. Jo, the two keys to successful task completion is to have (1) _____ (TWO words) and (2) _____ (TWO words). As for the former, when working together students collaboratively complete the writing task by providing language supports each other. If working alone, they could not achieve such an outcome. Regarding the latter, by informing them of voting for the best writing in advance, she creates a competitive atmosphere between groups, which accelerates helpful anxiety and then motivates them to make an extra effort for better performance.

Your Answer

(1) _____

(2) _____

NEW Build Up

Chapter 03

Receptive Skills

Chapter 03 Receptive Skills

정답 및 모범 답안 p. 242

01 Read the passage and follow the directions.

> **Lesson Procedure**
>
> Step 1 T shows a photo of people having a party and asks Ss to make a prediction on what they are celebrating.
>
> Step 2 T plays a listening script in three segments.
>
> Step 3 After listening to each segment, Ss guess the answer and write down the clues which lead them to think so.
>
> (1) Where is the conversation taking place?
> (2) What is the purpose of this conversation?
> (3) What will happen at the end?
>
> Step 4 Ss in pairs discuss their answers.
>
> Step 5 While listening to the conversation one more time, Ss find the answer to the following questions.
>
> (1) What is the address of the party venue?
> (2) Which bus should they take to get to the party place?
> (3) What is the dress code for men and women, respectively?
>
> T=teacher, Ss=students

Referring to the lesson procedure above, fill in each blank with the ONE most appropriate term.

> The lesson procedure focuses on two major listening strategies necessary to comprehend the whole text. In Step 1 and Step 3, students are asked to predict what occasion is in the listening script using the given photo and guess where and why the conversation takes place based on some clues. During the steps, in terms of comprehending process, students need to employ a/an (1) _____ listening strategy in that they are asked to use their background knowledge and life experience. On the other hand, in Step 5, they need to listen to specific details including the party venue, the bus number, and requested dress code. Through this step, students can practice a/an (2) _____ listening strategy that they divide and decode the listening text piece by piece using their knowledge on vocabulary, grammar, and sounds.

Your Answer   (1) _____

(2) _____

Guideline for Pre-service Teachers

02 Read the listening script and follow the directions.

Below is a listening script excerpted from today's listening lesson.

Listening Script

Setting: Two friends, Alex and Jamie, run into each other at a coffee shop.

Alex : Hey Jamie! Long time no see. How have you been?

Jamie : Alex! Wow, it's been ages. I'm doing well, thanks. How about you? How's everything going?

Alex : Pretty good, actually. Just keeping busy with work and a bit of travel here and there. How's the family?

Jamie : Everyone's great, thanks for asking. The kids are growing up fast and keeping us on our toes. Did you end up moving to the new place?

Alex : Yes, we moved last spring. It's been hectic but exciting to set up a new home. You should come over sometime!

Jamie : I'd love that! Let's definitely plan something soon. Have you been to any interesting places recently?

Alex : Yeah, I went to Portugal last month. It was amazing—beautiful beaches, great food, and the weather was perfect.

Jamie : That sounds fantastic!

(ellipsis)

Fill in each blank with the ONE most appropriate word.

> After listening to the given dialogue students are supposed to engage in two activities: True or False activity and then Ordering activity. The first activity focuses on comprehension by asking students to listen to a conversation and answer True/False questions based on specific details. These questions require them to pay attention to the personal experiences and interactions between Alex and Jamie, which are typical elements of (1) _____ dialogues, rather than the dialogues related to propositional facts. Moreover, the second activity requires students to reconstruct a conversation by arranging mixed-up lines in the correct order. Thus, this activity directly addresses (2) _____ by reinforcing understanding of how conversations are structured and how ideas and responses are connected logically.

Your Answer (1) _____

(2) _____

> Guideline for Pre-service Teachers

03 Read the passages and follow the directions.

A

What Makes Listening Difficult?

As teachers plan lessons and techniques for teaching listening skills, many characteristics of spoken language need to be taken into consideration. Second language learners need to pay special attention to such factors because they strongly influence the processing of speech, and can even block comprehension if they are not attended to. In other words, they can make the listening process difficult. They include some characteristics of spoken language such as clustering, redundancy, reduced forms, performance variables, colloquial language, rate of delivery, stress, rhythm, and intonation.

B

Listening Script

Simon : Hey, Janny. How's it going?
Janny : Pretty good, Simon. How was your weekend?
Simon : Aw, it was terrible. Really bad. I mean… the worst you could imagine. You know what I mean?
Janny : Yah, I've had those days. Well, like, what happened?
Simon : Well… you're not gonna believe this… my friend, you know Mike? — I think you met him at the party — anyway… he and I drove to Sydney Observatory, you know, the observatory in Millers Point? So, we were driving along when this dud in one SUV like a Hummer or something, comes up like three feet behind us and like tailgates us on these crazy roads up there, you know what they're like…

(…)

Below is an excerpt from the conversation between two English teachers talking about listening script above.

T1 : Hmm, Ms. Yoo. Is it too difficult for our students?
T2 : Difficult? Is it?
T1 : I mean, there are many reductions like gonna and I've.
T2 : I see. I agree that such reductions would not easy to hear for our students who are accustomed to only written English.
T1 : Also, the two speakers speak too fast. We need to slow down the speed when we play the listening file.
T2 : Do you really think so? Well, I understand what you mean but I think there are many pauses by the speakers. It would be okay for them to comprehend the conversation. Also, they can have more processing time and get more extra information with the little insertions like *I mean* and *you know* from the listening.
T1 : You mean, some _____ can help our students listening more easily, right?
T2 : That's right. For example, suppose the speaker repeats and elaborates his previous utterance, saying "*SUV, SUV like a Hummer or something.*" Such spoken characteristic can give listeners one more chance to listen for it even though they miss and misunderstand the previous information.
T1 : Okay, then, let's remind our students of this spoken characteristic before listening and see how they perform. If they have a problem with this, then we can try another one.
T2 : That's exactly what I am saying.

T=teacher

Fill in the blank in <B> with the ONE most appropriate word from <A>.

Your Answer

Guideline for Pre-service Teachers

04 Read the meeting note and follow the directions.

Meeting Note

- Date: April 20, 2023
- Subject: Reading Comprehension
- Topic: The importance of background knowledge for reading comprehension.
- Participants: Three English teachers (Ms. Park, Ms. Yoo, Ms. Kim)

Today we discussed how having prior knowledge about a topic can help students better understand a text. We used the concept of _____ to explain how prior experiences and knowledge can act as a mental framework for readers to make sense of new information. First of all, we talked about how social, political, and cultural aspects are often part of readers' _____, and recognizing these elements in a text can help them further their understanding of the text. We also explored how it can help them visualize aspects of a story and create mental images that make the text more engaging. We used the example of a novel describing a scene in a sunny park, and discussed how readers can use their prior experiences in parks to visualize the setting in their mind. Thus, we noted that not having enough _____ can make the readers difficult to establish context and visualize components of a text.

Below is the table of content mentioned in today's meeting.

Roles of _____ in Reading a Text	Description
1. Help establish context	These allow readers to understand the background, setting, and social/cultural context of a text.
2. Enhance comprehension	By drawing on their existing knowledge and experiences, readers can better understand and interpret a text. They also can use these to make inferences about what might happen next.
3. Aid in visualization	These allow readers to create mental images of scenes and settings described in the text.
4. Support critical thinking	By recognizing patterns and making connections, readers engage in critical thinking and analyze the text more deeply. These also help them evaluate the author's purpose and message, and make connections to their own lives and experiences.

Fill in the blanks with the ONE most appropriate word in common.

Your Answer _____

05 Read the passages and follow the directions.

A

Mr. Yu's Note

Today, I attended to a teacher's conference about how to help struggling readers. According to an article from the conference, there are seven cognitive strategies which students can use, when they struggle with understanding key contents in a text. The seven cognitive strategies of effective readers are:

- activating
- questioning
- searching-selecting
- summarizing
- predicting
- monitoring-clarifying
- visualizing-organizing

I believe that these cognitive strategies will change struggle readers into skilled one. By using these strategies students could extract, construct meaning from text and create knowledge structures in long-term memory. Thus, I decided to directly teach and model these strategies during the lesson. The following lesson represents one of these strategies, which can improve students comprehension and retention.

B

Below is a lesson template that Mr. Yu has prepared to teach one of cognitive strategies.

Lesson Template

Lesson Template for Teaching Cognitive Strategies		Lesson Plan for Teaching _____
1. Provide direct instruction regarding the cognitive strategy	a. Define and explain the strategy	This is restating in your own words the meaning of what you have read-using different words from those used in the original text-either in written form or a graphic representation.
	b. Explain the purpose of the strategy serves during reading	It enables a reader to determine what is most important to remember once the reading is completed. Many things we read have only one or two big ideas, and it is important to identify them and restate them for the purpose of retention.
	c. Describe the critical attributes of the strategy	• It is short. • It is to the point, containing the big idea of the text. • It omits trivial information and collapses lists into a word or phrase. • It is not a "photocopy" of the text.
	d. Provide concrete examples/ non-examples of the strategy	• **Good example**: report of a basketball or football game that captures the highlights. • **Non-example**: a paragraph that is too long, has far too many details, or is a complete retelling of the text rather than a statement of the main idea.

2. Model the strategy by thinking aloud	Choose a section of relatively easy text from your discipline and think aloud as you read it, and then also think aloud about how you would go.
3. Facilitate guided practice with students	Practice the strategy using easy-to-read content text: (1) with the whole class (2) with partners (3) independently

Fill in the blank in <B> with the ONE most appropriate word from <A>.

Your Answer _____

06 Review the lesson procedure below and follow the directions.

- Level: Intermediate
- Grade: 2nd grade in a middle school
- Time: 45 minutes
- Objectives:
  1) Students will be able to find the main idea and specific information from the text.
  2) Students will be able to present their own healthy eating tips.

Lesson Procedure

<u>Step 1</u> T provides a reading text and explains some new vocabulary from the text.

※ Adjectives to describe the healthfulness of food. Read and listen.
- **healthy/healthful**: is good for you.
- **unhealthy/unhealthful**: is bad for you.
- **fatty/high-fat**: contains a lot of oil.
- **salty**: contains a lot of salt.

[Reading text] Get Smart! Eating on the go

We know a daily diet of fast food can be bad for us. But fast food is quick and easy, and when we're on the go, it's sometimes a necessary choice. So here are some tips for fast-food fans:
- Choose the chicken. Have chicken rather than red meat. When in doubt, order the grilled chicken - not the fried.
- Go light on the sauce. Mayo, salad dressings, and other sauces are loaded with calories. Cut down on them, or cut them out altogether!
- Fill up on veggies. Ask for tomato, lettuce, onion, or other veggies on your sandwich. These low-calorie choices can help you avoid fried and other high-calorie options.
- Go for the regular size, not the extra-large. Super-size portions can super-size YOU.

(ellipsis)

Guideline for Pre-service Teachers

Step 2 T asks Ss to look at the title of the text and predict what the text is about. Ss present their ideas voluntarily. T checks the main idea of the text with the whole class.

Step 3 Ss are asked to independently read the text and answer the following comprehension check-up questions.
(1) What is the first tip that the text suggests?
(2) To cut calories, you should cut this. What is this?
(3) To avoid fried and high-calorie options, what should you include on your sandwich?

Step 4 T puts Ss in groups of four and makes them share the answers. T nominates a few groups to present the answers and then checks the answers with the whole class.

Step 5 T provides students with a discussion question as seen below. Ss in groups discuss healthy eating tips using vocabulary from the list.

※ Share healthy eating tips with your group members. Use the vocabulary list.

Categories of foods	Adjectives	Verbs
• grains • meat • seafood • sweets • dairy • products • fruit • vegetables • oils	• healthy/unhealthy • good/bad for you • high-calorie/low-calorie • fatty • salty • sweet • spicy	• skip • avoid • cut out • cut down on • fill up on

Step 6 Each group presents their eating tips. Ss listen to the tips and vote for one best tip.

Fill in each blank with the ONE most appropriate word.

> The reading lesson demonstrated above provides lots of vocabulary related to food and health based on the topic, "healthy eating tips". Also, this lesson takes the (1) _____ approach to language skills by requiring students to read, listen to, and speak about eating tips. That is, in Step 3, students read a text and find specific information using a/an (2) _____ strategy. Then, in Steps 5 and 6, students in groups speak about and listen to their own healthy eating tips.

Your Answer   (1) _____

　　　　　　　　(2) _____

Guideline for Pre-service Teachers

07 Review the two students' learning logs below and follow the directions.

> *Ms. Yoo is managing an after-school reading club and Suji and Woobin, her students wrote logs after taking her reading club as below.*
>
> **Suji's Log**
>
> It has been three months since I took Ms. Yoo's reading club. I can enjoy it because I can choose the texts that I want to read. Different from other classes, I don't have to care about any new words, expressions, or grammatical forms. Actually, many pre- and after-reading activities are helpful to analyze the text itself but they seem to be far from reading for pleasure. After taking the after-school reading club, also, only then did I realize that maintaining reading flow without stopping or being interrupted by any reading activities is to improve my reading fluency. Below is the list of texts or books that I have read so far.
>
> 1. Cambridge English Readers Level 2 The Big Picture
> 2. Penguin Readers Level 3 Michelle Obama
> 3. Macmillan Readers Elementary The Mark of Zorro
> 4. Penguin Readers Level 3 Mr. Bean in Town
>
> **Woobin's Log**
>
> In Ms. Yoo's reading club, I can choose reading texts for myself. Usually, I did not even think about reading real English books because my English proficiency is quite low. Actually, most authentic books that I want to read include too many unknown words and unfamiliar structures, which make me overwhelmed. Moreover, some sentences are too long and complex for me to understand. So, I hoped that Ms. Yoo helps me choose some authentic books even beginners like me can enjoy reading without feeling burdened. From the next reading club, I wish I could find some books suitable for my proficiency level. Below are examples of books I read in Ms. Yoo's reading club so far.
>
> 1. Anna Karenina (Novel by Leo Tolstoy)
> 2. The Power of Habit (Book by Charles Duhigg)
> 3. Harry Potter and the Philosopher's Stone (Novel by J. K. Rowling)
> 4. 10 Steps to Earning Awesome Grades (Book by Thomas Frank)

Fill in each blank with the ONE most appropriate word.

As seen in Ms. Yoo's reading lesson, a good way to improve the learner's knowledge of a foreign language is "free and voluntary reading". Such type of reading that two students have experienced in Ms. Yoo's after-school club is a/an (1) _____ reading where they choose their reading books for themselves and read longer texts for pleasure during the extended period of time. According to the list of books, Suji has read graded readers that are reading books of various genres, specially created for false beginners or intermediate-level learners of foreign languages. On the other hand, even in Ms. Yoo's reading club, Woobin only read books with too many unknown words and complex sentence structures. Consequently, he was a bit overwhelmed while reading the chosen authentic books. Therefore, from the next reading club, he hopes that he can choose authentic texts considering the (2) _____ of the books according to his reading proficiency.

Your Answer (1) _____

(2) _____

08 Read the conversation between a teacher and a student, and fill in each blank with the TWO most appropriate words.

> *Bomi, who has an intermediate level of English, visits the office of her English teacher, Ms. Choi, to talk about reading lessons.*

Ms. Choi : So, Bomi, what's up?
Bomi : I have something to talk to you!
Ms. Choi : Yeah, what is it about?
Bomi : I really enjoy reading books, so I read many books in Korean.
Ms. Choi : That's a good thing!
Bomi : Yes, it helps me a lot. So, I want to read English books a lot. But I have only a few English books that I can read at home. Besides, the texts in the textbook are excerpts from whole stories, aren't they?
Ms. Choi : So, you mean, it's not enough?
Bomi : Yeah, that's just it! And I want to read the entire stories, which are more interesting.
Ms. Choi : Okay. Let me see.
Bomi : I want you to come up with a great idea.
Ms. Choi : Well, how about having the reading lesson in the school library tomorrow? Then, you guys can have more chances to read stories in English. There are many books you can choose for yourself.
Bomi : That sounds great! I like the idea!
Ms. Choi : Yes, that's called (1) _____, whose purpose is reading for pleasure. Usually, all of you participate in a/an (2) _____ class where you read for information and practice reading strategies with some exercises.
Bomi : I see. Then, what's the difference?
Ms. Choi : For the next lesson, usually, you are not asked to gain every detail from the text. There is no comprehension test after reading. But I can ask you to review the book very briefly. How does it sound to you?
Bomi : Cool! I am already looking forward to it.

Your Answer (1) _____
(2) _____

Guideline for Pre-service Teachers

09 Read the passage in <A> and the teacher's journal in <B>, and follow the directions.

A

    The teaching and learning of reading skill in high schools, just like the other three skills, contains a lot of problems that have been criticized for a long time. Despite the fact that it is the most taught skill of the four, reading has not become any easier for students. As part of efforts to teach students reading skills effectively, researchers have provided several reading models. The first model takes a bottom-up reading process where the reader decodes, letter-by-letter, word-by-word the written symbols in the text and then reassembles the pieces to form meaning. The second model with a top-down reading process, suggests that efficient readers do not need to use all of the textual cues. Instead, they consider reading process as a "psycholinguistic guessing game". Lastly, the third model represents the interactive processing. Interaction refers to the constant interaction between the two processing skills. This model proposes that developing readers must work at perfecting both their language recognition skills and their interpretation skills.

B

Teacher's Journal

    Mr. Kim and I read an article on teaching reading and discussed how we can improve the way we teach reading. We realized that, in our reading lessons, the students were asked to focus on understanding separate pieces of information from the text without considering any higher-order relationship between them. As a result, the fragmented memory and heavy memory load disturbed their reading comprehension. So, we came up with the following activities to compensate the current reading process, leading to the _____ reading model.

Reading activities to be implemented:

- Graphic organizers to relate students' own experiences to the reading topic
- Activating vocabulary knowledge
- Visualizing what they read
- Finding moods and emotions

Fill in the blank in <B> with the ONE word from the passage in <A>.

Your Answer _____

Guideline for Pre-service Teachers

10 Read the conversation and follow the directions.

> Ms. Choi : Hi, Mr. Kim! Do you have a minute?
> Mr. Kim : Sure! How can I help you?
> Ms. Choi : It's about the reading texts I use in my lessons. My students find the topics from our current textbook a bit boring and uninteresting.
> Mr. Kim : Boring and uninteresting? What exactly do they find unappealing about them?
> Ms. Choi : They say the topics are outdated. They are interested in more authentic texts with relevant and current content.
> Mr. Kim : That's a common concern. But don't worry, I might have a solution that might work for you!
> Ms. Choi : Really? What is it?
> Mr. Kim : In my classes, I supplement textbook readings with additional materials both inside and outside the classroom.
> Ms. Choi : Outside the classroom? Like what?
> Mr. Kim : For example, every month, I take my students to the school library so they can choose interesting books on their own. This encourages them to engage with texts that capture their attention.
> Ms. Choi : They choose their own books? That's great! But, you teach intermediate students, right? My students are beginners and might struggle with reading English books on their own.
> Mr. Kim : Even for beginners, there are resources. Our library has a section of _____ designed for different proficiency levels. These books are specifically written to help learners gradually build their reading skills.
> Ms. Choi : Even for beginners?
> Mr. Kim : Absolutely! You know, _____ are an excellent stepping stone. They expose beginners to high-frequency vocabulary and help them progress to more advanced texts over time.
> Ms. Choi : That sounds perfect! Exactly what I needed. Thank you, Mr. Kim!
> Mr. Kim : No problem! Always happy to help.

Fill in the blanks with the SAME words.

Your Answer

Guideline for Pre-service Teachers

11 Read the dialogue and follow the directions.

Ms. Kim and Mr. Gang, two English teachers, are having a conversation about how they can make their reading classes more effective and meaningful.

Ms. Kim : Some of my students mentioned that my reading class was too demanding and a bit dull. Since then, I've been thinking about how I can make the class more engaging and effective.

Mr. Gang : That's a great point. What have you come up with so far?

Ms. Kim : Well, I decided to encourage students to explore books about their personal interests from the school library.

Mr. Gang : That's an interesting idea. How's it been going?

Ms. Kim : Unfortunately, the results haven't been quite what I hoped for. The wide range of proficiency levels among students is a big challenge for me. I think the problem is that I asked them to freely choose what they want to read without any guidance. Most students chose books that were either too easy or too difficult for them without considering their proficiency levels. In particular, low-level students seemed to struggle with understanding the text, which included lots of unfamiliar words and structural complexities beyond their current level.

Mr. Gang : Hmm... Ms. Kim, did you notice that our school library has a/an _____ section? It has books distinguished into beginner, false beginner, low intermediate, high intermediate and advanced levels.

Ms. Kim : Really? That's new to me.

Mr. Gang : Actually, I had the same trouble as you did. So, I suggested our school librarian prepare a/an _____ section in the corner of the library so that teachers like me can encourage students to read books corresponding to their proficiency levels.

Ms. Kim : That will completely address my concern!

Mr. Gang : If you refer to this section and guide your students, they can choose level-appropriate books and read smoothly and effectively.

Ms. Kim : That's exactly what I want!

Fill in the blanks with TWO words in common.

Your Answer _____

Guideline for Pre-service Teachers

12 Read the activity procedure and follow the directions.

Activity Procedure

STEP #1

T provides a picture about Korean Tranditional Chuseok and asks Ss in groups of four to discuss their thoughts and ideas while taking a close look at the picture.

STEP #2

T asks each group to present what they have shared voluntarily. T transcribes Ss' words on the board in an organized way to create the text.

STEP #3

The whole class reads the story aloud and discusses it. T asks if Ss want to make any corrections or additions to the story. Then, T marks the changes they suggest and makes further suggestions, if needed.

STEP #4

The final story can be read in a choral or echo style, or both. Ss can also read in small groups or pairs, and then individually.

STEP #5

T asks Ss in groups to create comprehension questions using the story. Each group switches the questions they have made with the other group and finds the answers to the questions.

STEP #6

T asks each group to present the questions they have received from the other group and the asnwers they have found.

STEP #7

Before finishing the lesson, T provides Ss with the following checklist.

Checklist for Students

* Read the following statements and respond with a checkmark (∨).

Statements	1	2	3
1. In group discussion, I talk about my ideas by using diverse words/expressions as many as possible.			
2. I listened carefully to my friends' thoughts and ideas.			
3. I understand all words and expressions used in the story.			
4. I pronounced the words clearly while reading my story aloud.			
5. I understand the whole story clearly and find the answers of comprehension questions correctly.			

1=No, 2=Sometimes, 3=Yes

Below is the comment about the activity procedure above. Complete the comment by filling in each blank with the ONE or THREE most appropriate word(s).

The activity procedure exemplifies the (1) _____ where students generate the reading text based on their personal experiences. After generating their own reading texts, to facilitate students' (2) _____ strategies, the teacher provides a checklist with which students can evaluate their own performance and participation during the lesson.

Your Answer (1) _____
(2) _____

Guideline for Pre-service Teachers

13 Read the activity procedure and follow the directions.

	Activity Procedure
Step 1	• The teacher displays six photos of students' school field trip to the fire station on the board. • T invites students to come to the front and collaboratively arrange the photos in the order that they visited the locations on the field trip day. • T facilitates the group activity, helping students verify the correct sequence and label each photo with a sequential number. • T forms six groups and assigns one photo to each group.
Step 2	• T instructs each group to collectively brainstorm and discuss how to describe the photo assigned to them. • Each group presents their descriptions, and T records the information shared by students on the board in an organized manner.
Step 3	• T guides all students to read aloud the sentences for photo number 1 displayed on the board. • T encourages students to provide any corrections needed and to suggest additional sentences. • T incorporates the students' feedback and offers suggestions to improve the sentences.
Step 4	• T asks Group 1 to read aloud the revised sentences for their assigned photo. • Following that, T also invites the other groups to do the same. • T involves the entire class by having all students read aloud the sentences displayed on the board.
Step 5	• T assigns each group the task of creating a poster on A3 size paper. • T instructs each group to present their poster to the class after the completion.

T=teacher, Ss=students

Complete the comments by filling in each blank with ONE or TWO word(s).

The activity is designed based on the (1) _____ approach, which is widely regarded as one of the most effective methods for second language readers. The strength of this approach lies in allowing students to collaboratively create their own reading material for the day's reading instruction. As demonstrated in the above lesson procedure, students talk about their school field trip to the fire station and the teacher transcribes their group descriptions which then become the material for the day's lesson. As a result, this approach can enhance students' (2) _____ motivation since it is based on a personalized experience that fulfills their curiosity, enjoyment, and engagement. Through this approach the teacher tailors the activity to align with individual students' unique interests, background knowledge, and language proficiency, setting it apart from conventional written text.

Your Answer   (1) _____

(2) _____

Guideline for Pre-service Teachers

14 Read the conversation and follow the directions.

> T1 : I've been finding it challenging to gauge my students' comprehension of the reading materials more accurately. Do you have any effective assessment techniques to share?
> T2 : Yes, I've developed a strategy that could be exactly what you need.
> T1 : I'm eager to hear about it. Could you describe how it is implemented?
> T2 : Of course. Start by selecting a passage tailored to your students' reading levels. Carefully eliminate certain words or phrases pivotal for grasping the main concepts or details of the text. Next, have your students read the passage and attempt to fill in the blanks based on their understanding of the context and the content.
> T1 : That sounds interesting. What's the purpose behind removing these words?
> T2 : The goal is to foster gaps that compel the students to deduce the missing information, encouraging deep thought and inference based on their reading.
> T1 : How do you determine which words to exclude?
> T2 : Focus on extracting words that are crucial to the text's meaning—like key nouns, verbs, or adjectives. The challenge should actively engage students in the reading without being overwhelming.
> T1 : Makes sense. And what is a good benchmark score for students to demonstrate adequate reading comprehension?
> T2 : Generally, aim for a minimum of 60% correctness. However, adjust this threshold as necessary, perhaps lowering it to 50% or raising it to 70%, depending on the specific objectives of your assessment and the current performance level of your students.
> T1 : Understood. So, it's best to tailor the scoring criteria to fit the educational goals and my students' progress. I'm excited to try this method. Thank you for the advice!
> T2 : You're welcome!

Fill in the blank with the TWO most appropriate words.

In the above conversation, T1 inquires about strategies to assess students' reading comprehension, and T2 introduces the _____ cloze procedure, which involves strategically removing critical words from a text to challenge students to fill in the gaps.

Your Answer _____

Guideline for Pre-service Teachers

15 Read the passage and follow the directions.

Ms. Lee designed the following cloze test and administered it to her students last week. In the test, the students were asked to choose the words that had been removed.

A Vocational Vacation

Once many students finish high school or college, they have the uncanny desire to travel as far away from home as possible. Visiting new places and seeing exotic locales around the world __1__ can be a great learning experience, but there is one big problem that these young travelers face—a lack of money. Most countries nowadays are __2__ young globetrotters by offering a six- to twelve-month working holiday for anyone between the ages of 18 and 35. This way, they will be able to experience new cultures while making enough money to survive.

In Australia, the working holiday program has been a phenomenal success. In its first year of existence, 1975, 2,000 working visas were __3__. By 2006, this number had increased to 113,000, which is estimated to have added US $1.3 billion to Australia's economy in that year. Many of the positions __4__ are in the hospitality industry or harvest work, but some travelers are getting jobs in finance, health care, and education.

For Australians, Britons, and New Zealanders, a popular place to spend a working holiday is Canada, where there are numerous ski and snowboard resorts.

1. (A) on leave
   (B) in person
   (C) off record
   (D) by surprise

2. (A) applying to
   (B) leading to
   (C) occurring to
   (D) catering to

3. (A) squeezed
   (B) issued
   (C) featured
   (D) inspired

4. (A) available
   (B) vacant
   (C) inclusive
   (D) essential

Complete the following comments by filling in the blanks with ONE or TWO word(s).

> Ms. Lee developed a/an (1) _____ cloze test where she selectively removed certain words with specific purposes. In this case, she only deleted content words. For each blank, students must choose the correct word from a list of options based on (2) _____ relationships between phrases. For example, the first blank tests if they understand the phrase that means experiencing new places firsthand. The second blank tests knowledge of the phrase that means providing for the needs of young travelers. The third requires the correct term for officially giving out visas. Finally, the fourth tests understanding of the word that describes job positions that can be applied for.

Your Answer (1) _____

(2) _____

16 Read the lesson procedure and follow the directions.

Lesson Procedure

1. The teacher introduces the topic with two visual aids: a 'no mobile phones' sign and a text message image, asking students to choose which aligns with their views.

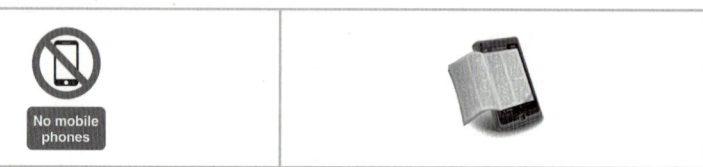

2. The teacher then shows a mini-drama on mobile phone use during lessons. Students receive the script and worksheet.
3. In pairs, students read the script, discussing the implied message about phone use in class.
4. They use online dictionaries or consult peers/teachers for unclear words.
5. Students write the message conveyed by the script on the worksheet.

[Worksheet]
※ Read the following parts of the script and write down the message they convey.

(1) Living without a mobile phone is a nightmare for Generation MZ.
→ _____.

(2) In the context of learning, the use of mobile phones represents a double-edged sword.
→ _____.

6. They conclude by discussing their agreement or disagreement with the drama's message.

※ Do you agree or disagree with the opinion from the drama? Share your opinions with your partner.

Referring to the lesson procedure above, fill in each blank with the ONE most appropriate word.

During the lesson, students read a mini-drama about mobile phone use, working in pairs to interpret and record its message. They concluded with a discussion to share their opinions on the author's viewpoint. The teacher guided students in deepening their understanding, initially focusing on (1) _____ comprehension of the information that was not explicitly stated in the scenes. Additionally, through pair discussions, students evaluated the message using (2) _____ comprehension skills, expressing their own ideas both for and against it.

Your Answer   (1) _____
　　　　　　　　(2) _____

NEW
Build Up

Chapter 04

Productive Skills

Chapter 04 Productive Skills

📖 정답 및 모범 답안 p. 243

01 Read the passage and follow the directions.

Lesson Procedure

Step 1: T introduces today's topic: asking for clarification. T asks Ss to imagine the situation when we might need to ask for clarification. (e.g. conversation between a newcomer to an area and a person living there.)

Step 2: T puts Ss in pairs and provides the following dialogue. Ss choose one role each between Jin, a Korean customer, and Alex, a store staff in a british store. Ss practice the given dialogue in pairs.

> Jin : How do I pay for my parking?
> Alex : Pay at the machine in the lobby before you exit. It's on level L.
> Jin : I'm sorry. Could you say that again?
> Alex : The ticket machine is in the lobby. Level L. Pay there.
> Jin : I apologize. Could you repeat that slowly?
> Alex : *(Slowly)* Pay at the machine. Level L. Show your receipt at the exit. You have 15 minutes to exit after you pay.

Step 3: T provides the following list of phrases that can be used to ask for clarification. T reads aloud one by one and Ss repeat after T. T makes Ss repeat after the phrases until they can read them naturally.

- Could you repeat that?
- Could you say that again?
- I'm sorry.. I don't understand.
- Would you mind repeating that?
- I didn't catch that. (I didn't hear what you said.)
- I don't get it. (I don't understand.)

Step 4: T provides the following dialogue between Mia, a newcomer to one town, and Patric, a working staff in a supermarket. Ss in pairs fill in each blank using the phrases above. When they complete, Ss practice the dialogue twice changing the role.

Mia　　: Can you tell me where to find the spaghetti sauce?
Patric : It's three rows down. Head all the way to the end. The sauces are next to the dried pasta.
Mia　　: I'm _____. I didn't _____ that.
Patric : Aisle 3. *(points)* At the very end of the row. Beside the pasta.
Mia　　: Thank you. Aisle 3. Beside the … Pesto?
Patric : Pasta.
Mia　　: Oh, Pasta! Sorry, English is not my first language.
Patric : No problem. That's what I'm here for.

T=teacher, Ss=students

Guideline for Pre-service Teachers

Complete the comments by filling in each blank with the ONE or TWO most appropriate word(s).

> The lesson procedure outlined above is designed to teach students one strategy for meaning negotiation when they do not understand what the other person is saying. Specifically, in Step 2, the teacher introduces a/an (1) _____ activity that includes phrases related to (2) _____. Then, in Step 3, the teacher explicitly teaches various phrases that students can use for (2) _____. Once students become familiar with these phrases, in Step 4, the teacher provides a new (1) _____ scenario for students to practice using the appropriate phrases after completing the initial dialogue.

Your Answer (1) _____

(2) _____

02 Read the passages and fill in the blank with the ONE most appropriate word.

> T : Okay, let's move on to a group activity. Guys, make a group of four!
> *(Ss sit in groups of four.)*
> T : This activity is called 'Let's go to Busan.' Have you been to Busan?
> Ss : Yes!
> T : How did you get there?
> S1 : I took a train.
> S2 : In my case, I took an airplane.
> T : Right, there are many different ways to get to Busan from Seoul. So, I will give you train, airplane, ship, and bus timetables. Based on the information from the timetables, find the best route to go to Busan.
> S3 : I have a question. The "best route" means the quickest way? Or the cheapest way?
> T : That's a good question! "Best route" means the cheapest way here. So, the budget to get to Busan is 200 thousand won for four people. Each transportation mode provides different discount types. For example, the train provides a 25 percent discount for four people travelling together. Also, the express bus provides a 20 percent discount for three people travelling together. Any questions? No? Okay, then I will give you 20 minutes. Let's start!
> *(T walks around the classroom to check the students' work and helps those who need help.)*

Guideline for Pre-service Teachers

[Timetables]

Train	Departure	Arrival	Price per person
KTX 293	13:55	16:22	50,000
KTX 139	14:00	16:40	51,000
KTX 295	14:15	16:45	52,000

※ KTX provides a 25% discount for groups of four people.

Bus	Departure	Arrival	Price per person
Express Bus 407	13:00	17:00	50,000
Express Bus 364	14:05	17:55	49,000
Express Bus 486	14:15	16:45	51,000

※ Express Bus provides a 20% discount for groups of three people.

. . .

T=teacher, Ss=students, S=student

The activity above requires students to derive some new information by inferring it from the information they have been given. This type of activity is called a/an _____ activity. In this lesson, students are given timetables for train, airplane, ship, and bus routes. Then, the teacher asks them to work out the best route to get from Seoul to Busan.

Your Answer _____

03 Read the passage and follow the directions.

> *Below is part of the pronunciation lesson conducted by Ms. Lee.*
>
> Ms. Lee : Guys, the sentence "I think I know" can be stressed differently depending on the meaning.
>
> *(Ms. Lee shows four sentences with their respective sound clips on the screen shared with students' individual tablets.)*
>
> > (a) **I** think I know. 🔊
> > (b) I **think** I know. 🔊
> > (c) I think **I** know. 🔊
> > (d) I think I **know**. 🔊
>
> Ms. Lee : In these four utterances, the bold typeface shows which word is stressed. If you listen to each sound clip, you will hear the sound and meaning differences among them. The differences are related to the context where the utterance occurs. Here are the interpretations of each sentence. Find your partner and match each interpretation with the appropriate sentence in pairs.
>
> *(Ms. Lee shows the following new sentences on the screen.)*
>
> > 1. I'm not entirely sure, but I think I know the answer.
> > 2. You may not know the answer, but I think I do.
> > 3. I am quite confident that I know the answer.
> > 4. You may not think I know the answer, but I'm pretty sure I do.
>
> *(Students use their tablets to play each sound clip, listen carefully to each one, and then match each sentence with the correct interpretation.)*

4. Productive Skills

Guideline for Pre-service Teachers

Complete the comments by filling in the blanks with the ONE most appropriate word in common.

> The lesson conducted by Ms. Lee focuses on how stress patterns can change the meaning of sentences, using the phrase "I think I know" as an example. She demonstrates this through different sound clips, each emphasizing a different word, which correlates with a specific meaning depending on the context. This exercise improves students' _____ by teaching them the importance of stress patterns in conveying meaning. By actively listening to variations of the sentence with different stressed words, students learn how stress impacts the sentence's meaning, helping them understand the relationship between stress and context. The use of tablets facilitates focused listening practice, enabling students to clearly hear and internalize the correct stress patterns. Engaging students in matching sentences with their correct interpretations reinforces their comprehension and retention. The repeated exposure and active involvement ensure students can apply these stress patterns in real-life conversations, making their speech clearer and easier to understand, thereby improving their overall spoken English _____.

Your Answer _____

04 Read the passage and fill in the blanks with the ONE most appropriate word.

Figure 1

What is needed to teach pronunciation effectively?

Teachers need to know….

Knowledge of the pronunciation features (e.g., articulation rules, occurrences in discourse)	Awareness of potential student problems (e.g., stemming from the students' L1 or diagnostic work)	Pedagogical priorities (i.e., which features should be taught and when)

Figure 1 displays the knowledge required for teachers to effectively teach pronunciation. According to this framework, teachers must first have a comprehensive understanding of the pronunciation features they are teaching. This involves knowing how articulators produce segmental features and how suprasegmental features convey meaning in discourse.

Second, teachers must be aware of factors influencing their students' acquisition of new pronunciation features. This includes understanding the problem stemming from the student's first language. For example, Korean students occasionally confuse sounds that can be represented by multiple phonetic variations in Hangul, leading to pronunciation errors. For example, they might mispronounce "fork" as "pork" or "right" as "light," due to the similarities between the sounds of "f" and "p," and "r" and "l." If teachers are aware of these examples of (1) _____ from the first language, they can more effectively assist Korean students with pronunciation.

Guideline for Pre-service Teachers

Finally, teachers, guided by curriculum guidelines, must make informed decisions about which aspects of pronunciation to focus on in each unit. This includes planning how and when to present these aspects. Teachers must assess the extent to which students' non-target-like pronunciation of segmentals and suprasegmentals interferes with (2) _____ (i.e., the ability to be understood.) and how important these features are for students' overall communicative needs.

Your Answer (1) _____

(2) _____

05 Read the passage and fill in the blank with THREE words from the passage.

> *Below is part of a conversation between two English teachers.*

T1 : What are you reading?
T2 : I'm reading an article about teaching pronunciation.
T1 : Interesting. What is it talking about? Stress and intonation?
T2 : Yes, they are part of it but I am looking for the best method to help them acquire clear pronunciation for specific sounds.
T1 : You mean, segmental units?
T2 : Right. Most of my students are fluent in speaking English. But sometimes when they speak fast, they mispronounce vowels like /ɜː/ into /ɑː/ and /ʌ/ into /ɜː/.
T1 : Hmm, they need a lot of practice for the vowel sounds. Did you try to provide such confusing words in pairs?
T2 : In pairs?
T1 : Yes. For example, you prepare pairs of words that have minimal phonetic difference.
T2 : Oh, yes I did. Actually, the article is talking about the same method as a solution.
T1 : Then, just do it. What's the matter?
T2 : There is one big difference between the method I used and what the article suggests.
T1 : Big difference? What is it?
T2 : The article suggests _____.
T1 : Can you explain more about it?
T2 : So, I used to give the list of words in pairs without context such as 'heard – hard', and 'firm and farm'. But, the article says I should provide them in a more contextualized manner. For example, I should give the pairs within example sentences describing the event in a *firm* and a *farm*. If needed, I can also add pictures to sentences. So, they can naturally pick up the sound difference within context.

Guideline for Pre-service Teachers

T1 : Oh, yes, I see what you mean. Context is one of the most important reference points for meaning or form. So, teaching language items with context allows students to clearly understand the difference in meaning or form.
T2 : You can say that again.

T=teacher

Your Answer

06 Read the conversation and follow the directions.

> *Joohee, who is a high school student, is now in the cafeteria of an international language school located in New York. She has been in this school for about a week and she is going to stay for a month during the summer vacation. She is in the line to choose some food for Dinner and Chef. Marco is welcoming her.*
>
> Marco : Hello, Joohee. What do you want to have?
> Joohee : Good evening, Chef. Marco. I want a rack [læk] of lamb.
> Marco : Excuse me?
> Joohee : A rack [læk] of lamb, over there.
> Marco : Oh, a rack [ræk] of lamb. I got it. Okay, then, what else?
> Joohee : Two pieces of pizza, please!
> Marco : Okay. Here you are, Joohee.
> Joohee : Oh, too thick [sɪk].
> Marco : Pardon me? You don't like it? or are you sick now?
> Joohee : Oh, no! I mean, can I get a thin [sɪn] one over there? This one is too think [sɪk].
> Marco : Ah-hah! You want a thinner one. Now, I do understand what you want. Here, let me change this for you.
> Joohee : Thank you, Chef. Marco.

Guideline for Pre-service Teachers

Complete the comments below by filling in each blank with the ONE most appropriate word.

> The conversation above highlights common pronunciation errors often made unconsciously by Korean students, largely due to the influence of their first language. Such pronunciation errors typically occur at the (1) _____ units. For instance, Joohee mispronounces the /r/ and /th/ sounds, which are absent in her native language. As seen in Chef. Marco's reactions, "Excuse me?" and "Pardon me?", to Joohee's incorrect utterances, some pronunciation errors can reduce speech (2) _____, leading to misunderstandings or communication breakdowns.

Your Answer (1) _____

(2) _____

07 Read the passage, and follow the directions.

Activity

Step 1

On one side of the worksheet, there are several sentences of varying length. On the other side, the sentences are represented by a series of numbers; The teacher reads out the sentences, and students underline the number(s) for the word that is (are) stressed. For example:

I bought my **sister** a **present**. ⇒ 1 – 2 – 3 – 4 – 5 – 6
Mike didn't break the window. ⇒ 1 – 2 – 3 – 4 – 5

Mix up the order in which the sentences appear on the left side. Say each sentence out loud, emphasizing the stressed word. Students must then match each sentence with its representation in numbers.

Step 2

Students in pairs discuss where to put stress in sentences according to different situations. After the discussion, they practice reading the dialogues out loud with their partners.

e.g., 1. A : Did you lose your credit card?
      B : No, Mike lost his credit card.

   2. A : Did you lose your credit card?
      B : No, I lost my wallet.

   3. A : Did you lose your credit card?
      B : No, I threw away the credit card because it was expired.

Guideline for Pre-service Teachers

Fill in the blanks with appropriate words.

> The activity demonstrated above focuses on practicing the pronunciation of (1) _____ (ONE word) aspects. Since they can have an even greater impact on (2) _____ (ONE word) than the mispronunciation of individual sounds, the activity aims to raise students' awareness to the relations between stress patterns and the intended meaning for successful future communication.

Your Answer   (1) _____

(2) _____

08 Read the passage and follow the directions.

> Contemporary approaches to pronunciation contrast significantly with earlier methods. Instead of focusing solely on developing a learner's articulatory skills from the bottom-up—merely mastering a list of phonemes and allophones—a top-down strategy is employed. This approach prioritizes the most pertinent pronunciation aspects. Rather than solely instructing the function of articulation within individual words or, at best, phrases, we emphasize its role within an entire discourse stream.
>
> ### Exercise in Worksheet
> 1. Read the following example aloud to yourself.
>   (1) Alfred said / the boss is stupid.
>   (2) Alfred / said the boss / is stupid.
> 2. Talk about the difference between (1) and (2) in pairs.

Complete the teaching note by filling in each blank with ONE word.

> ### Ms. Park's Teaching Note
> I believe that teaching learners about suprasegmentals can significantly impact on their comprehension of messages. Just as punctuation aids in processing written text, pronunciation facilitates the listener's understanding of spoken language. Illustrated in the above, (1) _____ in different places can alter meaning. For instance, Exercise (1) implies that Alfred said something about the boss, while Exercise (2) suggests that the boss said about Alfred. This example highlights how a single sentence can convey distinct messages through varying breaks. It adopts a/an (2) _____ approach to teaching pronunciation leading students to deduce the role of these suprasegmentals by comparing the provided sentences.

Your Answer (1) _____
  (2) _____

Guideline for Pre-service Teachers

09 Read the passages and follow the directions.

Lesson Procedure: Long Time No See!

Stage	Procedure
Listening	(. . .) • Ask Ss about two questions, 'what is the situation?' and 'what are they saying to each other?' for each scene. Then Ss play each conversation and contrast them to their predictions. • Give Ss Handout and draw attention to the gap-fill exercise. Ss complete together. **Handout** | Conversation 1	Conversation 2 | |---|---| | A: Good evening. B: Hi. A: Is anyone sitting here? B: No. A: Would you _____ if I joined you? B: Not _____. That would be lovely. A: Can I get you a drink? B: That's very _____. I'd love one. | A: It was lovely to see you again, Sue. We really enjoyed ourselves. Thank you so _____ for having us to stay. B: Not at all. It's _____. A: But it was really kind of you to put up with all of us, and the animals. B: It's no problem at all. | • Listen and pause after each conversation. Ss check. • Ask any questions about vocabulary.
Focus on pairs	• Lead Ss to focus on the functions of the pairs and show the function of each pair. • Ss match all the functions and check with their partner.
Speaking	• The whole class goes through each cue and then Ss practice the pairs individually. • Then Ss in pairs practice all the cues, paying attention to stress and intonation. • Ss switch the role and repeat the practice focusing on stress, rhythm, and intonation.

Ss=students

	A	B
Scene 1.	Would you mind if I joined you?	Not at all, that would be lovely.
Scene 2.	Thank you so much for having us to stay.	Not at all. It's my pleasure.
Scene 3.	Guess what? I passed the test!	What? Congratulations!
Scene 4.	Are you going to the theater tomorrow?	I'd love to, but I've already made plans.

Guideline for Pre-service Teachers

Considering the lesson procedure above, fill in each blank with a suitable term in ONE word.

> The lesson procedure above is a speaking lesson teaching (1) _____ pairs for intermediate/upper-intermediate students aimed at helping them to respond more appropriately to each other's utterances. It highlights the importance of listening carefully and how to reply with focusing on (2) _____, not segmentals, for more natural stress, rhythm, and intonation.

Your Answer   (1) _____

(2) _____

10 Read the conversation and follow the directions.

Ms. Kim	: Today, we are discussing environmental conservation. Please remember to only speak in English. Let's get started!
Min-ji	: Last weekend, I participated /pɑːrrˈtɪsɪpeɪtɪd/ in a clean-up drive. It was very rewarding /rɪˈwɔːrrdɪŋ/. *(Note: emphasis on the 'r' sounds)*
Hyun-woo	: That sounds great. Who did you go with?
Min-ji	: I went with my family.
Ji-hyun	: I think it's great when people who care about the planet do things like this.
	(After the discussion)
Ms. Kim	: Great job, everyone. I have a few questions. First, Min-ji, you emphasized the 'r' sounds in 'participated' and 'rewarding'. Was there a reason for that?
Min-ji	: Oh, I thought pronouncing the 'r' clearly would make me sound more native-like. Was it too strong? Then, I will try to soften it.
Ms. Kim	: Great effort, Min-ji! It's important to pay attention to pronunciation, but you don't need to stress the 'r' too much. I appreciate your attention to language. It's key to clear communication. Now, let's return to our main topic on how even small efforts, like clean-up drives, can have a big impact environmental conservation.

Fill in the blank with the ONE most appropriate term.

In the conversation between two students, Min-ji displays a linguistic phenomenon where learners overapply language rules or norms, typically in an effort to sound more correct or formal than necessary. Min-ji's overemphasis on the /r/ sound in words like "participated" and "rewarding" is a clear example of _____. Attempting to sound more like a native English speaker, she exaggerates the pronunciation, which actually makes her speech sound unnatural.

Your Answer _____

11 Read the passage below and follow the directions.

> *Before the teacher starts his lesson in a middle school English class, he asks students questions to warm up, starting with Kang-min.*
>
> T : What did you do last weekend, Kang-min?
> S : I visit my grandma in the hospital.
> T : Ah, you visited your grandma in the hospital?
> S : Yes, I visit her.
> T : I see. Did you do anything else?
> S : Yeah, Um, I see a movie with my best friend, Dong-hee.
> T : See?
> S : Sorry! I saw a movie with Dong-hee.
> T : Great! What movie did you see?
> S : I saw the movie "Dune."
>
> T=teacher, S=student

Complete the comments about the conversation by filling in each blank with the ONE most appropriate word.

> As seen in classroom conversation above, the teacher effectively uses both implicit (e.g., (1) _____) and explicit (e.g., repetition) feedback to address the student's grammatical errors. By continuing the conversation and providing opportunities for self-correction, the teacher facilitates the student's successful (2) _____ of past tense verbs. In other words, the student immediately responds to the teacher's feedback, trying to correct his previous error. Two types of student responses appear in this talk: one that produces an utterance still needing repair (e.g., "Yes, I visit her.") and the other that produces a repair (e.g., "I saw a movie with Dong-hee.") on which the teacher's feedback focused.

Your Answer (1) _____

(2) _____

Guideline for Pre-service Teachers

12 Read the passages and follow the directions.

Students	Feedback
A	Before writing the first draft, my teacher told us how to start an essay, how to finish it, and how to use connectives or transitions in writing. He always emphasizes organizing the writing, which is significantly helpful in improve my writing skills.
B	Whenever I write something, I have difficulty getting started. However, today, my teacher arranged for us to share ideas about a writing topic in groups. As a result, I was able to glean some ideas from my group members and easily began to write an essay.
C	After completing the first draft, the teacher encouraged us to peer-edit each other. Also, he provided a guideline for us: what to focus on and how to give feedback. On the checklist, the appropriate vocabulary use was treated more importantly than other factors. So, when I gave some feedback on my partner's first draft, I pointed out the wrong word choice.
D	When I talked about my second draft with my English teacher, I focused on my weaknesses and reviewed what needed to be improved. This consultation is always quite helpful in reflecting on my essays critically and writing a better version.

Complete the teacher's reflection by filling in each blank with the ONE most appropriate word.

Teacher's Reflection

The writing program in which the four students have participated is designed based on the (1) _____ writing approach. In class, I began by providing a brief explanation of essay writing. As Student A noted, teaching how to organize writing, even briefly, can be greatly helpful in encouraging students to start writing. Then, I asked students to work in groups to share their ideas about interesting topics and select one. Usually, I have students start writing individually. However, today, as Student B mentioned, I encouraged students to have a group discussion before writing, which helped some students reduce their anxiety and unnecessary tension. After completing their first drafts, students engaged in peer-editing to provide and receive feedback on their drafts using a checklist. As commented by Student C, I required students to focus on the appropriate word choice more than any other linguistic components. Prior to submitting their final work, I had a/an (2) _____ to discuss their writing pieces individually. As Student D pointed out, a crucial element of this writing approach is that I afforded them the opportunity to reflect deeply on their own writing and to enhance it through revision.

Your Answer (1) _____

(2) _____

Guideline for Pre-service Teachers

13 Read passages <A> and <B>, and follow the directions.

A

Pre-Writing Activity Procedure

- Duration: 10 minutes

- Preparation:
  1. In a pre-writing activity, it is important to find out what the students already know about the topic and to get them involved from the start.
  2. After choosing the writing topic "plastic pollution," the following pre-writing procedure begins.

- In class:
  1. Introduce the Topic
     Write the phrase "plastic pollution" inside a circle in the center of the board.
  2. Accept All Responses
     Ask students to call out any words or phrases they associate with "plastic pollution" as they come to their mind.
  3. Create a Spidergram
     As students call out words, write them around the circle, connecting them to the central topic to form a spidergram.

B
Student's Log

During the pre-writing activity on "plastic pollution," I was able to hear a variety of ideas from my classmates that I hadn't thought of before. This activity provided me with a broad range of perspectives and information related to plastic pollution such as "ocean waste," "microplastics," "recycling," and "single-use plastics." These ideas were particularly helpful during the freewriting stage. Additionally, since the teacher accepted all responses without immediate judgement and criticism, I felt comfortable participating without worrying about whether my ideas were off-topic. These two aspects made the activity highly beneficial for enhancing my understanding and preparation for writing on the topic.

Write the name of pre-writing activity in ONE word.

Your Answer _____

14 Read the email exchange between two English teachers, and fill in the blank with the TWO most appropriate words.

Email from Ms. Kim

Subject: Need Help Enhancing Student Writing Clarity

Dear Mr. Lee,

I hope this message finds you well. I am seeking assistance with a challenge I've encountered with my intermediate students. They struggle to write smoothly, often producing texts that lack cohesion and are quite choppy. This significantly impacts the clarity and readability of their writing. I'm looking for an engaging method to help them improve the connectivity and transitions in their writing. Any advice would be greatly appreciated.

Warm regards,
Ms. Kim

Response from Mr. Lee

Subject: Re: Need Help Enhancing Student Writing Clarity

Hello Ms. Kim,

It's always a pleasure to help. To address the challenge you've described, I suggest a practical exercise where you provide students with their original texts alongside revised versions that incorporate appropriate _____. By comparing two versions and identifying the differences, students can clearly see how these devices enhance writing clarity and flow.

[Text 1. Original Text]

　Jenny decided to go for a jog. It was late. She knew exercise could help her clear her mind. She laced up her running shoes. She realized she hadn't eaten since lunch.

(omitted)

[Text 2. Revised Version]

　Despite the late hour, Jenny decided to go for a jog; furthermore, she knew that exercise could help her clear her mind. However, as she laced up her running shoes, a thought struck her: she hadn't eaten since lunch.

(omitted)

The revised version will demonstrate a smoother, more logical flow, compared to the original version.

I hope this activity can help enhance your students' writing skills!

Best wishes,
Mr. Lee

15 Read the reading lesson procedure and follow the directions.

Below is part of a reading lesson plan for first-year middle school students to improve their reading comprehension and develop reflection.

Lesson Plan

Pre-stage

Step 1: T makes Ss recall what problems/difficulties they have faced while using social media.

Step 2: T puts Ss in groups to share what problems they have experienced and how they resolved them.

Step 3: T asks each pair to present what they talked about. T draws a table and writes down what Ss present as seen below.

	Difficulties	Solutions
1	Received mean messages from an anonymous person	Block the person's account
2		
3		...

While-stage

Step 4: T provides Ss with an editorial about Cyberbullying from newspapers. T reads the headline of the story and prompts students to predict the story. Ss voluntarily present their prediction. T asks students to read the text quickly and guess the main idea. Ss skim the text and find the main idea.

Step 5: T provides comprehension questions and asks students to find the answers while reading the text, once again, more carefully.

Step 6: T puts Ss in pairs and asks them to share the answers they found. T checks the answers with the whole class.

	Step 7: T puts Ss in groups and asks Ss to discuss the types of cyberbullying and think about solutions. The types and solutions can be drawn from the text or based on their own experiences as well. T asks Ss to fill in the blanks using what they discussed.

	Types of Cyberbullying	Solutions
1		
2		
3		
4		

Post-stage	Step 8: T asks each group to present what they discussed. After the presentation, T says cyberbullying is a serious crime and emphasizes the importance of fighting against it. Step 9: T gives students homework, in which they write a reflective log of what they have learned related to cyberbullying. T tells Ss to submit their logs by tonight, online, and also mentions that she will provide her responses to each log within this week.

Guideline for Pre-service Teachers

Fill in each blank with the TWO most appropriate words.

Below is an excerpt from a teacher talk briefly introducing today's lesson and wrapping it up.

T: Hello, everyone! Today, we're going to dive into the world of cyberbullying and social media challenges. Before we get started with our text on cyberbullying, I'm going to introduce you to the strategy of (1) _____. Using this strategy can help you have a comprehensive preview of the reading topic, and thus, enhance your reading comprehension skills. First up, we're going to recall our own experiences with social media difficulties. This will help us make a connection between what we're about to read and what we've personally experienced. Next, you'll explore the different types of cyberbullying and brainstorm some possible solutions in groups. After your group discussion, each of you will receive an editorial about cyberbullying. But wait! Before you start reading, I'll read the headline out loud and ask you to predict what the article might be about. Based on your predictions, you'll skim through the text to get the main idea. This will give you a good overview of the subject matter before you dive into the details of the text. Does that sound good to everyone?

(omitted)

T: Alright, everyone! As we're wrapping up today's lesson, I've got a writing assignment for you. This task will have you reflect on any cyberbullying experiences you've had and how you handled them. This will help cement what we've learned today. Also, your reflective logs will give me valuable insights and help me plan my next lesson more effectively. Plus, I'll be giving each of your logs a personalized response, which will help us build a stronger connection. Please email your writing journals at parkhyunsoo@daum.net by 11 p.m. I'll go through your logs and respond within the week. Starting this semester, we'll have a/an (2) _____ as homework every two weeks. Sound good?

Your Answer (1) _____
(2) _____

> Guideline for Pre-service Teachers

16 Read the students' learning logs and follow the directions.

A

Eunju's Learning Log

Today, my English teacher asked us to do a/an (1) _____, a kind of writing activity. First, my teacher read a short paragraph three times. After finishing the paragraph for the third time, she asked us to write the paragraph as we remembered it. To help us recollect what we heard, she put some keywords from the paragraph on the board. With keywords, then, we rewrote the paragraph as close as possible to the original sequence of events. After we completed our own paragraph, my teacher showed us the original text and asked us to compare our versions with the original text. Through this activity, I was able to use my listening and writing skills at the same time. Also, with some language support, it was a little bit demanding but enjoyable and exciting to me.

B

Minkyu's Learning Log

These days, I am writing a journal and getting the teacher's feedback on it every week. I enjoy it very much. There are several reasons that I like this writing activity. For this writing, I can choose the topics as I wish. Also, I can get my teacher's immediate feedback on what I write. Actually, this is a form of written communication but I feel as if it were a face to face conversation. Usually, my teacher does neither correct any errors from my writing, nor grade or evaluate the journal. Through the activity, I am having a good relation with my teacher and I can practice the mechanics of writing. With these various benefits, I like writing (2) _____ very much.

Identify the name of the writing activity that each student talks about in the learning log.

Your Answer   (1) _____
　　　　　　　　(2) _____

17 Read the passage, and follow the directions.

> *The activity below is a written conversation between Ms. Kim, an English teacher in a middle school, and her student, Sungjin.*

1st e-mail by Sungjin

July, 10

Hello, Mr. lee. Today, the class is very interesting. When you teach words, you show pictures, videos, and example sentences. *(ellipsis)* Thanks to these words, I can easily read the text, today. I love today's lesson!

Ms. Kim's Response

July, 15

Hi, Sungjin. I also feel really glad that you could read the text in class. As you know, vocabulary knowledge is quite important in reading comprehension. Thus, in the next lesson, you will be taught some new words so that you can expand your vocabulary knowledge as well as review today's words. See you soon!

4th e-mail by Sungjin

September, 19

Hello, Ms. Kim. Today's speaking class was very fun. I think Joon-ho did a very good job in making the presentation today. His PowerPoint slides and photos were very impressive. I want to learn how to use the program as well. Can you teach me how to use it? Or can you show us how to use it briefly? Thank you. :D

Ms. Kim's Response

September 25

Sungjin! Joon-ho did a good job but I think your presentation was amazing as well! I liked your story about the family trip to Japan. But, still, if you want to learn how to use visual aids for your presentation, I can help you! Of course, I can. Not only PowerPoint but there are also many useful tools for presentation! Next class, I will prepare a lesson introducing some of them. I hope you will enjoy the class!

Complete the teacher's note by filling in each blank with ONE word.

Ms. Kim's Teaching Note

This semester, I have been writing diaries with my students. It gives me more chances to communicate with them beyond the classroom. That's why I started this written conversation.

Actually, my class consists of 30 students, so it is difficult to have enough conversation with each of them during the class. While reading their diaries and then responding to them, I feel that I became much closer to my students than before. At first, they hesitated to write something and so did not enjoy writing dairies. Probably, they are bothered about making mistakes in writing. However, after several times of experiences, they realized that the content is more important than their grammatical mistakes. In their diaries, they usually like to talk about their daily lives to me. Sharing their daily routine with me, students and I are getting closer, which is the first purpose of this activity. I have thought establishing a good (1) _____ with my students like this is more important than anything in classroom teaching. Moreover, my second intention was to give them more chances to write and consequently improve their writing skills. During writing lessons, they usually feel a great deal of pressure for writing because they think their writing skills are not good enough. Hence, it is not easy to motivate them to write. However, as for this informal writing activity, students are willing to write something about themselves without being bothered about correct forms. Since they do writing regularly, their writing fluency as well as accuracy have improved a lot. Although their focal attention is placed on meaning, they pay peripheral attention to form. Such (2) _____ learning meaning unintentional or unplanned learning is the second aim of this writing activity. For example, Sungjin, at first, showed incorrect usage of the past tense and writing conventions like capitalization errors. However, he gradually acquired how to use them correctly while reading my written feedback with correct grammar and writing conventions.

Your Answer   (1) _____

(2) _____

18 Read the passage in <A> and the teacher's journal in <B>, and follow the directions.

A

   The process-oriented writing approach emphasizes the importance of developing students' ability to plan, identify issues and analyze, and implement possible solutions. In this approach, teachers train students to become self-aware and reflect on the activities and strategies they carry out while they write. In the classroom, teaching process writing means that students will engage in activities such as [figure 1] below. When students write, they do not follow a straight procedure. Instead, they can go back and forth in the stages allowing them to revise and edit even when the text has not been completed, engaging in a non-linear, exploratory, and generative process.

[Figure 1] A process model of writing instruction

   Selection of topic: by teacher and/or students
   Prewriting: brainstorming, collecting data, note-taking, outlining, etc.
   Composing: getting ideas down on paper.
   Response to draft: teacher/peers respond to ideas, organization and style.
   Revising: reorganizing, style, adjusting to readers, refining ideas.
   Response to revisions: teacher/peers respond to ideas, organization and style.
   Editing and _____: checking that the writing makes sense overall and then correcting spelling, grammar and syntax errors.
   Evaluation: teacher evaluates progress over the process.
   Publishing: by class circulation or presentation, websites, etc.
   Follow-up tasks: to address weaknesses

B
Teacher's Journal

Normally, to make the written works, higher-quality writers should focus on revising and editing process as well as the drafting itself. Hence, during the writing lesson I have intentionally emphasized these processes. So my students always revise and edit their own writings before the submission. However, I found that some students' final papers still had many mistakes uncorrected even after revision and editing works. Through a one-on-one conference with students, I figured out that they do not check surface errors while editing their writings. Thus, I am preparing a lesson to teach students how to catch errors like misspellings and mistakes in grammar and punctuation. The following five strategies will be introduced to develop their _____ skills, which enable them to edit their writings as accurately as possible before finalizing their works.

Strategies to be taught for the students:
1. Work with a printout, not your computer screen.
2. Read slow, and read every word.
3. Circle every punctuation mark.
4. Check only one kind of error at a time.
5. Don't rely entirely on spelling and grammar checking programs.

Based on the information in <A> and <B>, fill in the blanks in <A> and <B> with the ONE most appropriate word. Use the SAME word in both blanks.

Your Answer _____

19 Read the passages and follow the directions.

> *The following is an excerpt from a lesson procedure of intermediate level writing course.*
>
> ## Lesson Procedure
>
> Step A Modeling a text
>
> 1. T chooses a certain type of writing form to develop classroom activities. In this case, the type of text must match the students' needs and market needs where they will work later on.
> 2. T shows a model text and Ss discuss the text format by deconstructing, or manipulating the text.
> 3. Ss are directed to explicitly know and understand the function of the text (the communicative purpose of the text).
> 4. Ss, then, study the certain rhetorical structures, grammatical patterns, and vocabulary of the text, and then practice the procedure if necessary.
>
> Step B Joint construction
>
> 1. Ss are guided and helped by the teacher before they become a real independent writer of a certain text format taught and learned through three practical steps:
>   a) Ss reconstruct the certain type of text given. In this case, Ss may revise and paraphrase the vocabulary usage, the grammatical patterns, and textual devices, if necessary, by their own words.
>   b) T continuously guides Ss to discuss so that they understand well the given text type.
>   c) Ss review a modeling text and what they have practiced.
>
> Step C Independent construction of a text
>
> 1. T makes sure that Ss fully understand the features of a certain text such as the communicative purpose, structure element of the text, grammatical patterns usage, relevant vocabulary usage, and textual devices as well.
> 2. Ss independently write the certain type of text as what they have learned before.
>
> T=teacher, Ss=students

Fill in the blank with the ONE most appropriate word.

> The lesson procedure above consists of three steps which must be followed and implemented to teach and learn the target type of a text. According to the three steps, modeling a text, guided writing, and independent practice, the lesson procedure exemplifies cyclic teaching and learning writing focusing on _____ approach.

Your Answer _____

NEW Build Up

Chapter 05

Vocabulary & Grammar

Chapter 05

Vocabulary & Grammar

정답 및 모범 답안 p. 244

01 Read the two English teachers' conversation and follow the directions.

> Teacher 1 : I've been worrying about our students' vocabulary skills lately, especially since they're at a low intermediate level. You know, having a broad vocabulary is crucial for them to improve their proficiency level.
> Teacher 2 : I feel the same about my students. It's challenging to help them progress when they're not yet at an advanced level.
> Teacher 1 : Exactly. I don't want them to just memorize new words without understanding how to use them in context.
> Teacher 2 : That's a valid concern. We need to find a way to teach them new words effectively while also helping them understand how to use them naturally.
> Teacher 1 : I was thinking about using reading texts. For example, here's a passage I found :
>
>> Sarah, a true *adventurer*, decided to embark on an exciting *adventure* through the dense jungle. With her *adventurous* spirit, she ventured into the unknown, eager to explore. As an experienced *adventurer*, she navigated through the winding paths with ease. Along the way, she encountered a variety of wildlife, marveling at the colorful birds and playful monkeys. Despite the challenges she faced, Sarah's *adventurousness* never wavered. Eventually, she reached a tranquil river, where she spotted a family of otters playing in the water. Sarah smiled, knowing that every *adventure* brought new experiences and discoveries. With her *adventurous* heart fulfilled, she returned home, ready to plan her next thrilling escapade.

178

Teacher 2 : That's an interesting text! By presenting words with the same root together in a reading text, students can learn a broader range of vocabulary at once.
Teacher 1 : Right. I also believe that this approach is more efficient than just giving them a list of words.
Teacher 2 : Absolutely. Let's start looking for more engaging texts that cover a wide range of word families. This could really make a difference in their learning.

Fill in each blank with the ONE most appropriate word from the passage.

Teacher 1 and Teacher 2 discuss their concerns about their students' vocabulary skills at the low intermediate level. They agree that it's important for students to understand how to use new words in (1) _____ rather than just memorizing them. Teacher 1 suggests using reading texts that incorporate words with the same (2) _____ as seen in the provided example, to help students expand a wider range of vocabulary more effectively. Teacher 2 agrees with this approach, and they decide to find more engaging texts that cover a variety of word families to enhance their students' vocabulary learning.

Your Answer (1) _____

(2) _____

02 Read the passage and follow the directions.

Ms. Yoo Teaching Log

For teaching vocabulary explicitly, I often use a concordance program during lessons. Compared to incidental vocabulary learning, using a concordance program seems to be more effective to learn new words for my students in that it provides evidence of how the words are used in real situations based on millions of examples of the words. Besides, by analyzing the corpus data, I can teach students not only the meaning of new words, but also their collocations, frequency, and particular contexts they are used. Below is part of the lesson procedure for intentionally teaching vocabulary using a concordance program.

Lesson Procedure

1. T tells Ss that they will learn some keywords related to Covid-19 and explains that the importance of words will be decided based on how often they are used in real life.

2. T introduces a concordance program and models how to use it. T searches for the words, *lockdown* and *pandemic* on the program and shows their example sentences. Additionally, she shows them that the program can find how often the word is used in real life. *(e.g., pandemic: 8493 times, lockdown: 6053 times (at CNN news from 2019~))*

3. T puts Ss in groups of four and shows some words related to Covid 19 (e.g. *Coronavirus*, Vaccine, Quarantine, etc.). Then, T asks each group to search for the example sentences using the program and guess the meaning of words.

4. T checks Ss' answers on word meaning.

5. T tells Ss that, this time, they will rank the words based on how often they are used in real life. T asks Ss to guess the rank of the words.

[Ss' guessing]

Your keywords ranking	Actual keywords ranking
1. Coronavirus	1.
2. Vaccine	2.
3. Social distancing	3.
4. Quarantine	4.
...	...

6. T asks Ss to search for how often each word is actually used in real life (at CNN news from 2019~) using the concordance program and compare their own rank and the actual rank.

[Actual keywords ranking]

Your keywords ranking	Actual keywords ranking
1. Coronavirus	1. Coronavirus
2. Vaccine	2. Quarantine
3. Social distancing	3. Social distancing
4. Quarantine	4. Vaccine
...	...

7. T asks Ss to write down one example sentence of each word in order.

Actual keywords ranking	Example sentence
1. Coronavirus	In humans, coronaviruses can cause mild diseases like the common cold as well as more severe diseases.
2. Quarantine	
3. Social distancing	
4. Vaccine	
...	

5. Vocabulary & Grammar

Guideline for Pre-service Teachers

8. T checks the target words once again by asking the higher-ranking words in order.

> T: What is the second important keyword?
> Ss: Quarantine!
> T: Good. What is the third important keyword?
> Ss: Social distancing!

9. T wraps up the lesson emphasizing the usefulness of a concordancer.

Complete the comments about the lesson procedure above by filling in the blank with the ONE most appropriate word from the passage.

The lesson above shows how to teach keywords related to Covid 19 effectively using a concordance program. Ms. Yoo first asks students to find authentic example sentences of keywords using the program. Based on the sentences, she makes them guess the meaning of each keyword. Then, she asks students to search for the degree of importance of keywords based on the word _____. As seen in the lesson procedure, a concordance program can provide much more useful information on vocabulary than a paper dictionary does and thus help students effectively broaden their vocabulary knowledge.

Your Answer _____

03 Read the passage and follow the directions.

In the context of teaching vocabulary, English learners should actively engage in the process of acquiring and memorizing new words or phrases, especially if they are beginners.

Such process involves purposefully focusing attention on vocabulary learning activities, employing various strategies to understand and remember the meanings and usage of words, and consciously incorporating them into one's language skills. It also involves taking specific actions to enhance vocabulary acquisition, such as semantic mapping, word association activities, word family, and other memory techniques. Learners who engage in this type of learning are proactive in seeking out opportunities to expand their vocabulary and are actively involved in the learning process rather than relying solely on incidental exposure to new words.

Then, how many words English learners need to learn in this way? The number of words English learners need to learn in order to read a book smoothly varies depending on several factors, including the learner's current proficiency level, the complexity of the book's vocabulary, and the learner's language learning goals. However, a commonly cited estimate is that knowing around 95% of the words in a text allows for relatively fluent reading comprehension. Researchers have suggested that learning 2,000 to 3,000 words intentionally can facilitate reading at a basic level. This range of vocabulary typically includes high-frequency words and essential vocabulary necessary for basic communication.

Guideline for Pre-service Teachers

Fill in the blank with the ONE most appropriate word from the passage. You can modify the form of the word if needed.

> The passage above describes the vocabulary teaching method using activities such as semantic mapping, word association, word family, and other memory techniques with the purpose of focusing direct attention on vocabulary. Having a base of two or three thousand words is considered a minimum threshold for enabling learners to read a book smoothly. This type of learning is commonly referred to as _____ vocabulary learning.

Your Answer _____

04 Read the conversation and follow the directions.

> Teacher A and Teacher B, English teachers in a middle school, are talking about the vocabulary lessons both of them delivered.

Teacher A : I recently tried (1) _____ vocabulary learning and the results were very satisfying. Have you tried this?

Teacher B : Absolutely! During reading lessons, I lead students to pick up many new words naturally. It became a game-changer for boring vocabulary memorizing lessons.

Teacher A : Right? It's like students are learning without even realizing their learning vocabulary. Another good point is that they grasp word meanings within context.

Teacher B : Totally. And those "aha" moments when they figure out meanings from context are priceless.

Teacher A : Plus, it's a big boost for reading skills. They become better guessers, and it spills over into even their listening skills, too.

Teacher B : No doubt. It's learning without pressure, yet it stays with them.

Teacher A : You got it. Besides, it complements (2) _____ learning perfectly.

Teacher B : Oh, you mean, learning vocabulary like using mnemonic techniques or word associations?

Teacher A : Bingo! And even we can use semantic maps to connect related words explicitly.

Teacher B : Nice! So, (1) _____ vocabulary learning can be complemented by the explicit teaching of vocabulary.

Teacher A : Exactly. Balancing both, we're giving them a strong language toolkit.

Teacher B : High-five to that!

Fill in each blank with the ONE most appropriate word.

Your Answer　(1) _____

　　　　　　　　(2) _____

05 Read the passage and follow the directions.

Lesson Procedure

T : Okay, guys. Today we are going to play one game. Let's make a group of five.
(*Ss sit in groups.*)
T : Everyone is in your group?
Ss : Yes!
T : Great! Let me give you directions for the game first. Here we go. First of all, I will read out some words which have something in common. Then, you guys listen to the words and work out the missing suffix. Does everyone know what suffix means?
S1 : It is something we can add to the end of a word such as '-ly' and 'er'.
T : You're right! By adding suffix, you can form a different word with a different meaning. All right, then let's listen to the words and find out the missing suffix. If you guess correctly, it is five points. It will be minus one point for any incorrect guessing. And no points for a guess which is also true but isn't the answer that I am thinking of. I will give you this small whiteboard for each group. Write the answer and show me when I ask for. Is it clear? Yes? Okay, then, let's start!

[On the Board]

- broad + (   )
- wide + (   )
- length + (   )

(*Ss in groups figure out the suffix in common for the given words.*)
T : Did you find it? Let's check your answer! Show me the answer!
(*Ss in group raise the whiteboard with their own answers.*)

T : Group 1, '-er'. Group 2, '-er'. Group 3, '-en'. Group 4, '-ness'. Group 5, 'en'. Okay, the correct answer is '-en'! Congratulations, Group 3 and 5! The others also made a nice try but the answer was '-en'. Those words take '–en' to make verb forms. Great job!

T=teacher, Ss=students

Referring to the passage above, fill in each blank with the ONE or TWO most appropriate word(s).

The lesson above deals with word-learning strategies, which is a form of a/an (1) _____ vocabulary learning contrasting with implicit vocabulary learning. In this learning process, students are involved in activities where they learn directly vocabulary words. For example, the teacher directs students' attention to three words (i.e. broad, wide, and length) and the suffix '-en' that he/she chooses beforehand. By figuring out the suffix in common for the given words, students learn the word-learning strategy which is (2) _____ by guessing the common suffix to change the given adjective words into the verb forms. Learning such a strategy can help students free from excessive dependence on the dictionary and develop confidence in reading.

Your Answer (1) _____

(2) _____

Guideline for Pre-service Teachers

06 Read the passage and follow the directions.

> *(After reading one paragraph)*
> S1 : Mr. Oh. What's the meaning of "clumsy"?
> T : Okay, "clumsy". Does anyone know what the word means?
> *(T writes the word on the board.)*
> Ss : *(Silence)*
> T : Anyone? Okay, well, take a look at this sentence.
>   "His clumsy efforts to imitate a dancer were almost amusing."
>   Through the text we read so far, is Bernard a good dancer?
>   *(S1 raises her hand.)* Okay, Sumi?
> S1 : Well, no. He is not a good dancer yet. We can see this in the earlier sentences.
> T : Excellent! So, what do you think "clumsy" might mean?
> S2 : Mmm . . . not cool?
> T : Good, what else?
> S3 : Not smooth? Not skillful?
> T : Great! Okay, so "clumsy" means careless and awkward.
>   *(T writes synonyms on the board.)* Is that clear now?
> Ss : Yes! *(Ss nod in agreement.)*
>
> T=teacher, S=student, Ss=students

Considering the lesson above, fill in each blank with the ONE most appropriate word.

In this lesson, students engage in (1) _____ vocabulary teaching in that it starts with the word appeared in a paragraph they are reading, not with a long word list to memorize in advance. When students request meanings of vocabulary during class or when the teacher realizes that a word needs to be clarified, such vocabulary teaching happens. However, this vocabulary teaching needs to be separated from incidental vocabulary learning that students read the text and pick up some words unconsciously. Further, when students face with the unknown word "clumsy" and ask about its meaning, the teacher encouraged students to use the strategy of (2) _____ to figure out the meanings of the unknown word through contextual clues not directly giving the meaning of the word, "clumsy."

Your Answer (1) _____
(2) _____

Guideline for Pre-service Teachers

07 Read the materials evaluation and follow the directions.

Ms. Lee, who is an English teacher in a high school, conducted a material evaluation on a candidate textbook as below.

Evaluation Criteria	1	2	3	4
Content and Presentation				
Does the content serve as a window into learning about the target language culture (American, British, etc.)?			√	
Are the new vocabulary words recycled in subsequent lessons to reinforce their meaning and use?				√
Do instructions in the textbook tell students to read for comprehension?			√	
Do the activities facilitate students' use of grammar rules by creating situations in which these rules are needed?		√		
Are the texts interesting enough that students will enjoy reading them?			√	
Teacher's Manual and Supplementary Materials				
Does the manual provide teachers with exercises to help students practice and review vocabulary words?				√
Does the manual provide supplementary exercises for reinforcing grammar points from the text?			√	

Rating Scale : 1=Totally lacking, 2=Weak, 3=Adequate, 4=Good

Complete the teacher's reflection by filling in each blank with ONE word.

Ms. Lee's Reflection

This semester, I need to focus extensively on enhancing the vocabulary knowledge of my low-intermediate level students. Thus, I chose this new textbook, which exhibits two main strengths. First, in terms of content, this textbook employs the (1) _____ learning approach where words are recycled and reinforced in subsequent units. Through this approach, students deepen their understanding of words each time they encounter or review them. Besides, regarding the supplementary materials, the teacher's manual offers a wide range of vocabulary exercises for teachers. These exercises assist teachers in helping students review new words introduced in each unit. One example of the exercises involves accessing corpus data to extract the immediate context of specific words and phrases. By utilizing a/an (2) _____, teachers can extract authentic instances of many new words. This tool allows teachers to efficiently display numerous examples of specific words and phrases on the screen. Based on the examples from the screen, students can identify patterns and correct any misconceptions by studying extensive, naturally occurring examples in authentic texts.

Your Answer   (1) _____

(2) _____

Guideline for Pre-service Teachers

08 Read the passage and follow the directions.

A

Computer Lab Worksheet
English Composition

Name: _____

1. Write down the problems noted in your paper.

   > [Student's answer]
   >   a. Crazy mobs who contributed to ostracize her.
   >   b. bored and boring
   >   c. interested and interesting

2. Find a sentence from a corpus using a program on your computer, which uses the word/phrase (for each of the sentences you wrote above) in the desired way. Write the sentence below.

   > [Student's answer]
   >   a. Levin makes a special case for Debord as a film-maker whose aim was to contribute to the ultimate destruction of cinema as a spectacular medium.
   >   b. I'm bored . . . wasn't that a damn boring game!
   >   c. Helen is not interested in making lists about her life.

3. Describe how this word/phrase is used lexicogrammatically.

   > [Student's answer]
   >   a. After the phrase "contribute to": most of the sentences have a noun, not a verb.
   >   b. If something needs to be bored, it should be a passive position. However 'being' accompanies something active.
   >   c. "interested" for a passive thing and "interesting" for an active thing.

4. Rewrite your sentences using the information that you learned.

> [Student's answer]
>
> a. Crazy mobs who contributed to ostracizing her.
> b. The students are bored because of the boring class.
> c. The audiences were interested after the singer made the show interesting.

Fill in each blank in <B> with a suitable term from the worksheet in <A>. You can change the form of the word if necessary.

B

This sample activity was used in a composition class to help students recognize (1) _____ errors in their writing. A worksheet was provided for students to complete as shown in the sample. Students then followed the procedures below.

- List the (1) _____ problems that his/her instructor has marked.
- Find examples from an electronic (2) _____ that uses each item in the desired way and write one example down on the worksheet.
- Rewrite his/her original sentences using the information learned from the (2) _____.

Your Answer   (1) _____

(2) _____

Guideline for Pre-service Teachers

09 Read the activity below and follow the directions.

※ Read the story and follow the directions.

> Sumi, who was fourteen years old, loved using her smartphone. **One Saturday afternoon**, she decided to go to the park with her friends. **Since** they wanted to make a fun video for social media, they started exploring different areas of the park. **Suddenly**, her phone slipped out of her hand **and** it fell
> *(ellipsis)*

1. With your partner, answer the following questions.
   - What were Sumi and her friends doing in the park?
     _____
   - How did Sumi feel when her phone fell into the pond, and what did her friends do?
     _____

2. Group Discussion: When did you have fun without using any eletronic devices? Share your experiences in groups.

3. Review the grammatical structures with examples from the reading text in groups:
   - Time/Order Transition: One Saturday afternoon, Suddenly, By the end of the day
   - Cause-and-Effect Transition: Since, Therefore, As a result
   - Addition Transition: and

4. Combine the following sentences using transition words mentioned above:

   (1) Her phone slipped into the pond. She was making a video.
   _____

   (2) She was upset. He decided to enjoy the day.
   _____

Fill in each blank with the ONE or THREE most appropriate word(s).

The activity procedure is an integrative lesson that engages students in reading, speaking, and writing. With the reading passage, students can notice the transition words highlighted in bold. After reading, they work with a partner to answer comprehension questions. Next, they engage in a group discussion, sharing personal experiences, followed by a grammar review that focuses on the functions of transition words. The lesson ends with a/an (1) _____ activity, using the target forms to merge two sentences into one. Overall, the lesson uses a/an (2) _____ approach, drawing attention to grammar within context, unlike the traditional approach.

Your Answer   (1) _____

(2) _____

Guideline for Pre-service Teachers

10 Read the activity procedure and follow the directions.

Ms. Lee, who is the English teacher in a middle school, is just about to do an activity with her students. She has explained how to construct the form of the present progressive at the beginning of the lesson.

Activity Procedure

Step 1: T shows a short video clip of a story and asks Ss to talk about what they have watched.
Step 2: T makes Ss listen to the teacher's instruction about the activity and provides the activity slip.
Step 3: T asks Ss to do Task A while watching the video clip one more time.

Task A
※ Write the numbers for the following sentences in order in which they appear in the video clip.

- They are jogging along the riverbank. _____
- Anna is tying her shoelaces. _____
- Ben is stretching his arms and legs. _____
- Ben is laughing as a playful dog chases its tail nearby. _____
- Anna is pointing towards a group of birds. _____
- Ben is grabbing a stick and is teasing the dog. _____
- Anna is picking up a pebble and is tossing it across the water. _____
- Anna is drinking water from her bottle. _____
- They are taking a short break from their exercise. _____
- They are heading home. _____

Step 4: T asks Ss in pairs to check the answers, sharing information they have watched from the video. Then, T gives the answers to the whole class.

Step 5: T asks Ss to do Task B in pairs.

Task B
※ Read the sentence and check Progressive or Present.

	Progressive	Present
1. They are taking a short break from their exercise.	☐	☐
2. Ben stretches his arms and legs.	☐	☐
3. Anna is tying her shoelaces.	☐	☐
4. They head home.	☐	☐
5. Anna is pointing towards a group of birds	☐	☐

Step 6: T checks the answers with the whole class and reviews the verb forms used in each sentence.

Complete the comments by filling in each blank with the ONE or TWO most appropriate word(s).

05

Ms. Lee's lesson procedure is based on the (1) _____ theory which describes the process of strategies and mechanisms that learners use to link linguistic form with its meaning or function. In Task <A>, students are repeatedly exposed to present progressive sentences. They are then required to list these sentences in the sequential order presented in the video clip. Subsequently, in Task <B>, they encounter sentences framed in either the present progressive or present simple tense, depending on whether the action is ongoing or a habitual occurrence. The goal of this activity is to push learners to process the morphological marker '-ing', which they might overlook if specific time adverbs (e.g., 'often', 'usually', 'now') are provided. In essence, the activity affords students the opportunity to establish (2) _____ connections, ultimately enabling them to focus on grammar while understanding input.

Your Answer (1) _____

(2) _____

Guideline for Pre-service Teachers

11 Read the activity procedure and follow the directions.

Ms. Park, who is the English teacher in a middle school, is just about to have an activity with her students. She has already explained how to construct the form of the present progressive and the present single at the beginning of the lesson.

Activity Procedure

Step 1   Have students watch a short video clip and talk about it.
Step 2   Have students listen to the teacher's instruction about the activity and have the activity slip.
Step 3   Have students do this task A while watching the video clip again.

> A. Write the numbers for the following sentences in order in which they appear in the video clip.
>
> _____ Dooly and Douner are dancing.
> _____ Douner is looking for Dooly.
> _____ Douner is singing.
> _____ Dooly and Douner are watching television.
> _____ Dooly is listening to classical music.
> _____ Douner is talking on the phone.
> _____ Dooly and Douner are swimming.
> _____ Dooly is introduced her cat, Mimi.
> _____ Dooly and Douner are playing in the park.
> _____ Dooly is kissing Heedoing.

Step 4   Have students check the answers in pairs talking about what they have watched, and then give the answers in a whole class.

Step 5 Have students do the task B in pairs.

B. Yes or no?	Yes	No
1. Dooly and Douner play at the park often.	☐	☐
2. Dooly finds Douner.	☐	☐
3. Dooly likes to read.	☐	☐
4. Dooly loves the Teletubbies.	☐	☐
5. Douner has a cat.	☐	☐

Step 6 The teacher checks the answers with the students and review the form with usages.

Complete the comments by filling in each blank with ONE word.

Ms. Park gave her students the (1) _____ input activity which is manipulated in particular ways to push learners to become dependent on form and structure to get meaning. For example, in this activity, the students are exposed to 10 present progressive sentences at first while matching with the actions in the video clip. Then, they are exposed to 5 present simple sentences while finding out the general information about the characters. It is considered that Ms. Park tried to use the (2) _____ relationship while the students match the given forms with the given situation. In other words, the students have an opportunity to connect the form and the meaning, and finally construct the rules about the tenses on their own during this activity.

Your Answer (1) _____

(2) _____

12 Read the passage and follow the direction.

Ms. Lee's Teaching Log

Today, I designed a grammar lesson with these key strategies: introducing one concept at a time to prevent overwhelm, connecting grammar rules to their meanings for practical understanding, and encouraging active participation to enhance retention. Below are today's activities.

(After explaining how to use the passive form)

Activity Procedure

(1) Students listen to a short story titled "How to Make a Turkey Cheese Sandwich."
(2) Students match the pictures with the sentences from the original recipe.

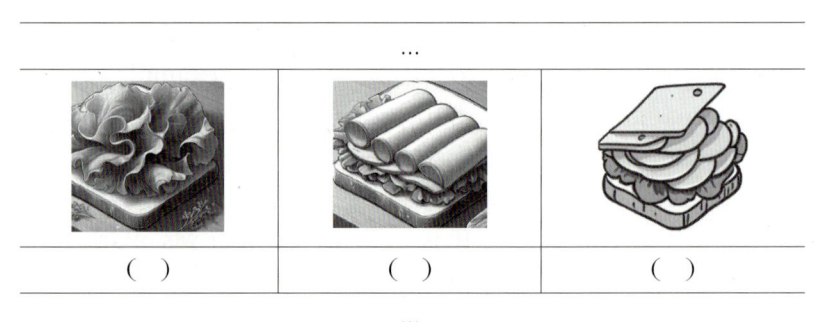

...

( )   ( )   ( )

...

[Audio Script]

　Lettuce leaves are placed on one slice. Slices of turkey are added on top of the lettuce. A slice of cheese is placed on the turkey.

(ellipsis)

(3) Students verify their answers in pairs.
(4) The teacher checks the answers with the students.
(5) The teacher has students match the picture and the correct sentence in the activity below.

• Lettuce leaves are placed on a slice of bread. ( ) • A slice of bread is placed on lettuce leaves. ( )	• The lettuce was added on top of slices of turkey. ( ) • Slices of turkey are added on top of the lettuce. ( )	• The turkey is placed on a slice of cheese. ( ) • A slice of cheese is placed on the turkey. ( )

Fill in the blank with the TWO most appropriate words.

Ms. Lee has designed a processing instruction based on the input processing approach, where students understand the target feature, the passive 'be + pp', in a controlled manner through the _____ activity.

Your Answer _____

Guideline for Pre-service Teachers

13 Read the passage and follow the directions.

    Mr. Yoo, an English teacher in a high school, participated in a Teacher conference about teaching grammar. Based on the following guidelines, he prepared a special type of form-focused activity that is communicative in nature.

> **Guidelines for designing _____ activity**
> - Present one thing at a time.
> - Keep meaning in focus.
> - Move from sentences to connected discourse.
> - Use both oral and written output.
> - Others must respond to the content of the output.
> - The learner must have some knowledge of the form or structure.

    In the process of designing, he carefully structured the activity expecting that the students can gain both fluency and accuracy through this activity. Below is the activity procedure.

Activity Procedure

Step 1. T explains Ss when to use "used to" and then how to do the following activity. After the explanation, T checks their comprehension.
Step 2. T puts Ss in pairs.
Step 3. T distributes the activity slip to Ss, respectively.
Step 4. T asks Ss to do the activity (1) individually and then to share their answers in pairs.

Activity Slip

(1) Tell what you used to do on weekends.
   Choose 'Yes' or 'No'.

	used to .... on weekends.	(Yes)	(No)
1.	go camping with family	☐	☐
2.	play soccer	☐	☐
3.	watch television	☐	☐
4.	play a board game	☐	☐
5.	take a nap	☐	☐
6.	read a comic book	☐	☐

(2) Write down four other activities that you used to do on weekends in the past but no longer engage in, and then share them with your partner.
   (Use 'I used to .... on weekends.')

_____
_____
_____
_____

Step 5. T puts Ss in groups of four, asks Ss to share what they have written in (2) and then take a vote for three most popular activities that their group members used to do on weekends.

Fill in the blank with the TWO most appropriate words from the passage.

Your Answer _____

> Guideline for Pre-service Teachers

14 Read the dialogue and follow the directions.

> *The following is an excerpt from a teacher-student conversation talking about a grammar activity.*
>
> T : Take a seat, Jihye. How may I help you?
> S : Well, Mr. Kim. I don't know grammar well, and grammar... is boring. I don't think we have to learn grammar.
> T : Really? Why do you think so?
> S : Because... I can learn grammar naturally when we listen and read texts a lot. So, I don't think learning grammar rules are necessary, which is so boring.
> T : Well, Jihye. I understand what you mean. But actually, learning grammar can be fun!
> S : Like how?
> T : I guess, you feel that the grammar lesson was boring because you tried to memorize the rules. Am I right?
> S : Exactly. I am tired of memorizing rules.
> T : Well, then, how about taking the next grammar lesson and talking with me again?
> S : Next grammar lesson? What will we do?
> T : Rather than simply providing grammar rules, I am preparing a fun activity that you guys figure out the rules. Do you want to check it really quick?
> S : Sure! I'd like to.
> T : Okay. There is a brief plan for the next lesson. First, I will give you a text which is a sheet of a tour leaflet of the city of London.
> *(T shows S the following activity plan.)*
>
> **Activity Procedure**
>
> 1. Presenting a leaflet with the following words:
>
> > William spent his summer vacations in London for the first time in 2012. When he arrived at Clink Hostel, the receptionist gave him the leaflet below. Take a look at the tour guide below:
> >
> > *(ellipsis)*

2. Look at the expressions below, taken from the leaflet:
   - the most important events
   - the best bars and nightclubs
   - the oldest buildings
   - the most majestic views
3. Answer the following questions.
   [Questions]
   a) Circle the nouns, as shown in the example: "the most important events"
   b) What words modify the word "events" in the given example?
   c) What words modify the word "views" in the example "the most majestic views"?
   d) How can we describe this pattern that modifies nouns?
   _____ + _____ + _____ + noun
   e) What is the difference in meaning between "majestic views" and "the most majestic views"?
   f) Why do you think we can find such structures in tour guides?
   g) Now, take a look at the example "the oldest buildings".
      Can you apply the same pattern to this case?
   h) If not, what is the pattern?
   _____ + _____ + noun
   i) Now, according to what you have answered, complete the rules in the chart:

Adjective	Rule	Example
(one syllable) old	the + adjective + _____	The oldest buildings.
(two or more syllables) important	the + _____ + adjective	The most important events.
(irregular) good	-	The best bars and nightclubs.

...

T=teacher, S=student

Guideline for Pre-service Teachers

Fill in the blank with the TWO most appropriate words.

> The lesson plan above describes a(an) _____, a pedagogical activity where students are provided with grammar rules in a text and required to perform some operation with it. The purpose of this activity is to arrive at an explicit understanding of some linguistic properties of the target language.

Your Answer _____

15 Read the conversation and follow the directions.

> *Two middle school English teachers are talking about how to teach exceptional grammar rules effectively.*
>
> Mr. Kim : May I have a moment of your time?
> Ms. Park : Of course, what can I assist you with?
> Mr. Kim : I am wondering if you could provide some advice on teaching grammar more effectively. Do you have any successful strategies for teaching grammar?
> Ms. Park : Let me think... Recently, I've been using the (1) _____ strategy in my grammar lessons.
> Mr. Kim : Is that such strategy where students make errors by overgeneralizing grammar rules?
> Ms. Park : Precisely. This technique sets up a situation where students can refine their initial assumptions with the partial information I provide. They get to discover the exceptions to the rules.
> Mr. Kim : So, it's a/an (2) _____ approach where students derive a general rule from specific instances.
> Ms. Park : That's correct!
> Mr. Kim : Alright, then, I will give it a try!
> Ms. Park : That sounds fantastic. Could you share your experience with me after you've tried it out?
> Mr. Kim : Absolutely, I'll keep you updated on how it goes.

Fill in the blank with the ONE or TWO most appropriate word(s).

Your Answer (1) _____
(2) _____

NEW Build Up

Chapter 06

Assessment

Chapter 06 Assessment

📖 정답 및 모범 답안 p. 245

01 Read the guidelines and follow the directions.

Guidelines for Individual Speech Program

Ms. Park, the head teacher of the English division at our high school, has planned a program to enhance the speaking skills of first-grade students gradually. Each week, two students will present their opinions in front of their peers, and teachers will give systematic feedback on their performance throughout the semester.

For Students

Script Submission Procedure
1. Submit the first script to your English teacher.
2. Get your first script with your teacher's comments.
3. Submit the second (final) script.

How to Prepare
1. Decide a topic to talk about.
2. Write a script that is one A4-size page in length.
3. Read your teacher's feedback and rewrite the script based on the feedback.
4. Use one of the visual aids such as PowerPoint, pictures, graphs, etc.
5. Practice, practice, and practice.

For Teachers

How to Grade
1. Make proper corrections for students' scripts in terms of grammar, vocabulary, and content.
2. Record each student's speech and upload the audio file into the school system.
3. Use the rubric below.

	Topic	Logically organized ideas	Pace of speaking and tone of voice	Visual aids	Connects with audience
Student 1					

4. Give systematic feedback and suggest how to improve their speaking skills.

Fill in each blank with the ONE most appropriate word.

　This weekly speech program includes a/an (1) _____ assessment in that the teacher evaluates students in the process of 'forming' their ongoing skills and helps them develop their speaking skills progressively. By receiving weekly feedback on their performances, students can identify the gap between what they achieved and what they missed. Based on the (2) _____ effect of this test, they can reinforce their strengths and improve their weakness in further study or lessons.

Your Answer (1) _____

(2) _____

> Guideline for Pre-service Teachers

02 Read the passage, and follow the directions.

Ms. Park's Teaching Log

I have always believed that pair work activities provide students with ample interaction time and offer teachers an opportunity to evaluate individual students. Consequently, I have incorporated pair work activities into both classroom testing and lessons. As needed, students' performances were evaluated during these activities. Most importantly, I need to carefully select pair work activities that align with the course objective. For instance, in the last conversation coursework, I aimed to assess whether students could maintain effective communication, which was the course objective for that lesson. Therefore, a paired conversation as an oral exam was a more appropriate form of classroom testing than a written exam or structured one-on-one interview. Additionally, I found that I could obtain better evaluation results when students were assessed using the same tasks used in the lesson. That's why I always coordinate classroom activities and testing within a single lesson. Below are the sample test and rubrics that I have developed.

[Practical English Conversation in Pairs]
Student A, Name: _____ (Total score: ____/15)
Student B, Name: _____ (Total score: ____/15)

Directions: Use expressions that you practiced in the last lesson. You will be given 10 minutes to complete the activities so it is important that you are prepared!

Part I. Greetings: /5 points
※ Students A and B:
1. Greet each other.
2. Have a conversation about music, sports, books, and any other topics according to their preference.

(Hint: Unit 1)

Part II. What's in your room?   /5 points

※ Students B and A:

1. B – Describe your room to A. A asks some questions about B's room.
2. A – Describe your room to B. B asks some questions about A's room.

(Hint: Unit 3)

Part III. Overall performance: /5 points
(Grammar, Fluency, Pronunciation, etc.)

Scoring for Parts I and II

Score	Descriptions
5	Followed all instructions, spoke clearly, no unnecessary pauses, native-like pacing, no unnecessary repetitions
4	Didn't follow all instructions, or, one or few errors, pauses, etc.
3	A few errors, pauses, etc., not very clear
2	Unprepared, many errors, unclear, poor pacing
1	Unprepared, incomplete, many errors, unclear, poor pacing

Scoring for Part III

Score	Descriptions
5	Very clear and well prepared
4	One or a few grammatical or pronunciation errors, pauses, etc.
3	Some grammatical and/or pronunciation errors, hard to understand at times
2	Hard to understand, many pronunciation and/or grammatical errors
1	Very hard to understand and incomplete

Fill in the blanks with the ONE or TWO appropriate word(s).

> The test designed by Ms. Park primarily incorporates pair work activities to assess students' conversation skills. She holds the view that the implementation of suitable pair work in the test is of utmost importance. All pair work activities, as mentioned in Ms. Park's teaching log, appear to be highly effective in not only promoting active interaction among students but also providing ample opportunities for teachers to evaluate. As stated in her teaching log, she aims to conduct learning activities and classroom testing concurrently within a single lesson, because she believes that the interconnection between lesson activities and classroom testing enhances the (1) _____ of the test which is one of testing principles. For scoring, Ms. Park plans to use a/an (2) _____ scoring rubric to assign scores based on the overall impression, both within each activity and across all activities and performances.

Your Answer (1) _____

(2) _____

03 Read the passage and follow the directions.

An English proficiency test was administered to 3rd graders ($n=300$) of a middle school. In order to check how well the test components contribute to the construct being measured, Ms. Kim, who is an English teacher, performed the following steps with the test results.

1. She divided the questions into even and odd numbers.
2. She scored each half of the test for each student.
3. She calculated the correlation coefficient for the two halves to learn the strength of the relationship between them.

Figure 1. Score of each student

Student	Score	Even questions	Odd questions
1	42	22	20
2	66	36	30
3	88	46	42
4	90	50	40
5	60	38	22
6	100	50	50
7	45	23	22
8	68	38	30
9	80	46	34
10	85	45	40
(ellipsis)			

Guideline for Pre-service Teachers

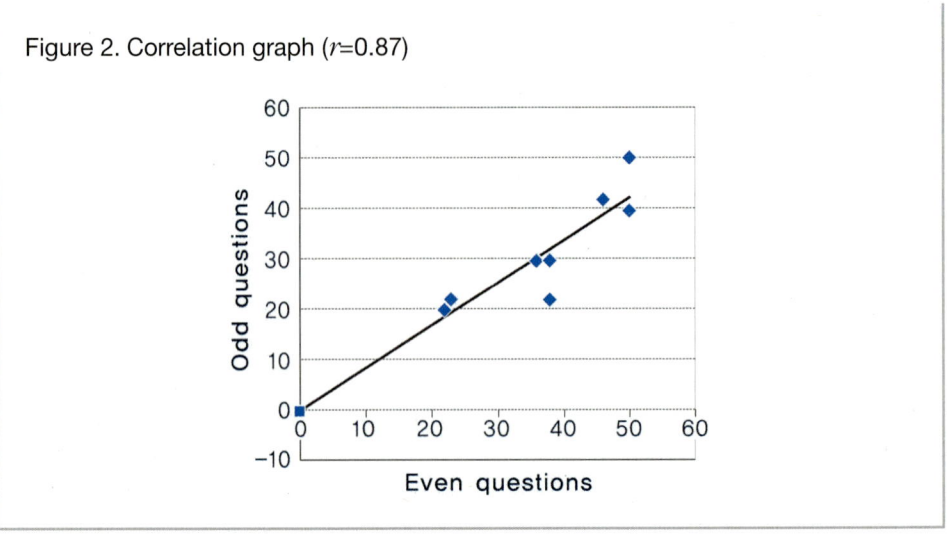

Figure 2. Correlation graph (*r*=0.87)

Fill in the blanks with the ONE most appropriate word in common.

Given the information and figures provided in the text, Ms. Kim intends to measure the internal consistency of the English proficiency test using the _____ method. For example, Figure 1 shows the scores of each student on even and odd questions, providing the data needed for the _____ reliability calculation. Figure 2 presents the correlation graph, illustrating the strength of the relationship between the two sets of scores. This approach helps ensure that the test items consistently reflect the construct being measured, thereby validating the test's reliability.

Your Answer _____

04 Read the passage and follow the directions.

  Ms. Cho is an English teacher in a middle school, recently conducted a reading test based on an excerpt from the book titled "Diary of a Wimpy Kid, The Ugly Truth". The test required students to fill in missing words in the text, choosing the correct verbs from a provided list. In scoring the test, I employed a/an (1) _____ scoring method that awards points for each blank filled correctly with a word from the list.

> **Directions:** Fill in the blanks using the correct words given in the box below.
>
>   It's _____ almost two and a half weeks since I and my ex-best friend, Rowley, ____ our big fight. To be honest, I _____ he would _____ come crawling back to me by now, but for some reasons that ____ not happened.
>   I'm actually starting to ____ a little concerned because school _____ back up in a few days and, if we ____ gonna get this friendship back on track, something ____ to happen quickly. If I and Rowley really _____ this go, that would stink, because the two of us ____ a pretty good thing going.
>
> > had, are, needs, get, starts, thought, have, been, let, has

  In the reading activity mentioned earlier, Ms. Cho utilized a/an (2) _____ cloze test, where she intentionally removed various tenses of verbs from the text. Ms. Choi has found this assessment tool to be highly effective. According to her, it provides a comprehensive evaluation of students' reading skills and language proficiency, with a particular emphasis on the correct usage of specific verb forms.

Fill in each blank with the most appropriate TWO words.

Your Answer (1) _____
(2) _____

05 Read the passage and follow the directions.

Test Result Graph

Ms. Park, who is an English teacher of a high school, is reviewing the results of the final-term for three classes that she has taught in the current semester. Each class has thirty students and the results were divided into ten levels.

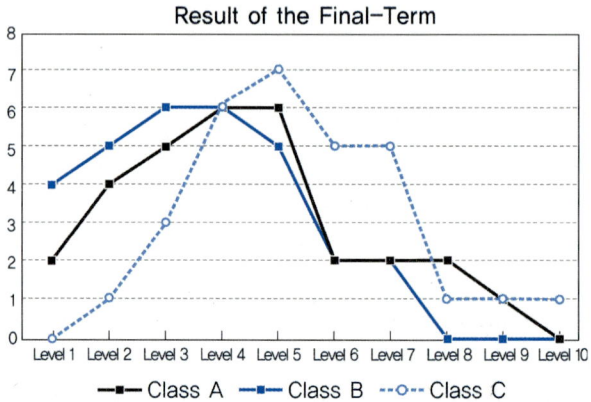

Result of the Final-Term
■— Class A   ■— Class B   --○-- Class C

* Level 1 is the highest and Level 10 is the lowest in Horizontal Axis.
* Numbers of students in Vertical Axis.

Teacher's Reflection

The final-term results are shown in the bell curves above. The performance gap between individual students is reflected in the curves of Class A, Class B, and Class C. I think Class B shows the most desirable result in terms of teaching and learning. However, I am concerned about the results of Class C because it seems that my lessons were quite demanding for the students. In order to figure this out more clearly, I want to assess how well the students have grasped the knowledge and information required for this semester. Also, I wonder if they struggled with any problems or challenges related to language skills. Once I find this out, I will be able to apply more effective lessons next semester.

Fill in each blank with the ONE most appropriate word.

> Ms. Park uses a/an (1) _____ test for her final-term assessment as evidenced with the bell curves that divide the results into ten levels, comparing students' performance relative to each other. With the results, she is concerned about the performance of Class C, where the results suggest that her lessons may have been too demanding. In order to reduce her concern about class C, it is advisable for Ms. Park to conduct a/an (2) _____ test. This would help her determine whether each student has mastered the specific content and skills expected for the course by measuring their performance against pre-defined criteria or standards, rather than comparing them to each other.

Your Answer   (1) _____

(2) _____

Guideline for Pre-service Teachers

06 Read the dialogue and follow the directions.

> *Below is part of the conversation between two English teachers discussing their upcoming achievement test.*

Mr. Park : Ms. Lee, I would like to discuss the achievement test for the next week.

Ms. Lee : What's on your mind? I hope it's nothing serious.

Mr. Park : Well, I have a concern about assessing students based on a bell-shaped curve and comparing their performance to that of other examinees. I don't think it is the best way to evaluate our students.

Ms. Lee : I understand your point, but I think providing test results with a percentile rank would be beneficial for them. It can help students set realistic goals for their academic progress, such as improving their rank. Don't you agree?

Mr. Park : That's true, but our primary aim should be to evaluate their individual achievements rather than solely their class rankings. Consider a scenario where all students have diligently studied and comprehended the material. In such cases, shouldn't they all be rewarded with high scores, regardless of their peers' performances?

Ms. Lee : Hmm, I see your point. So, do you have any better idea in mind?

Mr. Park : I've been considering assessing them based on a predetermined standard for satisfactory achievement. This will allow us to concentrate on evaluating the performance of each individual student.

Ms. Lee : I think that's a good idea!

Complete the following by filling in each blank with ONE word.

> Before having the above conversation, the two teachers developed a/an (1) _____ test which assesses each student's achievement relative to others, distinguishing between high and low level students in the class. However, following their discussion, they reached the consensus that this type of test was not suitable for their intended purpose. Consequently, they decided to convert the current test type into a/an (2) _____ test, which would allow them to accurately evaluate individual achievements according to the set criterion.

Your Answer   (1) _____

(2) _____

Guideline for Pre-service Teachers

07 Read the passages and follow the directions.

A

Ms. Choi's Teaching Log

　Last week, I conducted a listening test to check my students' listening proficiency. I provided a 5 minute-long listening script and students chose the correct answer for 10 questions while listening to the script. The test results were given to each student today. I recorded their scores and ranks out of 30 students on the result sheet. By figuring out their current listening levels compared to the others, I thought it would help my students to maximize motivation for learning English. Some of my students looked disappointed with their test results. However, I believe that they will overcome the depressed feeling soon and study hard to improve their listening skills.

B

Hye-rim's Learning Log

　According to the listening test results, I ranked only 20 out of 30 students in my class. After seeing my scores and ranks, I was so discouraged by the test results. What I expected from the test was not knowing how poor my English skill is comparing to the others. Instead, what does matter is whether I can pass the listening test or not. Thus, I hope my teacher uses (1) _____ testing to examine my own ability according to the predetermined learning criteria, not influenced by other students' performances. Instead of receiving the results only in a number score, I want to get some comments from the teacher on my test results. If the teacher tells me what I am good at and poor at, I will enhance my strengths and improve my weak points in listening skills. In other words, with the teacher's comment, the test can have positive (2) _____ since it makes me take the study more seriously.

222

Referring to the passages, fill in each blank with the ONE most appropriate word.

Your Answer (1) _____

(2) _____

Guideline for Pre-service Teachers

08 Read the passage below and fill in each blank with an appropriate term.

The following is part of testing items of the midterm drafted by Mr. Lee.

1. Choose the correct answer to complete the given sentence.
   Q. He may not come, but we'll get ready in case he _____.
   ① will   ② does   ③ is   ④ may

2. Choose the correct answer to complete the given sentence.
   Q. Then we _____ the loudest thunder you have ever heard!
   ① heard   ② did hear   ③ hear   ④ hearing

   Examples like these are known as (1) _____ test which is to measure one aspect of language at a time. These multiple-choice examples are decontextualized: each item consists of a single-sentence format with no other context provided, either within the item itself or in the previous parts of the text. In terms of testing principles, as one of objective test formats, multiple choice items have high reliability and practicality. However, these show low (2) _____ about overall proficiency unlike open-ended items.

Your Answer (1) _____

(2) _____

09 Read the passage in <A> and the conversation between a teacher and a student in <B>, and follow the directions.

A

Imagine being a teacher in a new classroom. You begin teaching a lesson only to be met with stares of confusion from your students. When you ask the students if they understand what you are teaching, they reply that they have no idea what you're talking about. Now imagine teaching the same class after conducting a pretest to determine what the students already know about the topic. Which scenario sounds preferable? Which would result in a better experience for both the teacher and the students? Of course, the latter would have a better result. The pretest in the latter case is a/an _____ that allows a teacher to determine students' individual strengths, weaknesses, knowledge, and skills before instruction. It is primarily used to identify students' difficulties and to guide lessons and curriculum planning.

B

The following is part of the individual conference that Ms. Kim had about the test results with one of her students, Hye-mi.

T : So, Hye-mi. How was the test?
S : It was good! Not too hard, not too easy.
T : That's great Did you check the results?
S : Yes, I did and... I did not know that my writing skill is lower than average.
T : Oh, well. That's why we take the _____. You can check your current language skills. Should we see the results closer then?
T : Yes.
T : Okay, for reading, you are at the top 3%. Great job!
S : Thank you. I guess it's because I have more vocabulary knowledge than usual students. I really like learning new vocabulary. It's very interesting.

Guideline for Pre-service Teachers

> T : I see! That's the secret! Then, let's see listening... it's top 5%, which is good and speaking is top 10% which is still good. But, writing! I think writing skill is something that you need to focus on for this semester.
> S : I know. Writing has been so difficult area for me since the first grade.
> T : Hmm... How about joining an English newspaper club? This semester I am going to take a charge of the club. I will let each student will write one news article every week. It can be a great practice for writing with lots of fun!
> S : That's a great idea! Thank you, Ms. Kim. I think I finally find the way to improve my writing skills. I did not expect that the test results can be useful this much!
> T : You're very right! That's the benefit of this test. It gives you ideas on which skills you need to focus on your future learning.
>
> T=teacher, S=student

Based on the information in <A> and <B>, fill in the blanks in <A> and <B> with the TWO most appropriate words. Use the SAME words in both blanks.

Your Answer _____

10 Read the conversation between two teachers and follow the directions.

> T1: Hi, Mr. Park. What are you doing?
> T2: Hi, Ms. Kim. I am reviewing my students' writing works. There are so many grammar mistakes. That's a big problem.
> T1: Didn't you have a multiple-choice grammar test last week? How was it?
> T2: Oh, most of them did great on that test. But maybe, it was not enough to check their grammar knowledge. They know the rules but obviously don't know how to apply them in writing.
> T1: Hmm... What about preparing for another test?
> T2: Another one? Do you have any good ideas?
> T1: For example, a dictation-based writing test. You read aloud a story two or three times, and then ask students to rewrite it. Through this test you can see if they understand the rules and use them properly. Furthermore, you can evaluate their listening & writing skills and vocabulary knowledge.
> T2: Feeding two birds with one scone! But... that could be an overwhelming activity for low-intermediate level students.
> T1: Don't worry. You can give some keywords so that they can listen and write the text within their proficiency level.
> T2: That sounds cool. Hmm, what do you think about the beginners? It could still be enough for them?
> T1: Well, for beginning level students, you can also add picture-cues to help them comprehend and remember the storyline.
> T2: Keywords and picture-cues! I guess that will be enough to support my students. Thank you, Mr. Park. I will try the new test and let you know how it works.
> T1: Cool!
>
> T=teacher

Guideline for Pre-service Teachers

Complete the comments by filling in the blank with the ONE most appropriate word.

> In the above dialogue, the two teachers are talking about testing students' grammar knowledge using a dictation-based writing test. The test described by the teachers here is a kind of _____ testing which requires a test taker to use several language skills at the same time such as listening and writing as well as grammatical knowledge.

Your Answer _____

11 Read the dialogue and identify the test type in TWO words.

Student–Teacher Meeting

T : Welcome, Come on in. Sun-ho, how are you today?
S : Hello, Mr. Choi. I am good. Thank you.
T : Take a seat. Everything is alright? How was the test?
S : Yes, it is all good. But I think there was something I could not understand during the test. The questions that I answered were different with my classmates'.
T : Oh, yes, Sun-ho. It could be. It would be a new test type for you. During the test, the computer checked your answers and chose the questions fit to your English proficiency. In short, it selects the questions just for you. So this test is also called as a tailored testing. That's why your questions were different with the others'.
S : A computer chose questions? I didn't know that. That's interesting.
T : One more fact about the test, you cannot review or change the answers to questions that you have already answered.
S : You're right. I wanted to review my answers but I couldn't. Then, where can I see my test results?
T : Do you remember the website that I showed you after the test? Log in that website, and you can find your test results.
S : Great. You've solved my doubts about this test! Thank you, Mr. Choi.
T : I am glad you said that. Okay then. Have a good afternoon.

T=teacher, S=student

Your Answer

> Guideline for Pre-service Teachers

12 Read the teacher's note and follow the directions.

Teacher's Note

Today, I conducted a new type of alternative assessment to gain a deeper understanding of my students' language performance. As teachers, we are constantly observing our students, and employing such an empirical tool can enhance the reliability and face validity of our feedback. The most important thing is to assess students without their awareness so that they can reduce any potential anxiety and maximize the naturalness of their linguistic performance.

During the alternative assessment, I focused on various aspects of student performance that can be effectively observed. Firstly, I paid attention to sentence-level oral production skills, such as the accurate pronunciation of target sounds and intonation patterns. This allowed me to identify areas of improvement and provide targeted feedback to enhance their spoken language proficiency. Furthermore, I also observed students' discourse-level skills, including their adherence to conversation rules and their ability to form appropriate questions. This gave me insights into their overall communication abilities and allowed me to address any specific challenges they might be facing. Finally, I observed students' interaction with their classmates. I looked for signs of cooperation and the frequency of their oral production during group activities. This provided valuable information about their ability to collaborate effectively and engage in meaningful discussions.

Fill in the blank with the ONE most appropriate word.

The teacher conducted a classroom _____ as alternative assessment to assess his/her students' language performance without their awareness, focusing on sentence-level oral production skills, discourse-level skills, and interaction with classmates. This helped the teacher identify areas for improvement, provide targeted feedback, and tailor his/her instructional strategies accordingly.

> Your Answer _____

13 Read <A> and fill in the blank in <B> with ONE word.

---- **A** ----

Teacher A: I think assessment is not all about testing. Students should have an opportunity throughout the class to be informally assessed. For example, as for listening, one important aspect of informal assessment is giving credit for the listening done in class or as homework. Listening takes practice, and it makes sense to assess the practice rather than putting complete emphasis on tests. Samples of a student's work contain the followings:
- a statement from the student that introduces this and tells why its contents were selected
- samples of classwork. This can be work specifically on listening or other work that includes listening.
- a sample of outside-of-class work. In addition to expected "academic homework" assignments, this may include summaries of non-academic listening experiences such as watching movies or TV or listening to a conversation in English.
- a reflection on learning: self-evaluation of strengths and weaknesses

---- **B** ----

The mentioned lists presented in <A> might mean collecting examples of completed listening tasks, as part of a/an _____ of work that is turned in at midterms and finals, through which students reflect on their progress.

Your Answer _____

14 Read the passages in <A> and <B> and fill in the blanks with the most appropriate terms.

> *Below is the conversation between two teachers reviewing the test results based on Table 1.*
>
> Ms. Jang : Hi, Mr. Lee. Do you have a minute to review the pilot test results?
>
> Mr. Lee : Sure, Ms. Jang. You used multiple-choice questions, right? Go ahead.
>
> Ms. Jang : Yes, that's correct. Let's take a look at the results in Table 1. The Y-axis shows item (1) _____, which indicates how well each question distinguishes between high and low-performing students. "Poor" (below 0.1, including negative values) means weak discrimination, "Fair" (0.1-0.3) is moderate, and "Good" (above 0.3) is strong.
>
> Mr. Lee : Got it. And what about the X-axis?
>
> Ms. Jang : The X-axis shows item (2) _____, which is the percentage of students who answered the question correctly.
>
> Mr. Lee : Any notable findings?
>
> Ms. Jang : Yes, 12 questions showed weak item (1) _____, meaning low scorers performed better on those than high scorers.
>
> Mr. Lee : So, those questions might be misleading?
>
> Ms. Jang : Exactly. I'll need to review those questions. Most of the questions, fall into the Medium and Easy levels for item (2) _____, as intended, but, ...
>
> Mr. Lee : Yeah, the problem is that 50% to 100% of students who answered correctly are in the low- performance group.
>
> Ms. Jang : That's the issue. That' why I need to thoroughly review the exam questions before actual exam.
>
> Mr. Lee : That sounds like a good idea.

Table 1

(Y)	Hard (0-50%)	Medium (50-85%)	Easy (85-100%)
Poor (< 0.1)	30	9, 15, 24, 25, 27, 28, 29	19, 20, 23, 26
Fair (0.1-0.3)		17, 21	
Good (>0.3)	18, 22	3, 4, 12	1, 2, 5, 6, 7, 8, 10, 11, 13, 14, 16

(X)

Your Answer

(1) _____

(2) _____

15 Read the passage and follow the directions.

> Ms. Park, a middle school English teacher, plans to administer the following tasks to diagnose her students' language proficiency.
>
> ### Tasks
>
> **Task A**
> Listen to the following sentences and indicate whether it talks about the present or the past. Write 1 for present and 2 for past.
>
> [Listening]
> 1. He shared the news to his friends right after his arrival. [ ]
> 2. I walk one Kilometer with my sister every morning. [ ]
>
> **Task B**
> By listening to the rise and fall of the voice, indicate the emotional status of the speaker.
>
> [Listening]
> 1. Really? curious ( ), surprised ( ), angry ( )
> 2. Really? curious ( ), surprised ( ), angry ( )
> 3. Really! curious ( ), surprised ( ), angry ( )
>
> **Task C**
> Read the question and choose the correct word to complete the sentence.
> * When I am thirsty, I get a _____.
>   a. drink   b. coat   c. ball   d. handkerchief
>
> **Task D**
> Read the question and choose the correct word to complete the sentence.
> * They told me that he had already _____.
>   a. going   b. went   c. go   d. gone

Complete the comments by filling in each blank with the ONE most appropriate word.

> Task A focuses on examining morphology, '-ed', by asking about the tense of each sentence. Task B seems to examine the understanding for intonation and meaning discrimination. Task C and D are the same multiple-choice questions but the focuses are different. Task C focuses on examining the vocabulary ability and Task D focuses on syntax. As seen in the tasks above, (1) _____ tests are constructed on the assumption that language is segmented into many small linguistic points and four language skills of listening, reading, speaking and writing. Each question has only one linguistic point in this testing method. Also, we can tell that this type of tests have high (2) _____ as each question has only one correct answer and thus human error, subjectivity, or bias may not enter into the scoring process.

Your Answer (1) _____

(2) _____

16 Read the passages and fill in the blanks with suitable words.

A

The following is the item discrimination table from the listening test result.

Item	1	2	3	4	5
High scorers with correct answer	3	4	1	3	2
Low scorers with correct answer	1	2	2	0	1
(1) _____ (TWO words)	0.5	0.5	-0.25	0.75	0.25

B

Ms. Park and Ms. Yoo reviewed the listening test result and analyzed it as follows.

The table in <A> shows how many high scores and low scores get a particular item correct. Generally, students who get any one question correct also have a relatively high score on the overall exam. However, according to this table, one item indicates that either the students who performed poorly on the test overall got the question correct or that the students with high overall test performance did not get the item correct. It is the case of Item 3. That is, Item 3 deteriorates the (2) _____ (TWO words) of the test as more low scorers find the correct answer than high scorers. Thus, this item might contain one of the following problems.

- There is a mistake on the scoring key.
- Poorly prepared students are guessing correctly.
- Well-prepared students are somehow justifying the wrong answer.

In all cases, action must be taken! So, since this item shows negative item difficulty, it should be revised or eliminated. Be certain that there is only one possible answer, that the question is written clearly, and that your answer key is correct.

Your Answer (1) _____

(2) _____

NEW Build Up

정답 및 모범 답안

정답 및 모범 답안

Chapter 01　Second Language Acquisition　　본문 p. 010

문항번호	정답	
01	(1) critical period	(2) inhibition
02	comprehensible input	
03	(1) comprehensible input	(2) comprehensible check
04	(1) focus-on-form / focus on form	(2) dictogloss
05	adjacency pairs	
06	(1) cohesive devices	(2) coherence
07	register	
08	register	
09	scaffolding	
10	acculturation	
11	social distance	
12	silent way	
13	(1) whole language	(2) intrinsic
14	(1) schemata	(2) prompts
15	blended learning	
16	inquiry-based	
17	multiple intelligence(s)	
18	interference	
19	(1) collocations	(2) interference
20	u-shaped	
21	fossilization	
22	fossilization	
23	personalization	
24	notice the gap	
25	(1) negative	(2) positive
26	(1) repetition	(2) pushed output

Chapter 02 Classroom Context

본문 p. 058

문항번호	정답	
1	readability (대소문자 무관)	
2	(1) blended	(2) dialogue journals
3	(1) functional	(2) contextualized
4	(1) facilitator	(2) recast
5	block time class (또는 block scheduling)	
6	drill	
7	Graphic organizers (첫 글자 대문자, 복수형만 가능)	
8	advance organizer	
9	Jigsaw (대소문자 무관)	
10	(1) referential questions	(2) display question
11	(1) referential questions	(2) repetition
12	(1) referential questions	(2) clarification request
13	digital literacy	
14	culture assimilator	
15	ambiguity tolerance	
16	(1) reflective	(2) field-dependent
17	(1) impulsive	(2) top-down
18	think-aloud	
19	metacognitive	
20	(1) word coinage	(2) literal translation
21	(1) strategic	(2) circumlocution
22	(1) peer scaffolding	(2) facilitative anxiety

Guideline for Pre-service Teachers

Chapter 03 Receptive Skills

본문 p. 100

문항번호	정답	
1	(1) top-down	(2) bottom-up
2	(1) interpersonal / interactional	(2) coherence
3	redundancy	
4	schemata (복수형만 가능)	
5	Summarizing (첫 글자 대문자)	
6	(1) integrated	(2) scanning
7	(1) extensive	(2) readability
8	(1) extensive reading	(2) intensive reading
9	interactive	
10	graded readers (복수형만 가능)	
11	graded reader	
12	(1) Language Experience Approach (대소문자 무관) (2) metacognitive	
13	(1) language experience	(2) intrinsic
14	rational deletion	
15	(1) rational deletion	(2) semantic
16	(1) interpretive / inferential	(2) evaluative / critical

Chapter 04 Productive Skills

본문 p. 136

문항번호	정답	
1	(1) role-play	(2) clarification requests
2	reasoning-gap	
3	intelligibility	
4	(1) interference	(2) intelligibility
5	contextualized minimal pairs	
6	(1) segmental	(2) intelligibility
7	(1) suprasegmental	(2) intelligibility
8	(1) pausing / pauses	(2) top-down
9	(1) adjacency	(2) suprasegmentals
10	hypercorrection	
11	(1) recast	(2) uptake
12	(1) process-oriented / process	(2) conference
13	brainstorming	
14	cohesive devices	
15	(1) advance organization(organizer)	(2) dialogue journal
16	(1) dicto-comp	(2) dialogue journals
17	(1) rapport	(2) incidental / implicit
18	proofreading	
19	genre-based	

Chapter 05 Vocabulary & Grammar

문항번호	정답	
1	(1) context	(2) root
2	frequency	
3	intentional	
4	(1) incidental	(2) intentional
5	(1) explicit	(2) word formation
6	(1) unplanned	(2) guessing
7	(1) spiral	(2) concordancer
8	(1) lexicogrammatical	(2) corpus
9	(1) sentence-combining	(2) focus on form / focus-on-form
10	(1) input processing	(2) form-meaning
11	(1) structured	(2) form-meaning
12	structured input	
13	structured output	
14	consciousness-raising task / CR task	
15	(1) garden path / garden-path	(2) inductive

Chapter 06 Assessment

본문 p. 210

문항번호	정답	
1	(1) formative	(2) washback
2	(1) content validity	(2) holistic
3	split-half	
4	(1) exact word	(2) rational deletion
5	(1) norm-referenced	(2) criterion-referenced
6	(1) norm-referenced	(2) criterion-referenced
7	(1) criterion-refereced	(2) washback
8	(1) discrete-point	(2) validity
9	diagnostic test	
10	integrative	
11	computer-adaptive testing(test)	
12	observation	
13	portfolio	
14	(1) discrimination	(2) difficulty / facility
15	(1) discrete-point	(2) reliability
16	(1) Item discrimination	(2) internal consistency

NEW
Build Up

박현수 영어교육론 Ⅳ-1 문제은행 [기입형]
Guideline for Pre-service Teachers

초판인쇄 | 2025. 7. 10.   **초판발행** | 2025. 7. 15.   **편저자** | 박현수
발행인 | 박 용   **발행처** | (주)박문각출판   **표지디자인** | 박문각 디자인팀
등록 | 2015년 4월 29일 제2019-000137호
주소 | 06654 서울시 서초구 효령로 283 서경빌딩   **팩스** | (02)584-2927
전화 | 교재주문·학습문의 (02)6466-7202

이 책의 무단 전재 또는 복제 행위는 저작권법 제136조에 의거, 5년 이하의 징역 또는 5,000만 원 이하의 벌금에 처하거나 이를 병과할 수 있습니다.

정가 45,000원(1, 2권 포함)
ISBN 979-11-7262-947-2 | ISBN 979-11-7262-946-5(세트)

저자와의
협의하에
인지생략

교원임용시험 전공영어 대비 [제1판]

NEW Build Up

박현수 영어교육론
Ⅳ-2 문제은행 [서술형]

Guideline for Pre-service Teachers

박현수 편저

Contents

Chapter 01 Second Language Acquisition

01 Language Learning Approach ··· 6
02 Learning Phenomenon ··· 50

Chapter 02 Classroom Context

01 Teaching Principles ··· 62
02 Textbook Evaluation or Modification ··· 88
03 Classroom Observation or Course Evaluation ··· 125
04 Instructional Techniques(classroom activities) or Syllabus ··· 136
05 Learner Variables ··· 176

Chapter 03 Receptive Skills

01 How to Teach Listening Skills ··· 196
02 How to Teach Reading Skills ··· 214
03 How to Improve the Receptive Skills ··· 233

Chapter 04 Productive Skills

01 How to Teach Speaking Skills ··· 250
02 How to Teach Writing Skills ··· 300

Chapter 05 Vocabulary & Grammar

01 How to Teach Vocabulary ··· 330
02 How to Teach Grammar ··· 346

Chapter 06 Assessment

01 Teaching Principles ··· 374
02 Testing Purpose, Types, and Methods ··· 392
03 Alternative Assessment ··· 413
04 Multiple-choice Item Testing ··· 425

정답 및 모범 답안 ··· 440

NEW
Build Up

Chapter 01

Second Language Acquisition

Chapter 01 · Second Language Acquisition

📖 정답 및 모범 답안 p. 440

1 Language Learning Approach

01 Read a teacher's belief in <A> and the conversation in <B>, and follow the directions.

A

　As a teacher, I'd like to share an insightful perspective on the concept of error analysis. It's a fascinating area that recognizes the reality of errors made by learners. These aren't just mistakes; they're valuable data. By examining, categorizing, and understanding these errors, we gain a deeper insight into the learning process itself. It guides us in tailoring our teaching methods and developing materials that address these challenges directly, making the learning experience more effective and enriching for our students.

　While analyzing errors, in general, we can identify three major types of them. The first is *interlingual transfer*, an error resulting from language transfer caused by the learner's native language. The second is *intralingual transfer*, which occurs due to faulty or partial learning of the target language, rather than language transfer. Intralingual errors may be caused by the influence of one target language item on another. The final category is *communication strategy errors*, which occur when learners attempt to communicate in the target language without full knowledge or competence. These errors often arise from using strategies such as avoidance, circumlocution, word coinage, and foreignizing, as learners try to navigate gaps in their linguistic knowledge.

B

Students are doing a problem-solving task about 'Air Pollution' in groups.

Aram : Okay, guys, let's think about how we can make the air cleaner. Any ideas?
Min-Ji : What if we say people should ride the bus and train more?
Chan-ho : That's a cool idea, Min-Ji. Riding buses and trains more.
Min-Ji : Oh, right. I sometimes forget to add '-s' to make words plural in English. In Korean, we don't do that much when we refer to non-living things.
Aram : No problem, Min-Ji! How about we also say people can ride bikes or walk?
Chan-ho : Good. Also, we can think about having more... umm... I'm not sure of the exact word... maybe... something like cleaning-trees? Sorry, my vocabulary is a bit limited.
Min-Ji : Cleaning-trees? Oh, you mean plants that make the air clean? We call them air-purifying plants.
Chan-ho : Ah-ha! Yes, then, air-purifying plants.
Aram : So we've got 1) using buses and trains, 2) riding bikes or walking, and 3) air-purifying plants. Anything else?

Based on the information in <A>, identify the TWO types of errors exemplified in the students' conversation from <B>. Then, explain your answers with evidence from <B>.

Your Answer

02 Read the passage in <A> and the interaction in <B>, and follow the directions.

A

Some research suggests that language development follows a predictable pattern. For example, one model outlines six stages in the development of question formation, each characterized by specific features.

Stage	Key feature	Example
1	Single words or phrases	• Why? • This? • To who?
2	SVO word order	This is picture?
3	Fronting wh-, do, or other word followed by SVO	• What he is doing?* • Does he going home?* • Is he is mad?*
4	• Inversion in yes/no questions with modal, or copula *be* • Inversion in wh-questions with a copula *be* (but not aux)	• Will they join us for dinner? • Is she mad about that? • What is this lady?
5	Inversion in wh-questions with Aux (e.g. is), do operator, or modal	• What is he doing? • What does she hold in her hand? • Where will she take this?
6	• Negative question with do operator • grammatical tag question	• Doesn't she want to come in? • He's a doctor, isn't he?

※ sentences with an asterisk * denote incorrectness.

Understanding these developmental stages can assist EFL teachers in assessing their students' language proficiency, thereby enabling them to set achievable learning objectives.

B

Two students are getting to know each other during their first week at a new school. They discuss their favorite sports, using question forms.

Jaemin : What is your favorite sport, Sara?

Sara : I love soccer. It's very exciting. What is yours?

Jaemin : Skateboarding for me. I love the thrill and freedom. Doesn't your brother play soccer, too?

Sara : Yes, he really loves it! We often play together. Will you play soccer with us someday?

Jaemin : Sounds great! This coming Sunday?

Sara : That sounds perfect! I'll check with my brother, but I'm sure he'll be excited too.

Based on <A>, identify the developmental stages of Jaemin and Sara, respectively. Then, explain your answers with evidence from <A> and <B>.

Your Answer

Guideline for Pre-service Teachers

03 Read the passage in <A> and the conversation in <B>. Then, follow the directions.

A

Language teachers and learners often encounter frustration when they find a gap between their knowledge of grammar rules and their ability to apply those rules seamlessly in listening, speaking, reading, and writing. This discrepancy can be attributed to the differences between declarative and procedural knowledge. Declarative knowledge pertains to understanding something; it allows a student to describe a grammar rule and apply it in pattern practice drills. Conversely, procedural knowledge involves knowing how to do something, enabling a student to use a grammar rule effectively in communication.

B

Ms. Kim, the English teacher at a middle school, has just finished explaining how to form the past tense for each verb covered in the textbook.

Teacher : Class! Can anyone tell me how we form the past tense for regular verbs?
Eunji : Sure, for regular verbs, we usually add "-ed" to the base form.
Teacher : Excellent, that's correct! Now, how about the past tense of the irregular verb?
Jaeho : Um, for irregular verbs, they don't follow the standard rule of adding '-ed' to form the past tense. Thus, we should memorize the unique past form of each verb.
Teacher : Great job, you've got it! By the way, Eunji, I heard you went to a party yesterday! Did you have fun? What did you do there?
Eunji : Um, I *danced* at the party until midnight!
Teacher : Until midnight? That sounds like a blast! Well done, Eunji! Then, Jaeho, what did you eat for dinner yesterday?
Jaeho : Uh, I *eated* spaghetti for dinner yesterday.
Teacher : Nice try! Jaeho, but you should say "ate," not "eated." Anyway, Spaghetti! It's one of my favorite dishes, too!

Referring to the terms in <A>, explain the difference between Eunji and Jaeho, providing corresponding evidence from <B>.

Your Answer

04 Read the passages and follow the directions.

A

Ms. Kim's Teaching Note

To initiate usual classroom dialogues, I pose questions to the students. Then, they listen to the questions and respond accordingly. If they have difficulty understanding the questions, they are expected to use meaning negotiation strategies such as comprehension checks, clarification requests, and confirmation checks. Through this kind of process, students can obtain _____, which can be mainly understood by listeners despite their not understanding all the words and structures in it. It is because I provide them with language input, which is slightly above their current proficiency level, but not too demanding. In short, whenever students interact with me in class, they can have opportunities to increase their comprehension.

B

Dialogue 1

T: Now, let's talk about your favorite appetizer. Minji?
S: Appe... can you say that again?
T: Appetizer. It's a small dish before your main meal!
S: Ah-hah! You mean, like soup or salad?
T: You're right!

Dialogue 2

T: Joonho, how was your weekend? What did you do?
S: I... go cinema this weekend.
T: You go...? Do you remember the past tense you learned last week?
S: Oh, yes. I went cinema this weekend.

Fill in the blank in <A> with the TWO most appropriate words. Then, choose ONE Dialogue in <B> that exemplifies the classroom dialogue explained in <A> and identify the types of meaning negotiation strategies used in that dialogue, citing each line.

Your Answer

05 Read the teaching note in <A> and the lesson procedure in <B>. Then, follow the directions.

A

Ms. Kim's Teaching Note

After attending a teacher's conference, I have decided to adopt a new teaching approach for my beginner-level students. This approach places a strong emphasis on immersing students in a natural and communicative target language environment. Consequently, I have chosen to conduct lessons exclusively in English to maximize my students' exposure to the natural use of the target language. Regarding classroom activities, it is crucial that they are comprehensible and aligned with the students' proficiency levels, rather than overwhelming them. Therefore, for my beginner-level students, I have designed a command-based activity based on comprehension and response through physical actions rather than verbal or written language production. Overall, my decision to implement this method is rooted in the belief that students should receive ample and understandable input, which will naturally foster the development of language output. Thus, during class, students predominantly listen to my instructions and are not pressured to speak until they become familiar with the target language. Only after they have gained a good grasp of the language, do I provide them with ample example sentences and encourage them to repeat these sentences without extensive explanations of grammatical rules.

B

Below is a part of the lesson procedure that Ms. Kim has designed for her beginner-level students.

Step	Procedure
Step 1	• T shows Ss a short video clip about people who are meeting for the first time. • T presents 14 target phrases on the board and reads aloud the phrases one by one. Ss listen to T's reading. (e.g. shake hands, bow, hug, kiss the person on the cheek, smile and say 'hi', stand very close, stand up, touch the person on the arm, look at the person directly, etc.) • T reads each phrase one more time with corresponding gestures to teach Ss the meaning of each phrase. • T asks Ss to do a pair activity. When one student reads the phrase, the other expresses the meaning in gesture. Ss take turns until they are accustomed to the phrases.
Step 2	• After sufficient exposure to target phrases, T gives Ss a checklist with the phrases. • T asks Ss to individually mark 'O' next to the actions they usually do and mark 'X' next to the ones they never do when meeting new people. When they finish, T puts Ss in groups and asks them to share their answers. • T writes a target sentence structure on the board. (e.g.) I usually/never sometimes _____. What about you? • T checks Ss' answers and encourages them to say using the target sentence.
Step 3	• T provides Ss with a role-play slip including many examples of the target structure. • T asks Ss in groups to practice the role-play. • Ss present their role-play on the front and T gives them feedback.

Guideline for Pre-service Teachers

Considering the information in <A> and <B>, write the name of the teaching approach that Ms. Kim describes and her major purpose of using the approach. Then, explain the teaching method she uses in Step 1 to achieve her purpose. Do NOT copy more than FOUR consecutive words from the passages.

Your Answer

06 Read the passage and follow the directions.

    The two middle school English teachers, Ms. Yoo and Mr. Kim, are in a teacher's meeting. They are discussing group activities in a communicative classroom.

Ms. Yoo : Mr. Kim, what types of group activities do you usually use?
Mr. Kim : Normally, I have students engage in grammar activities. After explicitly learning grammar rules, they answer the multiple-choice questions. Then, in pairs, they share the answers and have a chance to change their answers.
Ms. Yoo : That sounds great! But, those activities are sufficient to improve students' speaking skills? I think doing similar grammar activities will neither improve their communication skills nor motivate students to actively participate.
Mr. Kim : You're right! Some of my students have mentioned that answering grammar questions is not interesting anymore. Besides, I've noticed that teacher talking time (TTT) is greater than student talking time (STT) in my lessons. How can I increase their talking time and promote the active participation of all students in class? Do you have any ideas?
Ms. Yoo : What if you provide diverse authentic tasks instead of focusing on grammar activities?
Mr. Kim : Hmm, could you clarify a bit more?
Ms. Yoo : I mean, I prepare tasks that are authentic and relevant to students' real-life situations. During these authentic group activities, students actively participate and communicate in English to achieve their goals. This allows me to significantly increase STT during lessons. Furthermore, to facilitate their active participation, I assign each of them a specific role such as a group leader, a passage chooser, and an online manager. This leads all students to contribute to the group's outcomes and actively participate in the given tasks.

Guideline for Pre-service Teachers

> Mr. Kim : That sounds perfect! I have one more question, though. How do you handle situations where students resort to using Korean instead of English when communication breaks down? This seems to happen quite often during group activities, and it's challenging for me to monitor all the groups simultaneously.
>
> Ms. Yoo : It's likely because they might not know or have forgotten the English words. In my case, I encourage students to use alternative words they already know to convey a similar meaning. For instance, they can say "a ship" instead of "a yacht" if they are unsure how to express it in English.
>
> Mr. Kim : That's impressive! Thank you for your suggestion.

Identify the type of lesson that Ms. Yoo recommends for Mr. Kim and explain TWO advantages of the identified type of lesson. Then, write the alternative communication strategy Ms. Yoo suggests for Mr. Kim's students.

Your Answer

07 Read the teacher's note in <A> and the lesson plan in <B>, and follow the directions.

A

Today I participated in a teacher workshop talking about Task-based instruction (TBI) model, a dynamic approach to language teaching. According to the workshop, this model stands out as it prioritizes the use of authentic language and practical tasks to enhance learning. It's a shift from the more traditional methods that predominantly center around grammar and vocabulary. Below is the TBI plan model from the workshop.

Task-based Instruction Plan Model

Pre-task

Introduction to topic and tasks
Teacher explores the topic with the class, activating students' prior knowledge and introducing useful words and phrases. Learners may also be exposed to examples.

Task Cycle

Task	Planning	Report
Students do the task in pairs, or small groups. Teacher monitors; mistakes do not matter.	Students prepare for report. The teacher stands by and gives advice on language.	Students exchange or present report. Teacher listens and then comments.

Language Focus

Analysis	Practice
Students examine the target language.	Teacher conducts practice of new words.

B

The following is a task-based lesson plan with speaking development as one of its main purposes.

Time: 80 minutes
Level: High intermediate
Theme: Organizing a Celebration

Stage 1. Pre-task (10 min)
- A teacher shows students pictures of a celebration. (e.g., photographs of the family celebrating Christmas or someone's birthday)
- The teacher shows students a list of questions to activate their schematic knowledge about celebrations.
- Students work in pairs to answer the questions.

[Questions]
- What are some of the special occasions you celebrate with family or friends?
- What is your favorite celebration with friends or family?
- When was your last family celebration? How was it?
- What details make a celebration successful?

(...)

Stage 2. Task Cycle
(1) Task (10 min)
- The teacher instructs students to form groups of four and plan a celebration, covering all aspects including invitations and event details.
- Students in groups discuss various types of celebrations and related objects.
- The teacher walks around the classroom and monitors students' group performance.

(2) Planning (40 min)
- Students in groups plan the chosen celebration. (e.g., Christmas, Halloween, or birthday)
- Students prepare to report. Everybody needs to be involved. The teacher circulates and observes students' group conversation, giving students affective support to encourage their active participation.

(3) Report (8 min)
- The classroom is divided. Each group is assigned a place in the classroom to decorate and provide the environment for the chosen celebration.
- Students present the chosen celebration. After the presentation, classmates ask necessary questions.
- The teacher gives feedback on the content and quickly comments.
- Students vote and choose the best celebration.

Stage 3. Language Focus
(1) Analysis (7 min)
- The teacher writes sentences given by students on the board and leads students to examine them.
- The teacher highlights language he or she wants to address.
- The teacher encourages students to note down useful phrases and language.

(2) Practice (5 min)
The teacher assigns activities that incorporate the new vocabulary and structures learned in the lesson.

Choose the TWO Stages in <B> that do NOT correspond to the TBI plan model in <A>, and explain your answers with evidence from <A> and <B>.

Your Answer

08 Read the passages and follow the directions.

A

There are two significantly different types of L2 instruction, namely meaning-focused and form-focused instruction. The former (MFI) aims to provide exposure to rich input or opportunities for meaningful use of the L2 within context. The focus is on conveying meanings using the words and phrases to the best of the learners' abilities. On the other hand, the latter (FFI) refers to any planned or incidental instructional activity that is intended to draw language learners' attention to specific linguistic forms.

B

Lesson Procedure A

Step 1
T introduces today's topic, 'Planning for weekends'. T talks about his/her plans for next weekend. Then, T provides pictures of what people normally do on weekends. T talks about the pictures with the whole class using level-appropriate vocabulary and grammar.

Step 2
T puts students in groups of four. T asks students to share their plans for next weekend with group members. T emphasizes them to feel free to use easy vocabulary or expressions, not them being stressed by new vocabulary or complex sentence structures. Additionally, T asks Ss to choose the Top 3 plans discussed in their groups.

Step 3
T asks each group to present their group findings. While listening to the presentation, all the students vote for and pick up the three plans they like best.

Lesson Procedure B

1. Introduction (5 minutes):
   T introduces today's target form, *present perfect* using an example sentence, "I have visited Paris," and explains its usage.

2. Text Analysis & Clarification (10 minutes):
   - T distributes a short reading text about global warming. It includes several example sentences of the *present perfect* form. Each expression is underlined.
   - T asks Ss in pairs to figure out the usage and meaning of the underlined expressions.
   - T explains when and how to use the *present perfect* clearly.

3. Discussion (15 minutes):
   - T divides Ss into small groups (4 members).
   - T asks each group to discuss their own experiences related to global warming using the *present perfect* structure.
   - Walking around the class, T provides help as needed.

4. Presentation & Feedback (20 minutes):
   - T asks each group to present their discussion to the whole class.
   - Before wrapping up the lesson, T provides feedback on the errors related to the *present perfect* students have made in common.

Referring to terms in <A>, identify which type of instruction each lesson procedure in <B> exemplifies. Then, explain the reason of your choices with evidence from both <A> and <B>.

Your Answer

Guideline for Pre-service Teachers

09 Read the passage in <A> and the teacher's reflections in <B>. Then, follow the directions.

A

Content-Based Instruction (CBI) is the integration of content learning with the goals of language education. In essence, it involves studying a language alongside a specific subject, where the language learning is directed by the subject content. Currently, the two most popular CBI methods in classrooms are the immersion and adjunct models. The immersion model immerses L2 learners in an environment where the target language is primarily used. Learners study academic content, such as math, science, and history in the target language. Overall, this model is based on the idea that learners develop language skills more effectively while learning other subjects. On the other hand, the adjunct model is a team-teaching model linking subject-matter teachers and language teachers. It involves students enrolling in both a standard academic course and separate language lessons. In their language lessons, the emphasis is on assisting students to comprehend the language so they can grasp the content taught by the subject instructor. Additionally, the language teacher supports students in completing academic assignments.

B

Below are the reflections of teachers who are teaching advanced leveled students at a high school.

Eunji's Reflection

In my school, all subject classes are conducted in English. During these lessons, I am always encouraged to communicate solely in English. Today, in our Art class, we practiced sketching. My teacher demonstrated drawing techniques using specific English terms, and we followed her lead. Afterward, we shared our sketches in groups and provided feedback to one another, communicating exclusively in English. Thus, while taking the Art lessons, I can improve my language skills—including vocabulary, grammar, and communication skills. After the Art class, I attended history and science lessons, both conducted in English. Since I began studying all subjects in English, I have developed my language skills more effectively than when I received subject lessons in my first language.

Sungho's Reflection

At my school, all my subjects are taught in English. This semester, I enrolled in history, math, literature, and science classes. However, because my English proficiency level isn't high enough to fully comprehend lessons conducted in English, I often find it challenging to understand the content. Consequently, I enrolled in a language course designed to support each of my subject lessons. After consulting with my subject teachers, the language teacher offers lessons tailored to teach us subject-specific vocabulary and strategies. This helps us better understand texts from subjects like history or science that contain unfamiliar words. Without these supportive language lessons, I would have struggled with specific terms in each class. Thanks to these lessons, I can now fully comprehend the content of subject lessons and actively participate in the classes.

Guideline for Pre-service Teachers

Considering the information in <A> and in <B>, identify the specific type of content-based instruction that Eunji and Sungho each participate in and, then, write the reason for your choice.

Your Answer

10 Read the passages and follow the directions.

A

In a typical conversation centered on making an invitation, there exists a common overarching sequence of interactional moves:

Step 1: Greeting
Step 2: Preliminary moves toward a forthcoming invitation
Step 3: Making an invitation
Step 4: Questions about the invitation
Step 5: Answers to the questions
Step 6: Short negotiation
Step 7: Acceptance/Rejection of the invitation
Step 8: Reply to acceptance/Rejection of the invitation
Step 9: Thanking/Closing

B

Below is a conversation between two friends. Jisoo is an ESL student with a low-intermediate level of English, and Sam is a native English speaker who moved from Australia to Korea.

Sam : Hey, Jisoo! How are you?
Jisoo : Hi, Sam! I'm good, thanks. What about you?
Sam : I'm doing well. Do you have any plans this weekend?
Jisoo : Not really.
Sam : Actually, I'm having a home party this Saturday to celebrate my birthday, and I'd love for you to come.
Jisoo : Oh, that sounds fun! Who else will be there?
Sam : It'll be a small gathering with some of our mutual friends.
Jisoo : What time does the party start?
Sam : The party starts at 7 P.M., and it'll go on until late. So feel free to drop by anytime!
Jisoo : *(She asks him again as she understands.)* So, I can come to your house at any time?

Guideline for Pre-service Teachers

> Sam : Yes, you can come at any time! You're welcome to come whenever you can.
> Jisoo : Cool! I'll definitely be there to celebrate with you.
> Sam : *(He smiles.)* See you on Saturday then!
> Jisoo : Thanks for inviting me! I'm looking forward to it.

Referring to <A> identify the utterance that corresponds to Step 2 and Step 8, respectively. Then, write the negotiation strategy that Jisoo uses to check her understanding of Sam's statement and cite the corresponding utterance.

Your Answer

11 Read the passage in <A> and the conversation in <B> and follow the directions.

A

Effective conversation hinges on cohesion, achieved through the use of grammatical devices like substitution, ellipsis, conjunction, etc. These devices ensure the conversation's parts are interlinked and coherently organized, facilitating a smooth discourse flow.

Devices	Sub-categories	Examples
Substitution	Nominal	Can I have another drink? This <u>one</u> is finished.
	Verbal	A: You look great. B: So <u>do</u> you.
	Clausal	A: Is she happy? B: I think <u>so</u>.
Ellipsis	Nominal	Nelly liked the green tiles, I preferred the blue <u>(*)</u>.
	Verbal	A: Will anyone be waiting? B: Jim <u>will</u> (*).
	Clausal	A: What does it look like? B: (*) A tape recorder.
Conjunction	Adversative	I didn't study. <u>However</u>, I still passed.
	Additive	He didn't study. <u>In addition</u>, he failed.
	Temporal	She studied hard. <u>Then</u> she passed the test.
	Causal	They studied hard. <u>Therefore</u>, they deserve to pass.

...

(*) denotes ellipsis.

Guideline for Pre-service Teachers

B

S1: Can you finish the assignment by tomorrow?
S2: Yes, I can. I think the assignment will take me all night. Have you finished the assignment?
S1: I haven't even started yet.
S2: You should have started earlier. I can help you with the assignment.
S1: That's okay. By the way, did the teacher mention anything about an extension?
S2: Nope. Maybe she might give us some information about the extension later.
S1: I think so, too.

S=student

Based on <A>, identify the specific grammatical devices (including sub-categories) used in the conversation from <B>. Then, explain your answers with concrete examples in <B>.

Your Answer

12 Read the passage in <A> and the conversation in <B>, and follow the directions.

A

Cohesive devices are words or phrases that are used to connect and link ideas within a text or discourse. They are essential in learning English because they enhance the understandability of the language. Cohesive devices help create a logical flow of ideas, improve readability, and make the text or speech more engaging for the listener or reader. Some researchers have identified four general categories of cohesive devices used in texts:

- **Reference**: This category involves the relationships between nouns or pronouns and the objects they refer to.
- **Ellipsis**: It occurs when certain words or phrases are omitted in a sentence, but their meaning can be understood from the context.
- **Substitution**: Instead of omitting words, substitution involves replacing a specific word or phrase with a more general one to maintain coherence and avoid repetition.
- **Conjunctions**: These are words or phrases used to connect words, phrases, or clauses in a sentence, establishing logical relationships (e.g., comparison, cause and effect, etc.) between them.

By understanding and using these cohesive devices effectively, learners can improve their English language skills and communicate more coherently.

Guideline for Pre-service Teachers

B

Two students are talking about their dream jobs.

S1: What is your dream job?
S2: Hmm, ... a teacher! How about you?
S1: Well, I want to be a writer. Writing stories is truly inspires me. I really love it.
S2: Terrific! I can see your passion.
S1: Thank you! Can you imagine the impact that my writing can have on others?
S2: Sure. Just like teachers can shape students' lives, they can make a lasting impression. In the same way, writers can influence readers through storytelling.
S1: Yeah, you're right!

S=student

Based on \<A\>, identify the categories of cohesive devices that S1 and S2 use, respectively. Then, write the concrete example(s) of identified category from \<B\>.

Your Answer
_____
_____
_____
_____

13 Read the passages in <A> and <B>, and follow the directions.

A

Ms. Park's Teaching Log

During a discussion with fellow teachers on enhancing students' communicative competence, we concluded that a comprehensive approach, incorporating all four components of communicative competence is essential for fostering our students' ability to communicate effectively. These components include grammatical competence, which focuses on the mastery of language structures; discourse competence, which involves the ability to combine ideas to achieve cohesion in form and coherence in thought; _____ competence, which entails understanding the various social contexts in which language is used; and strategic competence, which is about using strategies to overcome communication problems and to enhance the effectiveness of communication. By integrating these aspects into our teaching, we can provide a more rounded and effective language education.

B

Activity 1

※ Below are sentences extracted from a short story, but they are in the wrong order. Rearrange them to correspond with the narrative's coherent thought.

1. They all agreed it was an unforgettable day.
2. It started to rain, and everyone scrambled to find shelter.
3. The family packed a basket full of sandwiches, fruits, and drinks.
4. The rain stopped, the family saw a beautiful rainbow.
5. The family decided to have a picnic by the lake.

→ Original sequence : ( ) ( ) ( ) ( ) ( )

After arranging the sentences in the correct order, write the story down in a paragraph by adding at least two references and conjunctions.

_____
_____
_____

Activity 2

When you are unsure of the exact word, how do you avoid a breakdown in communication? You explain or describe the unknown word. Let's practice!

Jihoon is looking for a needle but describes it instead because he does not know the word "needle."

Teacher : What are you looking for, Jihoon?
Student : I'm looking for a small, thin thing. It's _____.
Teacher : Oh, you mean a needle?
Student : Yes, that's it! A needle. I was looking for a needle. Thank you!

- Intended idea: needle
- Your answer: It's _____.

(Potential answer: It's very sharp at one end and has a hole at the other end.)

Fill in the blank in <A> with the ONE most appropriate word. Then, identify which of the four components of communicative competence each activity in <B> aims to develop. Support your choices with evidence from <B>. Do not copy more than FOUR consecutive words from the passage.

Your Answer   _____

_____
_____
_____
_____

14 Read <A> and <B> and follow the directions.

— **A** —

Communication can be explained as the process of transmitting information from one person, place or group to another. It is through communication that we share messages. There are three integral elements of communication, i.e. Sender, Message, and Receiver. A mode is the means of communicating, i.e. the medium through which communication is processed. There are three modes of communication: Interpersonal Communication, Interpretive Communication, and Presentational Communication. Below is the table overviewing three modes of communication.

Interpersonal	Interpretive	Presentational
Two-way communication with active negotiation of meaning among individuals	One-way communication with no resource for the active negotiation of meaning with the writer, speaker, or producer	One-way communication intended for an audience of readers, listeners, or viewers
• spontaneous • meaningful	Reader, listener or viewer interprets what the author, speaker, or producer wants the receiver of the message to understand	• Presentation of information; not exchange • No direct opportunity for the active negotiation of meaning exists

Guideline for Pre-service Teachers

B

Case A

Alex just read the article about 'New jobs for 2030' through online news websites. Below is the part of the text messages that he shared with his friend, Sarah, through kakaotalk.

Alex : Just read about New jobs for 2030—"Nano-Medic Specialists" and "AI Ethicists".
Sarah : Say that again…?
Alex : "Nano-Medic Specialists" who use tiny tools inside bodies and "AI Ethicists" who watch over AI ethics.
Sarah : Sounds complex. How do you even train for those?
Alex : You'd need a mix of medical/engineering for Nano-Medics and ethics/tech for AI Ethicists.
Mike : Are these jobs real though?
Alex : Yeah, the article seems legit, not just sci-fi. It's cool how the job landscape's changing, right?

Case B

Jungmin just read the novel "The Ants" and wrote the following log.

I just finished "The Ants" by Bernard Werber. It's a book about ants and how they live together. The author seems to want us to think about how ants and people are alike. He also wants us to care about the environment. The ants' world is kind of like ours, so we can learn from them. This book makes us think about how everything is connected and how we fit into the big world.

Considering the information in <A>, identify the mode of communication that each case exemplifies in <B> and write the reason for each of your choices.

15 Read the passage and follow the directions.

> *Ms. Kim and Ms. Yoo, English teachers at a middle school, believe that current English lessons should be student-centered instruction. Below are the teaching notes of two teachers talking about how to actualize student-centered instruction.*

Ms. Kim's Teaching Note

I believe that current English lessons should be student-centered instructions. Thus, in designing classroom activities, I make students play an active role in their learning process by providing them with various group activities. For example, I use one special group activity to teach my students how to take charge of their learning. Specifically, in my writing class, students are asked to share their writing works with their classmates to exchange feedback. Not only do they receive feedback from their friends, but they also provide feedback to them. By critiquing each other's work, they have ownership of their learning and become active learners. In this activity, my students use a checklist to support the process as seen below.

[Checklist]
a. What do you like the most about the writing?
b. What is the main idea?
c. Who is the audience, and what is the purpose?
d. What convincing details does the writer use?
e. Where could the writer add details to make the piece more convincing?
f. What areas in the writing seem unclear?
g. How could the writer make the piece clearer?

Ms. Yoo's Teaching Note

From the perspective of student-centered instruction, I firmly believe that collaboration is a pivotal element. So, when I design my English lessons, I make it a point to incorporate various group works for my students. Especially, I ask them to use a specific strategy in which they support one another whenever necessary. For example, in reading activities, if lower-level students are having a difficult time understanding and answering comprehension questions, advanced students in the same group can offer explanations about the questions and help them find the answers. What's fascinating about this strategy is that the assistance from peers tends to align better with each individual's current proficiency level by providing tailored support. This can be more effective than guidance solely from the teacher.

Based on the teaching notes, explain how Ms. Kim and Ms. Yoo actualize student-centered instruction in their lessons, respectively. Then, write the potential benefit of using each identified way from the teacher's perspective.

Your Answer

16 Read the passages and follow the directions.

A

The _____ theory works in four stages—concrete experience, reflective observation, abstract conceptualization, and active experimentation. The first two stages of the cycle involve grasping an experience, and the second two focus on transforming an experience. Effective learning is seen as the learner goes through the cycle.

- Concrete experience: being involved in a new experience.
- Reflective observation: watching others or developing observations about one's own experience.
- Abstract conceptualization: creating theories to explain observations.
- Active experimentation: using theories to solve problems, and make decisions.

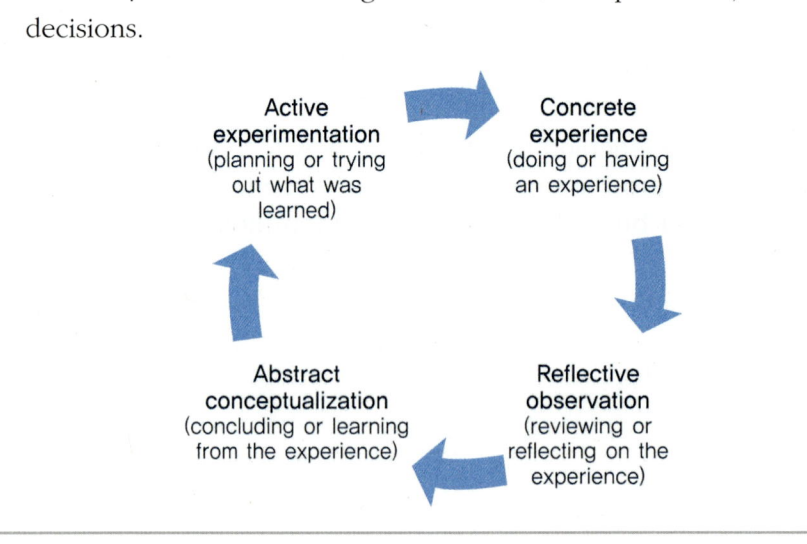

B

Minsoo's Log

Today's visit to the animal farm was quite an adventure. After interacting with the farmers and spending time with the animals, I took a moment to reflect on everything I had experienced. This included observing the animals' behavior and connecting it with my existing knowledge. This step allowed me to carefully analyze and comprehend the significance of my visit, as well as understand its impact on me.

Eunji's Log

Volunteering at the senior center was an enlightening experience. After spending time with the elderly residents and understanding their needs, I felt inspired to try something different. I thought to myself, why not organize a group activity to bring them joy? Consequently, I decided to lead a painting session that would allow them to express their creativity. I hope this initiative can bring smiles to their faces and positively impact their days.

Fill in the blank in <A> with TWO words. Based on the information in <A>, identify the stage of the learning that each student in <B> describes and write the reason for your choices with evidence.

Your Answer

Guideline for Pre-service Teachers

17 Read the passages and follow the directions.

A

Ms. Yoo's Teaching Note

Today, I implemented a new type of learning: _____ instruction. This dynamic approach to active learning ignites curiosity, deepens understanding of concepts, fosters a love for learning, and prepares students for a lifelong journey of asking questions and seeking answers. Thus, I have preferred this kind of instruction to traditional teaching methods that primarily involve the transmission of facts by the teacher. There are two advantages to conducting this lesson. First, it can foster the development of higher-order thinking skills, more specifically, critical thinking. Instead of rote learning, students engage in activities where they analyze data, evaluate necessary evidence, and draw conclusions based on their own findings, thereby the activities can enhance their critical thinking skills. Second, it could maximize their motivation and engagement for the lesson. Allowing students to explore real-world problems makes their learning more relevant and applicable. In other words, connecting real-world problems to their learning can lead them to stay engaged and motivated to learn. Based on these two ideas, today's lesson was very satisfying for both myself and my students. Below is an outline of the lesson procedure I conducted today.

B

	Procedures
Week 1 (Setting a hypothesis and basic knowledge)	• T activates Ss' schemata by showing a short video clip about today's topic: the water quality of the Han River. • T presents a question on the board: "Would you recommend your friends to swim in the Han River?" • T asks Ss to contemplate the question and share their opinions. • In groups, Ss discuss Seoul's water supply through the Han River based on the materials provided by T.
Week 2 (Finding Answers)	• T delivers a lecture about water pollution and asks Ss to discuss the types of pollutants that might be present in the water. • T introduces basic water tests and water sampling using water-test kits. • Ss start forming their hypotheses to answer the question. • Ss record all observations and hypotheses in their notebooks. • Ss embark on a field trip to the Han River, collecting water samples in groups for analysis. • Ss document all analyzed data that may affect the water quality of the Han River.
Week 3 (Presenting Answers)	• Ss compare their data with that of other groups to gain an overall picture of the Han River's water quality. • Ss prepare for their presentations. • In groups, Ss present their findings and answers. • Both Ss and T exchange feedback.

Guideline for Pre-service Teachers

Fill in the blank with the ONE most appropriate word. Then, write TWO benefits of the learning type mentioned in Ms. Yoo's Teaching Note, comparing to traditional teaching methods. Do NOT copy more than FOUR consecutive words from the passages.

Your Answer

18 Read the passages and follow the directions.

A

A common question among educators is "What is the difference between inquiry-based learning and project-based learning?" It can certainly be confusing, not only in differentiating between the two but also in deciding which method will work best for your class.

Inquiry-based learning is a student-led process that begins with their own questions and wonderings. It is an approach to learning that emphasizes questions, ideas, and the natural curiosity of students. With inquiry-based learning, student questions are at the center of their learning journey.

Project-based learning involves a long-term approach to teaching and learning where students solve real-world problems. In this approach, the goal is for students to produce a tangible, and meaningful product. While this approach also begins with a challenge or question, the goal is a bit different. The focus is more on the output of the learning journey—in other words, what students produce through extensive investigation and the application of skills.

In summary, inquiry-based learning is about the journey of exploring and questioning, while project-based learning is about the destination—a final product demonstrating the learning process. Both approaches value student engagement and teacher facilitation, but they differ in focus and end results.

B

Below is part of the lesson plan designed by one English teacher in a middle school.

Lesson Plan

Grade Level: 3rd graders, middle school
Objective: Students research impulse buying and reasonable consumption, then create a promotional video advocating for reasonable consumption.
Duration: Around three months

Materials:
- Computers with internet
- Research materials
- Video recording and editing tools
- Projector

Activities

Weeks 1-4: Research Phase
- Introduce project; form groups
- Research impulse buying and reasonable consumption
- Weekly group discussions and regular meetings with the teacher

Weeks 5-8: Planning and Scripting
- Brainstorm ideas to make the video
- Write the script and create storyboards to outline their video's visual and narrative structure
- Peer and teacher feedback on scripts and storyboards

Weeks 9-12: Video Production
- Film and edit the video
- Add sound effects and finalize the edit
- Peer and teacher review of rough cuts

Final Week: Presentation
- Groups present their videos
- Class discussion on the impact and message of each video
- Reflect on what they learned

Assessment:
- Ongoing: Participation, script, and storyboard
- Final: Promotional video

Based on the information in <A>, identify the type of instruction described in <B> and write TWO reasons for your choice with evidence from <B>.

Your Answer

Guideline for Pre-service Teachers

19 Read the passages and follow the directions.

A

Below is the list of instructional techniques that Ms. Yoo prepares for her foreign students who are facing _____ in the multicultural classes.

- Culture capsule: It is a brief description, usually one or two paragraphs, of some aspect of the target culture, followed by or incorporated with contrasting information about the students' native culture. Culture capsules can be written by teachers or students.

- Culture island: A culture island is an area in the classroom where posters, maps, objects, and pictures of people, lifestyles, or customs of other cultures are displayed to attract learners' attention, evoke comments, and help students develop a mental image.

- Artifact study: It is designed to help students discern the cultural significance of certain unfamiliar objects from the target culture. The activity involves students in giving descriptions and forming hypotheses about the function of the unknown object.

- Cultoons: These are like visual culture assimilators. Students are given a series of (usually) four pictures depicting points of surprise or possible misunderstanding for persons coming into the target culture. The situations are also described verbally by the teacher or by the students who read the accompanying written descriptions. Students may be asked if they think the reactions of the characters in the cultoons seem appropriate or not. After the misunderstandings or surprises are clearly in mind, the students read explanations of what was happening and why there was misunderstanding.

B

Ms. Yoo's Teaching Note

As an English teacher for 2nd graders in a middle school, I am managing multicultural classes from this semester. During the lessons, I noticed that some foreign students who recently moved to Korea are facing challenges in adapting to the Korean language and culture because of _____, cultural conflict occurred between Korean and their own cultures. In response to this, I decided to create a special lesson to help them gain a better understanding of Korean culture. For this purpose, I chose to use the cultural product of Norigae. During the culture lesson, I divided the students into groups and presented them with the unfamiliar object, Norigae. Each group read a short explanation about it and then had a group discussion to guess when and how Korean people use it. Following the discussions, each group presented their own ideas about Norigae in groups. After the group presentations, I provided a comprehensive explanation of Norigae, highlighting its significance as a symbol of good luck and protection in Korean culture. After the lesson, I received feedback from the students that reading a story about Norigae and engaging in discussions about its cultural significance allowed them to deepen their understanding of Korean culture. They expressed that the activity gave them hope and confidence that they can successfully acculturate to Korean culture.

Fill in the blanks in <A> and <B> with TWO words in common. Then, referring to <A>, identify the instructional technique that Ms. Yoo uses to teach Korean culture to her foreign students in <B> and write the effect of the identified teaching technique.

Your Answer

2. Learning Phenomenon

01 Read the passages, and follow the directions.

A

Many studies show that declarative knowledge can become procedural knowledge in the sense that "learners can lose awareness of the structure over time, and learners can be aware of the structure of implicit knowledge when attempting to access it". However, it is manifest that the development of procedural knowledge takes longer time than the development of declarative knowledge. Thus, teachers often use different types of corrective feedback to assist the development of procedural knowledge. With the help of corrective feedback, L2 learners can achieve native-like proficiency after going through three stages: 1) declarative knowledge stage, 2) procedural knowledge stage, and 3) automatizing stage. In the first stage, learners develop declarative knowledge of the language. Declarative knowledge is the learners' knowledge of all the conscious facts about the language and the learners' ability to articulate those facts. However, they may not necessarily be able to apply the knowledge correctly. In the second stage, learners are developing procedural knowledge. Procedural knowledge is the learners' intuitive application of linguistic knowledge to produce responses in the target language. They subconsciously use the language correctly. In the third stage, they eventually develop automatizing stage which enables them to automatize their knowledge and fluently use the language.

B

Suji's Learning Log

In today's class, the teacher asked us about our favorite places to go. I gladly volunteered to speak and said, "I like to go to the beach because my sister also like to go there." The teacher pointed out my errors saying that "Put '-s' after the verb 'like'. Say 'my sister also likes'". Then, I continued speaking and the teacher kept jumping in with feedback on the same kind of errors. I already knew the third-person singular rule but I just could not use it properly while speaking. I think, it was only a minor mistake. After several times of direct corrections by my teacher, I felt nervous and didn't want to continue speaking. I was really so embarrassed that I wanted to ask her not to correct my errors too directly. Only with indirect correction, I would have noticed my mistakes.

Ms. Kim's Teaching Note

I am teaching 3rd graders in a middle school, who are intermediate level students. Today, I asked my students to talk about their favorite places. Some students who are very passionate about speaking English spontaneously started to share their favorite places with other classmates. Most of them used correct grammar but, only Suji didn't. Surprisingly, Suji is also a high intermediate level student, but she kept dropping the third person singular '-s'. For the first and the second time, I just let her continue speaking hoping that she fixes her errors by herself. However, the third time of making the same error, I could not help giving direct correction. Although she is a fluent speaker, she was making the same mistake again and again. I was worried that such an incorrect form becomes permanently internalized into her interlanguage system. That's why I directly corrected her utterances. After several times of corrections, she started to use the correct grammar.

Guideline for Pre-service Teachers

Referring to the terms in <A>, identify the knowledge stage of Suji and write the reason of your choice based on <B>. Then, explain why Ms. Kim could not help giving direct correction to Suji's error. Do NOT copy more than FOUR consecutive words from the passages.

Your Answer

02 Review the two teachers' conversation below and follow the directions.

Two middle school English teachers, Ms. Park and Ms. Kim, are discussing the result of the writing test administered last week.

Ms. Kim : Ms. Park, did you check the writing test score?
Ms. Park : Yes, I did… The results were not so satisfactory. You did?
Ms. Kim : Yeah, and same here. I was disappointed with the results. For the last month, I fully focused on improving their writing ability but their writings in the test were just full of errors. Especially, the grammar part.
Ms. Park : Hmm, what did we miss?
Ms. Kim : I think the cause of grammatical errors is due to their native language. When I checked the errors, errors were frequently affected by their native language.
Ms. Park : Can you give me one example?
Ms. Kim : For instance, they kept dropping articles for nouns because Korean does not have articles. It's an entirely new item to them. So, I concluded that I should have compared all grammar rules of English and Korean in advance and taught the differences preemptively. If I had done so, they would not have made any errors.
Ms. Park : Well, it might. But, not all errors are caused by the grammatical differences between English and Korean. Besides, we cannot predict all types of difficulties before the actual errors happen. So, I think, it is better to focus on the point that students' confusion between English rules matters even further.
Ms. Kim : You mean, the errors like 'intelligentest'?
Ms. Park : Exactly! 'Intelligentest' does not relate to the grammar rules of Korean at all. Rather, it is because they misapply the target language rule to where it does not apply. I think this is the major cause of errors.
Ms. Kim : Hmm… Whatever the reason is, we need to find some other possible errors and help students not to make any errors.
Ms. Park : You don't need to be too negative about their errors. I believe making errors is just a part of a language learning process.

Guideline for Pre-service Teachers

Identify the cause of the error that each teacher exemplifies in the conversation, respectively. Then, addressing the hypothesis of Second Language Acquisition that Ms. Kim refers to, write her idea on how to deal with students' errors.

Your Answer

03 Read the passage in <A> and a teacher's note in <B> and follow the directions.

A

A researcher provides a brief sketch of the u-shaped curve, common in first language acquisition, and also found in second language learners. U-shaped learning denotes one frequent developmental path when new cognitive skills are developed. Imagine a curve shaped like a letter "U" in a graph with the x-axis depicting time, and the y-axis depicting the learner's level of skill. Learners often start out with seemingly high levels of skill, but then go through a certain phase in which students undergo a dip in performance. Then later, learners return to the high levels of performance once again. For example, a Korean student learned the expression 'Do you come to ~ ?'. But later, the student may use 'Do you go to ~ ?' instead of 'come to', and finally, she again uses 'Do you come to ~ ?'.

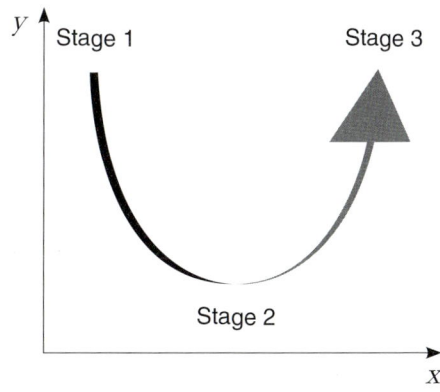

U-shaped learning

Guideline for Pre-service Teachers

B

Teacher's Note

    Whenever I teach a new target form to my students, interestingly, they show a three stage-based learning pattern. For example, when I taught the verb 'broke' in transitive and ergative contexts, in the beginning, they accepted both uses of the verb: they judged "He broke the vase" and "The vase broke" to be good English. However, at the next lesson, they rejected the _____ construction: they judged "The vase broke" to be incorrect English. Then, later they accepted both uses more correctly. While observing such a pattern of learning, I wondered why students go through regression. So I checked one research article. According to the article, this occurs when students' monitor is down due to either stress or relaxation. Besides, it usually lasts for very brief periods of time. Through this article, I clearly understand that this temporary regression is natural and inevitable for language learning.

Fill in the blank with the ONE word from <B>. Then, explain the "a certain phase" underlined in <A>, citing concrete examples from <B>.

Your Answer

04 Review the lesson procedure and follow the directions.

A

Types of Errors

1. **Overgeneralization**: This is the use of one form or construction in one context and extending its application to other contexts where it should not apply.
2. **Hypercorrection**: Sometimes too much effort from teachers in correcting their students' errors induces the students to make errors in otherwise correct forms. Students make mistakes in grammar, punctuation, or pronunciation that result from trying too hard to be correct.
3. **Fossilization**: Some errors, especially errors in pronunciation, persist for long periods and become quite difficult to get rid of.
4. **Avoidance**: Some syntactic structures are difficult to be produced by some learners. Consequently, these learners avoid these structures and use instead simpler structures.

B

Below is part of the conversation between a teacher and students.

T   : Juwan, how was your trip to Jeju Island [ˈaɪlənd]?
Juwan : Jeju Island [áislənd] was beautiful! My grandparents also came with us!
T   : They came to Jeju Island [ˈaɪlənd] with your family?
Juwan : Yes, on Jeju Island [áislənd], there are so many fresh seafood dishes!
T   : You must have a good time in Jeju!
Juwan : Indeed!
T   : How about Minju? Did you have a good weekend?
Minju : Yes, I did. I went to Seoul Zoo. It's Right [laɪt] next to my house.

T	: Minju. Repeat after me, *(T emphasizes the /r/ sound.)* Right. [**raɪt**] Right. [**raɪt**]
Minju	: Right. [**raɪt**]
T	: Great! Sometimes, Korean students pronounce the /r/ sound like the /l/ sound because the two sounds come from the same underlying consonant 'ㄹ' of the Korean language. So, you should be careful when pronouncing the 'r' sound.
Minju	: I see. I will try my best. *(She looks nervous.)*
Juwan	: Minju, were there many animals?
Minju	: Yes, there were so many cute animals like pandas, monkeys, giraffes, zebras, and so on. Especially, I was so lucky [**ˈrʌki**] that I could feed a baby lion [**ˈraɪən**] by myself. *(After the teacher's correction, Minju starts to pronounce both 'r' and 'l' sounds into the 'r' sound.)*
Juwan	: Feeding a baby lion [**ˈlaɪən**]? Wow, that's amazing!

Based on the information in <A>, identify TWO types of errors the students show in <B>. Then, explain each type of the identified errors using concrete evidence from <B>.

Your Answer

NEW Build Up

Chapter 02

Classroom Context

Chapter 02 Classroom Context

1 Teaching Principles

01 Read the passages in <A> and <B>, and follow the directions.

A

　Ms. Kim, a new middle school English teacher, conducted a survey focused on classroom management within the realm of English education. She engaged 70 local English teachers to cast their votes for the one most important principle they believe in for effective classroom management. Her objective was to identify the prevailing classroom management principles favored by her peers and subsequently incorporate them into her own teaching practices. She analyzed the survey responses, and the results are shown below.

No.	Classroom Management Principles	Vote Counts
1	Establish clear teacher and student roles.	8
2	Articulate unambiguous objectives and goals.	6
3	Be flexible.	7
4	Allow students some choices in lesson topics and activities.	15
5	Take a personal interest in students.	8
6	Be fair to all students.	6
7	Exhibit enthusiasm and a positive attitude yourself.	7
8	Challenge students of both higher and lower levels of ability.	13

Lesson A

Below are parts of classroom conversation between a teacher and students during English lessons.

T : Good morning, class! It's writing time, and I hope you're all feeling inspired from our discussion on environmental destruction in our previous lesson. Today, I've prepared two different writing worksheets for you to choose from.
S1 : What are the options, Ms. Yoo?
T : The first worksheet has 10 lines where you can freely express your thoughts and reflections, so, you'll write a full paragraph on your own.
S2 : What about the other one?
T : The second worksheet offers more guidance. It starts with a 5-line summary of the book's content, followed by 3 lines for your personal reflections. To help you get started, the first reflection line begins with, "One thing that struck me about the story was…". Additionally, there's a 'useful expressions' box at the bottom of the worksheet that you can incorporate into your reflective sentences.
S3 : Which one would be better for me?
T : The choice depends on your comfort level with writing. If you're confident and want to challenge yourself, go for the first option. If you prefer a bit more guidance, choose the second option.
S4 : Got it, thanks for the clarification, Ms. Yoo!

Guideline for Pre-service Teachers

Lesson B

T : Welcome, class! Today, we're going to have a fun reading session. I've prepared a selection of short stories for you to choose from.
S1 : That sounds exciting, Ms. Park!
S2 : I love story time!
T : I'm glad to hear that! I want to make our reading time more engaging for everyone. Take a moment to look over the options, and once you've made your choice, we'll spend some time reading our selected stories.
(T conducts a vote to choose one story for today and the students choose a mystery.)
T : Great choice! The mystery story can be quite captivating. Alright, we have a mystery story. After we've finished reading, you'll have the opportunity to choose an activity related to the story—whether it's a group discussion, a creative writing task, or even a presentation. This way, you not only get to choose what you read, but also how we explore the story further.

T=teacher, S=student

Based on the survey results in <A>, identify the two management principles that the majority of teachers consider the most important. Then, choose the lesson where each identified principle is key to being applied, respectively, and explain your choices with evidence from <A> and <B>.

Your Answer

02 Read the passages in <A> and <B>, and follow the directions.

A

In a recent gathering, 50 middle school teachers convened to vote on what they considered the most important principles for designing a lesson. This assembly aimed to identify key priorities and best practices in teaching various language skills effectively. After a thoughtful discussion, each teacher cast their vote for the principles they found most beneficial. The results were as follows:

No	Design Principles	Vote counts
1	Describe the goal of the lesson.	5
2	Provide a schema building task.	11
3	Provide students with authentic language models.	6
4	Make students use diverse skills in class.	6
5	Provide students with a challenging task.	5
6	Give feedback on the task students have completed.	4
7	Give students chances to think creatively.	13

B

After the survey, Ms. Yoo developed activities by applying some of the principles.

Activity 1

Before listening to a script, students work in pairs to predict the good things and bad things about using a mobile phone in class.

Good things	Bad things
-	-
-	-
-	-

Activity 2

- Students listen to a story of Dave, Anne, and Denise talking about what it is like to live in another country. None of them live in the country where they were born. Students make a note of the places they hear.
- Students listen again. Students in groups complete the table showing where these three people were born and where they are living now.

[Table]

Name	Where from	Where now
Dave	-	-
Anne	-	-
Denise	-	-

Activity 3

Students in pairs make a list of the things they wonder about Australian culture. Mr. Hemsworth, a foreign teacher from Australia, is invited to the class. Students interview Mr. Hemsworth and find out what he finds interesting, unusual, strange, good, and not so good about Australia.

Activity 4

Students work in pairs.

※ **Directions**: Read the text carefully and write your conclusion in one paragraph. Be descriptive and think about how to resolve the mystery of Hawthorn Manor. After finishing writing, be prepared to share your conclusion with the class.

[Reading Text]

In a small town, there was an old house called Hawthorn Manor. People said the house was haunted. At night, strange lights could be seen, and odd music could be heard. One afternoon, three friends, Lily, Mark, and Sam, decided to explore the house. They wanted to see if the stories were true. As they walked up to the house, the wind started to blow, and the sky turned gray. They were scared but excited. They opened the old door and stepped inside. The house was dusty and the floors creaked. They split up to look around. Lily went upstairs, Mark went to the library, and Sam went to the kitchen. Suddenly, they heard a loud noise from the basement. They met up and slowly went down the stairs. The basement was dark and cold. In the corner, they saw an old chest. With shaking hands, they opened the chest and...

(ellipsis)

※ Write Your Conclusion Below:

___

Based on the two most popular design principles in <A>, identify the ONE activity in <B> where each principle has been applied, respectively. Then, explain your answers with evidence from <A> and <B>.

Your Answer

03 Read the passages in <A> and <B>, and follow the directions.

A

　Designing effective listening activities is essential in language learning, as it enhances students' comprehension and interaction with spoken language. Because listening is a cornerstone of language acquisition, it aids in mastering sounds, rhythms, and intonations, thereby supporting other language skills. Therefore, teachers need to know the key principles for developing these activities, as this knowledge significantly impacts students' language learning success and communication proficiency. Below is the list of design principles and descriptions for listening activities.

Design Principles	Descriptions
Matching activities to students' levels and interests	When planning activities, consider students' current English proficiency and preferences. Ensure activities are neither too easy nor too difficult to keep them engaged and motivated.
Using diverse kinds of listening materials	Use a mix of listening materials like news reports, podcasts, songs, conversations, and lectures. This helps students get better at understanding English in various situations and settings.
Providing interactive activities	Give students interactive activities like Q&A sessions, or having discussions. This provides students with opportunities to use English in genuine conversations.
Focusing on listening strategies	Set clear goals for improving listening skills, such as guessing what will be said next, finding the gist and key information, making inferences.
Providing feedback and evaluation	Give students specific feedback on effectively using listening strategies and improving their skills.

B

The following is a listening lesson plan prepared by Ms. Kang, a middle school English teacher, for her students, based on design principles of listening activity.

Lesson Procedure

Step 1	T prepares several short audio clips of news reports covering recent global events from international news channels for teenagers.
Step 2	• Students are divided into small groups, and each group is assigned a news report clip about different types of car accidents. • After listening to their assigned news report, students individually complete the worksheet. [Worksheet] 1. What is the main idea of the listening clip? _____ 2. When, where, and why did the accident happen? ※ When: _____ ※ Where: _____ ※ Why: _____
Step 3	• After listening, each group discusses and prepares a summary of the main content of their news report. • Then, each group presents their news report in front of the other groups. • After each group's presentations, students from the other groups have the opportunity to ask and answer questions to clarify information and explore specific points from the presentation.
Step 4	T evaluates the accuracy and clarity of each group's news report summary and presentation.

Based on the information in <A>, identify each design principle demonstrated in Step 2 and Step 3 of the lesson procedure in <B>. Then, explain your answers with evidence from <A> and <B>.

Your Answer _____
_____
_____
_____
_____

04 Read the passages in <A> and <B>, and follow the directions.

A

Authentic materials refer to real-life resources used in educational contexts to provide learners with genuine and culturally relevant content. These materials can include newspaper articles, advertisements, videos, podcasts, interviews, and more. By incorporating a variety of authentic materials beyond textbooks, teachers can achieve several purposes. The purposes a teacher can achieve by using authentic materials in class can be listed as follows:

- To promote cultural awareness: Authentic materials expose students to diverse cultures, perspectives, and experiences, fostering empathy and cultural understanding.
- To increase engagement: Authentic materials are often more interesting and relevant to students' lives, increasing their motivation and engagement in reading lessons.
- To support authentic language acquisition: Authentic materials offer genuine language input, helping English language learners develop their language proficiency in context.
- To provide students with real-life examples of the topic being studied: Authentic materials, including articles, videos, interviews, advertisements, and more, can offer concrete examples of how the subject matter is applied or experienced in everyday life.

Guideline for Pre-service Teachers

B

Ms. Yoo is teaching first-year high school students and is preparing for her reading class for the upcoming week. After carefully reviewing the textbook materials, she decides to enhance her students' learning experiences by incorporating additional authentic materials. For Lesson 3, which focuses on environmental issues, she plans to introduce a video documentary that explores real-life examples of environmental challenges such as deforestation and endangered species. This video will provide students with concrete instances of the problems that will be discussed in class. In preparation for Lesson 5, which covers the civil rights movement, Ms. Yoo is eager to develop students' cultural sensitivity and enhance their understanding. To achieve this goal, she plans to distribute copies of a transcript of Martin Luther King, Jr.'s speech. Originally published during the civil rights era, the speech will help students gain a deeper understanding of the culture and social atmosphere of American society at that time.

Based on <A>, identify the purpose of using authentic material that Ms. Yoo intends to achieve in Lesson 3 and Lesson 5, respectively. Then, explain your answers with evidence from <B>.

Your Answer

05 Read the passages and follow the directions.

A

　After reading an article about the importance of action research, two English teachers, Ms. Park and Ms. Yoo, conducted action research on their recent English lessons. The following are classroom principles that Ms. Park and Ms. Yoo want to achieve through action research.

Principle 1. Facilitate active learning with hands-on activities
Principle 2. Conduct formative assessment techniques to evaluate their students' progress
Principle 3. Encourage collaborative learning to promote peer-to-peer support
Principle 4. Use English as the primary language of instruction and communication
Principle 5. Provide authentic tasks that reflect real-life situations

---
B

　The following are the results of the action research showing the percentages of English and Korean used during the two teachers' English lessons:

Ms. Park's Class
- Ratio of Teacher talk using English in class: 30%
- Ratio of Teacher talk using Korean in class: 70%
- Ratio of Student talk using English in class: 15%

Ms. Yoo's Class
- Ratio of Teacher talk using English in class: 60%
- Ratio of Teacher talk using Korean in class: 40%
- Ratio of Student talk using English in class: 30%

Below are the teaching notes from the two teachers.

Ms. Park's Teaching Note

Since my students are at a low-intermediate level of English, I use both English and Korean during lessons to avoid overwhelming them with too much English. Before conducting the action research, I thought I used at least 50% English in class. However, the results showed that I am only using English for 30% of the lesson time, which was much less than I expected. Additionally, my students only use English for 15% of their speaking in class. Based on these results, I realized that both my students and I need to use more English in class. Therefore, I plan to increase my use of English to more than 50% by giving more instructions in English. I also plan to incorporate more group discussions where students are required to speak only in English. Through more opportunities to use English, I believe they can improve their fluency and acquire the language more effectively.

Ms. Yoo's Teaching Note

As I teach advanced level students, 60% of class time is conducted in English. However, I use Korean when teaching new vocabulary or complex grammar and explaining new topics. As a result of the action research, I realized that my students need to use more English during class. They currently only use English for around 30% of their speaking in class, which is not enough. Therefore, I am going to provide them with more opportunities to speak English. As one way, I will create a reward system where students who speak more English in class are recognized and rewarded. I hope that this reward system can encourage my students to communicate more in English, and help them be more fluent.

Considering the information in <A> and <B>, identify ONE classroom principle that both teachers want to achieve through action research. Then, write the solution(s) that each teacher has chosen to achieve the identified principle.

Your Answer

Guideline for Pre-service Teachers

06 Read the passages and follow the directions.

A

Ms. Park, a middle school English teacher, attended a workshop for desigining good speaking lessons and gained a lot of useful information to facilitate students' speaking skills. Below is part of the suggestions from the workshop.

Teaching Principles

How to facilitate speaking skills
(1) Create a supportive and affective classroom environment.
(2) Model and guide sentence construction.
(3) Focus on meaningful and authentic communication.
(4) Offer language support and feedback.
(5) Encourage active listening for dynamic interaction.

B

Ms. Park's Teaching Log

Today, I designed a lesson plan for my intermediate level students. When I began designing the lesson, my intention was clear: promoting speaking skills. Thus, I carefully planned the activity where students need to share their own experiences and opinions. First, students in pairs will briefly share their most memorable travel experience they have had. Meanwhile, they should use descriptive language as much as they could. After the pair work, in groups, they will make a plan for summer vacation. During the discussion, students are expected to actively share their thoughts, ideas, and experiences to plan the best summer vacation. While reviewing the speaking activity, however, I realized that students need to use some interaction strategies to maintain the effective communication among them. Accordingly, I decided to introduce strategies that students need while listening to the others, such as asking for clarification, and responding appropriately (e.g., nodding, providing feedback). At last, I finalized the activity as I desired, which could definitely improve my students' speaking abilities. Already I am looking forward to the next lesson.

Identify TWO teaching principles from <A> that Ms. Park has employed in her class and provide evidence for each identified one from <B>.

07 Read the passages and follow the directions.

A

Ms. Park, an English teacher, attended to a workshop for language teachers where she gained a lot of useful information to promote student learning. Below is part of the suggestions from the workshop.

Teachers should ...
(1) Provide real-life contexts and authentic materials.
(2) Encourage group work and collaborative projects.
(3) Offer students necessary learning strategies.
(4) Incorporate digital technology in lessons to engage the digital-native generation.
(5) Involve students in self-/peer-evaluation instead of evaluating them alone.

B

Ms. Park's Reflection

After attending the recent teacher workshop, I tried to bring some of the ideas into my class. In today's reading lesson, I provided students with an article about World Festivals from a magazine. According to the suggestion from the workshop, introducing real-life situations in the reading lesson not only helps students understand English better but also gives them insight into the culture behind the language. During the lesson, the students were more engaged than in the other lessons because they could learn language and culture simultaneously. Additionally, I introduced essential metacognitive strategies to foster students' autonomy. In particular, when engaging in self-directed learning outside the classroom, students need to use these strategies by planning, monitoring, and evaluating what they listen to or read. After several periods of instruction on these strategies, students became able to employ various strategies freely, thereby becoming more autonomous and independent learners.

Based on <A> and <B>, identify TWO suggestions that Ms. Park has applied in her lesson and provide some evidence that shows how the teacher has implemented each suggestion. Then, write the objective behind the teacher's implementation of each suggestion, from <B>.

Your Answer

08 Read the Mr. Kim's note in <A> and class observation note in <B>, and follow the directions.

A

Mr. Kim's Note

As a high school English teacher preparing to teach mixed-level 1st graders, I attended a highly informative teacher workshop. The workshop highlighted the importance of flexibility and understanding in managing a class with students of different levels. It provided a range of effective strategies for managing a mixed-level classroom, aimed at efficiently addressing the varied needs of my students. Below, I've outlined some of the recommended strategies from the workshop.

Strategy 1. Provide the same learning materials (e.g. reading text) to every student but adjust the support according to each student's needs to help them complete tasks.

Strategy 2. Conduct an assessment at the beginning to accurately determine each student's proficiency level, ensuring appropriate instruction and support.

Strategy 3. Use language level that is accessible to all students during whole class activities, ensuring that everyone can participate and understand.

Strategy 4. Tailor feedback to students based on their proficiency levels, ensuring it is more relevant and helpful for their specific needs.

Strategy 5. Enhance the learning experience with digital tools that adapt to individual students' needs.

B

Below is the observation note that Ms. Choi, a senior English teacher, has written after observing Mr. Kim's English class, which was conducted for 27 students.

Observation Note on Mr. Kim's English Reading Lesson

Pre-lesson Preparation:
- Mr. Kim conducted a proficiency test to determine the English levels of the students before the lesson.
- Students were divided into three groups based on their levels: High (6 students), Intermediate (15 students), and Low (6 students), and were seated in the left, center, and right sections of the classroom, respectively. Within these groups, students formed groups of three for the upcoming activities.

Schematic Knowledge Activation:
- At the start of the lesson, Mr. Kim engaged the students with the topic of volunteering, employing high-level vocabulary to challenge them and activate their prior knowledge.
- This approach, however, seemed to cause comprehension difficulties for some students, particularly those with lower proficiency levels.

Reading Activity:
- All students were provided with the same reading text related to volunteering.
- To assess understanding, Mr. Kim distributed different worksheets to each group based on their proficiency levels:
  ∨ High Level: Summarize the key ideas from the text. (Write the answer in one paragraph on the worksheet.)
  ∨ Intermediate Level: Read the questions and answer them using words or phrases. (Questions are provided on the worksheet.)
  ∨ Low Level: Match questions with their corresponding answers. (Questions and answers are provided on the worksheet.)
- While circulating and providing feedback, Mr. Kim maintained uniformity in feedback regarding content and language level across all groups to ensure fairness in the lesson.

Guideline for Pre-service Teachers

> Speaking Activity:
> - Following the reading session, each group engaged in a writing activity to plan future volunteering activities.
> - Directed to use digital tools tailored to their level:
>   ∨ High Level: Tools that assist in writing detailed plan sentences.
>   ∨ Intermediate Level: Tools that offer grammar corrections and necessary vocabulary.
>   ∨ Low Level: Tools that provide volunteering ideas, necessary words, and grammar support.
> - Utilizing these tools, students presented their volunteering plans.

Based on <A> and <B>, identify the TWO strategies that Mr. Kim does not follow in his mixed level class. Then, explain how the lesson deviates from the identified strategies with evidence from <A> and <B>.

Your Answer

09 Read the passages and follow the directions.

A

Below are teaching principles for communication oriented English lessons.

Principle (1) Use authentic language.
Principle (2) Provide diverse linguistic forms within context.
Principle (3) Provide language at the discourse or suprasentential level.
Principle (4) Give students an opportunity to express their ideas and opinions.
Principle (5) Give students the chance to correct errors by themselves.
Principle (6) Assess students' ongoing skills in a communicative way.
Principle (7) Encourage students to reflect what they learned.

B

Below is the lesson procedure that Ms. Park, an English teacher, designed for her students based on some teaching principles mentioned above.

Step 1
　　The teacher distributes a handout that has a copy of a sports column from a recent newspaper.

Step 2
　　The teacher tells the students to underline the reporter's predictions and to say which ones, they think, the reporter feels most certain of and which he feels least certain of.
e.g. Korea <u>is very likely to</u> win the World Cup this year.
　　　Italy can win <u>if</u> they play as well as they have lately.
　　　France <u>probably</u> will not be a contender again.
　　　England <u>may</u> have an outside chance.

Step 3
　　The teacher asks students to rewrite the sentences of the reporter's predictions using their own predictions and words.

Guideline for Pre-service Teachers

Step 4

  The teacher puts students in groups of four. The teacher asks them to share their prediction about which country will win the World Cup this year using the underlined phrases and choose the most common prediction among group members.

Step 5

  Each group presents their discussion outcome. While listening to the presentation, the teacher immediately corrects any grammatical errors that the presenter makes.

Step 6

  As an evaluation process, the teacher gives a multiple choice item test related to the target function, *prediction*.

Step 7

  Closing the lesson, the teacher tells students to write their learning log about today's lesson as homework and upload it into the class blog by 10 p.m.

Based on the information in <A> and <B>, identify TWO teaching principles that are not applied in Ms. Park's lesson. And then, explain how the identified principles are differently applied into Ms. Park's lesson in <B>.

Your Answer

10 Read the passage in <A> and the lesson plan in <B>, and follow the directions.

A

For language teachers, integrating culture into lessons is essential. Presenting cultural aspects neutrally helps create a "third culture" in the classroom, allowing students to explore both their own and the target cultures without judgment. This approach helps students understand how their own culture affects their perceptions and interactions, enhancing their ability to communicate across cultural boundaries. Here are five suggestions for teaching language and culture together:

(1) Identify students' cultural interests and needs through surveys or interviews.
(2) Include cultural contexts in vocabulary lessons to highlight the nuances and implications of new words.
(3) Encourage students to share their experiences to enhance their understanding of cultural differences.
(4) Have students research cultural events in groups and present the outcome using visual aids.
(5) Encourage students to reflect on their performance and provide feedback to enhance their learning.

B

Below is part of a lesson plan designed by Ms. Kim, a middle school English teacher, for teaching culture.

Objective: Students will be able to
1. use vocabulary related to cultural customs and traditions in context.
2. describe and discuss various cultural festivals around the world.

Guideline for Pre-service Teachers

Lesson Procedure

Introduction to Cultural Concepts:
- Begin the lesson by asking students questions to elicit their ideas about what culture means and why it's important to learn about different cultures.
- Introduce today's topic and a story chosen by the teacher: 'Cultural Festivals Around the World.'

Vocabulary Development and Personal Connection:
- Have students read a story about world festivals and underline the new words in the story.
- Explain the meanings of the new words (ceremony, tradition, carnival, ritual, etc.), informing students of their connotations.
- Ask students to read the story again and share in pairs their experiences with Korean festivals. Then, have them compare these experiences with the festivals described in the story, discussing similarities and differences.

Research and Information Gathering:
Divide students into small groups and assign each group a festival to research using the provided materials (e.g., newspapers and articles). If needed, students can search online for related websites or videos.

Presentation of Research Findings:
- Each group prepares their presentation with visual aids, such as slideshows, posters, or videos, to enhance it.
- Have each group present the festival they have researched to the class, using the key vocabulary they just learned.

Reflection and Personal Insight:
- Ask students to write a reflection on what they have learned and how they performed today.
- Encourage them to consider what new insights they gained and how the day's learning has expanded their understanding of cultural diversity.

From the five suggestions provided in <A>, identify TWO that are not implemented in Ms. Kim's lesson from <B>. Then, explain how Ms. Kim's lesson deviates from the identified suggestions, with specific evidence from <A> and <B>.

2 Textbook Evaluation or Modification

01 Read the passages and follow the directions.

A

T1 reads an article and shares it with T2

T1 : Hey, I just read an interesting article about form-focused instruction (FFI) and its effects on L2 oral production. According to the article, FFI can actually improve both the complexity and accuracy of students' language use.

T2 : Really? I thought FFI was just for teaching grammar rules.

T1 : Well, that's one aspect of it. But there are actually two types of FFI: focus-on-formS (FonFs) and focus-on-form (FonF). FonFs is more focused on explicit instruction of grammar rules, while FonF is more focused on raising learners' awareness of language features through communicative activities.

T2 : I see. If so, can FFI help students acquire better oral production?

T1 : The article suggests that both FonF and FonFs can improve students' oral production since FonF prioritizes fluency and FonFs accuracy. However, the effectiveness of each type may vary depending on the students' proficiency level.

T2 : That's interesting. So, which type should we use for our students?

T1 : Well, the research indicates that FonFs is more suitable for low-proficiency learners as it provides them with explicit knowledge of basic grammar rules. As for FonF, it is more beneficial for high-proficiency learners as it allows them to integrate their existing knowledge of grammar with new information in a communicative context. However, the article also recommends using a variety of activities as each type has different impacts on the improvement of students' proficiency. In short, we need to prepare diverse FonFs and FonF activities for different proficiency levels of students.

T2 : That makes sense. I think we should try to incorporate both types of instruction in our lessons to maximize the effectiveness of FFI.

T1 : Agreed. And if you're interested, I can send you the article so you can read more about it.
T2 : Yes, please do. I think it's important for us to stay informed about effective teaching strategies like FFI.

T=teacher

B

Evaluation Criteria	Textbook A	Textbook B	Textbook C
1. Does it introduce up-to-date topics?	3	2	1
2. Does it provide enough communicative activities?	1	2	3
3. Does it provide different types of activities based on students' proficiency levels?	2	3	1
4. Does it provide both FonFs and FonF type intructions?	1	3	2
5. Does it provide enough new vocabulary?	2	1	3

...

3=Excellent, 2=Okay, 1=Poor

Based on the conversation between the two teachers in <A>, which textbook in <B> is the most suitable for their classes? And why? Write TWO reasons of your choice. Do NOT copy more than FOUR consecutive words from the passages.

Your Answer

Guideline for Pre-service Teachers

02 Read <A> and <B> and follow the directions.

A

Category	Description	Textbook A	Textbook B
Language Level	• Does the textbook match the language proficiency of intermediate level students? • Are the vocabulary and grammar used in the textbook suitable for learners at this level?	Y	Y
Organization	• Is the textbook organized in a logical and structured manner? • Are topics and lessons presented in a way that builds upon previous knowledge?	Y	N
Content	• Does the textbook feature content that is interesting and relatable to the students? • Are there examples, stories, or activities that capture the students' attention?	Y	N
Practicality	• Does the textbook provide practical language skills that students can use in real-life situations? • Are the language concepts applicable to everyday communication?	Y	Y
Skills Development	• Does the textbook offer a balanced approach to developing listening, speaking, reading, and writing skills? • Are there exercises and activities that target these language skills integratively?	N	Y
Activities	• Are there diverse interactive activities facilitating authentic language use such as discussions and survey activities? • Does the textbook cater to different learning styles and preferences?	N	Y

Yes=Y, No=N

B

Students' Log

As an intermediate-level student, I have some concerns about the current textbook. First, I feel it is a bit too advanced for our level, making it hard for us to keep up with the vocabulary and sentence structures. I've, also, noticed that the book focuses more on reading and writing, with fewer chances to practice listening and speaking. This imbalance is making it difficult for me to practice and improve all aspects of my language skills. Moreover, I wish for more interactive activities, instead of just traditional exercises like grammar drills. These activities are not only fun but also help me use the language in real-life situations. Given these concerns, I plan to ask my teacher for a new textbook or additional resources to help address these issues.

Based on <A>, choose ONE appropriate textbook for the student in <B> and write THREE reasons of your choice based on the characteristics of the chosen textbook.

Your Answer

Guideline for Pre-service Teachers

03 Read the passages and follow the directions.

A

Below are the results of the textbook evaluation.

Textbook Criteria	Textbook A	Textbook B
1. Is it suitable for teaching students with different proficiency levels?	N	Y
2. Does it offer sections on cultural guidance?	Y	N
3. Does it cover various speech styles?	Y	N
4. Does it provide additional vocabulary and grammar learning?	Y	N
5. Does it provide learning opportunities using multimedia during lessons?	N	Y
6. Are there opportunities to learn various learning strategies?	N	Y

B

Ms. Yoo : Ms. Park! Have you had a chance to look at the new textbooks for the upcoming semester?

Ms. Park : Yes, I did. It's quite a decision, isn't it? Which one did you go for?

Ms. Yoo : Well, after carefully evaluating them, I chose the textbook based on certain criteria. First of all, I chose the textbook which offers some fantastic cultural sections, giving our students a broader perspective.

Ms. Park : That sounds intriguing. What's your second criterion?

Ms. Yoo : Second, it covers various speech styles, which I believe will help our students become more versatile and confident communicators.

Ms. Park : Those are excellent reasons. What's your third one?

Ms. Yoo : Finally, it provides additional vocabulary and grammar learning, especially useful for promoting self-directed learning among our students.

Ms. Park : I see your points. Now, let me share how I chose the textbook. First, I like that it's designed for level-differentiated lessons, which I believe is essential for accommodating our students' diverse proficiency levels.
Ms. Yoo : That's an important consideration. What's your second reason?
Ms. Park : Second, it offers opportunities to use multimedia for learning, making our lessons more engaging and interactive.
Ms. Yoo : That's a compelling feature. What's your third reason?
Ms. Park : Lastly, it gives our students a chance to acquire valuable learning strategies, which can be a significant asset in their language acquisition journey.
Ms. Yoo : Those are solid reasons, Ms. Park. It's interesting how our teaching styles and priorities can lead us to different choices, but both seem like excellent options for our students.
Ms. Park : Absolutely, Ms. Yoo. It's all about what will best serve our students' needs. Let's collaborate and make this semester a successful and engaging one for them.
Ms. Yoo : Definitely, Ms. Park. Here's to a great semester ahead!

Based on the conversation in <B>, choose the textbook that is more appropriate for each teacher in <A>. Then, write the reasons for each of your choices based on the characteristics of each textbook from <A>.

Your Answer

Guideline for Pre-service Teachers

04 Read the students' feedback in <A> and follow the directions.

A

Mr. Park requested his first-year high school students to write and hand in feedback regarding the English textbook they are using this semester. Referring to the feedback, Mr. Park will choose the new textbook for the next semester.

Students' Feedback

S1	Providing feedback on the textbook I used was a bit challenging due to my mixed feelings about it. On one hand, I didn't like the design of each page, particularly the narrow spacing of paragraphs which made it difficult for me to jot down important notes in the right places. Additionally, the small font size made focused reading difficult. Despite these challenges, I was able to significantly expand my vocabulary through this textbook.
S2	Some of the topics from the reading texts were completely unfamiliar and not interesting to me. So, some of the reading lessons were boring or too difficult. Although my teacher provided many reading activities, the lessons based on unfamiliar reading topics didn't still motivate me. If the reading texts had topics that were more related to my life or experiences, I believe my reading lessons would have been more exciting.
S3	I'm confident in my English reading skills, so I didn't encounter significant difficulties with this textbook. However, I do believe it could be improved by including more visual aids to help understand the flow of a story more easily. Additionally, if there were a greater of variety of activities or projects, it would have motivated me more to improve my language skills. As most activities focused on checking comprehension after listening to or reading texts, I found it somewhat lacking in terms of fostering a balanced improvement in all four language skills.

B

Below are the textbook evaluation results of the three new textbooks.

Evaluation Criteria	Textbook A	Textbook B	Textbook C
Presentation of the Text	4	2	3
Appropriateness for Course	3	2	4
Relevance of content to students' lives	4	4	2
Exercises and Activities that cover all four skills	4	3	2
Appropriateness of the level of Vocabulary and Grammar	2	4	4

4=excellent, 3=good, 2=adequate, 1=poor

Based on the information in <A> and <B>, choose the ONE most appropriate textbook to replace the current textbook for the sake of the students. Then, explain how the new textbook can compensate for the weak points of the current textbook with supporting evidence from <A> and <B>.

Your Answer

Guideline for Pre-service Teachers

05 Read the dialogue and follow the directions.

> *Teacher A and Teacher B, who are English teachers at a middle school, are discussing new textbook for the 2nd graders.*
>
> Ms. Park : I've been thinking, maybe we should look into a new textbook for the 2nd graders next year.
> Mr. Kang : Do you think that is necessary?
> Ms. Park : Absolutely. The current one just isn't sparking their interest or curiosity. It's either too dull or too difficult for them.
> Mr. Kang : I see where you're coming from. Some of the reading materials in the current textbook don't really relate to their daily lives. It's hard to get them motivated.
> Ms. Park : That's my point! It's tough to keep them engaged with unrelated texts.
> Mr. Kang : I couldn't agree more.
> Ms. Park : So, what if we additionally provide students with more engaging reading texts? Like stories! What is even better, stories are something that all students regardless of their proficiency level can understand. Moreover, episodically well organized stories can be closely related to students' real lives, and are therefore more easily retained, and recalled as well than any texts less episodically structured.
> Mr. Kang : That's an excellent suggestion! If so, students will be able to understand and remember the interesting parts better. Let me look over some sample stories for our students.

Identify the hypothesis that underlies key criterion for Ms. Park's text selection and then explain the advantages of the identified hypothesis from the teachers' perspective.

| Your Answer |

06 Read the teacher's note in <A> and news scripts in <B>. Then, follow the directions.

A

Below is part of a note written by a teacher who teaches English to 3rd-grade students in a middle school.

Teacher's Note

For the upcoming listening lesson for my 3rd-grade students, I plan to incorporate a news clip as the primary listening material. My goal in this selection is to expose my students to authentic, real-world language, particularly spoken language. To ensure the authenticity of the clip, it should first present information in a natural flow, emphasizing the connections between different pieces of information. Particular attention will be given to the use of transitions that connect distinct pieces of information seamlessly. Next, the news clip should be conversational including some natural speech elements like fillers and colloquial language. This approach aims to enhance their comprehension skills and acquaint them with the everyday language they are likely to encounter outside our classroom setting. After the listening activity, I plan to distribute the news clip's script to the students. This will help reinforce their understanding, allow them to review what they've listened to, analyze the language structure, and familiarize themselves with any new vocabulary or phrases.

Guideline for Pre-service Teachers

B

News Script A

Newscaster : Good morning and welcome to our news program. We have some important stories to share with you today. Let's go live with our reporter Jessica Cho, hi Jessica, there are a lot of people there this morning!

Reporter : Hi Bill, you can say that again. Good morning to all our viewers, here I am at the community center of Seocho this morning. Many many people are here to celebrate the opening of a new library. Well, you know, donors and volunteers in the community have been striving to build this library for two years. It's so amazing, isn't it? This library has books, computers, and other cool stuff for everyone in the area. Naturally, people are excited and happy this morning with this opening as you can see. Well, now, let's talk to some of them to hear what this library means to them.

(omitted)

News Script B

Newscaster : You are watching our news program. We have some important stories to share with you today. We have our reporter Jessica Cho. Jessica, could you tell me what happened?

Reporter : This is the community center of Seocho, where hundreds of people have come together for a very special occasion. They want to celebrate the opening of a new library. It was constructed with the generous support of donors and volunteers from the community. This library will offer books, computers, and other educational resources to everyone in the area. People are thrilled and delighted about this project. They express their pleasure with their expressions and gestures. They are conversing with each other, sharing stories and praises. Let's listen to some of them and find out what this library means to them.

(omitted)

From <B> choose a more suitable news script for the teacher's lesson in <A>. Then, based on information in <A> and <B> write the reason for your choice with evidence from <A> and <B>.

Your Answer

Guideline for Pre-service Teachers

07 Read the passages and follow the directions.

A

Textbook evaluation is essential because it ensures materials meet students' learning needs and educational goals, facilitating effective knowledge acquisition. For teachers, it helps them select suitable resources and enhance teaching efficacy. Ultimately, this process improves the overall educational experience and helps ensure that students are well-prepared for real-world challenges. Below is the checklist that teachers can use in evaluating different textbooks.

Criteria		Textbook A Y	Textbook A N	Textbook B Y	Textbook B N	Textbook C Y	Textbook C N
Content & Activity	Engaging Themes: High quality and relevance of themes		√	√			√
	Real-World Application: Connection of content to real-life situations	√		√		√	
	Comprehensive Coverage: Inclusion of all necessary language skills	√			√	√	
	Interactive Exercises: Variety and interactivity of exercises		√	√		√	
	Cultural Diversity: Representation of diverse cultures	√		√			√
Language Development	Advanced Grammar: Exploring complex grammatical structures and rules	√			√	√	
	Vocabulary Development: Systematic approach to building vocabulary	√		√			√
Skills Development	Reading and Listening: Development of reading and listening competencies		√	√			√
	Speaking Practice: Opportunities for practicing speaking	√			√		√
	Writing Skills: Support for developing writing abilities		√	√		√	
Technological Integration	Technology Integration: Use of technology to enhance learning	√		√			√

Y=Yes, N=No

B

Below is the conversation between two English teachers discussing the results of their recent textbook evaluation for their 3rd-grade middle school students.

Mr. Kim : The textbook that we chose really stands out with its engaging thematic units, doesn't it? The interactive exercises and cultural insights are exactly what we've been looking for.

Ms. Park : Absolutely! Also, the integration of technology in each chapter is a huge plus for our digital-savvy students. Besides, it provides diverse reading and listening activities. However, the textbook appears to lack adequate speaking practice opportunities for discussions and presentations.

Mr. Kim : Good point. What if we supplement with bi-weekly speaking workshops? We could use topics from the textbook to develop their discussion and presentation skills.

Ms. Park : I like that. It will give our students the practical speaking experience they need. One more thing, I wish the textbook offered more complex grammar exercises, like advanced tenses and conditionals, to improve students' writing and speaking with richer, more nuanced expressions.

Mr. Kim : Agreed. Regarding the grammar, maybe a concise online exercise for each unit could help reinforce their grammar proficiency. Something concise but effective.

Ms. Park : Exactly! Something that students can do at their own pace but still aligns with our lesson themes.

Mr. Kim : Perfect. Then, we can maintain the strengths of the textbook while addressing its limitations in a practical way. Let's finalize this plan.

Based on the information in <A> and <B>, identify the ONE textbook that Mr. Kim and Ms. Park have selected for their English lessons. Then, write TWO weak points of the chosen textbook and the corresponding supplementary strategy that they plan to implement to overcome these weaknesses with evidence from <B>.

Your Answer

08 Read the passages and follow the directions.

A

A good teacher is constantly adapting texts to bridge the gaps that exist between a textbook and learners' needs. This can be achieved by the following techniques.

1. **Adding:** In the technique of adding, the teacher supplements existing materials, providing additional content. This can be done by either *extending* or *expanding* the materials. When extending an activity, the teacher supplies more of the same type of material, thus making a quantitative change. On the other hand, expanding involves adding something different to the materials, constituting a qualitative change.

2. **Deleting:** Much like adding, materials can be deleted both quantitatively (subtracting) and qualitatively (abridging). *Subtracting* refers to reducing the length of materials in a quantitative manner. Conversely, *abridging* involves omitting materials qualitatively, effecting changes that are more significant than mere subtracting.

3. **Simplifying:** When simplifying, the teacher might reword instructions or text to make them more accessible to learners, or alter an entire activity to make it more manageable for both learners and teachers.

B

Mr. Park and Ms. Yoo are English teachers in a middle school. In their teaching journals below, they describe their recent experiences with textbook adaptation.

Mr. Park's Teaching Journal

Early in this semester, I closely examined the current textbook and its alignment with the needs of our low-intermediate level students. It became apparent that the textbook was lacking in one crucial aspect: speaking activities. Given the importance of developing conversational skills, this gap was a significant concern. Upon realizing this limitation, I decided to take action. It was evident that our students needed more opportunities to practice speaking in English. To address this problem, I made the decision to supplement the existing materials by adding more diverse types of speaking activities, with a particular focus on role-play and discussion exercises. The rationale behind this choice was clear: By incorporating role-play and discussion activities, I can provide my students with practical, real-life contexts for using the language. These activities will encourage them to engage in meaningful conversations, express their opinions, and collaborate with their peers.

Ms. Yoo's Teaching Journal

In my recent teaching sessions, I've been closely assessing the needs of my low-intermediate level students. It has become increasingly evident that some of the reading texts and writing activities in the current textbook were posing challenges beyond the students' current proficiency level. To address this problem, I decided to revise certain reading texts to make them more accessible to my students. I found that by changing the vocabulary and sentence structures with easier versions, I could ensure that the content remained engaging and informative without overwhelming our students. Furthermore, I noticed that some of the complex writing activities were causing frustration for both the students and me as their teacher. To make these tasks less daunting, I broke them down into smaller, more achievable steps. This approach not only reduced anxiety among the students but also facilitated a more structured learning process. As I implemented these changes, I observed a positive shift in the classroom dynamic: The students appeared more confident when tackling the reading texts, and their comprehension improved. They were also more willing to engage in writing activities, as the simplified tasks allowed them to build their skills gradually.

Using the terms provided in <A>, identify the textbook adaptation technique that Mr. Park and Ms. Yoo each employ, respectively. Then, explain how they apply each technique, providing supporting evidence from <B>.

Your Answer

09 Read the passages in <A> and <B>, and follow the directions.

A

By implementing some modifications, textbooks can be tailored to the specific needs and language abilities of second language learners, making the learning experience more accessible, engaging, and effective. Here are some strategies:

- adding: It means to add necessary materials.
- deleting: It refers to omission of some exercises quantitatively by answering only a proportion of it or qualitatively by omitting a tedious and boring exercise.
- modifying: It can involve rewriting to change the content, or restructuring to change the way the task is carried out in class.
- simplifying: It is rewording or paraphrasing the text without damaging its authenticity. It usually involves adapting the language level of texts.
- reordering: This procedure refers to the possibility of putting the parts of a course book in a different order.

B

Ms. Yoo's Teaching Note

Today, I want to reflect on the recent textbook modifications that I made to support my students. By adapting teaching materials, I aimed to enhance their learning experience and promote a deeper understanding of the content. During the last class, I taught Unit 3 about 'Wildlife Conservation'. I noticed that some words in the textbook were too demanding for my students, so I replaced them with easier alternatives. For example:

Original sentence: "Biodiversity is crucial for protecting various species."
Adapted sentence: "The variety of plants and animals is crucial for protecting various species."

By using language that matches their proficiency level, I helped them better understand the material and created a more supportive learning environment. Moreover, since the textbook only provided a reading text about wildlife conservation, I prepared supplementary materials to give my students additional support. Firstly, I showed a short video clip that included an interview with wildlife experts and some example cases of their efforts. The video could provide visual context and foster a deeper understanding of the topic. Additionally, I created an infographic to present statistics and key information about wildlife conservation. This helped students grasp important facts and figures, making the content more accessible and memorable.

After the lesson, I realized that the textbook adaptations I made enhanced my students' comprehension, engagement, and overall learning outcomes. Hence, I will continue to monitor their progress and explore further ways for textbook adaptation to create more effective learning environment.

Based on <A> and <B>, identify the TWO strategies that Ms. Yoo has applied to adapt the textbook for her students. Then, explain your answers with evidence from <A> and <B>.

Your Answer

10 Read the passage and follow the directions.

A

Materials can undergo adaptation for various reasons, and this process can be accomplished through a variety of techniques, as outlined below.

- **Addition**: When there appears to be insufficient coverage, teachers may choose to supplement textbooks with additional texts or exercise materials.
- **Reduction**: Teachers may shorten an activity to reduce its weight or emphasis.
- **Replacement**: Text or exercise materials deemed inadequate, for any reason, can be substituted with more suitable alternatives.
- **Reordering**: If teachers find that the sequence in which the content is presented in the textbooks is not ideal for their students, they can, then, opt for a different progression through the textbooks than the one initially prescribed by the writer.
- **Simplifying**: Teachers may rephrase instructions or text to make them more accessible to learners.

B

Ms. Park's Note

I am currently teaching advanced-level English to third-year middle school students. After conducting a needs analysis, I discovered that while the topics introduced in the textbooks are quite engaging, the language level of the text is too simplistic for my students. To be frank, the existing reading texts are more suited for intermediate levels rather than advanced ones. However, topics such as Global Warming and the World Economy, which are covered in the textbook, seem to captivate my students. Consequently, I decided to replace the reading text from the textbook with an article on the same topic, Global Warming, sourced from The New York Times. The New York Times is a daily newspaper intended for a general English-speaking audience, hence the language used is more authentic and complex. Therefore, this new reading text will undoubtedly present a more challenging and engaging task for my advanced students.

Mr. Jung's Note

This semester I am teaching English to first-year middle school students who are at a low-intermediate proficiency level. At the start of the semester, I conducted individual conferences with my students to identify the topics they found most interesting. As an educator for low-intermediate level students, I believe that fostering their motivation to learn English is crucial when designing lessons. Based on the results of the conferences, I selected the top three topics according to their interest and popularity: K-pop culture, Future jobs, and Social Media. Fortunately, these topics are covered in Chapters 7, 5, and 1 of our reading textbook, respectively. Therefore, to align with their interests, I decided to rearrange the order of the chapters. We will begin with Chapter 7 on K-pop culture, followed by Chapter 5 on Future jobs, and finally Chapter 1 on Social Media.

Referring to \<A\> and \<B\>, identify each technique that Ms. Park and Mr. Jung use for material adaptation and write some evidence of how the identified techniques are applied into their lessons, respectively.

Your Answer

Guideline for Pre-service Teachers

11 Read the passages in <A> and <B>, and follow the directions.

A

Ms. Kim's Teaching Note

Today, I spent some time reflecting on what really makes a course effective. I've come to realize that a significant part of this is doing a deep dive into the materials we use. It's not just about having resources; it's about ensuring those resources truly resonate with our goals and meet the needs of our students. With this in mind, I decided to evaluate the new textbook. I used a comprehensive checklist including criteria such as student motivation, appropriateness for student level, availability of supplementary materials, alignment with curriculum objectives, quality of teacher's manual, cultural content, and layout and design. Based on these criteria, I evaluated the new textbook to examine how well the content aligns with my course objectives and whether it's suitable for my students. Below is the evaluation result.

Criteria	Scale		
	Yes	Somewhat	No
Does the textbook effectively engage and motivate students?	√		
Is the textbook language appropriately tailored to the students' proficiency level?		√	
Are additional learning resources included with the textbook?			√
Does the textbook meet the curricular objectives?	√		
Is the teacher's manual comprehensive and supportive?		√	
Does the textbook provide a significant amount of relevant cultural information?			√
Is the textbook's layout user-friendly, clear, and visually appealing?		√	

After carefully considering the seven criteria on the checklist, I marked five as either "somewhat" or "no." I devised strategies to adapt the material concerning three of these criteria. However, for the remaining two, I decided to ask for help. Consequently, I emailed Mr. Choi, a head teacher, to seek his advice on these two challenging criteria.

B

From	choi-go@school.korea
To	cheers.k@school.korea
Subject	Re: Asking for advice

Dear Ms. Kim,

I understand the challenges and concerns you are facing in the present.

For the first issue, I suggest incorporating multimedia resources that align with the textbook's themes. This approach can significantly enrich the learners' experience and facilitate a deeper understanding of the content. Multimedia resources, such as videos, podcasts, and interactive games, provide varied and engaging ways for students to interact with the material.

Regarding the second concern, a potential solution could be to simplify the textbook language. This could involve reducing the level of vocabulary or using less complex grammatical structures. By adjusting the language, the textbook could become more accessible to your students, thereby facilitating a smoother learning process.

Please feel free to reach out if you need further assistance in implementing these suggestions or if you have any other concerns.

Best regards,

Choi, Go

Based on <A> and <B>, identify the TWO problems that Ms. Kim asks Mr. Choi for advice on. Then, explain Mr. Choi's recommendations for adapting the material to address each identified problem. Do NOT copy more than FOUR consecutive words from the passages.

Your Answer

12 Read the evaluation results in <A> and the conversation in <B> and follow the directions.

A

The table below shows the results of the textbook evaluation conducted by two teachers. According to the results, they will create supplementary teaching materials for the categories they both identified as "Poor".

Categories of Evaluation (Subskills & Skills)	Mr. Park 3	Mr. Park 2	Mr. Park 1	Ms. Yoo 3	Ms. Yoo 2	Ms. Yoo 1
1. Do reading topics relate to real-life issues and encourage critical thinking in comparison to native speaker texts?	√				√	
2. Are there pre-listening activities accompanying listening materials to aid comprehension?		√				√
3. Are there various activities promoting meaningful communication between students?		√				√
4. Is new vocabulary introduced at an appropriate rate and reviewed in subsequent units?		√			√	
5. Are grammar points presented with simple examples and explanations?	√				√	
6. Are there diverse types of writing practices?		√				√
7. Is there ample focus on recognizing and producing stress patterns, intonation, and individual sounds?	√				√	

3=Excellent, 2=Good, 1=Poor

B

Mr. Park and Ms. Yoo, who are the English teachers of a high school, are talking about the results of textbook evaluation.

Mr. Park : After reviewing the textbook, I felt the listening materials were engaging but lacked pre-listening activities. I believe these activities are key to setting the context and providing necessary knowledge.

Ms. Yoo : I'm on the same page, Mr. Park. What if we make students watch related videos or visit relevant websites in the pre-listening phase?

Mr. Park : Good idea. Then, the videos and websites will give students some background information and activate their schematic knowledge.

Ms. Yoo : Correct! Next, on the speaking front, I noticed that the exercises are mostly individual speech presentations. I think we should diversify activities to facilitate genuine communication among students.

Mr. Park : Well, how about adding some group activities such as problem-solving tasks and discussions? These will foster more meaningful communication between students.

Ms. Yoo : I like that. Additionally, given that our students are high-intermediate level, the current textbook only provides controlled writing exercises. How about giving them different types of writing activities?

Mr. Park : That sounds great. Then, let's provide them with freer writing exercises. Then, they will have opportunities to write about their personal experiences or opinions.

Ms. Yoo : That's an excellent idea. Then, we can give them more autonomy.

Mr. Park : Are we done now? Then, how about preparing these supplementary materials until next week?

Ms. Yoo : Absolutely.

Considering the information in <A> and <B>, write THREE supplementary teaching materials/activities that Mr. Park and Ms. Yoo need to prepare for their lessons. Then, explain how each supplement can compensate for the problems of the current textbook.

Your Answer

Guideline for Pre-service Teachers

13 Read the passages in <A> and <B>, and follow the directions.

A

After the workshop, I realized the importance of adapting materials to fit learners' needs, goals, and the learning environment. I will now actively assess and adjust my materials to improve teaching effectiveness, addressing any mismatches with student levels, objectives, or context, and maximizing the materials' potential. Below is an example of the choices involved in this process.

1. Reasons
    (1) Personalizing: Increasing the relevance of content by relating it to learners' interests.
    (2) Individualizing: Adapting the learning styles and proficiency levels of both individuals and the entire class.
    (3) Localizing: Adapting the content to reflect the regional culture and context relevant to the target language's teaching.
    (4) Modernizing: Using current and authentic English. Some materials may lack familiarity with current English usage, making them outdated, misleading, or even incorrect.

2. Adaptation Techniques
    (1) Adding   (2) Deleting   (3) Modifying
    (4) Simplifying   (5) Reordering

3. Content Areas
    (1) Language   (2) Activities   (3) Topic
    (4) Skills   (5) Classroom management

B

Ms. Lee teaches 3rd-grade students at a low-intermediate level in middle school. After planning a lesson on 'storytelling,' she reviewed it to ensure it was suitable for her students. Typically, they prefer pictorial activities over non-pictorial ones when exploring the day's topic. However, she realized that the worksheet she had prepared only introduced storytelling tips without effectively engaging the low-intermediate level students. Additionally, she found that the chosen text was too advanced for them. As a result, she decided to adapt the teaching materials to better align with her students' individual learning preferences and current skill level. Below are the original and modified lesson plans.

Original Lesson Plan

Title: Storytelling
Duration: 60 minutes
Materials: Storytelling tips handout, storybook, whiteboard, markers

Step 1: Introduction
- Greet the students and introduce the topic of storytelling.
- Distribute a worksheet introducing some storytelling tips.

Step 2: Reading Activity
- Divide the class into pairs.
- In pairs, students talk about some tips they found from the text after reading it individually.

[Text] Storytelling Tips

Storytelling is a captivating art that has the power to engage and transport your audience to different worlds. Whether you're sharing a personal experience, reading a story, or presenting information, here are some essential tips to make your storytelling more compelling:

> (1) Know Your Audience: Consider the age, interests, and background of your audience. Tailor your story to connect with their distinct perspectives and experiences.
> (2) Engaging Opening: Start with an attention-grabbing opening line or scene to hook your listeners from the beginning.
>
> (...)

Step 3: Story Sharing
- Each pair shares a brief story of their own experience considering the tips from the text.
- Ask students to provide feedback on what they found interesting or engaging from the partner's story.

Step 4: Wrap-Up
- Encourage students to share their thoughts and experiences about storytelling.
- Assign reading homework related to storytelling for the next class.

Modified Lesson Plan

Title: Storytelling
Duration: 60 minutes
Materials: Video related to the theme, storytelling tips handout, storybook, whiteboard, markers

Step 1: Introduction with Video
- Greet the students and introduce the topic of storytelling.
- Show the video clip related to storytelling tips.
- Share the video content briefly with the whole class to provide context for the storytelling activity.
- Distribute a worksheet introducing some storytelling tips.

Step 2: Reading Activity
- Divide the class into pairs.
- In pairs, students talk about some tips they found from the text after reading it individually.

[Text] Storytelling Tips

　　Storytelling is an interesting skill that can take your listeners to new places. Whether you're talking about something personal, reading a story, or giving information, here are some important tips to make your storytelling better:

(1) Know Your Audience: Know the age, interests, and background of your audience. Design your story to connect with them.
(2) Interesting Start: Start with an interesting first line or scene to grab your listeners' attention right away.

(...)

Step 3: Story Sharing
- Each pair shares a brief story of their own experience considering the tips from the video and the text.
- Ask students to provide feedback on what they found interesting or engaging from the partner's story.

Step 4: Wrap-Up
- Encourage students to share their thoughts and experiences about storytelling.
- Assign reading and watching homework related to storytelling for the next class.

Referring to the terms in <A>, identify the Reason why Ms. Lee wants to adapt the materials, and explain Technique(s) and Content Area(s) that she chooses for material adaptation reflected in <B>.

Your Answer

14 Read the passages in <A> and <B> and follow the directions.

A

English teachers have several factors to consider when creating classroom tasks. One of the key considerations is whether the activity is appropriately challenging for our students—neither too difficult nor too easy. The following are factors that teachers should consider when creating tasks, along with corresponding questions:

Factors	Questions
Text	• How dense/complex are the texts that learners are required to process? • How relevant/irrelevant is the content to the learners' experience? • How much contextual support is provided?
Task	• How many steps are involved in the task? • How relevant and meaningful is the task? • How much time is available? • What degree of grammatical accuracy is required? • How much rehearsal time is available?
Learner	• Motivation of learners • Prior knowledge of content • Degree of linguistic knowledge • Skill level and extent of cultural knowledge • Degree of familiarity with task type itself

---
B

T1 : Hi there, Ms. Jin! Shall we discuss our problem-solving task?

T2 : Hello, Mr. Lee. Yes, let's start.

T1 : I believe our topic, 'Traffic Congestion in Front of the School,' is closely related to students' real lives, and the text we've chosen clearly outlines the problem.

T2 : I agree. The level of vocabulary and grammar is accessible for them. Regarding the task process—from understanding the problems to deciding on a solution—the steps are clear and logical.

T1 : My concern is whether we're providing enough time for presentation practice.
T2 : Presentation practice is essential. We should allocate more time for it, ensuring students feel confident about their actual presentations.
T1 : You're right. So, let's adjust the plan to include about half an hour for students to feel ready. What do you think?
T2 : Perfect! Also, we need to consider if students have enough background knowledge on the topic.
T1 : True. The topic 'Traffic Congestion in Front of the School,' while relevant, might be challenging without previous knowledge. Perhaps, we should provide additional materials for a better understanding.
T2 : A background video followed by a Q&A session could bridge that gap and engage students.
T1 : Excellent idea. I'll look for a suitable video and share it with you for review. We'll add it to our lesson plan.
T2 : Sure, let's work on it together.

T=teacher

Based on the information provided in <A>, identify the TWO factors that teachers in <B> consider to reduce the task difficulty. Then, explain how the strategies related to these factors will support students in completing the task, using concrete evidence from both <A> and <B>.

Your Answer

15 Read the passages in <A> and <B>, and follow the directions.

A

Ms. Lee, a middle school English teacher, recently attended a material development workshop where she explored various factors affecting task difficulty. Recognizing the direct impact of these factors on student learning and engagement, she decided to modify her textbook tasks to better accommodate her low-intermediate-level students. Her aim is to create tasks that are optimally challenging, thereby boosting student motivation and facilitating deeper learning. Below is part of the workshop material she explored.

Set of Factors Related to Task Difficulty

(1) How many sub-steps are involved in the task?
(2) How much time is available?
(3) How relevant and meaningful is the task?
(4) What degree of grammatical accuracy is required?
(5) How much assistance is provided?

B

Based on what she has learned at the workshop, Ms. Lee modified one of the speaking activities from the textbook as shown below.

The Original Task

What You Will Do:
You will be divided into groups of five, and each group will be assigned a different country. First, research the assigned country's culture, exploring areas such as food, traditions, festivals, and social norms. Second, do a group discussion, and write your group's outcomes in a complete paragraph. Lastly, each group will present their findings.

The Adapted Task

What You Will Do:

Step 1. **Topic-related vocabulary**: You'll start by learning basic vocabulary related to the country's culture.

- **Traditions**: Practices and customs passed down through generations
- **Festivals**: Celebratory events, often with historical or religious significance
- **Cuisine**: Traditional foods and cooking styles unique to a country

(...)

Step 2. **Discussion preparation**: You will be divided into groups of five, and each group will be assigned a different country. You will have guiding questions to help you focus on basic aspects, like food, sports, and clothing of that country.

[Questions]

Food:
- What are some traditional dishes in this country?
- Are there any special foods eaten on holidays or celebrations?

Sports:
- What are the most popular sports in this country?
- Are there any traditional sports unique to this country?

Clothing:
- What traditional clothing is worn in this country?
- How does the climate of the country influence its traditional clothing?

> Step 3. Group discussion: Have a group discussion based on the guiding questions. After your discussion, you will write your group's findings using the following template.
>
> > **Introduction to (country)'s Culture**
> > Group: _____
> > 1. Food
> >   - traditional dishes: _____
> >   - special foods for holidays: _____
> > 2. Sports
> >   - the most popular sports: _____
> >   - traditional sports: _____
> >   (...)
>
> Step 4. Planning and rehearsal: Plan your presentation and rehearse it.
>
> Step 5. Presentation: Present your findings based on the group rehearsal.

Based on <A>, identify the TWO factors that Ms. Lee applied to lower the difficulty of the original task in <B>. Then, explain how each factor is addressed in the adapted task, providing concrete evidence from <A> and <B>.

Your Answer _____

3 Classroom Observation or Course Evaluation

01 Read the passage and follow the directions.

Below is the lesson procedure that Ms. Kim prepares to teach key vocabulary related to clothing using a role-play activity.

Lesson Procedure

Level: Low-intermediate
Time: 15 minutes
Preparation: Prepare 27 cards, each with a picture, to cover all the possible permutations of the following colors, fabrics, and items of clothing. The items can be increased and/or varied if required:

⊙ Target Vocabulary

[Colors]	[Fabrics]	[Clothing Items]
red	woolen	dress
blue	cotton	shirt
black	nylon	sweater

The cards should look like this:

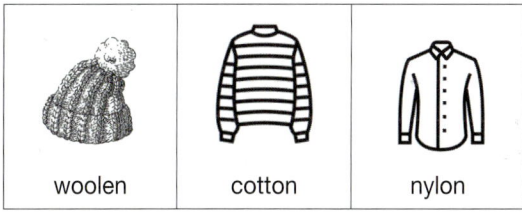

| woolen | cotton | nylon |

Procedure

1. Set up a clothing store situation. Show some picture cards to students and ask them to describe what to purchase using colors, fabrics, and clothing items. Then, ask the students to show the cards by indicating fashion items they want to purchase and complete a substitution table on the board as follows:
  ※ I'd like [a red woolen dress,] please.
       [blue cotton sweater,]
       [black nylon shirt,]

Guideline for Pre-service Teachers

2. Take the role of the sales clerk, and ask the students to take turns asking for something in the shop. Whenever a student asks for something, you should hand over a picture, making an error in either the color, the fabric, or the item of clothing. The student then has to correct the error using appropriate stress. The dialogue should go like this:

Student: I'd like a red COTTON dress, please.
Teacher: Here you are. *(giving a blue cotton dress)*
Student: No. I asked for a RED cotton dress, not a BLUE one.

or

Student: I'd like a BLACK woolen shirt, please.
Teacher: Here you are. *(giving a black woolen skirt)*
Student: No. I said a black woolen SHIRT, not a black woolen SKIRT.

* capital letter denotes stress.

3. Once they have gotten the hang of the exercise, divide the cards among pairs of students for independent practice.

Referring to the lesson procedure above, write TWO major lesson objectives.

Your Answer

02 Read the passages and follow the directions.

A

Below are lesson objectives suggested from a teacher's conference for teaching middle school 2nd graders this semester.

Students will be able to:
- listen to a dialogue and explain the content.
- ask for reasons and make decisions.
- read a text and retell the story.
- listen to a dialogue and take notes on details.
- use strategies to open and close conversations.
- talk about their own experiences.
- revise a writing based on grammatical feedback.

B

Stage 1	• T shows a video clip of Arctic animals. • T asks Ss in pairs to talk about what they have seen in the video clip. • T preteaches the target vocabulary words.
Stage 2	• T asks Ss to listen to a three-minute dialogue talking about Arctic animals and to find the main idea. • T talks about the main idea with Ss. • T asks Ss to listen to the dialogue two more times and think about key information.
Stage 3	• T puts Ss in groups of four. • T instructs Ss to collaboratively write a summary based on key information. • T plays the listening file one final time and asks Ss to write down as many additional information as they can. • T instructs Ss to revise and finalize their writing based on the additional notes they have taken.
Stage 4	• T asks Ss to exchange their summaries with another group. • T prompts Ss to read the other group's summary and find any grammatical errors. • T asks Ss to return the summaries with feedback to the respective groups. • T asks Ss to check the feedback from the other groups. Ss revise their summaries by correcting their grammatical errors in the original text and then submit the final summaries.

Guideline for Pre-service Teachers

From <A>, choose TWO lesson objectives that the lesson procedure in <B> is designed for, providing each stage to actualize the chosen objective. Then, explain the reasons of your choices.

Your Answer

03 Read the passage in <A> and the teaching procedure in <B>, and follow the directions.

A

Ms. Kim, a middle school English teacher, uses a comprehensive approach to assess her students' needs through interviews and diagnostic tests. This enables her to effectively tailor her lesson objectives to develop both receptive and productive skills in English. The following are lesson objectives she had outlined for this semester.

Lesson Objectives

[Receptive skills]
Students can
- identify the main idea and details from a written text.
- identify the author's purpose and point of view in a spoken text.
- infer the meaning of unknown words using contextual clues in reading tasks.
- distinguish between fact and opinion in spoken texts.

[Productive skills]
Students can
- orally present facts supported by clear arguments or evidence.
- organize ideas logically and coherently in writing tasks.
- employ a variety of sentence structures and descriptive language.
- use various idiomatic expressions in a discussion.

B

Teaching Procedure

Ms. Kim has designed an English lesson for her third-year students, focusing on achieving two specific objectives she had outlined.

Stage 1	• T introduces the topic of environmental conservation and shows a short video clip related to the topic. • T asks questions about the content from the video clip to activate students' schematic knowledge.
Stage 2	• T asks about students' personal experiences with environmental conservation, using specific guiding questions. • T pre-teaches new vocabulary from the reading text based on example sentences and definitions.
Stage 3	• T provides a reading passage titled "Personal Efforts to Protect the Environment". • T asks Ss to skim the text to identify the gist of the text. • T checks the answer with Ss. • T provides five comprehension questions asking about the facts and details in the text. • Ss reread the text and find the answers to the questions. • T checks the answers with the whole class.
Stage 4	• T puts Ss in groups of four and asks them to share their own ideas for protecting the environment. • T asks each group to choose the five best ways to protect the environment based on the discussion.
Stage 5	• T instructs Ss in groups to write a paragraph introducing the top five environmental protection ideas. • Ss focus on organizing their ideas clearly and logically.
Stage 6	• After a brief training on giving feedback, groups exchange paragraphs. • Ss use a checklist to give and receive feedback on clarity and coherence in writing. • Ss rewrite their drafts based on the feedback received from their peers.
Stage 7	• T asks Ss to post their revised paragraphs to the class blog for T's feedback. • T wraps up the lesson by highlighting the key skills practiced.

T=teacher, Ss=students

Identify ONE objective for receptive skills and ONE for productive skills from <A> that the teaching procedure in <B> targets. Then, explain how each objective is addressed, specifying the Step(s) and providing evidence from <B>.

Your Answer

Guideline for Pre-service Teachers

04 Read the class observation checklist and the summary written by a teacher after observing a colleague's class. Then, follow the directions.

A

Lesson Observation Checklist: Speaking Lesson for 3rd Graders in Middle School

Areas	Criteria	Scale
Lesson preparation	• Lesson objectives are clear and appropriate for the lesson. • Adequate and relevant speaking activities are prepared based on students' level.	1-2-3-4-5 1-2-3-4-5
Instructional strategies	• Use of diverse and effective instructional methods. • Facilitation of student participation and active engagement. • Incorporation of timely and constructive feedback.	1-2-3-4-5 1-2-3-4-5 1-2-3-4-5
Affective aspects	• Positive rapport and interaction with students. • Creation of an inclusive environment where students feel safe and valued.	1-2-3-4-5 1-2-3-4-5

* Scale: 1(Poor)~5(Excellent)

B

Summary After Class Observation

- The teacher actively interacted with students and established a strong rapport with them.
- The teacher used a balanced mix of group discussions and individual tasks, which encouraged students to participate to a certain extent.
- The teacher used real-life situations and visual aids, which somewhat maintained students' engagement.
- The teacher prepared many speaking activities, but some of them seemed too complex for the students' proficiency level.

From the lesson observation checklist in <A>, identify one area that represents the strongest aspect of the lesson, and another that represents the weakest. Then, support each of your choices with details from the summary. Do NOT copy more than FOUR consecutive words from the passages.

Your Answer

Guideline for Pre-service Teachers

05 Read the passages and follow the directions.

A

Student's Log

During today's lesson, I came to realize the importance of my teacher's guidance during activities. Rather than relying solely on verbal instructions, she demonstrated the day's activity, which made it more engaging and comprehensible for us. If she had only provided verbal explanations, we might have struggled to understand the task, leading to confusion. However, by demonstrating an example through classroom interaction, she made it easier for us to follow along. Specifically, today's topic was our dream jobs. She started a conversation by asking us about our dream jobs. Based on her questions, we circled and crossed out potential dream jobs on our worksheets. Moreover, before we began the activity, she ensured our understanding by conducting a comprehension check on the activity procedure. Her hands-on guidance today significantly enhanced our learning experience.

B

[Worksheet]
※ What do you want to be in the future? Circle three jobs you want to have. Cross out three that you don't want to be. Write three other jobs you would like to have.

*doctor   nurse   police officer   soldier   teacher
architect   artist   baker   businessperson   carpenter
engineer   firefighter   gardner   lawyer   model*

Three other jobs you would like to be ...
1._____   2._____   3._____

Teacher A's Lesson

T explains how to do the activity with the worksheet.

Teacher : Now, you are going to talk about jobs you want to have in the future. I want you to circle three jobs you want to have, cross out three you don't want to have, and add three more jobs you want to have.

Teacher B's Lesson

Teacher : Jinah, what is your dream job?
Jinah : I want to be a teacher.
Teacher : Great. Then, will you circle on 'teacher' from the list? Eunji, do you want to be a babysitter?
Eunji : No. Not at all.
Teacher : Okay, then let's cross off 'babysitter' from the list. Minchul, what do you want to be in the future?
Minchul : Soccer player.
Teacher : Hum... do you see a soccer player on the list?
(T points to the worksheet on the screen.)
Class : No.
Teacher : Then, you can write down 'soccer player' in one of the blanks below.
Minchul : I see.
Teacher : Everyone, read the instructions aloud together.
(The class read the instructions.)
Teacher : What do you circle?
Class : Three jobs that we want to do.
Teacher : What do you cross out?
Class : Three jobs that we don't want to do.

Referring to the student's log in <A>, identify the ONE specific lesson in <B> that the student likely has participated in. Then, explain TWO reasons for your choice with evidence from <B>.

Your Answer

4 Instructional Techniques(classroom activities) or Syllabus

01 Read the passages and follow the directions.

Syllabus A

Units	Functions	Grammar Activation	Activities
Unit 1. Self-introduction (Total 7 periods)	• Greeting people • Asking for/ giving personal information	• WH- questions • Present and past of 'to be'	• Role-play • Simulation

Syllabus B

Units	Grammar	Vocabulary / Pronunciation	Activities
Unit 1. What did you do on weekends? (Total 7 periods)	• Past tense: regular verbs and irregular verbs • Prepositions in time expressions	• Hobbies (reading books, riding a bike, jogging) • Word Stress	• Pattern drill activities • Choral reading

B

Below is an excerpt from the e-mail that a Head teacher in the English department has sent to English Teachers.

Dear colleagues

As we prepare for the upcoming semester, I want to share my core belief that shapes our syllabus: Language is a tool for communication, not just a subject to be mastered. This belief will be at the heart of how we approach language teaching. Thus, our lessons will shift the focus away from traditional grammar and vocabulary drills. Instead, we'll concentrate on teaching specific language functions essential for communication, such as making requests, expressing emotions, and participating in conversations. The aim is to equip students with good command of English by appropriately using these functions outside the classroom. Besides, another key aspect of our syllabus will be engaging students in activities that mimic real-life situations. These practical exercises will allow students to apply the language functions they learn in class to scenarios they are likely to encounter in everyday life. By practicing in contexts that mirror the real world, students will develop their ability to communicate more naturally and confidently in English. Overall, our objective is to transform language learning into an engaging and interactive experience, rooted in practical application. By prioritizing these principles, we aim to empower our students to use English as an effective communication tool!

If you have any questions related to my suggestion, please feel free to e-mail me.

Best regards,
Ms. Choi
Head Teacher in the English Department

Guideline for Pre-service Teachers

Identify the type of each syllabus exemplified in <A>, respectively. Then, based on <B>, choose ONE syllabus that the teachers should use for the upcoming semester and write TWO reasons of your choice with corresponding evidence from <A>.

Your Answer

02 Read the conversation in <A> and the draft of the syllabus in <B>, and follow the directions.

A

T1 : Hello, Ms. Park! I hope you're doing well. I've been working on our syllabus for the upcoming English lessons with our high-intermediate level students.

T2 : Hi, Ms. Yoo! That's great to hear. Let's discuss how we can design the syllabus effectively. What components should we focus on?

T1 : Well, to start, I believe we should carefully select topics for the syllabus that are both practical and directly relevant to real-life situations. Examples could include greetings and introductions, daily routines, and food and dining.

T2 : Those topics sound relevant. Now, let's think about the functions. How can we ensure they are practical and functional for our students?

T1 : To make the functions more practical, we could focus on key areas like introducing oneself and others, describing everyday activities, and practicing making requests or ordering food at restaurants.

T2 : Great! Moving on to skills, how do you think we should approach developing these in our students?

T1 : I believe that introducing reading texts as supplementary material will help improve vocabulary and comprehension, in addition to focusing on speaking and listening activities.

T2 : That's a well-rounded approach. Now, when it comes to activities, diversifying our speaking exercises is essential. How about incorporating group discussions and survey to encourage more interaction?

T1 : That's an excellent idea. It will keep the class engaging and dynamic while aligning with our chosen components.

T2 : Lastly, how do we plan to effectively integrate grammar and vocabulary?

T1 : For grammar, we can introduce indirect questions, modal verbs, present perfect tense, frequent adverbs, time expressions, and the use of imperatives, aligning them with themes like greetings, daily routines, and food and dining. As for vocabulary, we should immerse them in relevant terms, phrases, and vocabulary specific to each unit's topic.

T2 : Perfect! To summarize our discussion: we'll include practical themes, emphasize functional language, enhance skills with supplementary reading, diversify speaking activities, and tailor grammar and vocabulary to each unit. It looks like we're on the right track for designing a comprehensive syllabus.

T1 : Absolutely, Ms. Park. With this approach, we can create a well-structured syllabus that will truly benefit our students in the upcoming semester.

B

This is the draft of the syllabus T1 and T2 wrote.

Components	Unit 1	Unit 2	Unit 3
Topics	Meeting and greeting people	Daily routines	Ordering food
Functions	Introducing oneself and others	Describing activities	Making requests
Skills	Speaking and listening	Speaking and listening	Speaking and listening
Activities	Structured role-play about greetings and introduction	Dialogue practice on daily activities	Menu ordering structured role-play
Grammar	• Indirect questions • Modal verbs for politeness	• Present perfect • Adverbs of frequency and time expressions	Imperatives for making requests
Vocabulary	Basic greetings and phrases	Daily routine vocabulary	Food-related vocabulary

Based on <A>, choose the TWO components in <B> that do NOT correspond to the teachers' ideas about their syllabus. Then, explain your answers with evidence from <A> and <B>.

Your Answer

Guideline for Pre-service Teachers

03 Read the passages and follow the directions.

A

Ms. Kim's Teaching Log

While communicative approaches have gained prominence, I believe that prioritizing the teaching of forms, structures, and rules of language is crucial. There are two key benefits to explicitly teaching forms in our classroom: improved accuracy and enhanced confidence. Firstly, when we teach grammar, vocabulary, and pronunciation rules explicitly, students gain a solid foundation in the language. They learn to communicate accurately, reducing errors that might hinder comprehension. This allows them to express themselves precisely and convey their ideas effectively. Secondly, when they understand the rules and patterns, they are more likely to take risks in speaking and writing. They feel empowered to experiment with the language and are less afraid of making mistakes. This increased confidence leads to greater engagement in class activities and a more positive attitude toward language learning.

Mr. Choi's Teaching Log

I believe that task-based learning is a potent method that offers numerous advantages for our students. Here are two key reasons why incorporating tasks into our lessons is so effective. First, task-based instruction simulates real-life language use. When we present students with tasks, such as problem-solving, decision-making, or creative projects, we're replicating authentic situations they may encounter outside the classroom. This relevance motivates students because they see the immediate practical application of what they're learning. It bridges the gap between classroom learning and the real world, making the language more meaningful and engaging. Second, tasks provide a rich context for language acquisition. Instead of focusing solely on isolated grammar rules or vocabulary lists, tasks encourage students to use the language naturally and purposefully. They have to communicate, negotiate meaning, and make linguistic choices to complete the task successfully. This context-driven approach enhances comprehension and retention. Students learn not just "about" the language, but also how to "use" it effectively in various situations, fostering a deeper understanding.

B

Syllabus A

Course Objective: To develop students' practical communication skills for real-world scenarios.

Chapter	Task	Pedagogical task
1. Let's prepare for traveling.	Task 1. Plan a Trip to a Foreign Country	• Choosing a destination • Booking flights • Creating an itinerary • Packing essentials • Understanding travel documents (e.g., passport, visa)
	Task 2. Navigate Through an Airport	• Role-play: Students take on the roles of travelers, airline staff, and security personnel. • Vocabulary: Key airport and travel-related vocabulary • Asking for directions • Checking in at the airline counter • Security procedures (e.g., screening, restrictions on liquids)
2. Do you know how to book an accommodation?	Task 1. Check-In and Check-Out at a Hotel	• Role-play: Students take on the roles of hotel guests and hotel staff. • Vocabulary: Hotel-related terms (e.g., reservation, reception, key card) • Checking in (providing identification, paying, getting room keys) • Room types and amenities • Checking out (e.g., settling bills, returning key cards)

Syllabus B

Course Objective: To provide students with a strong foundation in English grammar and sentence structure.

Week	Chapter	Rules & Patterns
1. Nouns	1. What is a noun?	• Common nouns vs. proper nouns • Countable vs. uncountable nouns
1. Nouns	2. Types of Nouns	• Common nouns and their role in everyday language • Proper nouns and their capitalization rules • Collective nouns (e.g., team, family) • Abstract nouns (e.g., love, happiness)
2. Verbs	3. What is a verb?	• Verbs as action words • Identifying verbs in sentences • Transitive vs. intransitive verbs
2. Verbs	4. Verb Tenses	• Present simple tense (e.g., I work, he works) • Past simple tense (e.g., I worked, he worked)

Based on <A>, choose ONE syllabus that is appropriate for each teacher from <B>. Then, write TWO reasons for each of your choices in terms of syllabus construction and course objective in <B>.

Your Answer

04 Read the passages in <A> and <B>, and follow the directions.

A

Teachers can play many roles in the course of teaching. Teachers' roles are often best described using metaphors, such as "teacher as manufacturer," "teacher as doctor," "teacher as judge," "teacher as gardener," and others. Some of these metaphors clearly pave the way to interaction. Below are some roles that teachers can play in the process of teaching:

Teacher as Controller	A role that is sometimes expected in educational institutions is that of a controller, in charge of every moment of a lesson. Control is an important element of structuring a lesson and successfully carrying out interactive techniques.
Teacher as Director	In some interactive classroom settings, the teacher may take on the role of a director, similar to a conductor of an orchestra. As students engage in either rehearsed or spontaneous language performances, it is the teacher's job to ensure that the process flows smoothly and efficiently by providing clear directions.
Teacher as Assessor	The teacher takes on the role of assessor to evaluate how well students are performing or have performed. Feedback and correction are then organized and implemented.
Teacher as Facilitator	The facilitating role requires the teacher to step away from a directive approach and allow students, with the teacher's guidance, to choose the topics they wish to learn and find their own ways to complete tasks. By offering skills, strategies, and resources (such as words, expressions, etc.) to enhance productivity, the facilitator makes it easier for students to engage in the learning process.
Teacher as Participant	By playing the role of participant, the teacher becomes an equal collaborator, participating in discussions, group work, or activities just like the students. For example, in a class discussion, rather than solely moderating or guiding, the teacher might contribute their own thoughts and ideas, responding to student input as a fellow learner.

B

Below are the classroom conversations excerpted from two middle school English lessons. Teacher A is teaching intermediate level students, whereas Teacher B is teaching beginner level students. Based on their respective classroom activity, each teacher plays a different role of a teacher in class.

Teacher A

T : Good afternoon, class! Today, we're going to have a debate on an important topic. I've divided you into two teams, and each team will present arguments for and against the topic.
(Teacher assigns specific roles and responsibilities to students in each team.)

T : Team A, you will be arguing in favor of stricter environmental regulations. Team B, you'll argue against them. Remember, we've been studying this topic, so use the information we've discussed in your arguments.
(Teacher initiates the debate, ensuring that each team has equal speaking time, follows the rules of debate, and maintains a respectful tone.)

T : Team A, it's your turn to present your arguments. Be concise and persuasive.

Teacher B

T : Hello, class! Today, we are going to talk about something fun. What do you want to talk about?
Yoonhee : Movies?
T : Yes, Yoonhee! Movies are great topic. Let's keep it simple. What kind of movies do you like? Scary, funny, or love story?
Binjin : Can we talk about different types of movies? Like, action, comedy?
T : Good idea, Binjin! Those are called 'genres.' Let's each pick a genre to talk about. Jaebum, what genre do you like?

Jaebum : I like funny movies. Comedy.
T : Good, Jaebum! Comedy movies make us laugh. When we talk about comedy, we can use words like 'funny,' 'laugh,' and 'joke.' Now, Jaebum, please tell us about a funny movie you like, using these related words.

Based on <A>, identify the role in <A> that each teacher in <B> has played in class. Then, explain your answers with evidence from <A> and <B>.

Your Answer

05 Read the passages <A> and <B>, and follow the directions.

A

It is essential to plan English listening practice that caters to different learning styles to ensure the success of ESL students. When activities match their learning preferences, students are more likely to thrive. These listening activities will help them express themselves, gain valuable language experience, and address key learning styles.

1. Blindfolding
   Prepare action cards in advance. Put students into pairs, assigning 'Leader' and 'Follower' roles. The blindfolded 'Follower' follows verbal directions from the 'Leader' to complete the action on the card.

2. Who, What, Where
   In this activity, students will brainstorm and infer meaning from visual clues. Show a short video clip of a conversation and have students guess who the people are, what they are discussing, and where the scene is set.

3. Reported Interview
   In this activity, students pair up, interview each other, and take notes. Then, they collaborate to write an introductory paragraph about their partner, focusing on details that highlight each person's special talents.

4. Cloze Lyrics
   You can use a song for a cloze activity by replacing every fifth word in the lyrics with a blank or by targeting specific words. As students listen, they'll fill in the blanks.

5. Name That Product
   Play the audio from a TV commercial to the students and ask them to identify what product is being advertised, without seeing the video. Vintage commercials work best for this purpose due to their exaggerated dialogues and over-the-top praise for the product.

B

Minsoo

Minsoo excels in learning settings where he can actively participate and use physical movement. He enjoys tasks that involve physical activities, such as moving around the classroom or going on field trips. This approach helps him understand and retain information effectively, as he prefers engaging in actions over passive listening. Minsoo's enthusiasm for learning through action is evident in his active participation in lessons that involve movement and hands-on activities.

Jisoo

Jisoo thrives in environments that encourage interaction and collaboration. She is good at understanding others' feelings, making her an excellent team player. As a result, Jisoo enjoys group activities, such as pair discussions. Her effective communication and collaboration not only contribute positively to group dynamics but also enhance her learning experience.

Among the activities presented in <A>, choose the most suitable activity for each student described in <B>. Then, explain your answers with evidence from <A> and <B>.

Your Answer

Guideline for Pre-service Teachers

06 Read the two teachers' teaching notes in <A> and three tasks in <B>, and follow the directions.

───── A ─────

Mr. Park's Teaching Note

I am planning to teach how to write a story for my low intermediate level students. Considering their proficiency level, I will provide students with some pictures as a writing stimulus so that they can use these pictures to create a story. Also, to lower task complexity, I will arrange students to use simple present tense only. In my writing task, students will able to write appropriate sentences by following the sequence of the given pictures.

Ms. Yoo's Teaching Note

For my high intermediate level students, I'd like to teach them how to write a summary of a story. As the first step, I will provide a series of questions which can serve as an outline for their summary. Accordingly, by answering to the questions, students will complete the initial draft of their writing. Next week, then, I will arrange the editing and revising session for them.

───── B ─────

Task 1

Choose the word with the correct spelling to fit the sentence, then write the word in the space provided.

1. I tried to stop the car, but the _____ didn't work.
    a. braicks
    b. brecks
    c. brakes
    d. bracks

Task 2

Describe the Minji's daily routine in eight sentences.

She gets up at eight o'clock.
She has a breakfast at 8:30.
...

Task 3

Students read a short story and answer the following questions. The answers will be used for a summary of the story.

1. Where did the story take place?
2. Who were the people in the story?
3. What happened first? and then? and then?
4. What happened at the end?
5. What is the moral of this story?

Based on <A>, identify ONE task in <B> that is appropriate for each teacher. Then, explain your answers with evidence from <A> and <B>.

Your Answer

Guideline for Pre-service Teachers

07 Read the passage in <A> and the activity procedure in <B>. Then, follow the directions.

A

There are four ways to teach culture in the classroom: E-mail surveys, Culture capsules, Culture assimilators, and Culture minidramas. In an E-mail survey, students communicate with their target language counterparts and investigate information about their daily routines, school, and interests. In Culture capsules, students read/listen to a brief description that illustrates the differences between Korean and the target culture along with several illustrative photos or relevant realia. Then, they engage in a comparative discussion about the differences between Korean and American cultures. Following their discussion, they participate in activities designed to integrate other skills based on their findings. In Culture assimilators, students listen to a description or watch an incident of cross-cultural interaction in which miscommunication occurs between a Korean and a member of the target culture. They choose from a list of alternatives an explanation of the episode and finally, they read feedback paragraphs that explain whether each alternative is likely and why. In culture minidramas, students listen to, watch, or read a series of episodes in which misunderstanding is taking place. They are led in discussion in order to understand how misunderstandings arise when wrong conclusions are reached about the target culture based on one's cultural understanding.

B
Activity Procedure

- Instruct the students to take a sheet of paper and divide it with a line into two halves labeled "Similarities" and "Differences."
- Inform the students that they will be watching a video clip containing information about big holidays, *Chuseok* in Korea and *Thanksgiving Day* in America.
- Ask the students to write down three similarities and three differences between Korean and American holidays, *Chuseok* and *Thanksgiving Day* while watching the video clip twice.
- Put Ss in groups of four and make them have a discussion on the similarities and differences they have observed.
- Have each group create a short script using one of the differences they observed and then do a role-play. Then, conduct a vote to determine the funniest performance.

Referring to the terms in <A>, identify the way of teaching culture exemplified in <B>, and explain the reason for your choice with evidence from <B>. Do NOT copy more than FOUR consecutive words from the passages.

Your Answer

08 Read the passages and follow the directions.

A

Classroom activities such as jigsaw, information gap, problem-solving, decision-making, and opinion exchange can aid students in engaging with the learning process and assuming responsibility for knowledge construction. Below is a table illustrating the characteristics of these tasks.

Table 1

Task Type	Interactant relationship	Interactant requirement	Goal orientation	Outcome options
Jigsaw	two-way	required	convergent	closed
Information gap	one-way OR two-way	required	convergent	closed
Problem solving	one-way OR two-way	optional	convergent	closed
Decision making	one-way OR two-way	optional	convergent	open
Opinion exchange	one-way OR two-way	optional	divergent	open

B

Below are the reflections from students who have taken part in one type of communication activity exemplified in <A>.

Student A's Reflection

In this activity, we were all in groups and each of us had different pieces of information. We had to communicate with each other to gather all the information, whether we wanted to or not. Based on the shared information, we also had to work towards a common goal to complete the task. In the end, all groups achieved the same outcome. After completing the task, our teacher checked our group outcomes and provided appropriate feedback. Thanks to the nature of this activity, we actively communicated and provided necessary support within our groups. If I had attempted this task alone, I might have given up.

New Build Up 영어교육론 **Ⅳ**-2

Student B's Reflection

This task was aimed at selecting one group opinion from five possible alternatives. Unlike jigsaw or information-gap activity, not all group members had to express their opinions to complete the task. Some shy students simply continued to listen to others' ideas. However, all our group members actively participated in the task and decided on our group opinion. Interestingly, since all groups chose different opinions, we were able to enjoy a variety of group presentations. At the end of the class, our teacher provided positive feedback on each group's outcome, emphasizing the importance of diverse opinions.

Referring to Table 1 in <A>, identify the type of task that each student in <B> has engaged in and then write THREE characteristics of the identified task, respectively.

Your Answer

09 Read the passages and follow the directions.

A

Ms. Park's Note

Today, I facilitated a classroom debate on a topic I thought would engage the students: "Should students have homework on weekends?" I divided the class into six groups, further splitting them into two teams. Team A argued for weekend homework, while Team B was against it. After a 15-minute brainstorming session, each team participated in the debate, presenting their arguments in turns. My goal was to foster critical thinking and improve their communication and collaboration skills through this engaging activity. However, the activity didn't go as smoothly as expected. While the topic was of interest to the students, some found it challenging to debate without adequate guidance and preparation. This experience made me understand that debate activities might be too demanding and inappropriate for some students without proper guidance. Moreover, groups with lower English proficiency struggled with communication and collaboration. Without a more proficient member to guide them, they felt unprepared despite investing considerable time. Reflecting on these challenges, I plan to modify my approach to speaking lessons in the future. Instead of debates, I'll introduce a new activity where students are asked to extract and infer new information from the given information. I'm also considering a revised grouping strategy where lower proficiency students are paired with higher proficiency ones to promote collaboration and mutual support within the groups.

B

Eunji's Reflective Log

Today, we engaged in a debate activity during our English-speaking class. The activity was structured in groups, aiming to provide each student with an equal opportunity to express their views. However, my personal experience was not as expected. Despite having several chances to participate, I found the activity challenging due to the absence of reference materials. This led to considerable hesitation and contemplation on my part about what to say. I observed that many of my classmates in other groups encountered similar difficulties. Moreover, the proficiency levels within our group were quite similar. Consequently, those of us with lower proficiency levels faced challenges in communication and collaboration, which seemed contrary to Ms. Park's objectives. For future sessions, I believe a different approach might be more effective. If we were provided with some reference materials or background information for the activity, I think I could participate more actively. Additionally, having group members with higher proficiency levels could facilitate smoother communication and collaboration within the group.

Based on the information in <A> and <B>, identify the problems that students have encountered in the activity and write the name of the new activity and the grouping type that Ms. Park will implement to solve the problems.

Your Answer

Guideline for Pre-service Teachers

10 Read the passages in <A> and <B> and follow the directions.

A

Language teachers use questions to engage their students actively with the language material. An effective questioning technique is one that elicits prompt, motivated, relevant, and full responses. However, if their questions result in long silences, are only answered by the strongest students, dominate the class, or consistently elicit only brief or unsuccessful answers, then there is probably something wrong. Thus, when teachers fail to elicit any response from the learners, they often need to modify their questions. There are a number of modifications devised by teachers, including *syntactic modifications* such as making the topic salient or decomposing complex structures and *semantic modifications* such as paraphrasing difficult words and disambiguation.

B

Classroom 1

During an English lesson, the teacher introduces a challenging text for discussion and begins by asking about the significance of the protagonist's actions in the narrative.

T : Today, we are going to dive into a thought-provoking text. Let's start with a question to get us thinking. How do the actions of the protagonist shape our understanding of the story?
S1 : Um, pro.. protagonist?
T : Oh, yes. Let me clarify. So, how do the actions of the main character shape our understanding of the story?
S1 : Oh, I see. The main character's actions are crucial because they're the key to saving his family.
T : Exactly! You've got it! The main character's actions often serve as the backbone of the story, guiding us through the narrative and revealing key themes. Great job engaging with the question!

Classroom 2

In an English classroom, a teacher initiates a discussion about the basic needs of trees and how to care for them.

T : Good morning, everyone! Today, we're going to talk about how trees grow. Sounds interesting, doesn't it?
S : Yes!
T : Great! So, who can tell me what trees need to be healthy and strong, and how we can help them to grow?
S1 : *(looking confused)* Um, could you say that again? It was a bit much to follow.
T : Of course! I'll break it down. First off, what do trees need to be healthy and strong?
S1 : They need sunlight, water, and good soil.
T : Exactly right! And how can we help them grow?
S2 : By watering them and ensuring they're not crowded, so they have room to expand.
T : Fantastic! Well done, everyone!

T=teacher, S=student

Based on the information in <A>, identify the type of modification that each classroom conversation in <B> exemplifies, respectively. Then explain your answers with evidence from <A> and <B>.

Your Answer

Guideline for Pre-service Teachers

11 Read the passages and follow the directions.

A

The following are the three most common types of modifications observed in conversations between Native and Non-native speakers.

Categories	Types
Modifications of input	(a) Replacing low-frequency vocabulary with more common items when speaking to low proficiency learners. (b) Avoiding idiomatic expressions with lower-level learners.
Modifications of interaction	(a) Using comprehension checks (b) Incorporating pausing
Modifications of information choice	(a) Adjusting the level of descriptive detail (b) Ensuring explicitness in logical development (c) Explaining assumed socio-cultural gaps (e.g. meaning of gestures)

B

Below are two types of teacher talk that Ms. Park has used to narrate a story based on a sequence of six pictures. The students have the same series of pictures but in jumbled order. Their task is to number the pictures to match the story told by the teacher.

Original Teacher Talk	Modified Teacher Talk that Ms. Park has used
(1) the man then thought this was very funny (2) a blind man with his little begging tin	(1) the man (1.0) then (1.0) thought (1.0) this was very (1.5) funny (2) a blind man with a tin + this tin is to collect money + he was begging people + to give him money

( ) : Interval between words (in seconds)
+ : explicitness

Based on <A>, identify the categories of modifications that Ms. Park applies for her students and explain your answers with evidence from <B>.

Your Answer

Guideline for Pre-service Teachers

12 Read the passages and follow the directions.

A

After participating in a teacher workshop focused on creating an interactive classroom, Mr. Kim, a middle school English teacher, realized the significance of teachers' questions. The workshop materials introduced the categories of teacher questions. Below are parts of the workshop materials.

※ *The table below provides typical six categories of teacher questions.*

Categories of Questions

Category	Descriptions
Knowledge question	Eliciting factual answers, testing recall and recognition of information
Inference question	Forming conclusions that are not directly stated in instructional materials
Application question	Applying information heard or read to new situations
Analysis question	Breaking down into parts, relating parts to the whole
Synthesis question	Combining elements into a new pattern
Evaluation question	Making a judgement of good and bad, right or wrong, according to some set of criteria, and stating why

---
B

Below are examples of classroom conversations between a teacher and students. Teacher initiates the conversation by asking a specific type of teacher question.

Conversation 1

Mr. Kim : Today, we've read about renewable energy sources. Now, let's think about how we can utilize this knowledge. Imagine our school decides to become more eco-friendly. Based on what we've read, let's discuss how we could use renewable energy sources to achieve this goal.

Student 1 : We could put solar panels on the school roof to make electricity. This would help us use less energy from sources that can run out.
Student 2 : I like that idea, but what if it's cloudy? We could also put windmills in the schoolyard so we have another way to get energy.
Student 3 : Those are good thoughts, but how do we make sure it doesn't cost too much? Maybe we could try something small to start, like putting lights in the garden that run on solar power.

Conversation 2

Mr. Kim : Let's review what we covered last week about the water cycle. Can anyone tell me what evaporation is?
Student 1 : Isn't it when water turns into vapor and goes up into the sky?
Mr. Kim : Almost correct, but can you explain in more detail what exactly causes water to turn into vapor?
Student 1 : Um, is it because of the sun heating the water?
Mr. Kim : Exactly! The sun's heat causes water from oceans, lakes, and rivers to evaporate into the atmosphere.

Based on the information in <A>, identify each type of teacher question exemplified in Conversation 1 and Conversation 2, respectively. Then, provide the reasons of your choices with evidence from both <A> and <B>.

Guideline for Pre-service Teachers

13 Read the passages in <A> and <B>, and follow the directions.

A

Digital technology is currently being used in various ways in our education, and among them, reading applications provide students with various ways to enhance their reading skills. These applications offer support for students to access texts more easily, understand difficult words, and improve reading speed and comprehension through various activities and exercises. Below are some apps that students can use for their English learning.

[App 1] Bookopolis
- Description: Bookopolis is an online platform designed to engage students in reading and foster a love for literature. It offers a social networking experience where students can discover exciting books and participate in online discussions about books or reading challenges.
- Features: Book recommendations, personalized reading lists, reading challenges and discussions, badges and rewards

[App 2] Lexia Reading
- Description: Lexia Reading is a research-based program designed to help students develop foundational reading skills. It offers personalized learning programs and progress monitoring tools to support students at their individual levels.
- Features: Individualized learning programs, skill-specific activities, real-time progress monitoring

[App 3] LitPick
- Description: LitPick is a website that allows students to read and review books before they are published. Students can join as reviewers, read books, write reviews, and contribute to a global community of young readers.
- Features: Book review assignments, reading contests, author interviews, reader forums

B

Sarah

Sarah is a 1st-year middle school student who struggles to find books that interest her. She often feels overwhelmed when browsing through the library shelves and doesn't know where to begin. Sarah is also hesitant to share her thoughts on books with her classmates face to face, as she tends to be shy. She is looking for an app that can provide personalized help tailored to her needs. She hopes to receive book recommendations that will help her discover new books aligned with her interests. Additionally, she is seeking opportunities to discuss ideas and share her opinions on books online, where she feels more confident.

Jaewon

Jawon is a 3rd-year middle school student who loves reading and has a talent for writing detailed book reviews. However, he often feels that his reviews go unnoticed and wishes to reach a larger audience with his critiques. Jawon is passionate about literature and enjoys analyzing themes and characters in depth. He is looking for an app that will help him showcase his writing talent to a wider community of readers. Through the app, he hopes to share his insightful reviews with other book enthusiasts around the world.

Based on the information in <A> and <B>, identify the single best App that fits each student's needs. Then, explain why this app is the best choice for each student by referencing its description or features from <A> that aligns with their preferences and requirements outlined in <B>.

Your Answer

14 Read the passages in <A> and <B>, and follow the directions.

A

Here are the posts written by two English teachers on an online teacher community dedicated to sharing ideas and offering assistance regarding the use of assessment tools:

Teacher 1's Post

Hello, everyone.

I hope you're all doing well. I teach middle school students and I am currently in search of an appropriate online assessment tool to evaluate their linguistic knowledge throughout the course. I am seeking an assessment tool that can deliver immediate results and also foster competition among my students. Do any of you have any recommendations for online assessment tools that have proven effective in assessing vocabulary and grammar for middle school students? I would greatly appreciate any insights or suggestions you might have.

Teacher 2's Post

Hello, fellow teachers,

I'm currently searching for an online assessment tool to evaluate my students' speaking skills. Specifically, I'm looking for a tool that allows students to post their presentation. Ideally, it should enable students to freely record their presentation when given a topic prompt. It would be great if the tool also supports peer evaluation. If any of you have recommendations for such an assessment tool, I would greatly appreciate your insights and suggestions. Thank you in advance for your assistance!

B

Tool 1

This is an efficient online assessment tool that simplifies the assessment process for both students and educators. Students can effortlessly upload their written assignments, whether directly as text or as files and documents. Educators benefit from the time-saving features as well. They can download all student submissions at once, complete with comments and feedback.

Tool 2

This is an innovative online assessment tool designed to elevate comprehension abilities. This platform offers customizable reading levels and diverse reading formats to cater to individual student needs. Real-time progress tracking and adaptive assessments ensure personalized learning experiences. Interactive questions and immediate feedback promote critical thinking and comprehension skills.

Tool 3

This is an innovative online assessment tool that not only enables students to freely upload their speaking performance on a chosen topic but also fosters peer feedback. As students watch each other's presentation and give and receive feedback, they can simultaneously refine their speaking levels, all the while gaining confidence in their abilities.

Tool 4

This is an online quiz maker designed for the continuous assessment of students' vocabulary and grammar in a language course. Educators can make multiple-choice questions online and ask students to answer them instantly by using their portable devices. It incorporates functions to promote friendly rivalry among students while providing immediate test results (showing the name who wins the first place, etc).

Tool 5

This is a cutting-edge online assessment tool crafted to evaluate and enhance students' clear pronunciation skills. This innovative platform is dedicated to helping educators gauge and improve students' articulation, and phonetic accuracy. It offers a variety of pronunciation exercises, encompassing sounds, words, and phrases, ensuring thorough assessment coverage.

Based on <A>, for each teacher, suggest the ONE most appropriate tool in <B> that satisfies their needs. Then, explain your answers with evidence from <B>. Do NOT copy more than FOUR consecutive words from the passages.

Your Answer

15 Examine the evaluation results of a teaching tool by a review committee in <A> and read Ms. Jang's comments in <B>. Then, follow the directions.

A

Evaluation of Three CMC Tools

Criteria		Tool A	Tool B	Tool C
User Experience	User-friendly design	Good	Okay	Good
	Supportive features for diverse learners (e.g., subtitles, text-to-speech technology)	Okay	Good	Poor
Content Quality	Accuracy and relevance of the educational content	Poor	Good	Poor
	Alignment with curriculum standards and learning objectives	Good	Good	Good
Engagement and Interactivity	Variety and effectiveness of interactive elements	Good	Okay	Good
	Real-time feedback support	Poor	Good	Poor
Assessment and Tracking Features	Availability and variety of assessment tools	Poor	Okay	Good
	Detailed analytics for educators	Okay	Good	Good
Security and Privacy	Security features to protect user data	Okay	Good	Okay

2. Classroom Context

Guideline for Pre-service Teachers

B

Ms. Jang's Comments

To enhance English interaction among my students, I plan to integrate a Computer-Mediated Communication (CMC) tool into my lessons. The ideal CMC tool must meet specific criteria: it should support students with relatively low proficiency levels by offering comprehensive support features, such as providing subtitles and assistive technology that reads the text aloud. Additionally, I seek a tool that provides instant feedback so that students can promptly recognize language errors and self-correct them. Furthermore, the tool should offer comprehensive analytics on each student's performance and learning progress, allowing me to give personalized instruction tailored to individual needs. With these key features, I am confident that the chosen tool will cultivate a dynamic and inclusive learning environment, ensuring every student's success.

Considering the information in <A> and <B>, choose the ONE CMC tool you would recommend for Ms. Jang and provide THREE reasons for recommending it based on its characteristics.

Your Answer

16 Read the passages in <A> and <B>, and follow the directions.

A

Below are the teaching logs written by two English teachers.

Teacher 1's Teaching Log

Recently, it has become evident that many students are struggling to understand the meanings of words in their reading assignments. This concerns me because it hinders their comprehension and affects their overall engagement and confidence as readers. While my students have appropriate grammar skills, their vocabulary is relatively limited. As a result, I feel a strong need to provide explicit vocabulary lessons. Vocabulary knowledge varies significantly among students, depending on their proficiency levels. Therefore, I plan to find an app that allows for explicit vocabulary instruction during lessons. I hope to find one that can recommend and teach words suitable for each student's proficiency, ensuring they receive instruction tailored to their individual needs.

Teacher 2's Teaching Log

I'm concerned about my students' English listening skills, particularly their difficulty in identifying specific pieces of information when listening to English audio. They often struggle to find details, leading to incomplete understanding. As their teacher, I feel responsible for addressing these issues and providing the necessary support. In the coming weeks, I plan to teach various strategies to improve their listening comprehension. To support this, I am looking for an application that promotes active engagement and immediate application of various listening strategies. I hope this will help my students enhance their English listening skills.

B

App 1

This program focuses on improving students' speaking skills through interactive exercises and speaking activities. It provides opportunities for students to practice speaking in simulated real-life situations, such as conversations, presentations, and role-plays. Feedback and pronunciation practice are integrated to help students develop clear and confident speech.

App 2

This program uses engaging activities to explicitly teach students new words and their meanings. It includes quizzes, games, and discussions that allow students to interact with the content and deepen their understanding. Additionally, adaptive learning algorithms adjust the learning experience based on each student's proficiency, ensuring that vocabulary instruction is tailored to individual needs or abilities.

App 3

This program aims to teach grammar concepts in a clear and structured manner. It provides comprehensive lessons on grammar rules, including explanations, examples, and practice exercises. Interactive quizzes and drills help reinforce understanding and mastery of grammar concepts, covering topics such as verb tenses, sentence structure, and parts of speech.

App 4

Focused on improving reading comprehension, this program offers a variety of reading materials and comprehension exercises. Students have access to authentic texts, including articles, stories, and passages, covering a range of topics and genres. Interactive features such as highlighting, annotating, and comprehension questions support active reading and deeper understanding.

App 5

This program is designed to enhance students' listening comprehension skills through targeted exercises that focus on various listening strategies. What makes this program unique is its specialization in helping students practice skills such as listening for specific information, identifying important details, and understanding main ideas. Additionally, it features a real-time application of these strategies, allowing students to assess their comprehension immediately after each exercise.

Based on the information provided in <A>, suggest the ONE most suitable App from <B> for each teacher, taking into account their specific needs. Then, support your answers with evidence from <B>.

Your Answer

17 Read the passages, and follow the directions.

A

Digital technology equips students with an array of new tools for effective language learning. Here are some apps that can enhance their English learning experience:

App 1

Quick Overview: An app that corrects grammatical errors in real-time, offering explanations to enhance understanding.
Key Features:
- Instant Corrections: Fixes errors as you type.
- Feedback: Provides reasons for corrections.
- Progress Tracker: Highlights areas of improvement.

App 2

Quick Overview: An AI-based app for practicing natural English conversations, simulating interactions with native speakers.
Key Features:
- AI Dialogues: Engages in realistic conversations.
- Pronunciation Aid: Gives feedback on pronunciation during the speech.
- Diverse Scenarios: Includes various speaking situations.

App 3

Quick Overview: A vocabulary game that adjusts to the user's level, making learning new words fun and interactive.
Key Features:
- Level-Based Learning: Tailors vocabulary to user level.
- Engaging Games: Focuses on word-definition matches.
- Progress Tracking: Monitors and rewards learning advancement.

B

Below are activities developed by Mr. Park to teach his students learning strategies.

Activity 1

Before You Listen

Work in pairs. Look at the ad on page 134 for a bicycle shop from the yellow pages of the telephone book. What things do you think you might hear on a telephone message for this store? Make a list. Then compare your answers with one other student's.

1. _____
2. _____
3. _____

Activity 2

E. Listen for Numbers

Read these questions about the story asking How *far* and How *long*. Then listen to the story again and answer with the questions.

1. How long are they going to be on vacation? _____
2. How far is from Ohio to the Shenandoah National Park? _____
3. How long are they going to stay at the park? _____
4. How far is it from the park to Wilmington? _____
5. How long are they going to stay in North Carolina? _____
6. How far is it from Wilmington to Orlando? _____
7. How far are they staying from Disney World? _____
8. How far is it from Orlando back to Columbus? _____

Referring to the terms in <A>, identify ONE (or TWO) strategy(ies) that each activity requires in <B>. Then, explain your answers with evidence from both <A> and <B>.

Your Answer

_____
_____
_____
_____

03 Read the passages and follow the directions.

A

Language learning strategies are classified in different ways. Oxford (1990) divides learning strategies into two big categories: direct and indirect strategies. Direct strategies deal with language while indirect strategies deal with the general management of learning. Furthermore, Oxford classified direct strategies and indirect strategies into 3 types, respectively. The direct strategies include memory strategies, cognitive strategies, and compensation strategies, while indirect strategies include metacognitive strategies, affective strategies, and social strategies. The different types of learning strategies can be seen in the following table.

	Categories	Types
Learning Strategies	Direct strategies: dealing with language	memory strategies
		cognitive strategies
		compensation strategies
	Indirect strategies: dealing with the general management of learning	metacognitive strategies
		affective strategies
		social strategies

B

Ms. Kim's Teaching Note

I am teaching low-intermediate level students in a middle school. Based on the results of a diagnostic test conducted earlier this semester, their reading proficiency was relatively low compared to other language skills (e.g. listening, and speaking). Thus, I am planning to have a special reading lesson to teach them how skilled readers read a text. Skilled readers understand and monitor their reading process while naturally and automatically using appropriate reading strategies. Hence, I prepared the following lesson to help my students plan and monitor necessary reading strategies as good readers.

Guideline for Pre-service Teachers

Lesson Procedure

1. I provide Ss with an interesting short story to read.
2. I talk about some reading strategies for today with the whole class. (ex. predicting, visualizing, questioning, clarifying, etc.) I state the purposes for learning reading strategies.
3. I let Ss know that I will be stopping at different points to think about what I have read.
4. I begin reading aloud the story and demonstrate my thinking as I read. (ex. "I don't know this word. Does it have a prefix or a suffix to guess what it means? Are there any clues that may help?") I talk about how to analyze and understand what I just read.
6. While modeling how to use each reading strategy, I write down some of my thoughts on the board. (ex. I can predict that ~, I can picture ~, This reminds me of ~, etc) and ask Ss to decide which strategy I have modeled each time.
7. After the demonstration, I ask Ss to read a portion of a story with a partner and take turns vocalizing their thoughts while they read to each other.

Based on \<A\> and \<B\>, identify the category and its specific type that Ms. Kim intends to teach her students. Then, explain the teaching technique that Ms. Kim uses in \<B\> to facilitate the identified strategies.

Your Answer

04 Read the passages and follow the directions.

A

Strategies for Reading Comprehension

For most second language learners who are already literate in a previous language, reading comprehension is primarily a matter of developing appropriate, and efficient comprehension strategies. Some strategies are related to bottom-up processes, and others enhance the top-down processes. Below are five strategies that can be readily integrated into your classroom techniques.

Strategy 1. Identify the purpose in reading.
Strategy 2. Use efficient silent reading technique for improving fluency.
Strategy 3. Scan the text for specific information.
Strategy 4. Use the visual aid to help readers comprehend the ideas or events.
Strategy 5. Guess and infer implied meaning between the lines.

B

Below are the students' logs after taking the reading lesson today.

Student A's Log

In today's English class, I participated in a unique reading activity. Unlike our usual routine where we read a text and answer questions about it, today our teacher introduced a different approach. She gave us an engaging story that was about 10 pages long. Before we started reading, she gave a short overview of the story. She advised us to avoid vocalizing the words while reading, suggesting that we process the content in chunks, not word-by-word, for better comprehension. The aim was to improve our reading fluency by letting us read the text silently and continuously. She allotted 50 minutes for this task. I really liked the story and read it without getting distracted. I enjoyed the story and remained focused throughout. When I encountered unfamiliar words, I inferred their meanings from the context, allowing me to maintain a steady reading pace. This was my first experience of reading at such a speed. As an English learner, I typically read at a slower pace. Today's independent reading activity notably improved my reading speed and fluency.

Guideline for Pre-service Teachers

Student B's Log

In today's reading class, my teacher gave us a fun group activity to help understand a complex story. First, we read through the story twice quickly, focusing on grasping its main point and important parts. Then, the teacher put us in groups of four to work together. He gave us a worksheet and asked us to draw a map that showed what happened in the story. My friends and I started by writing down the main idea at the top. From there, we outlined elements such as the characters, the challenges they faced, the reasons behind those challenges, their reactions, and the story's conclusion. Importantly, we connected all these things back to the main idea to show the whole story. Making this semantic map helped me a lot. It prevented me from feeling overwhelmed by the lengthy and complex narrative. It helped me organize the story structure effectively and made everything clear.

Based on <A>, identify ONE reading strategy that each student in <B> describes in their logs and write the major benefit of using each strategy from the student's viewpoint.

Your Answer

05 Read the passage in <A> and the conversation in <B>. Then, follow the directions.

A

Strategic competence refers to a person's ability to keep the communication going when there is a communication breakdown or to enhance the effectiveness of the communication. It means being able to get one's message across through the use of repetition, modulation of volume, and other methods listed below. This ability holds particular significance for English language learners at lower proficiency levels. Common instances of strategic competence include *avoidance, circumlocution, word coinage, prefabricated patterns, appeal to authority,* and *keeping the floor.*

B

Emily, a native English speaker is a seller at a sneaker shop, and Minsoo, a beginner-level English speaker, is trying to buy a pair of sneakers. Last night, he looked for several expressions and memorized useful stock phrases. Below is an excerpt from the conversation between them.

Emily : Good afternoon. Welcome to Emily's Sneaker Shop! We have some awesome sneakers for you today.
Minsoo : Hi! Good afternoon. *(He chooses one pair of sneakers. So he uses a memorized stock phrase and asks the price.)* How much?
Emily : They're on sale today for just 10 dollars!
Minsoo : Great! *(He recalls the line he memorized again.)* Can I try these?
Emily : Of course. What size are you?
Minsoo : Size 270.
Emily : *(Bring the sneakers)* Try these sneakers! You're going to love them!
Minsoo : *(He tries on red sneakers. He wants to ask if there is another color but he cannot remember what to say.)* Well... Do you have different, I mean... colors, like, different colors?
Emily : *(looking around)* Yes! we have blue, green, and black ones too!
Minsoo : Awesome! Then, a black one, please!
Emily : Sure! (Bring the black one)

Guideline for Pre-service Teachers

Referring to terms in <A>, explain all communication strategies that Minsoo uses in <B> and provide corresponding evidence for each strategy from <B>.

Your Answer

06 Read the passage in <A> and the conversation in <B>, and follow the directions.

A

In the process of meaning negotiation, uptake refers to an interlocutor's immediate response to his or her partner's signal of noncomprehension. In uptake, the interlocutor often uses a variety of communication strategies such as circumlocution, word coinage, message abandonment, topic change, foreignizing, and literal translation.

B

The following is part of a teacher-student classroom conversation that includes meaning negotiation.

T : Good morning, class. Today we're discussing animals that can live both in water and on land. Who can give me an example?
S1: There's a hopswimmer!
T : *(looking curious)* A "hopswimmer"? Can you explain what you mean?
S1: *(trying to explain)* It's an animal hops around the ponds and swims. But, actually, I don't know what it is called.
T : Haha! You might be thinking of a toad! Now, can anyone tell me about the features of this animal?
S2: They have a lung [long]. A good lung [long].
T : Can you say that again?
S2: They have...sort of... Never mind.
T : No worries! Language can be tricky sometimes. Let's open it up to the class to help out.

T=teacher, S=student

Considering the information in <A> and <B>, identify the utterances where the uptake takes place and then, explain the communication strategies used in the identified utterances.

Your Answer

07 Read the passages and follow the directions.

A

Subject: Feedback and Request for Help with Group Activities

Dear Ms. Kim,

My name is Jimmy, and I'd like to provide feedback on our recent English classes. First, I am really enjoying your lessons. In particular, I love the topics that are closely related to our daily lives and the diverse activities that facilitate the development of our language skills. Moreover, I love group activities, too, which seem to make a dynamic classroom and accelerate mutual communication between us. However, if there is one thing I feel wanting, communication breakdowns frequently occur during group activities due to different proficiency levels. For example, as a high-intermediate level student, my job is to help lower-level students smoothly complete the group task. However, whenever I explained verbally how to attack the task, there were communication breakdowns between us. Lower-level students seemed not to understand what I said. Particularly, they did not understand some words I used. However, I do not know how to say these words into much easier ones or expressions. Another problem is that lower-level students pretend to understand everything even though they do not understand it at all. To avoid communication breakdowns, thus, they need to request for elaboration or let me know they have no understanding. Therefore, I hope you also teach lower-level students the most effective way to overcome such a communication problem. I believe that learning effective communication strategies will benefit all of us by improving understanding and communication.

Thank you for your time, and I look forward to hearing from you.

Sincerely,
Jimmy

Guideline for Pre-service Teachers

B
Ms. Kim's Teaching Note

I recently received an email from one of my students, Jimmy, requesting that I teach some communication strategies during my English lessons. He expressed his desire to overcome communication barriers that arise between students with different proficiency levels. As a result, I have planned a lesson to teach my students appropriate communication strategies in our next lesson. Firstly, for higher-level students, I will introduce a "speed game" where they will need to explain or describe words to their partner. In this game, one student will become the "narrator" (Student A) and the other will become the "player" (Student B). The narrator will be given a set of words and will need to provide descriptions and examples of the target word to help the player identify what the word is. The game is played in pairs, and the pair who figures out the most words will be the winner. As for lower-level students, I will teach them the strategy of directly asking for clarification. By asking questions like "Can you say that again?" or "Pardon me?", they can tell their group members that they have zero understanding of the preceding words or concepts. Then, higher-level students in their groups would provide simpler explanations or additional information to help them better comprehend difficult words or concepts. Overall, these strategies can facilitate communication among students with different proficiency levels and foster a more inclusive and collaborative learning environment.

Identify TWO types of communication strategies that Ms. Kim plans to teach in <B>. Then, write how each strategy can help students with different proficiency levels to solve the communication problems described in <A>.

Your Answer

08 Read the passages in <A> and <B>, and follow the directions.

A

Communication strategies, also known as compensatory strategies, are vital in helping students prevent communication breakdowns during conversations. These types of communication strategies include avoidance (e.g., phonological, syntactic, and lexical); code switching, word coinage, appeal to authority (e.g., direct and indirect), using prefabricated patterns, and foreignizing. Actually, these strategies enable students to engage more effectively in conversations, particularly when communicating in a second language.

B

Two students, Min-ho and Ji-hyun, reflect on their performances in an English-speaking class after watching their presentation recordings. They discuss the strategies they used to overcome their individual challenges.

Min-ho : Hey Ji-hyun, did you get a chance to watch our presentation recordings from the speaking lesson?
Ji-hyun : Yeah, I just finished reviewing mine. What about you, Min-ho? How was yours?
Min-ho : I watched mine, too, and I realized I was quite strategic in my topic selection.
Ji-hyun : Oh? You chose future technology as your topic, which sounds pretty challenging. Why did you pick that one?
Min-ho : Honestly, I chose it because I'm not good at using past tense. Most of the other topics the teacher suggested involved talking about past experiences. But, by choosing future technology, I could stick to future tense.
Ji-hyun : That was really smart. I think it was a great way to manage your difficulty at the time.

Guideline for Pre-service Teachers

> Min-ho : Yeah, I felt much more at ease with a tense I'm confident in.
> Ji-hyun : Speaking of strategies, I noticed something in my own presentation, too. When discussing the causes of the Korean War, I said, 'The invasion started in 1950 by...?' with a rising intonation and then looked at my teacher with a confused expression. Then she filled in, 'North Korean forces.'
> Min-ho : That's a clever move.
> Ji-hyun : Exactly. Watching the recording of my presentation was a great learning experience. It made me realize that even if my English isn't perfect, I can still go through a presentation by using different speaking strategies.
> Min-ho : Absolutely.

Based on terms in <A>, identify the specific communication strategies that Min-ho and Ji-hyun employed in their presentations. Then, explain your choices with evidence from <B>.

Your Answer _____

_____

_____

_____

_____

NEW Build Up

Chapter 03

Receptive Skills

Chapter 03

Receptive Skills

정답 및 모범 답안 p. 453

1 How to Teach Listening Skills

01 Read the passages in <A> and <B>, and follow the directions.

― A ―

Ms. Park, a middle school English teacher, introduces a listening activity designed for her high-intermediate students. She emphasizes the importance of this activity in providing a comprehensive learning experience that not only improves language proficiency but also fosters teamwork and critical thinking among students. Ms. Park has invited five colleagues to observe the class and provide feedback to further refine her teaching methods.

Activity Procedure

1. Preparation	• T starts the lesson by briefly explaining the activity and its benefits. • T introduces new vocabulary from the listening script, using visuals, synonyms, and example sentences to ensure comprehension.
2. Listening for Meaning	• T reads a script at a natural pace, asking students to listen without taking notes. • After the first listening, students share their understanding of the story's general plot and main ideas in pairs.
3. Listening for Note-Taking	T reads the script again, this time allowing students to take brief notes on key phrases they have listened.
4. Text Reconstruction in Groups	• T puts Ss in groups of four and asks them to combine their notes and reconstruct the text paying attention to the content and language form. • Each group discusses and negotiates the wording, grammar, and structure, promoting collaborative learning. • T walks around the classroom and provides help for groups.

5. Text Comparison	• Groups present their reconstructed texts, and T displays the original script. • Each group compares their own version and the original script, highlighting similarities and differences in both content and language usage.

After the lesson, Ms. Park invites her colleagues to share their observations and insights. Each observer provides short comments.

B

The followings are parts of the comments from the five teachers after observing Ms. Park's lesson.

- Teacher 1: I was particularly impressed by how the teacher introduced new vocabulary before the main activity, which seemed to help students feel more prepared and confident.
- Teacher 2: Following several listenings, students were supposed to reconstruct the text, taking into account its original content using the notes they have made. Consequently, the objective of the lesson necessitates that students concentrate on structure.
- Teacher 3: The students were clearly engaged and collaborating effectively particularly during the "Text Reconstruction in Groups" and "Text Comparison" stages.
- Teacher 4: In this lesson, the teacher effectively acted her role by controlling students in reconstructing the text.
- Teacher 5: The activity effectively combined listening, speaking, writing, and collaborative learning. It was wonderful to see the students' active involvement and teamwork.

Identify the TWO teachers in <B> whose comments are NOT correct. Then, explain your answers with evidence from <A> and <B>.

Your Answer

Guideline for Pre-service Teachers

02 Read the passages and follow the directions.

A

Listening Activity Procedure

1. T asks Ss to listen to the following recorded speech.

> Crash! was perhaps the most famous pop group of that time. It consisted of three female singers, with no band. They came originally from Manchester, and began singing in local clubs, but their fame soon spread throughout the British Isles and then all over the world. Their hairstyle and clothes were imitated by a whole generation of teenager, and thousands came to hear them sing, bought recordings of their songs or went to see their films.

2. T makes Ss answer the multiple-choice questions below.

   (1) Crash! was _____.
      a) notorious   b) well-known
      c) unpopular   d) local

   (2) The group was composed of _____.
      a) three boys   b) two girls and a boy
      c) two boys and a girl   d) three girls

   (3) The group was from _____.
      a) Britain   b) France
      c) Brazil   d) Egypt

   (4) A lot of young people wanted to _____.
      a) sing like them   b) look like them
      c) live in Manchester   d) all of these

3. T checks the answers with the whole class.

B
Students' Reflections

S1: In today's listening lesson, my teacher asked us to answer multiple-choice questions after listening to a recorded speech. So, I tried to listen to the recording very carefully but I couldn't remember all. That's why I couldn't give the correct answers to most of the questions. I thought about the reasons carefully. Then, I realized that I had not known what to listen to before listening so, I had no choice but to catch every detail from the recorded speech. Without a clear purpose for listening, the listening activity was too demanding for me and I could not catch that many details. If I had had a chance to see the questions in advance of listening, I would have listened to the script more effectively.

S2: Today's listening lesson was very demanding for me. Usually, my teacher introduces the topic for the day and provides us with related photos or personal questions to check my current knowledge and experience about the topic. However, today, there was no step for it. Without any preparation, the teacher asked us to directly listen to the recording. Thus, it was quite difficult to understand what the recording was about. Although I tried my best to find out what the story was about, it was fruitless and I could not answer the multiple-choice questions precisely.

S=student

Considering the information in <A> and <B>, suggest what the teacher should prepare to compensate for the listening lesson that students mentioned in <B> and write the reasons for your answer.

Your Answer

03 Read the listening activity procedure in <A> and the conversation in <B>. Then follow the directions.

A

Mr. Choi is an English teacher in a middle school teaching low-intermediate level students. Below is a listening activity procedure designed by Mr. Choi.

Step 1	Listen to the recording about *The Internet of Things (IoT) and a smart farm*. [Listening Script] The Internet of Things (IoT) has provided ways to improve nearly every industry imaginable. In agriculture, IoT has not only provided solutions to often time-consuming and tedious tasks but is totally changing the way we think about agriculture. What exactly is a smart farm, though? Here is a rundown of what smart farming is and how it's changing agriculture. What Is a Smart Farm? Smart farming refers to managing farms using modern Information and communication technologies to increase the quantity and quality of products while optimizing the human labor required.

Step 2	• Look at the words below.
	• Use a dictionary to check the meaning of any you are not sure about.
	  - **Nouns**: The Internet of Things (IoT), industry, agriculture, rundown, technologies
	  - **Verbs**: provide, improve, manage, increase, optimize
	  - **Adjectives**: imaginable, time-consuming, tedious, required

Step 3	After listening to the recording again, fill in the blanks. _____ has provided ways to _____ nearly every industry imaginable. ___ agriculture, IoT has not _____ provided solutions to often _____ and tedious tasks _____ is totally changing the ____ we think about agriculture. _____ exactly is a smart _____, though? Here is a _____ of what smart farming _____ and how it's changing _____.

200

B

Mr. Choi, a new English teacher in a middle school, seeks advice from the senior teacher, Ms. Yoo, regarding the listening activity he has designed.

Mr. Choi : Ms. Yoo, do you have a moment to review the listening activity I've created? It's my first lesson plan for teaching listening to first graders, and I want the activity to be well-suited for my students.

Ms. Yoo : Of course. May I take a look? *(She examines the procedure.)* Well… I'm wondering if your students are familiar with the topic, *a smart farm*. Do you think they have sufficient background knowledge about it?

Mr. Choi : To be honest, Probably not. I chose this topic because it is one of the up-to-date topics these days.

Ms. Yoo : If your students do not have enough topic knowledge, they can fail to comprehend their listening. So, before listening, check if they already have knowledge related to the topic or not.

Mr. Choi : If they don't, what should I do?

Ms. Yoo : In that case, you should activate students' schemata through a brainstorming session as a pre-listening activity. Also, if necessary, you can provide some essential information.

Mr. Choi : That's a good idea! I'll include a pre-listening activity. Is there anything else?

Ms. Yoo : Well, I'm still wondering if the lesson you planned mainly focuses on listening.

Mr. Choi : Definitely, I planned a listening lesson.

Ms. Yoo : Actually, the listening activity you planned seems too demanding because it has lots of blanks. Also, as an after-listening activity, it requires students' reading and writing skills, rather than listening skills, which results in increasing the cognitive load for low-intermediate students.

Mr. Choi : Hmm, you're right. Anyway, I want to facilitate their listening comprehension only. Then, how should I modify the task? Any recommendations?

Guideline for Pre-service Teachers

> Ms. Yoo : How about asking students to fill in the blank while listening? I mean you arrange students to dictate some key words so that they can focus on listening itself.
> Mr. Choi : You say a partial dictation activity?
> Ms. Yoo : Exactly!
> Mr. Choi : Perfect, I'll modify the task then. Thank you for your valuable advice, Ms. Yoo.

Based on the information in <A> and <B>, identify TWO issues(challenges) that may arise during Mr. Choi's listening lesson. Then, discuss how the solutions suggested in <B> can address these issues.

Your Answer

04 Read the passages and follow the directions.

A

The importance of comprehension cannot be overstated in the realm of education. Comprehension, often viewed through the lens of constructivism, hinges on the active engagement of students' prior knowledge. To facilitate effective comprehension, it is essential to employ pre-activities that activate and harness students' existing knowledge and experiences. These pre-activities serve as the key to unlocking meaningful learning experiences. They allow students to draw upon their *socio-cultural knowledge*, which encompasses the cultural, social, and historical context that shapes their understanding of the world. Consideration of sociocultural aspects of language is increasingly important in English language teaching because it allows learners to explore the contexts the target language functions in, and how these contexts affect linguistic choices. Furthermore, *linguistic knowledge* plays a pivotal role in comprehension. Language is not merely a medium of communication; it is a tool that structures our thoughts and understanding. Pre-activities that tap into students' *linguistic knowledge*, including vocabulary and grammatical structures, empower them to decode and interpret text effectively. This linguistic foundation serves as a scaffold upon which comprehension can be built. In addition to *socio-cultural* and *linguistic knowledge, extratextual knowledge* also plays a vital role. It encompasses the broader, real-world context that extends beyond the boundaries of the text itself. Pre-activities that encourage students to bring their *extratextual knowledge* into the learning process enable them to make connections between what they will read and their understanding of the world around them. This bridges the gap between the theoretical content of the text and its practical applications.

B

Ms. Choi's Lesson

Below is part of the teacher's talk during her lesson.

Today, I'd like to talk to you about an exciting topic related to our listening comprehension goals: "tip culture." Let me explain this briefly. I'm sure many of you have heard about tipping when you visit restaurants and cafes, or even when you receive certain services. Tipping is the practice of giving extra money, known as a "tip," to someone who has provided you with a service. But here's the interesting part: tipping culture can vary widely from one country to another. In some places, tipping is customary and expected, while in others, it's not as common. Does that make sense to everyone?

Ms. Kim's Lesson

Below is part of the classroom conversation between the teacher and students.

Ms. Kim : Good morning, everyone!
Students : Good morning!
Ms. Kim : Today, we have an exciting topic to explore—future technology. But before we dive into our reading activity, let's have a brainstorming session. I want to hear about your own experiences and thoughts regarding future technology.
Student 1 : Well, I recently read about self-driving cars. It's amazing how they might change the way we commute.
Ms. Kim : That's a great point! Self-driving cars do have the potential to revolutionize transportation. Anybody else have thoughts on self-driving cars or other futuristic modes of transportation?
Student 2 : I'm fascinated by the idea of hyperloop transportation. It could make long-distance travel much faster and more energy-efficient.

Based on <A>, identify the type of schematic knowledge that each teacher wants to activate for successful text comprehension. Then, support your choice with evidence from <B>.

Your Answer

Guideline for Pre-service Teachers

05 Read the passages and follow the directions.

A

Students' Reflections

Jaebum	Native English speakers speak at such a fast pace that I often find it necessary to listen to their speech several times to fully comprehend the meaning. In listening, unlike reading, I am unable to go back to the previous line while listening to a story because the next one quickly follows. But, I really want to avoid repeated listening. What shall I do? Are there any effective strategies to understand the story only with one time of listening?
Mina	When I listen to the spoken text, I have a strong desire to understand every word. If I happen to miss any words during the listening process, I feel like I've failed, all of which make me get worried and stressed. I tried to focus on the most important and specific information more effectively but, I couldn't. That's why I ask for some help from Ms. Yoo. In the next class, I hope she can give us chances to practice some corresponding listening strategies.

B
Ms. Yoo's Teaching Reflection

In reflecting on my teaching experiences, I have observed that many of my middle school students encounter similar listening challenges to those mentioned by Jaebum and Mina. One common issue is the rate of delivery, particularly for students at the low intermediate level like Jaebum. He struggles to keep up with the normal speed of native speakers. To address this, my plan is to teach him about one characteristic of spoken language. More specifically, in most conversations, speakers often employ rephrasing, repetitions, and elaborations. For listeners, these can provide additional information or extra time to process the information they have just heard or missed. Thus, teaching Jaebum these features will assist him in clarifying the meaning of what he might have misunderstood in the fast flow of spoken language. On the other hand, Mina faces difficulties in selectively listening to key information. To tackle this problem, I will provide pre-set questions before listening to the spoken text. These questions can help students like Mina focus on specific information related to them during the listening. In the way mentioned before, I will continue to help my students solve their listening problems and enhance their listening comprehension more and more.

Based on <A> and <B>, identify the characteristic of the spoken language that Ms. Yoo will teach Jaebum and write how it can help him. Additionally, explain the listening strategy that Ms. Yoo will teach Mina to solve her listening problem with evidence from <B>.

Your Answer

Guideline for Pre-service Teachers

06 Read the passages and follow the directions.

A
Lesson Procedure

Step 1	• Put a box and a ball on the front table. • Move the ball and the box while saying the sentences. 　e.g. A ball is on the box. 　　　The ball is above the box. (Target forms: under, above, below, by, next to, between, in front of, opposite, behind) • Check students' comprehension with interactions.
Step 2	• Provide students with some pictures. • Have students listen to an audio file and select the right picture describing the sentence from the listening file. 　e.g. listening script: 　　　1) The treasure was hidden beneath the old oak tree. 　　　2) She placed her keys behind the vase on the shelf. 　　　3) The stars twinkled above us in the clear night sky. • Check the answers with the whole class.
Step 3	• Have students listen to another audio file. • This time, ask them to listen to short sentences and draw what they hear on their notes. 　e.g. There are two squares of varying sizes. A smaller one is positioned in front of a larger one. • Check the answers with the whole class.
Step 4	• Distribute a picture of three students and a worksheet. • Have students listen to a new audio file and write the action that each person is doing in order. 　e.g. Who is Minji? She is the one riding a swing. So, who is the boy playing in front of Minji? He is Jiwhoo. 　　Minji: riding a swing. 　　Jiwhoo: _____ 　　Sean: _____ • Check the answers with the whole class.

B
Student's Log

Today's listening activity was a perfect fit for improving my listening skills. Unlike previous lessons where listening tasks were often coupled with extensive reading and writing adding to my cognitive load and overwhelming me, today's session was purely focused on listening. This allowed me to truly concentrate solely on understanding the content by attentively listening to the provided scripts. The absence of reading or writing tasks seemed to be well-suited for my current level and helped reduce my cognitive load on the task. Most importantly, I was able to fully comprehend all the information from the audio files, marking my first successful completion of a listening task.

Explain the listening technique described in Steps 3 and 4 with respective evidence from <A> and then, write the primary benefit of the identified technique from the student's perspective in <B>.

Your Answer

07 Read the passages and follow the directions.

A

Below are the basic types of oral production.

1. Imitative: Students simply imitate a word or phrase or possibly a sentence. Although this is a purely phonetic level of oral production, a number of prosodic (intonation, rhythm, etc.), lexical, and grammatical properties of language may be included in the performance criteria.
2. Intensive: Students need to produce only a limited amount of language in a highly control context. They must be aware of semantic properties to respond, but interaction with an interlocutor is minimal at best.
3. Responsive: It includes interaction and test comprehension but at the limited level of very short conversations, standard greetings with small talk, simple questions and answers, and the like. It tends to start with genuine referential questions in which the respondent is given more opportunity to produce meaningful language.
4. Interactive: It includes multiple exchanges and/or multiple participants. Interaction can be broken down into two types: *transactional* language and *interpersonal* exchanges.
5. Extensive: The tasks include speeches, oral presentations, and story-telling, during which the opportunity for oral interaction from listeners is either highly limited or ruled out altogether.

B

Activity A

※ Students hear the questions and respond with ONE or TWO sentences at most.

1. What do you think about the weather today?
2. What is your favorite foreign language to learn?
3. Have you ever been to the United States?
4. What other countries have you visited?

Activity B

※ Students see the following six-picture sequence and tell the story that these pictures describe. The teacher will listen to your story without asking questions or giving feedback and comments.

Based on <A>, identify the type of oral production that each activity in <B> focuses on, respectively. Then, write the reason of your answers with evidence from <A> and <B>.

Your Answer

Guideline for Pre-service Teachers

08 Read <A> and <B> and follow the directions.

--- A ---

Below is a table showing the differences between extensive listening and intensive listening.

	Extensive listening	Intensive listening
Objective	For pleasure	For information
Listening material	Chosen by Students	Chosen by Teacher
Advantage		Allow students to practice listening focusing on certain elements of spoken language
Disadvantage	• Difficult to assess students' listening • Difficult to know what problems students are having	

--- B ---

Ms. Park's Teaching Note

Today, I conducted an English lesson in a classroom that was equipped with as many computers as there were students. I had asked my students to search online for their own materials that they wanted to listen to. The objective of today's listening session was purely for enjoyment and overall improvement in English. It was evident that the students enjoyed their listening experience without the pressure of completing listening tasks. The topics of the listening materials varied greatly, reflecting the diverse interests of the students. As a result, I was unable to assess whether each student fully understood the content they were listening to. However, I ensured that my students were deeply engaged and felt motivated during today's listening lesson, which was a departure from our usual lessons.

Mr. Kim's Teaching Note

Today, I chose a video clip about the soccer player, Lee Kang-in as the listening material, anticipating that the students would enjoy the lesson based on this interesting topic. However, the outcome was not as expected. To ensure accurate comprehension and to help students distinguish confusing sound streams, I frequently paused the video, sometimes as often as every 5 seconds. Although the video clip was only three minutes long, these frequent pauses resulted in the students only being able to listen to one-third of the spoken text. While repeated listening can sometimes aid in understanding the content and sounds more effectively, it was not always the case in today's lesson. Due to time constraints and the frequent repetition, we were only able to cover a small portion of today's content.

Referring to Table in <A>, identify each listening method employed by Ms. Park and Mr. Kim. Then, using the information in <B>, discuss the advantages of extensive listening and the challenges of intensive listening from the perspectives of Ms. Park and Mr. Kim.

Your Answer

Guideline for Pre-service Teachers

2 How to Teach Reading Skills

01 Read the passages in <A> and <B>, and follow the directions.

A

Mr. Kim, an experienced middle school English teacher, noticed a shared interest among his colleagues in improving reading proficiency for low-intermediate students. To support this goal, he developed a workshop to enhance reading class effectiveness and compiled the materials detailed below.

> **Plan for Effective Reading Lessons**
>
> 1. Key factors affecting students' reading skills
>   (1) The role of affect and culture
>   (2) Schematic and background knowledge
>   (3) Reading strategies
>   (4) Extensive reading
>   (5) Reading rate, fluency, and automaticity
>
> 2. Teaching Principles
>   A. Conduct an integrated course including a focus on reading skills
>   B. Offer reading on relevant, interesting, and motivating topics
>   C. Balance between authenticity and readability in choosing texts
>   D. Encourage the development of reading strategies
>   E. Include both bottom-up and top-down techniques
>   F. Design pre-, while-, and post-reading phases

B

Below is the lesson plan designed by Mr. Jung, a novice English teacher, who participated in the workshop for effective reading lessons, followed by the student's log after attending Mr. Jung's class.

Lesson Procedure Conducted by Mr. Jung

- Pre-reading Phase (15 minutes):
  1. Begin the lesson by discussing the importance of reading skills and how they are useful in real-life situations.
  2. Introduce the reading topic chosen based on students' interest briefly and activate schemata by asking students what they know or think about the topic.
  3. Provide a short video related to the topic and help students have sufficient background knowledge.

- While-reading Phase (30 minutes): Distribute the authentic reading text to the students.
  1. Introduce some reading strategies—predicting, skimming, scanning, and summarizing—for effective reading.
  2. Instruct students to make predictions about the content based on the title and headings, skim through the text to get a general idea, scan for specific information, and summarize each paragraph as they go along.
  3. Allow students to work in pairs to apply the strategies and share their thoughts.
  4. As the students are reading, walk around the classroom, observing their engagement and noting any struggles or questions they may have. Offer guidance and clarification as needed.

Guideline for Pre-service Teachers

> **[Text]** *Chimpanzees are dying from our colds — these scientists are trying to save them.*
>
> - Humans are increasingly passing pathogens to animal populations, imperilling endangered species such as chimpanzees and gorillas.
>
> There was something wrong with the chimpanzees. For weeks, a community of 205 animals in Uganda's Kibale National Park had been coughing, sneezing and looking generally miserable. But no one could say for sure what ailed them, even as the animals began to die. (...)

- **Post-reading Phase (15 minutes):** Initiate a class discussion about the reading text.
    1. Ask open-ended questions related to the text, promoting critical thinking and analysis.
    2. Discuss the effectiveness of each reading strategy and how it helped them comprehend the text.
    3. Based on the observation during the while-reading phase, address any common misconceptions or difficulties that arose by providing explanations or examples.

Student's Log After Taking Mr. Jung's class

Today, I attended Mr. Jung's reading class where we explored various useful reading strategies. The class was engaging thanks to the interesting reading material. However, the text, sourced from a science magazine, seemed a bit too advanced for most of us who are the low intermediate-level. The vocabulary and grammar were too demanding, which made it difficult for us to fully comprehend the content. In future classes, I hope that Mr. Jung might select reading texts that are better aligned with our proficiency levels or perhaps teach us new vocabulary before reading. Despite this challenge, I appreciate Mr. Jung's teaching efforts and am eagerly looking forward to the next class.

Referring to <A>, identify TWO teaching factors that Mr. Jung incorporates into his lesson plan from <B>, and ONE teaching principle that he does not adhere to. Then, explain your answers with evidence from both <A> and <B>.

Your Answer

Guideline for Pre-service Teachers

02 Read the conversation in <A> and the outline of the lesson plan in <B>, and follow the directions.

A

T1 : Mr. Kim, could we discuss our English lessons for next week? I'd like to finalize the lesson plan as soon as possible.

T2 : Certainly. What's the proposed topic for our next lesson?

T1 : I'm thinking of focusing on successful YouTubers. It seems to be a topic that really interests my students lately.

T2 : Same here. It's definitely relevant. Maybe we could give them some tips on creating a successful YouTube channel?

T1 : That's a great idea. I'd like to start by eliciting what they already know about YouTubers.

T2 : How about we introduce a short video clip on the subject before they start reading? Would that work for you?

T1 : An interview with a YouTuber, perhaps? I love that idea! I'll find a suitable video. I also want to use a strategy where students make predictions about the content before watching—like guessing what the video might be about just by looking at the title or the first scene.

T2 : Excellent. And during the reading, how should we guide their comprehension?

T1 : First, they could skim the passage to get an overall understanding after briefly predicting what it's about, and then extract specific tips for creating a successful YouTube channel.

T2 : Skimming followed by scanning. I like it. Could we also incorporate some inferential reading? It might be beneficial at their intermediate level.

T1 : Inferential reading? Yes, that could definitely deepen their understanding. And after reading, how should we incorporate speaking or writing skills?

T2 : Let's focus on writing this time. They've had plenty of speaking practice recently.

T1 : Agreed. How about a group writing activity where they draft a script for a YouTube channel based on the tips they've learned?

T2 : That's perfect. Could we also provide a script template to guide them?

T1 : Absolutely. I'll prepare a template and a sample script for reference. I'll share them with you for feedback once they're ready. Is that okay?

T2 : That would be very helpful, thank you. And how will we assess their work?

T1 : What about starting with peer feedback? It could be a valuable learning exercise.

T2 : Peer feedback is an excellent idea. After they've given and received specific feedback, we can evaluate their revised scripts using clear criteria. Does that sound good?

T1 : That sounds very clear. I'll draft the lesson plan based on our discussion and send it to you for review later today.

T2 : I look forward to seeing it, Ms. Lee. Thanks for taking the lead on this.

B

This is the outline of the reading lesson T1 wrote.

※ *Components of the lesson plan: Grade, Subject, Date, Topic, Lesson period, Lesson objectives, Material needed, Target skills, Pre-reading, While-reading, Post-reading, Assessment*

Lesson Plan

Grade: 3rd grade	Subject: English	Date: Sep 10, 2024
Topic: Build A Successful Youtube Channel		Lesson period: 3/5

Lesson Objectives:
- Students will be able to predict the content of the listening and reading passages.
- Students will be able to find the useful tips to be successful YouTubers.
- Students will be able to write an outline for a YouTube video in groups.
- Students will be able to give feedback to each other.

Material Needed:	Target Skills: integrated skills
• Interview video • Reading passage • Writing worksheet	• Listening • Reading • Writing

Pre-reading
- Introduce a short interview video (3 min) of a successful YouTuber.
- Ask students to brainstorm about YouTubers to activate their prior knowledge.
- Make students predict the video content based on its title and the picture of the first scene.
- Watch the video clip and talk about the content with the whole class.

While-reading
- Provide a reading passage titled "How to build a successful YouTube channel".
- Make students briefly predict the contents of the passage.
- Ask students to skim the text to find the main idea.
- Ask students to scan the tips to build a successful YouTube channel.

Post-reading
- Make students in groups write a short script for their YouTube video using a template.
- Make students present their scripts.

Assessment:
- Make students vote for the best group script.
- Teacher assessment based on evaluation criteria.

Based on <A>, identify the TWO steps in <B> that do NOT correspond to the teachers' ideas about their lesson plan. Then explain your answers with evidence from <A> and <B>.

03 Read the passages in <A> and <B>, and follow the directions.

A

Ms. Jung's Teaching Log

I believe using diverse reading activities is essential for improving students' reading skills and sparking their interest. In my lessons, I incorporate a variety of activities to help students practice understanding and interpreting texts. Here are some examples.

- **Graphic Organizers**: Tools like story maps, character charts, and Venn diagrams help students organize and visualize information from a text. Story maps track plot elements, character charts analyze traits and relationships, and Venn diagrams compare and contrast text elements.
- **Reading Response Journals**: It is a versatile and valuable tool in the language classroom, designed to encourage active engagement, critical thinking, and personal reflection on texts. It helps students improve their reading comprehension, writing skills, and overall language development, while also fostering independent learning and meaningful connections with the material. Through regular use, it promotes both academic growth and a lasting habit of thoughtful reading.
- **Reading Comprehension**: Comprehension questions based on reading passages help students practice key skills. By adjusting the levels of questions, educators can prompt students to move beyond simply identifying main ideas and encourage them to engage in higher-level critical thinking about characters and themes. This approach supports a deeper analysis and understanding of the text.
- **Book Talks**: In book talks, students write reviews, or summaries, and discuss themes, characters, and your overall opinions. This activity helps them articulate their thoughts, opinions, and recommendations in a more structured and in-depth way, fostering both communication skills and a deeper understanding of the reading material.

Today, I planned reading activities based on last week's diagnostic tests. While my students excel in surface-level understanding, they struggle with deeper comprehension. These activities aim to help them explore texts more deeply and improve their comprehension.

B

Activity 1

Title: The Mystery of the Missing Key

Once upon a time, in a small town nestled between the mountains, there was a mysterious old mansion. The mansion had been abandoned for years, and locals whispered that it was haunted. Despite the rumors, Sarah and her friends decided to explore the mansion one sunny afternoon. (...)

※ Instructions: Read the passage above carefully and write the answers of the following questions in a phrase or in a sentence.

[Questions]
1. How does the setting help create the mood of the story?
2. What clues does the author provide that suggest what might happen in the future?
3. How do Sarah's personality traits shape her decisions and actions throughout the story?

Activity 2

※ Instructions: After reading a short story, answer the following questions in pairs.

- Summary: Write a brief summary of the plot with your partner.
  _____
  _____
  _____

- Character Analysis: Talk about the main characters and their roles in pairs.
  _____
  _____
  _____

- **Themes and Symbols**: Discuss the main theme and any important symbols in pairs.
  _____
  _____
  _____

- **Personal Opinion**: Share your opinion about the book in pairs. What did you like or dislike? Why?
  _____
  _____
  _____

- **Recommendation**: Would you recommend this book to others? Write your reasons individually and share them in pairs.
  _____
  _____
  _____

Based on <A>, identify each type of reading activity exemplified in <B>, respectively. Then, explain ONE common reason that the teacher used both activities with evidence from <A> and <B>. Do NOT copy more than FOUR consecutive words from the passages.

Your Answer _____

_____
_____
_____
_____

04 Read the passage in <A> and the conversation in <B>, and follow the directions.

A

When it comes to academic contexts such as reading thick textbooks or academic journal articles, the sheer volume of material can initially feel overwhelming. However, there are several reading strategies that can help learners cope and become more efficient readers. Let's explore these strategies in detail using the following table:

Reading Strategies

Strategies	Description
Surveying	Quickly assess whether a text is worth reading in detail by examining the author, title, introduction, etc.
Skimming	Rapidly read through a text to identify main ideas, focusing on the introduction, first sentences of paragraphs, etc.
Scanning	Search the text for specific information by scanning or searching for key words or phrases.
Inferencing	Use your background knowledge, context clues, and critical thinking to infer or deduce information that is not directly stated such as drawing conclusions and understanding implied meanings.
Guessing Unknown Words	Develop the skill of inferring the meaning of unknown words from context rather than stopping to look up every word which can be time-consuming.

B

Ms. Park, a middle school English teacher, is talking with her student, Jihae, about her reading comprehension test results.

Teacher : Jihae, let's discuss your recent reading test results. I must say, you did an excellent job understanding the main ideas of the passages. Well done!

Jihae : Thank you, Ms. Park! I'm glad to hear that. Finding the main ideas comes relatively easily to me. However, I struggled with inferring information from the text. I find it challenging to guess something that is not explicitly stated. Could you offer any advice on how I can improve in this area?

Teacher : Certainly, Jihae! Inferring information from a text is crucial for enhancing your reading comprehension. Firstly, focus on reading between the lines by paying attention to contextual hints within the passage and utilizing your prior knowledge.

Jihae : Hmm, could you please explain in more detail how to do that?

Teacher : When you read a text, for instance, ask yourself questions like "What does this line imply?" and "What details support that implication?". Then, seek answers to these questions based on your own experiences, textual clues, or specific details provided in the passage. This approach will assist you in deducing the implied meaning of the passage.

Jihae : That sounds like a solid plan, Ms. Park! I will try to apply this strategy to my next reading, as you suggested. Thank you for the advice.

Teacher : You're welcome, Jihae! Remember, I'm here to help anytime and anywhere. Feel free to ask if you need any assistance. Keep up the good work!

Based on <A>, identify Jihae's strong and weak reading strategies discussed in the conversation in <B>. Then, write the concrete solution that Ms. Park offers to Jihae from <B>.

05 Read the passages and follow the directions.

A

Mr. Kim's Teaching Note

These days, I am focusing on improving my students' listening skills. Based on a diagnostic test, I recognized that their difficulties in listening were because of lack of essential listening strategies. Thus, I decided to teach two necessary listening strategies. First, before listening, I will provide information related to the listening material, such as the title, visuals, and pre-set questions. This will enable them to effectively anticipate the content before listening. Additionally, I will teach how to figure out the hidden meaning between the lines. To do that, I will give students some questions asking about implied meaning of certain utterances from the material. Then, I will guide students in identifying some clues related to the hidden meaning from the text. Once they have completed this exercise, I will ask them to share their ideas with their group members. In this way, they will be able to uncover hidden messages and meanings not explicitly mentioned. I am confident that teaching these strategies will contribute to enhancing their listening abilities and overall language proficiency.

B

The following is part of lesson procedure that aims to improve students' listening strategies.

- Before listening, T provides a news title 'Top 3 K-Movies' and some pictures related to the news clip.
- Then, T asks Ss to anticipate what the news story is going to be about. Ss freely talk about their anticipations.
- T distributes a handout including 10 short answer questions about the news clip. Ss are asked to answer the questions based on their guessing.
- Ss watch the news clip about 'Top 3 K-Movies'.
- Ss in pairs check if their predictions were right, sharing their answers.
- Ss listen to the news piece once again and, if needed, Ss change the answers of the questions.
- T provides two additional questions below and asks Ss to figure out the answers in groups.

> Q1. What is the implied meaning of 'We did it' from the news clip? and what are some clues?
> Q2. What is the underlying intention of the last utterance from the news reporter? and what makes you think so?

- T asks each group to present their answers and checks the answers together with the whole class.

Based on <A> and <B>, identify TWO listening strategies that Mr. Kim plans to teach. Then, explain your answers with evidence from <B>.

Your Answer

06 Read the passage in <A> and the conversation in <B>. Then follow the directions.

A

Comprehension strategies are sets of steps that good readers use to make sense of text. Comprehension strategy instruction helps students become purposeful and active readers who are in control of their own reading comprehension. These strategies have research-based evidence for improving text comprehension.

1. Monitoring comprehension:
    - Students who are good at monitoring their comprehension know when they understand what they read and when they do not.
    - They have strategies to "fix" problems in their understanding as the problems arise.

2. Answering questions (Question-Answer strategy):
    - This strategy aims to enhance students' question-answering skills by encouraging them to provide comprehensive responses.
    - Students address questions related to the text from multiple angles, identifying whether their answers are based on explicit text information, implicit inferences, or background knowledge.

3. Generating questions:
    - By generating questions, students become aware of their comprehension and understanding.
    - Students learn to ask themselves questions that require them to combine information from different segments of text, such as main idea questions.

4. Recognizing story structure:
    - In story structure instruction, students learn to identify content categories like characters, setting, events, problem, and resolution.
    - Analysis of story structure improves students' comprehension.

5. Summarizing:
    - Summarizing requires students to determine what is important in what they are reading and to put it into their own words.
    - Instruction in summarizing helps students identify the main idea, connect central ideas, eliminate unnecessary information, and remember what they read.

B

Ms. Yoo, a middle school English teacher, taught her students reading strategies in a reading lesson using a story. Before finishing the lesson, she asked her students to share their performance during the lesson.

Ms. Yoo : Alright, Guys! You all did a great job, today! Before we finish today's reading lesson, shall we talk about the strategy we used to comprehend the story? Yes, Minjae, are you going to be first?

Minjae : So, when I started reading the text, the first thing I did was quickly go through the whole thing, trying to get a feel for what the author was trying to say. Then, I started looking more closely at how the story is put together and what the relationships of the main characters are. Doing this really helped me understand the text better and get the main idea that the author was trying to get across. All in all, it was a pretty cool experience reading it.

Ms. Yoo : Very good. Does anyone else want to share?

Eunhee : Alright, so here's what I did. I really wanted to dive deep into what I was reading. So, I examined pre-set questions that were all about the story. Each question was a bit different, so I had to handle them in their own way. It was kind of like peeling an onion—I read the story three times. The first time, I just got the surface meaning of the story. The second time, I started noticing things that were beyond the text. And the third time, that's when I really started thinking critically about it, using what I already knew. Those questions were a big help in understanding the deeper meaning of the story.

Ms. Yoo : That's impressive, Eunhee! Thank you all for sharing your experiences.

Referring to <A>, identify the ONE most appropriate comprehension strategy that each student in <B> uses as they read the story. Then, write the evidence for your answers from <B>.

Your Answer

3 How to Improve the Receptive skills

01 Read the passage in <A> and the teaching procedure in <B>, and follow the directions.

A

The English department at a middle school has announced specific lesson objectives for English lessons. The following are the lesson objectives that English teachers should incorporate into their lessons for this semester.

[For listening skills]
Students will be able to
- predict the main idea of a listening material.
- look for the general gist of the listening material.
- outline or take notes on the listening material.
- associate the topic with their prior knowledge and opinions.
- apply test-taking strategies for listening comprehension.

[For reading skills]
Students will be able to
- find the main idea of the reading material.
- engage in a group activity using textual and extratextual information.
- answer questions about details from the reading material.
- provide a new ending to the reading material.
- summarize orally what is read.

Guideline for Pre-service Teachers

B

Lesson Procedure

Step 1. T introduces today's listening topic and pre-teaches some necessary vocabulary related to the listening material.

- resume - a summary of a person's work and education
- responsibilities - things that must be done
- to oversee - to make sure something is done, to supervise
- to keep track of - to be aware of or notice something
- inventory - the number of items a store has
- to handle - to take care of, to deal with
- to be transferred - to be moved from one place to another, especially within a company or organization

Step 2. Ss listen to a conversation between Mr. Kim (employer) and Sungmin Lee (job applicant) in a job interview.

Step 3. T asks Ss to determine whether the following statements are true or false.
   a) Sungmin was a boss at Computer Country. (T/F)
   b) Sungmin liked taking care of angry customers in her previous job. (T/F)
   c) Sungmin's husband has a new job in a new city. (T/F)

Step 4. T puts Ss in pairs and provides the following questions. Based on the questions, Ss share their own experiences or ideas on the topic with each other.
   a) Have you ever been in a job interview? How was it?
   b) What did you learn after listening to the conversation?
   c) If you were Sungmin, how would answer the interview question?

Step 5. T introduces a reading text about a job interview, 'Interview Process Steps.'

Step 6. T asks Ss to read the text individually. T encourages them to underline the part they think is interesting.

Step 7. T asks Ss to present what they have underlined from the reading material.

Step 8. T puts Ss in groups of four and provides each group with a handout containing discussion questions related to the reading text. T encourages them to have a discussion by using both the information given from the reading text and their own experiences and ideas.

[Discussion Questions]
1. What are the key tips for a successful job interview mentioned in the text?
2. Have you encountered any of these tips before in your own experiences?
3. Which tip do you find most valuable, and why?

Step 9. T brings the class back together and asks each group to share their findings and insights from the group discussion.

T=teacher, Ss=students

Identify ONE lesson objective for listening skills and ONE lesson objective for reading skills from <A> that the teaching procedure in <B> targets. Then, explain how each lesson objective is incorporated, addressing the corresponding Step, respectively.

Your Answer

Guideline for Pre-service Teachers

02 Read the passages and follow the directions.

A

Reading comprehension is the ability to process information that we have read and to understand its meaning. The five levels of comprehension are the literal, reorganization, infererential, evaluative, and appreciative level. Below are short explanations of each comprehension level.

1. Literal level: Students focus on information explicitly stated in the text.
2. Reorganization level: Students have to organize for themselves some of the information explicitly expressed. They have to summarize information or handle it in a different sequence.
3. Inferential level: Students are required to go beyond the immediate text. They have to make use of their own experience and intuition, and possibly guess intended meaning or predict outcomes.
4. Evaluative level: Students are required to make judgement. They have to make use of their own knowledge of a particular subject.
5. Appreciative level: At this advanced level of response to a text, students have to be emotionally and aesthetically sensitive to what they are reading.

B

Mr. Kim's students need to read and answer the following text and questions. Additionally, two students of Mr. Kim's class make comments on their reading comprehension skills.

Text

Jeremy is about forty years old and his hair is starting to go grey. Everybody knows Jeremy because he is an actor. He has done his job very well for twenty years and enjoys acting quite a lot. Recently, Jeremy has a plan to appear in a famous director's film as the protagonist of the story. However, all of sudden, the movie director suggested that Jeremy should change his character. Jeremy knows the director wants a younger man to take his role and doesn't care what happens to Jeremy. The new role could never be as good as his old one. He has no one to discuss the problem with at home and this makes it worse.

Questions
(1) The story implies that a youthful and attractive appearance is often more important than age and experience in the very competitive world of movie filming. Is is true or false to you?
(2) Jeremy will probably not accept a new role and decide to resign instead. Agree or disagree? and Why?

Students' Comments
Jihye : While reading a text, I feel difficulties in guessing the hidden meanings or the ending of the story. Thus, I need to practice how to think beyond the text level using my own personal experiences.
Jungho : Sometimes, I blindly believe that the opinions or ideas of a text or a writer are always true, which I realize they are not so true eventually. Thus, to improve my reading comprehension skills, I need to develop making my own judgements regarding the writer's opinions or ideas.

Based on <A>, identify the comprehension level of Question (1) and (2) in <B>, respectively. Then, choose the proper Question for each student and write the reason of your choice with evidence from <A> and <B>. Do NOT copy more than FOUR consecutive words from the passages.

Your Answer

Guideline for Pre-service Teachers

03 Read the passages and follow the directions.

A

What is reading comprehension or understanding? Below is one contemporary definition: Reading comprehension is finding information, inferencing, evaluating, reacting emotionally, and creating new ideas from the author's written content. There are four different types of comprehension levels:

- Literal Comprehension
  It is the reader's ability to find out ideas and information that are directly stated in the text.

- Inferential Comprehension
  It is the reader's ability to extract ideas and information not directly stated in the text, using prior or background knowledge to assist in such understanding.

- Critical Comprehension
  It is the reader's ability to respond with personal judgments and ideas about the content of the text, using his or her past knowledge and thoughts on the subject.

- Creative Comprehension
  It is the reader's "emotional" response to the content of the text. This level of comprehension also includes creating new ideas from what was learned in school and life.

B

Sungjin's Learning Log

Date: November 15, 2023
Group members: Eunbin, Hyejin, Joonho
Reading activity:
  First, I quickly glanced over all the contents of the lesson to guess the main idea. Then, we talked about the main idea and some details of the passage in a group. Next, we tried to write down our judgement on the writer's intention collaboratively.

Reflection:

I enjoyed working together with my classmates while answering reading comprehension questions. It was not difficult to answer questions asking about some details explicitly mentioned in the passage. I didn't need to think about the answer. I only had to understand the question precisely and find where the sentence with the answer was located in the passage. However, some of the comprehension questions in the reading lesson were quite demanding. I struggled to answer these questions because they required me to critically analyze what the writer was trying to say using my prior experience and knowledge. After reading the passage several times, I was finally able to answer the questions. Discussing this experience with my classmates, I realized that reaching this level of comprehension is essential for fully understanding the reading material. Additionally, collaborating with my classmates was an enjoyable experience.

Based on <A> and <B>, identify the comprehension level that Sungjin finds easy and difficult, respectively. Then, explain the reason for your choice with evidence from <B>. Do NOT copy more than FOUR consecutive words from the passages.

Your Answer

Guideline for Pre-service Teachers

04 Read <A> and <B>, and follow the directions.

A

Comprehension Level

1. **Literal level**: Answers are directly and explicitly expressed in the text. Students can answer the questions using the words of the text.
2. **Reorganization level**: Students obtain information from various parts of the text by putting them together in a new way.
3. **Inferential level**: Students consider what is implied but not explicitly stated. They make conclusions about the material presented in the text to come up with insights that are not explicitly stated in the text.
4. **Evaluative level**: Students formulate a response based on their previous reading experience, their life experience, and their opinions on the issues relevant to the text.
5. **Creative level**: At this advanced level of response to a text, students have to be emotionally and aesthetically sensitive to what he is reading. It also requires some appreciation of literary techniques.

B

Reading Text

On September 8th, the Korean national soccer team beat Brazil 2-1 in the World Cup championship game held in Qatar. The victory was the greatest moment in Korean sports history. As a matter of fact, it was the first time an Asian country won the World Cup. It was anyone's game as the score was tied 1-1 deep into the second half of the game. But, with just 26 seconds left in the game, one of the youngest members of the Korean team, Jeong Wooyeong (23) scored an incredible goal. When the game ended, Korean fans stormed the streets all over Korea. Fireworks and car horns could be seen and heard everywhere. Crowds that gathered around City Hall celebrated for hours after the game. On the other side of the globe, fans wiped away their tears from their painted faces in Brazil. Thousands of fans walked around with expressions of disbelief and disappointment.

Below is parts of the conversation between two English teachers teaching 2nd graders in a middle school.

T1 : Hi, Mr. Kim. What are you doing?
T2 : Hi, Ms. Park. I am reviewing my next reading lesson plan. I want to modify it a little bit.
T1 : So, what do you want to fix?
T2 : A few comprehension questions need to be fixed. These questions are too complex and difficult compared to students' current level.
T1 : On what level are they?
T2 : Low intermediate level. Can you check up the text and the questions I prepared?
T1 : Sure! *(T1 reads the text and checks the question.)* Okay, let's see. 'What is the author's attitude or tone toward Korea's winning of the World Cup?' Hmm...the author's attitude is not mentioned in the text. Isn't it?
T2 : That's the point. That's why it is too demanding for my students who are not ready to figure out hidden meanings yet.
T1 : How about asking for the information easily found in the text? Like, 'When did the Korean team score the second goal?'. It's clearly mentioned in the seventh line of the text.
T2 : That's good!! Thank you, Ms. Park.

T=teacher

Based the categorization in \<A\>, explain the comprehension level of the question that T2 originally plans to give. Then, write the comprehension level that T1 suggests to T2 and explain why the new question is more suitable for T2's reading lesson. Do not copy more than FOUR consecutive words from the text.

Your Answer

(Guideline for Pre-service Teachers)

05 Read the passages and follow the directions.

A

When good readers involve themselves with any type of written discourse, they work on several processes simultaneously to produce understanding of the incoming text. The higher level of processing is driven by readers' expectations and understandings of the context, the topic, the nature of the text, and the nature of the world. The lower level of processing is triggered by the words, and phrases that the readers read as they attempt to decode a text and assign meaning. The text itself carries only some clues to the meanings that are encoded within it; readers must use their knowledge of the language to recognize keywords, phrases, and sentences.

B

Below is part of the lesson plan that Ms. Choi prepared for her students.

Stage 1	• T shows a video clip of metaverse. • After watching the video clip, students in pairs share what they already knew about metaverse and what they newly learn from the video. • T previews some new words from the text.
Stage 2	• T asks Ss to skim the text about metaverse and think about the main idea. • T checks the main idea with the whole class.
Stage 3	• T provides Ss with comprehension questions on literal and inferential levels. • Ss read the text individually to find out the answers explicitly stated in the text and to infer the writer's intention beyond the text. • T asks Ss to present their answers and check them with the whole class.

Stage 4	• T provides a discussion question related to the metaverse and puts Ss in groups of four. (e.g. "Metaverse will have positive or negative effects on human evolution. What do you think?") • Ss in groups discuss the question while sharing their individual opinions. • Ss choose one group opinion.
Stage 5	• T asks each group to present their group opinion based on two supporting ideas. • Ss vote for one group that presents the most persuasive opinion.

Referring to <A>, identify TWO stages presented in <B> which require both levels of processing. Then, explain the reasons for your choice with some evidence. Do NOT copy more than FOUR consecutive words from the passages.

Your Answer

06 Read the passages and follow the directions.

A

Five Types of Reading Comprehension

1. Lexical comprehension: understand key vocabulary in the text.
   - Preview vocabulary before reading the story or text.
   - Review new vocabulary during or after the text.

2. Literal comprehension: answer who, what, when, and where questions.
   - Look in the text to find the answers written in the story.
   - Ask questions from the beginning, middle, and end of the story.

3. Interpretive comprehension: answer what if, why, and how questions.
   - Understand 'facts' that are not explicitly stated in the story.
   - Illustrations may help to infer meaning.

4. Applied comprehension: relate the story to your opinion.
   - Not a simple question that can be marked right or wrong.
   - Challenge students to support their answers with logic or reason.

5. Affective comprehension: understand social and emotional aspects
   - Preview social scripts to ensure understanding of plot development.
   - Connect motive to plot and character development.

B

Below are two examples of reading activities.

Activity 1

※ If something is true, or it really happened, it is a fact. If something is what someone thinks or believes, it is an opinion. As you read Marco's letter from Uncle Ben, think about what parts are fact and what parts are opinion.

> [Text]
> Marco got a letter from his Uncle Ben, the airplane pilot. Uncle Ben has traveled all over the world.
>
> Dear Marco,
> This is my third time visiting Paris, and I think it is one of the most beautiful cities in the world. Paris, as I'm sure you know, is the capital of France. Today I walked along the Avenue des Champs-Elysees, which is the most famous street in Paris. I think it may be the most famous street in the world. It is lined with beautiful trees, fountains, and flowers. There are shops, theaters, restaurants, and many sidewalk cafes. *(ellipsis)*

※ Here are some things Uncle Ben said in his letter. Which ones are facts and which are Uncle Ben's opinions? Circle the word "fact" or the word "opinion."

1. This is Uncle Ben's third time visiting Paris.   (fact) (opinion)
2. Paris is one of the most beautiful cities in the world. (fact) (opinion)
3. Paris is the capital city of France.   (fact) (opinion)
4. The Avenue des Champs-Elysees may be the most famous street in the world.   (fact) (opinion)
5. On the Champs-Elysees, there are shops, theaters, and restaurants.
                                                          (fact) (opinion)

Activity 2

※ As you read the story, think about what you already know and what you newly know from the story. Try to figure out what the story means by thinking about what makes the most sense.

> [Text] The Kingly Lion
>
> The animals of the field and forest had a Lion as their King. When anyone had a problem, he took it to the Lion King, and the Lion King helped to solve it. When anyone had an argument, they took it to the Lion King, and he helped to settle it. The Lion King never made demands that were in his own interest. He wanted only what was best for each and every animal. Day after day, the Lion King thought about nothing but the animals who were his subjects. Then he sat down and wrote out a Royal Order. He called all the animals to come before him. He stood on a hilltop and watched the animals come together from far and near. He waited for them to settle.
>
> "Hear ye, hear ye!" the Lion began, in his deep and rumbling voice. "I have written out my orders for a new way of doing things that will be better for all. From this day forward, the Wolf and the Lamb shall agree to live in peace. The Panther and the Goat shall live in peace. The Tiger and the Deer, and the Dog and the Rabbit—all shall live together in perfect peace and harmony.

※ Use what you already know and what the story says to make inferences:

1. Why did the animals bring their problems to the Lion?
   A. The animals knew the Lion was powerful.
   B. The animals knew the Lion was fair.
   C. The animals feared that the Lion would punish them.

2. Why did the Lion write a Royal Order?
   A. The Lion wanted the best for animals.
   B. The Lion was tired of the animals bringing their problems to him.
   C. The Lion wanted to be King of the field and forest.

Based on <A>, identify the level of reading comprehension that each Activity in <B> exemplifies and write the reason for each with evidence from <B>.

Your Answer

Build Up

Chapter
04

Productive Skills

Chapter 04 Productive Skills

정답 및 모범 답안 p. 457

1 How to Teach Speaking Skills

01 Read the passages in <A> and <B>, and follow the directions.

A

Below are the posts written by two students on an online community where students can share their concerns and ideas, and help each other with English lessons.

Student 1's Post

Overcoming My Speaking Challenges

Hello everyone,

I hope you're all doing well. I wanted to share something that's been on my mind lately. Recently, my confidence in speaking English has decreased because I'm afraid of making mistakes. Public criticism when I make mistakes has also affected my confidence, making it harder for me to speak fluently. As a result, I often hesitate during conversations and feel like I'm not expressing myself as effectively as I could. I believe having some time to track my progress and reflect on areas for improvement would help. I was wondering if anyone has suggestions for activities we could try in class to address these issues. A relaxed, low-pressure environment would really help us become more confident English speakers. Let's brainstorm some ideas!

Looking forward to your suggestions.

Student 2's Post

Vocabulary Challenge in Understanding Conversations

Hi everyone,

I hope you're all having a great day. I wanted to share something I've been struggling with recently. My limited vocabulary often makes it difficult for me to understand conversations in English. Sometimes, I get lost during discussions, and it can be frustrating. Even though I know some words, I struggle to use them appropriately in context. Hopefully, our English teacher will give us some opportunities to focus on both the meaning and proper usage of words through various activities. I think this would be incredibly helpful for me, and I'm sure others would benefit as well. If anyone has ideas or suggestions for how we can work on this together, please feel free to share.

B

Activity 1

Students sit in a circle. One student starts a story with a sentence. The next student adds to it with another sentence, continuing around the group. The goal is to collaboratively create a fun and imaginative story, promoting creativity and spontaneity. As they build the story together, all students experience a sense of achievement through active participation.

Activity 2

The activity includes smaller, supportive groups, where students not only take turns speaking but also engage in role-playing conversations or discussions on everyday topics, focusing on fluency over mistakes. The teacher can rotate between groups, providing personalized encouragement and private feedback. Finally, weekly reflection sessions where students share their progress privately with the teacher could help track improvement and build confidence over time.

Guideline for Pre-service Teachers

Activity 3

The teacher introduces several websites on multicultural customs to students. Each student selects a country and its culture that interest them while browsing websites. They research and prepare a short presentation about that culture's customs, traditions, and interesting facts. During class, students take turns presenting their findings, promoting cross-cultural awareness and public speaking skills.

Activity 4

The teacher introduces new words with examples in different contexts, such as formal and informal settings. Students are then asked to determine the meanings based on context and practice using target words in group activities, role-playing, and weekly reviews to reinforce correct usage. This approach helps students confidently apply vocabulary in various real-life situations.

Choose the ONE most appropriate activity in <B> that could satisfy Student 1 and Student 2, respectively, and then support your choices with evidence from <B>. Do NOT copy more than FOUR consecutive words from the passages.

Your Answer

02 Read the passages in <A> and <B>, and follow the directions.

A

Research suggests that L2 learners employ various oral communication skills to enhance their speaking skills. These skills can be classified into two types: microskills and macroskills. Below are some specific strategies from each type.

Microskills

(1) Produce reduced forms of words and phrases.
(2) Monitor their own oral production and use various strategic devices to enhance the clarity of the message. (e.g., pauses, fillers, self-corrections)
(3) Produce fluent speech at different rates of delivery.

Macroskills

(1) Use facial features, kinesics, body language and other nonverbal cues.
(2) Use a series of speaking strategies. (e.g., emphasizing key words, rephrasing, and appealing for help)
(3) Use contrastive marker(s) in spoken discourse.

Guideline for Pre-service Teachers

B

Mr. Kim, a middle school English teacher, taught his students various speaking strategies to enhance their communicative competence. Afterward, he asked two students to engage in a conversation on a specific topic to assess whether they were applying those skills. The following is an excerpt from the recorded conversation between the two students.

Eunha : Sungjin! Did you see that new video on SNS? It was so funny!
Sungjin : Yeah, I saw it. But honestly, Eunha, I think we spend way too much time on social media these days. It is becoming a real problem for students.
Eunha : I disagree that it is that bad. SNS helps us connect with friends and stay updated.
Sungjin : Nevertheless, Eunha, spending too much time online can affect our studies and health. It is important to find a balance.
Eunha : I understand where you're comin' from, Sungjin. I believe it is all about self-control. We can learn to use SNS wisely without gettin' addicted.

Identify the ONE specific speaking strategy in <A> that Eunha and Sungjin use during the dialogue in <B>, respectively. Then, explain your answers with evidence from <A> and <B>.

Your Answer

03 Read the passages in <A> and <B>, and follow the directions.

A

A group of 10 English teachers gathered to discuss enhancing the communicative aspect of speaking lessons. They shared insights and compiled a list of tips aimed at making speaking activities more engaging and reflective of real-world communication. To prioritize these strategies, each teacher voted for the two tips they considered most crucial. The voting results are shown below.

No	Tips	Vote counts
1	Activities should mimic authentic communication scenarios that learners might encounter outside the classroom.	2
2	Promote collaborative decision-making, where students work together to achieve shared conclusions on specified topics.	5
3	Incorporate real-life materials like news articles, videos, podcasts, and social media content.	1
4	Design activities that encourage learners to take charge of their learning. This can involve allowing them to make choices within activities, set their learning goals, or assess their progress.	2
5	Incorporate cultural aspects into communicative activities to promote cultural awareness and understanding.	1
6	Provide different support where needed. For learners who are more proficient than the others, you can reduce the support. For learners who are less proficient than the others, you can give more support.	6
7	Combine different language skills within a single activity. A task might involve reading a text, discussing it, and then writing a response, which integrates reading, speaking, and writing skills.	3

B

After the survey, Ms. Park, an English teacher, designed speaking activities by applying some of the tips.

Activity 1

※ **Directions**: Work in pairs. Choose one role card. If you are fluent, choose Card A. If you are not fluent enough, choose Card B. Read each role card and plan a vacation plan in pairs.

Card A (Travel Agent)	Card B (Customer)
As a travel agent, your task is to help your customer plan their dream vacation. You'll need to gather information about their preferences, budget, and any specific requirements they might have. Based on this, you'll suggest suitable destinations, accommodation options, activities, and transportation tips. While you can use online resources for this activity, remember to base your suggestions on general knowledge about popular travel destinations, common travel practices, and typical tourist activities.	As a customer, fill in the table below and share it with your travel agent. <table><tr><td>Your budget</td><td></td></tr><tr><td>Travel dates</td><td></td></tr><tr><td>Interests</td><td></td></tr><tr><td>Any specific needs</td><td></td></tr></table> Ask the travel agent to plan your vacation using the expressions below: • Could you suggest places that are **[adjective]**? • I prefer **[activity/place]** over **[alternative]**. • I'd like to know more about **[place]**. • I'm not sure about **[suggestion]**. Do we have other options? (…)

Activity 2

※ **Directions**: Work in groups. You will create and share a story, practicing your speaking and writing skills. Your group will choose a theme, start a story, each contribute to it, and then share it with the class. Use the template below.

Story Writing Template

Group Number/Name: _____
Theme: _____
Opening Scene/Character Introduction:
- Written by: _____ (Name)
- (Write your 3-5 opening sentences here)
  _____
  _____
  _____

Second Contribution:
- Written by: _____ (Name)
- (Continue the story with your 3-5 sentences here)

Third Contribution:
- Written by: _____ (Name)
- (Add to the story with your 3-5 sentences here)

Continue in the same pattern until each group member has contributed.

Final Part of the Story:
- Written by: _____ (Name)
- (Conclude the story with your 3-5 sentences here)

Guideline for Pre-service Teachers

Activity 3

※ **Directions**: Work in groups. Discuss and decide on the best theme for an upcoming class party. Share your ideas and perspectives to collectively decide on one option. Remember, any of the options can be correct; the goal is to make a decision through group discussion and consensus.

- Option 1: Superhero Soiree - A party where everyone dresses up as their favorite superheroes.
- Option 2: Retro Rewind - A throwback party celebrating a past decade of choice (e.g., '80s, '90s).
- Option 3: Around the World - A multicultural party where each corner of the room represents a different country or culture.

Based on <A>, identify the ONE activity in <B> that each of the two most popular tips has been applied to, respectively. Then support your answers with evidence from <A> and <B>.

Your Answer

04 Read the passages in <A> and <B>, and follow the directions.

A

Ms. Yoo, a high school English teacher, has introduced a new speaking course called "Effective Communication" to help students develop discourse competence. To prepare, she conducted thorough research, consulting books and seeking advice from experienced teachers. This led to the creation of her teaching plan shown below.

Teaching Plan for 'Effective Communication Strategies'

1. Teaching Contents

Discourse Competence	Cohesion	The way that a text makes sense syntactically. Common cohesive devices include forms of reference, ellipsis, substitution, lexical cohesion, and conjunction.
	Coherence	The way that a text is made semantically meaningful. That is, within a discourse, multiple sentences logically follow each other.
	Genre Structure	The specific organizational patterns, conventions, and structures that are characteristic of different types of texts or speeches, known as genres.
	Conversational Structure	The patterns and norms that govern spoken interactions: turn-taking, topic initiation and closure, managing interruptions, and recognizing and interpreting verbal and non-verbal cues in dialogue.

2. Teaching Principles
(1) Encourage the use of authentic language in meaningful contexts.
(2) Provide chances for both peer feedback and teacher feedback.
(3) Focus on both fluency and accuracy.
(4) Give students opportunities to nominate topics, and ask questions.
(5) Encourage the development of speaking strategies.

B

Below is one of the lesson plans that Ms. Yoo has developed to implement her speaking course.

1. Introduction
- Introduce the basic structure of debates. (e.g., opening statements, argument presentation, rebuttals, etc)
- Introduce key expressions used in debates by structure.

Key expressions

• Opening statements
  - I firmly believe that...
  - My position is clear...
• Argument presentation
  - Firstly...
  - One critical point to consider is...
• Rebuttals
  - However, it's important to note that...
  - Contrary to what has been argued...
(...)

- Introduce necessary oral communication strategies generally used in debates. (e.g., asking for clarification, using fillers to gain time to process, using nonverbal expressions, etc.)

2. Practice Session
Have Ss practice the introduced expressions in pairs, focusing on pronunciation, fluency, and correct usage in a debate context.

3. Preparation for Group Discussion
   - Divide Ss into small groups and provide a discussion topic related to students' real-life experiences. (e.g., Is online learning as effective as traditional classroom education?)
   - Ask groups to prepare for a mini-debate using the learned expressions.

4. Mini-Debate
   - Ask groups to conduct their mini-debates on the given topic.
   - Emphasis on using the expressions taught in the lesson and oral communication strategies.
   - Observe the mini-debate and make notes for feedback.

5. Peer Feedback and Teacher Input
   - Ask each group to provide feedback to their group members focusing on the use of expressions and adherence to debate structure.
   - Provide additional feedback and correct any misuse of expressions.

6. Wrap-up
   - Summarize the key expressions and their effective use in debates.
   - Encourage students to think about how they can use these expressions in other real-life scenarios.

Based on <A>, identify the ONE teaching content that Ms. Yoo mainly focuses on and the ONE teaching principle that she does NOT conform to in her lesson plan in <B>. Then explain your answers with evidence from <A> and <B>.

Your Answer

05 Read the passage in <A> and the teacher's log in <B>, and follow the directions.

A

　Second language learners often face difficulties in understanding spoken English due to specific features inherent in the language. These challenges can stem from the use of reduced forms and contractions, idioms and colloquialisms, and the wide variety of accents and dialects further complicate listening comprehension. To mitigate these difficulties, it is crucial for teachers to directly instruct students on these various features of spoken English. The descriptions for each feature are as follows:

- **Reduced Forms**: In spoken English, words are often pronounced more quickly and can be contracted or reduced, such as "gonna" for "going to" or "wanna" for "want to."
- **Colloquial Expressions**: English speakers frequently use idiomatic expressions and slang, which may not be literal and can be confusing for learners to understand without knowledge of the cultural context.
- **Variety of Accents**: The wide range of English accents and dialects can make comprehension difficult, as learners may be more familiar with one type of accent (e.g., American English) and struggle to understand others (e.g., British, Australian, or regional dialects).
- **Stress and Intonation**: English relies heavily on stress and intonation to convey meaning, which can be challenging for learners whose native languages use different systems of stress and intonation.
- **Use of Fillers and Pauses**: Native speakers often use fillers ("um," "uh," "you know") and natural pauses, which can disrupt the flow for learners who are trying to follow the conversation.

B

Ms. Kim's Teaching Log

Today's listening lessons focused on familiarizing students with some features of spoken English, a crucial step towards enhancing their comprehension of natural English dialogue. In the first listening activity, we started by diving into expressions like "Catch some Z's" (to get some sleep) and "hustle" (to work hard), aiming to enhance their understanding of spoken English in real-world contexts. The students' initial reactions were a mix of amusement and confusion. However, as we practiced listening to these informal expressions in various dialogues, their ability to pick up on and understand them visibly improved. In the second listening activity, we tackled speech shortcuts, focusing on examples like "gimme" for "give me" and "lemme" for "let me." Students practiced identifying these contractions in audio clips and engaged in a vibrant discussion about how these forms are often used in fast and casual conversation, thereby enhancing their ability to comprehend the natural flow of spoken English as I intended. Reflecting on today's lessons, it's clear that directly teaching these aspects of spoken English significantly boosts students' listening skills. They're not just learning to recognize words but also to understand how native speakers naturally communicate.

Based on <A>, identify the feature of spoken English that Ms. Kim focuses on in each listening activity mentioned in <B>. Then, write the key objective for each listening activity, citing evidence from <B>.

Your Answer

06 Read the passages and follow the directions.

A

Factors Contributing to Difficulty of Speaking Tasks

1. **Clustering**: Fluent speech is phrasal, not word by word. Learners can organize their output both cognitively and physically through clustering.

2. **Redundancy**: Learners can capitalize on redundancy, a feature of spoken language that allows a speaker to make meaning clearer.

3. **Reduced forms**: Contractions, elisions, reduced vowels, and other similar characteristics all pose special problems in teaching spoken English. Students who don't learn colloquial contractions can sometimes develop a bookish quality of speaking.

4. **Performance variables**: Learners can be taught how to pause and hesitate. For example, in English our "thinking time" is not silent; we insert certain fillers.

5. **Colloquial language**: Make sure your students are reasonably well acquainted with the words, idioms, and phrases of colloquial language and they get practice in producing these forms. They are used very often informally in a daily life and help your students hold fluent conversations.

6. **Rate of delivery**: One of your tasks in teaching spoken English is to help learners achieve an acceptable speed along with other attributes of fluency.

B

Student A's Log

Today, we had a lesson on speaking English more naturally. My teacher explained that in English, there are words and phrases used with specific meanings in certain situations. She introduced us to some idioms. She said that "Break a leg!" actually means 'I wish you good luck', and "piece of cake" means 'something that is very easy'. These idioms can't be understood by their literal meanings, so we need to know their actual meanings. Although the expressions seemed unfamiliar, after practicing a few times, it feels like I can speak more naturally. Moreover, I think I'll be able to better understand casual conversations of native speakers in their daily lives.

Student B's Log

I took a speaking lesson on how to speak naturally today. To speak English smoothly, we learned about various language features, particularly how to keep the conversation flowing. When doing impromptu speaking, we often need time to think about the next words. However, if there's a long pause without speaking, it can make the listener feel awkward or think that we can't speak well. To fill these gaps naturally, we learned to use phrases like "I mean," "you know," "um," "well," "uh," etc. While practicing this, I found that my speaking flow improved, and I feel like my English speaking skills have become better, sounding more like a native speaker.

Based on <A>, identify the aspect (factor) of speech that each student in <B> has learned during their speaking class. Then, explain how each aspect contributes to the improvement of their speaking skills with evidence in <B>.

Your Answer

Guideline for Pre-service Teachers

07 Read the passages and follow the directions.

A

Types of Classroom Speaking Performance

1. **Imitative**: A very limited portion of classroom speaking time may legitimately be spent generating rehearsed, imitative speech, where, for example, learners practice an intonation contour or try to pinpoint a certain vowel sound.

2. **Intensive**: This includes any speaking performance that is designed to practice some phonological or grammatical aspect of language. Intensive speaking can be self-initiated or it can even form part of some pair work activity, where learners are going over certain forms of language.

3. **Responsive**: A good deal of student speech in the classroom is responsive: short replies to teacher- or student-initiated questions or comments. These replies are usually sufficient and do not extend into dialogues.

4. **Transactional dialogue**: This is carried out for the purpose of conveying or exchanging specific information. This is an extended form of responsive language. Conversations, for example, may have more of a negotiating nature to them than responsive speech.

5. **Interpersonal dialogue**: This is carried out more for the purpose of maintaining social relationships than for the transmission of facts or information. These conversations are a little trickier for learners because they can involve some or all of the following factors: a casual register, colloquial language, emotionally charged language, slang, ellipsis, sarcasm, and hidden meanings that require understanding "between the lines".

6. **Extensive**: Students at intermediate to advanced levels are sometimes asked to give extended monologues in the form of oral reports, summaries, or perhaps short speeches. Here the register is more formal and deliberative. These monologues can be planned or impromptu.

B

Below is the speaking activity that Ms. Lee has designed for her low-intermediate level students.

Student A's Worksheet

※ **Directions**: You are a telephone salesperson for the Best Wear Company. Your partner is a customer. Your partner calls to order some items from your company's catalog. Take the order and fill out the order form. Make sure you have written the order correctly by asking your partner to confirm it. Don't look at your partner's page!

- Ordered by:
    Name _____
    Address _____
    City _____
    State _____
    Telephone _____

Item number	Quantity	Color	Size	Description	Unit price	Total

- Method of Payment
    ( ) store account   ( ) credit card
    ( ) check   ( ) debit card

Student B's Worksheet

※ **Directions**: You want to place a catalog order. Your partner is a telephone salesperson. Look at the catalog page below. Choose two items you want to buy. Call the Best Wear Company and give your order to your partner. Make sure that your partner takes the order correctly by confirming the information. Don't look at your partner's page!

Guideline for Pre-service Teachers

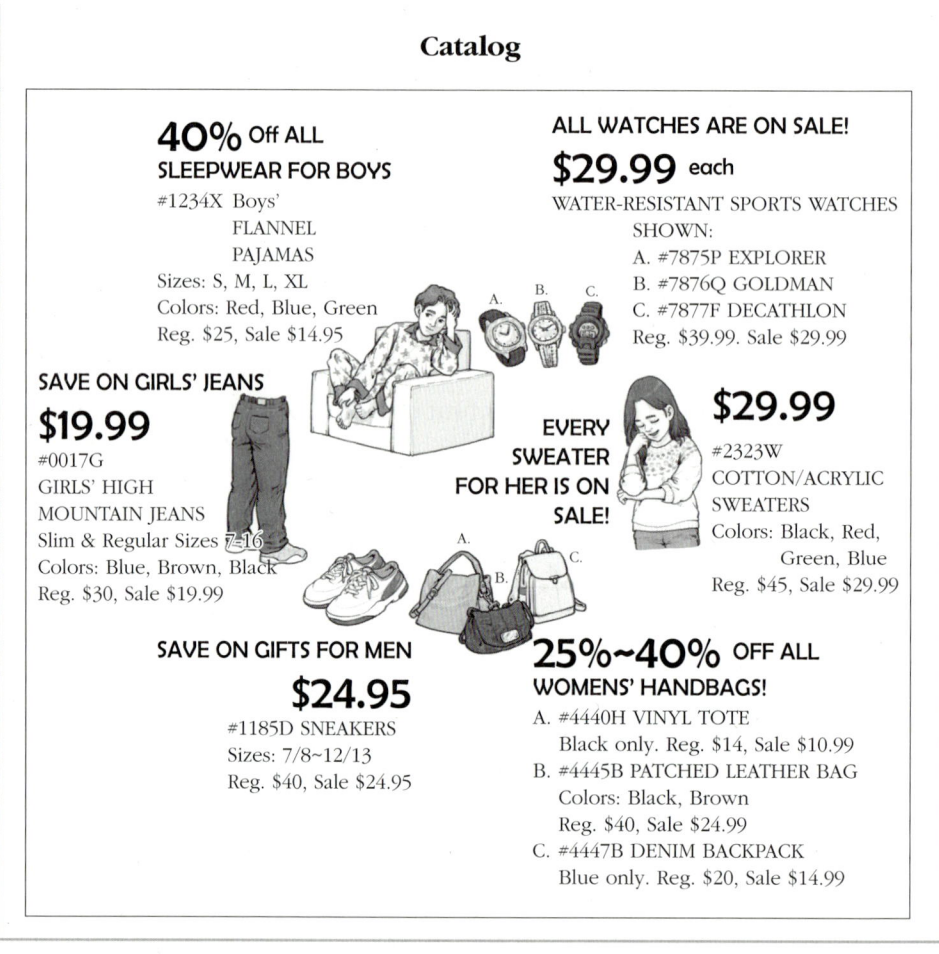

Write the name of the activity exemplified in <B>. Also, referring to the terms in <A>, identify the speaking performance of the identified activity, adding some evidence from both <A> and <B>.

Your Answer

08 Read the passages in <A> and <B>, and follow the directions.

A

English teachers use classroom activities related to various micro and macro strategies to enhance students' pronunciation. Here are some specific activities from each level.

1. Micro-level: This level focuses on the pronunciation of individual phonemes.

   (1) Phoneme Practice: Practice individual consonants and vowels to develop basic pronunciation skills.
   (2) Minimal Pair Exercises: Use pairs of words with similar sounds (e.g., "ship" and "sheep") to distinguish and practice subtle pronunciation differences.
   (3) Phonetic Symbols Study: Learn the accurate ways to pronounce various phonemes using the International Phonetic Alphabet (IPA). (e.g., /e/, /æ/, /ɒ/, etc.)
   (4) Vowel and Consonant Combination Drills: Practice words or syllables combining vowels and consonants to enhance pronunciation accuracy.

2. Macro-level: This level focuses on elements of pronunciation that go beyond individual syllables, such as rhythm, stress, intonation, and linking.

   (1) Stress Practice: Identify and practice stressed parts of words and sentences to create natural intonation patterns.
   (2) Intonation Pattern Drills: Practice intonation patterns for different types of sentences, such as questions, commands, and exclamations.
   (3) Linking Practice: Practice common linking phenomena in natural speech (e.g., "don't you" becoming "don'cha") to improve fluency.
   (4) Role-play Practice: Engage in role-plays or conversational practices that mimic real-life situations to practice using appropriate intonation or rhythm in different contexts.

Guideline for Pre-service Teachers

B

Ms. Kim, a middle school English teacher, created tailored speaking activities for students with pronunciation challenges. Below are parts of the activities and comments from participants, Kyuhee and Wonji.

Activity 1

"at" Sound Practice:
- Cat
- Fat
- Hat

"ba" Sound Practice:
- Basket
- Bakery
- Baseball

...

Kyuhee's Comments

Today, I practiced some words, focusing on the specific sound combinations in each case to improve my pronunciation. I repeated each word in the list in chorus. Overall, I think today's practice helped me become more accurate in pronouncing the specific sounds.

Activity 2

※ Pair up and practice the following script paying close attention to the intonation patterns.

  Scene: At a restaurant

Jamie : Good evening! Can I start you off with something to drink? (*Rising intonation on "drink", indicating a question*)

Alex : Hmm, could I have a glass of iced tea, please? (*Rising intonation on "please", indicating a polite request*)

Jamie : Of course! Would you like lemon or peach flavor? (*Rising intonation on "peach flavor", indicating an invitation for the listener to make a choice*)

Alex : Lemon sounds refreshing, thank you. (*Falling intonation on "thank you", indicating gratitude*)

...

Wonji's Comments

  Today's activity was very engaging and practical to enhance my English speaking skills. Taking on the role of Alex, the customer, I was challenged to use appropriate intonation patterns to make my utterances sound natural and polite.

Identify the ONE specific activity in <A> that Kyuhee and Wonji each practiced during their speaking lesson from <B>. Then explain your answers with evidence from <A> and <B>.

Your Answer

Guideline for Pre-service Teachers

09 Read the passage in <A> and the teaching procedures in <B>, and follow the directions.

A

When it comes to teaching pronunciation, it is important to focus on various aspects of speech that contribute to clear and effective communication. The following table provides simple descriptions of four pronunciation elements: *articulation, stress, rhythm,* and *intonation.*

Elements	Description
Articulation	Articulation refers to how sounds are formed and produced in speech. It involves the precise movement and coordination of the speech organs such as the lips, tongue, and teeth to produce individual sounds and words accurately.
Stress	Stress refers to the emphasis or prominence placed on certain syllables or words within a sentence or utterance. It helps convey meaning, highlight important information, and add clarity and emphasis to the message.
Rhythm	Rhythm pertains to the pattern of stressed and unstressed syllables in speech. It involves the appropriate timing and grouping of syllables to create a natural speech flow.
Intonation	Intonation relates to the rise and fall of pitch and the melodic patterns in speech. It conveys the meaning differences in terms of emotional tones, attitude, and communicative intent of the speaker.

B

Teaching Procedure 1

1. Introduce the sounds /p/ and /f/ and explain their lip position and airflow differences.
2. Practice minimal pairs (e.g., "pat" and "fat", "pool" and "fool") with students repeating after the teacher to emphasize the distinction.
3. Guide students to focus on lip position and airflow while repeating the words multiple times.
4. Engage students in activities where they produce words or sentences using the /p/ and /f/ sounds.

Teaching Procedure 2

1. Provide three example sentences that demonstrate meaning differences based on different types of modulation:
   a) "You're going?" (a rising pattern, expressing surprise)
   b) "You're going." (a falling pattern, stating a fact)
   c) "You're going!" (a falling-rising pattern, expressing excitement or encouragement)
2. Engage students in this activity where they practice different types of modulation to convey various meanings.
3. Offer feedback and guidance as students practice using modulation to express different emotions or intentions.
4. Reinforce the concept of modulation's impact on meaning and encourage continued practice in varied contexts.

Based on <A>, identify the specific pronunciation elements that Teaching procedure 1 and 2 focus on in <B>, respectively. Then, explain your choices with evidence from <A> and <B>.

Your Answer

10 Read the passage and the teaching journals, and follow the directions.

A

Current approaches to pronunciation markedly differ from earlier methods. Instead of solely focusing on developing a learner's articulatory skills from the bottom-up, treating it as the mastery of a phoneme and allophone inventory, modern techniques employ a top-down approach that places significant emphasis on the most pertinent pronunciation aspects within discourse context. Rather than confining instruction to articulation within individual words or phrases at best, that is, we now turn to delve into its significance across entire stretches of discourse to enhance the intelligibility of the conveyed message.

B

Teacher A

A significant number of my students face difficulty in producing the [v] sound due to its absence in the Korean language, often substituting it with the [b] sound. To address this challenge and aid students in distinguishing these similar sounds, I designed today's lesson around minimal pairs. I guided them to focus on one pair at a time, allowing them to closely compare the [v] and [b] sounds. For example, students practiced saying 'vest' followed by 'best.' Through consistent repetition, students made notable progress in distinguishing these sounds at the end of the class.

Teacher B

Teaching learners about stress and intonation can significantly enhance their message comprehension. Initially, I presented the sentence "I didn't say he stole your money." and exemplified the shifting of stress depending on context.

(e.g.)
- Stressed on "I": "**I** didn't say he stole your money." (Someone else said he stole the other's money.)
- Stressed on "didn't": "I **didn't** say he stole your money." (Implies you didn't say he stole someone's money.)
- Stressed on "he": "I didn't say **he** stole your money." (Someone else stole it.)

Subsequently, I organized them into groups to identify nuances in meaning. As they encountered challenges in discerning these differences, I supplemented the sentence within a dialogue showcasing distinct stress patterns. By engaging with the dialogues, and considering the context, students gained a deeper grasp of how stress modulation within a sentence can distinctly alter its intended message.

Referring to the terms in <A>, identify each approach to pronunciation instruction that Teacher A and B take in class by adding the supporting evidence from <B>. Do NOT copy more than FOUR consecutive words from the passage.

Your Answer

Guideline for Pre-service Teachers

11 Read the passage and follow the directions.

> *Below is part of the conversation between two English teachers talking about teaching pronunciation.*
>
> Ms. Kim : Hello, Mr. Jin. What are you up to?
>
> Mr. Jin : Hi, Ms. Kim. I'm reading an article about effective pronunciation teaching methods. Recently, my students have been consistently struggling with pronunciation, particularly with distinguishing sounds like /r/ and /l/, as well as /p/ and /f/.
>
> Ms. Kim : Could you elaborate a bit?
>
> Mr. Jin : Certainly. For instance, they find it challenging to differentiate between words like "alive" and "arrive," or "coffee" and "copy." This leads to the issue of _____ in regard to whether the message they intend to convey is understood or not by their listeners.
>
> Ms. Kim : That's indeed a significant challenge. It highlights the importance of explicitly teaching pronunciation.
>
> Mr. Jin : I couldn't agree more. Do you happen to have any effective strategies for teaching pronunciation?
>
> Ms. Kim : Well.. how about providing minimal pairs which contain confusing sounds?
>
> Mr. Jin : Minimal pairs?
>
> Ms. Kim : Yes, but it's essential to provide them within a meaningful context. This approach helps students naturally distinguish individual sounds in context.
>
> Mr. Jin : Could you provide some examples?
>
> Ms. Kim : Of course. Let's say you want to teach the difference between 'ch' /tʃ/ and 'j' /dʒ/. You could offer sentences like "The crowd cheered the speaker" and "The crowd jeered the speaker." The words 'cheered' and 'jeered' only have a single sound variation, yet their meanings are completely opposite. This contextual approach allows students to grasp the sound difference more effectively.

> Mr. Jin : I understand. So, teaching the differences between individual sounds within a meaningful context helps students naturally comprehend the distinctions in meaning. Right?
> Ms. Kim : Exactly!

Fill in the blank with the ONE most appropriate word. Then, write the solution that Ms. Kim is recommending to address Mr. Jin's students' pronunciation problem and explain how it helps students.

Your Answer

Guideline for Pre-service Teachers

12 Read the passages and follow the directions.

A

Student's Reflection

Today's lesson was quite interesting as the lesson topic is closely related to our school lives. Many students bring their mobile phones to school, and teachers consistently advise against using them in class. So, today, we had a valuable opportunity to discuss the school policy on mobile phone usage in-depth. In our group work, we were divided into those in favor and those against the use of mobile phones. However, unfortunately, we couldn't discuss the topic so effectively. We had difficulties expressing our opinions because we lacked experience in debating in English. If the teacher had provided us with key expressions commonly used in debates, we could have shared our ideas effectively and fluently.

Teacher's Reflection

My students have a strong attachment to their mobile phones and carry them at all times. However, our school policy strictly prohibits mobile phone use in class. Nevertheless, some students secretly send texts and watch videos of their favorite celebrities during lessons, in violation of the school policy. This led me to organize a classroom debate on the subject of mobile phone use. To start, I distributed a school newspaper article discussing mobile phone use in school. Since today's topic is directly related to students' real lives, they enjoyed reading it and had no trouble sharing what they had read from the article. However, the challenge arose when they struggled to articulate their arguments fluently. As I observed their performance, it became evident that I should have provided them with essential expressions to help them clearly present their opinions, both in favor and against the debate question. Moreover, during the discussion, many students displayed pauses and hesitations. This prompted me to realize that they needed preparation time before the actual debate.

B
Lesson Procedure

- Students: 1st graders in a high school
- Proficiency: Multiple levels

Step 1 : The teacher distributes a school newspaper article about using mobile phones in school.

Step 2 : T asks students to read the article individually. Then, T puts students in pairs and asks them to share the main idea and details they have found from the article.

Step 3 : T divides Ss into groups of four and introduces the debating question.

> [Debating Question]
> *Do you agree or disagree with using mobile phones in school? Why?*

Step 4 : Each member chooses one side, either pro or con, and discusses the debating question.

T=teacher, Ss=students

Based on <A>, identify ONE good point and ONE problem of this lesson. Then, choose TWO steps in <B> and write how to revise each to solve the identified problem from the teacher's point of view.

Your Answer

13 Read the passages in <A> and <B>, and follow the directions.

A

Ms. Kim's Note

Attending a workshop on improving classroom interaction has been enlightening. As a middle school teacher, I now better understand the importance of interaction in education. This is particularly relevant today, as communicative language teaching increasingly emphasizes interaction as the foundation of effective communication. This workshop highlighted the critical role of fostering interaction to engage and empower students, ultimately improving their learning outcomes. Below are some effective strategies I learned to facilitate interaction in the classroom:

Strategies for Promoting Interaction

(1) Respond to students with praise and recognition.
(2) Pose questions that elicit genuine responses from students.
(3) Promote meaning negotiation and self-correction through group work.
(4) Encourage self- or peer-evaluation among students.
(5) Delay error correction until the end of the communication.

B

After participating in the workshop, Ms. Kim conducted several English lessons. Below are excerpts from the classroom interactions taken from her lessons.

Classroom 1

T : Alright, class, let's continue with our lesson. Sunho? Where do you want to go for your summer vacation?

S1 : I want to go to Hawaii! I heard the weather is very warm year-round. I like warm weather.

T : Hawaii! And yes, the place is indeed very warm. How about Eunji? For your dream vacation, where do you want to go?

S2 : I want to go to Paris! I want to see the Eiffel Tower.

T : Paris also sounds nice! Visiting the Eiffel Tower is a must-do for many travelers to Paris! Guys, just like this, we all have different dream vacation destinations, right?

Ss : Yes!

T : So from now on, we're going to do a decision-making group activity. Please keep in mind that during your discussions, respect everyone's ideas and make a decision. Is it clear?

Ss : Got it!

T : Excellent. In your groups, please decide on a destination for your dream vacation. Each person should share their preference and reasons for choosing that place.

(Ss break into groups and begin discussing their vacation destination choices. T observes student interactions and takes notes some errors most students frequently made during the group work.)

T : Well done, everyone! I observed some great discussions. Now, let's briefly go over the choices you made and address some common errors I noticed during your interactions.

Guideline for Pre-service Teachers

Classroom 2

T : Everyone! Today, we're going to do a picture-description activity in your groups. Make groups of four and collaboratively describe this picture. Don't forget to assign your own roles. Leaders, please ensure that every member participates in the description. The writer, please write down your group's description. *(T continues explaining each role.)*
Is everything clear? Great! Let's get started then!

(Ss break into groups and begin the picture-description activity.)
S1 : So, uh, in this picture, there is a palm [fam] tree.
S2 : I didn't catch that. Can you say that again?
S1 : There is… a palm [pɑːm] tree.
S2 : Oh, I see. A palm tree.
S3 : Next to it, three people are playing volleyball.

(Later in the class)
T : Now, let's move on to the next step. In your groups, has everyone written down your group's description?
Ss : Yes!
T : Okay, then, pass your descriptions to the group on your left. I'm handing out the checklists now. Please use them to provide constructive feedback to your classmates.

(Each group exchanges descriptions and works in groups again. T walks around the classroom.)
T : Constructive comments can help us improve our communication skills. Keep up the good work, everyone!

T=teacher, S=student, Ss=students

Based on <A>, identify TWO strategies that each classroom interaction in <B> has mainly exemplified, respectively. Then, explain your answers with evidence from <A> and <B>.

Your Answer

4. Productive Skills

> Guideline for Pre-service Teachers

14 Read the passage in <A> and the interaction in <B>, and follow the directions.

A

　　Teacher's corrective feedback can take various forms and is commonly seen as a continuum, ranging from explicit to implicit. In explicit feedback, the teacher provides linguistic information that directly addresses the non-target-like nature of the produced utterance. On the other hand, implicit feedback is a more indirect and subtle way of indicating that a learner's utterance may have issues. In practice, the teacher follows a sequential order of prompts, starting with less explicit feedback and gradually moving towards more explicit feedback. The choice of feedback depends on whether the learner is capable of producing the correct form. This approach aims to provide learners with feedback that is tailored to their current level of proficiency and understanding. As a result, the student comprehends the feedback and becomes capable of self-correcting errors. Some researchers have designed a set of guidelines for providing students with tailored feedback, as follows:

Types of Feedback

No 1. Pause
No 2. Repeat the erroneous phrase/sentence as a question
No 3. Repeat just the error
No 4. Ask the student what is wrong with the utterance
No 5. Ask an 'either/or' question
No 6. Provide the correct language
No 7. Provide an explanation

> **B**
>
> Teacher : Can anyone tell me what you and your family did yesterday? Yes, Sungjin?
> Student : We was at the park yesterday.
> Teacher : We was at the park?
> Student : Yes, we was there.
> Teacher : Can you think about what might be wrong with 'we was'?
> Student : Um, it sounds right to me.
> Teacher : Is it 'we was' or 'we were'?
> Student : Oh, it should be 'we were at the park yesterday.'
> Teacher : Exactly, 'we were'. Nicely corrected!

Based on <A>, identify all the types of feedback that the teacher uses to address the student's error in <B>. Then, explain how the teacher adjusts the feedback when the student repeatedly fails to recognize the error, and write the outcome of these adjustments.

Your Answer

Guideline for Pre-service Teachers

15 Read the passages <A> and <B>, and follow the directions.

A

In English speaking lessons, the method of providing feedback on student errors depends on the focus of the activity. For activities focusing on *accuracy*, feedback should be provided immediately to address any mistakes. However, for activities aimed at *fluency*, feedback should be given when the overall conversation has finished to avoid disrupting the flow of communication. Feedback can be adjusted to fit the context and goals of the speaking exercise. Some common types of feedback include recast, clarification request, explicit correction, metalinguistic feedback, and pinpointing.

B

Conversation 1

T : Today, we're going to practice using the past perfect tense. I'll give you each a question, and I'd like you to answer using the past perfect tense. Let's start with you, Aram!
S1 : Sure, I'm ready.
T : Can you tell us about a task you had completed before you left your house to come to school today?
S1 : Yes, I had finished my breakfast before I left my house this morning.
T : Well done! Now, let's move on to Jisun. Jisun, can you describe something you had done over the weekend before you met your friends?
S2 : Certainly. I have completed all my homework before …
T : *(Interrupting)* Have completed?
S2 : Oops, I had completed all my homework before I met my friends at the cinema on Sunday afternoon.
T : Excellent! Let's hear from Jooho. Jooho, can you talk about a book you had read before you started the one you're reading now?
S3 : I have read 'To Kill a Mockingbird' before …
T : *(Interrupting)* Have read?
S3 : Well, I read 'To Kill a Mockingbird' before …

T : *(Interrupting)* Remember, we're focusing on the past perfect tense for things done before other past events. Let's try again.
S3 : I had read 'To Kill a Mockingbird' before I started '1Q84' last week.
T : Very nice!

Conversation 2

T : Alright, everyone, for this activity, let's talk about what you did last weekend with your group members. Don't worry about making mistakes. Confidence is key here!

Students are chatting in groups, occasionally making errors, but they continue speaking confidently as encouraged.

S1 : So, last Saturday, I go to the park and see a lot of people there.
S2 : Really? I visit my grandmother's house last Saturday.
S3 : That's cool! Last week, I cooked a meal of a new recipe.
(ellipsis)
T : *(After the activity)* It sounds like you all had busy weekends. Eunji, you went to the park and saw a lot of people.
S1 : Oh, yes! There were lots of people when I arrived at the park. There was a music festival, and it was amazing!
T : A music festival sounds like a lot of fun! And Sungjin, you visited your grandmother's house last Saturday.
S2 : Yes, I visited her. We had a great time together.

T=teacher, S=student

Based on <A>, identify the focus of activity and the type(s) of feedback presented in Conversation 1 and Conversation 2, respectively. Then, explain when and why the identified feedback type(s) are used in each conversation, based on evidence from <A> and <B>.

16 Read the passages and follow the directions.

A

Ms. Choi's Teaching Note

During a recent group discussion activity, I noticed that many of my students were making similar grammatical errors. Specifically, I observed that they were struggling to distinguish between adjectives that end in '-ed' versus '-ing'. Despite having learned the rule, they were still making mistakes. During the activity, I attempted to correct every errors by interrupting their conversation and pointing them out. However, I found that this error correction method did not seem to be effective, as they continued to struggle with using the two forms correctly. Moreover, they seemed to speak less during the speaking activity. After that class, I spoke with some of my students and they commented that my frequent interruptions to correct their errors were demotivating them and raised their affective filter. Based on this feedback, I realized that my error correction method was not appropriate and that I need to develop a more effective error correction strategy.

B

Ms. Park's Teaching Note

Recently, I heard that Ms. Choi has difficulty fixing her students' grammatical errors. In my opinion, error correction method should vary depending on the purpose of the lesson. For instance, if the class goal is accuracy, it is appropriate to correct the errors related to the target grammar immediately. However, if the focus is on fluency, it is more effective to address the errors related to the target grammar after the speaking activity as a follow-up treatment. Therefore, my suggestion to Ms. Choi would be to let her students engage in speaking activities without interrupting their conversation flow, and address any errors later in the class.

Explain why Ms. Choi's error correction method from <A> is problematic. Then, based on <B>, write the error correction method that Ms. Park will suggest for Ms. Choi.

Your Answer

17 Read the passages and follow the directions.

A

In a teacher-student interaction, a teacher can provide feedback in response to a learner's production, which is associated with inaccuracy. It can take one of two forms: implicit or explicit. Implicit feedback occurs when there is no overt indicator of an error being committed, whereas explicit feedback involves clear indications. Implicit feedback can manifest through clarification requests, and recasts during communicative interactions. On the other hand, explicit feedback takes various forms such as *explicit correction, elicitation, repetition*, and *metalinguistic feedback*. Thus, during the interaction, the student receives indications that their conversational patterns have not been understood correctly, and their immediate reactions to such indications are referred to as uptake. There are two types of student uptake: (a) *repair*: the student's utterance successfully repairs the initial problem and (b) *needs repair*: the student's response fails to successfully repair the initial utterance and still needs repair.

B

Below is a conversation between a teacher and a student.

S: Ms. Kim! I have some news to share!
T: What's up? Tell me.
S: Well, my sister buy a car.
T: She bought a car!
S: Yes, she bought a car.
T: Wow, that's great! How old is she?
S: She have just turned 20.
T: Nice. Getting a car is a step towards independence.

T=teacher, S=student

Based on <A>, explain the teacher's feedback and the student's uptake, citing each line from <B>.

Your Answer

Guideline for Pre-service Teachers

18 Read the passages and follow the directions.

A

Teacher feedback refers to the teacher's verbal and nonverbal responses or actions which he/she provides to students' ideas or actions. Feedback can be categorized in two ways: positive and negative feedback. For instance, positive feedback indicates that the one does understand the other clearly, whereas negative feedback indicates a lack of one's understanding or an error of the utterance.

B

Two middle school students, Minji and Junho, have a conversation about their hobbies with their English teacher, Mr. Choi. Minji is an advanced level student and Junho, a low-intermediate level one.

Mr. Choi : Let's talk about our favorite hobbies. Minji, what's your favorite hobby?
Minji : I really enjoy playing the guitar. It's so much fun strumming the strings.
Mr. Choi : That's wonderful, Minji! Playing the guitar is a great way to express yourself. Now, Junho, what's your favorite hobby?
Junho : Um, my favorite hobby is *paint*.
Mr. Choi : Your favorite hobby is....?
Junho : Painting! My hobby is painting!
Mr. Choi : That's fantastic, Junho. Painting is a great way to facilitate your creativity. And what about you, Minji? Do you have any other hobbies you enjoy?
Minji : Well, besides playing the guitar, I like taking a photo, *either*.
Mr. Choi : That's impressive. What kinds of camera do you usually use?
Minji : I use my polaroid camera. Oh, I use my Iphone camera, *either*!
Mr. Choi : Great, Minji.

* Italicized words indicate students' errors.

Referring to the terms in <A>, explain the reason Junho can correct his error but Minji cannot correct her errors, respectively, with evidence from <B>. Then, write the potential problem that Minji can have in this situation.

Your Answer

Guideline for Pre-service Teachers

19 Read the passages and follow the directions.

A

Current research on corrective feedback underscores the crucial role of feedback in achieving successful oral communicative competence acquisition. Consequently, it is imperative that we utilize a range of feedback strategies, including *recast, repetition, clarification requests, elicitation,* and *metalinguistic feedback.* It is paramount to bear in mind the principles of maintaining communicative flow, using either implicit or explicit types of feedback, fostering self-correction among students, and taking into account the affective state and linguistic stage of the learner. Inappropriate feedback can result in students embedding incorrect forms within their cognitive framework.

B

The following is the excerpt from a conversation between an English teacher and his student, Seojoon, during a picture-description activity. This activity was centered around practicing the present progressive tense, a grammar form that the student had covered the previous week in class.

T : Alright, Seojoon! Who is he? Yes! It's Mr. Kim. Now, what is he doing?
Seojoon : He is PLANT a tree.
T : Exactly! He is planting a tree! He looks nice, doesn't he?
Seojoon : Yeah!
T : How about the next picture? What can you see there? Who are they? What are they doing?
Seojoon : Three children are PLANT flowers.
T : Do you remember how to use the present progressive?
Seojoon : Yes, it's 'be+ Ving' form.
T : That's right. Three children are?
Seojoon : Three children are planting flowers!

Referring to terms in <A>, identify all types of feedback mentioned in <B> with corresponding utterances, and explain the reasons why the teacher modifies the type of feedback in the conversation.

Your Answer

Guideline for Pre-service Teachers

20 Read the passage and follow the directions.

> Below is an excerpt from a classroom conversation between an English teacher and her students. When students make errors, she either provides feedback to encourage them to correct these mistakes or she repeats the errors, hoping they will notice and address them. By providing corrective feedback to her students, she pushes her students to use grammatically and sociolinguistically correct utterances, a pedagogical concept known as _____ according to Swain.
>
> T : Kyungmin, what did you do last weekend?
> S1 : On Saturday, I *watches* a movie with my sister.
> T : *watches?*
> S1 : Oh, sorry, I *watched* a movie with my sister.
> T : That's right, Kyungmin. And what about you, Lisa? What did you do?
> S2 : I *visit* my grandparents in the countryside.
> T : Lisa, how do we say it already happened?
> S2 : Oh, I *visited* my grandparents in the countryside.
> T : Perfect, Lisa! It sounds like you both had a nice weekend.
>
> T=teacher, S=student

Fill in the blank with the TWO most appropriate words. Then, explain TWO types of corrective feedback (using ONE word) that the teacher provides to her students by providing corresponding feedback utterances in the classroom conversation.

Your Answer

21 Read the passage in <A> and the examples in <B>, and follow the directions.

A

There are various methods for implementing focus on form. A fundamental distinction is made between 'Planned focus on form' and 'Incidental focus on form'. For both types, a communicative task is essential. Planned focus on form involves predetermined linguistic forms through the use of specific tasks designed to elicit these forms within meaningful language use. On the other hand, incidental focus on form uses unfocused tasks aimed at eliciting general language samples rather than specific forms. There may be instances where no particular attention to form is given, though sometimes, either teachers or students might choose to focus incidentally on various forms during the task. Below is the summary of the different types of focus on form.

Types	Descriptions
Planned focus on form	Use of focused communicative tasks with predetermined targets
A1. Enriched input	Input flood or input enhancement
A2. Focused communicative tasks	Communicative tasks that have been designed to elicit the use of a specific linguistic form in the context of meaning-centered language use
Incidental focus on form	Unfocused communicative tasks
B1. Pre-emptive	The teacher or a student brings a linguistic form into the discussion even though no error has been committed.
B2. Reactive	The teacher or another student responds to an error that a student makes in the context of a communicative activity.

B

Example 1

In an English language classroom, the teacher has organized a communicative task for middle school students, focusing on using past simple tense to talk about their favorite childhood memories.

T : Good morning, class. Today, we're going to share our favorite childhood memories. I'd like you to use the past simple tense to describe what you did. For instance, I could say, "When I was a child, I visited my grandparents every summer." Who would like to start?

S1 : I can start, Mr. Lee. When I was a child, I played a lot of soccer with my neighborhood friends.

T : That's great, Ji-hoon! You used "played" correctly in the past simple tense. Any others? Yes, Min-ah!

S2 : Last year, I went to Jeju Island with my family.

T : Perfect, Min-ah! "Went" is the correct past simple form of "go".

Example 2

In an English language classroom, students are engaged in a group discussion about environmental conservation. Students are sharing their opinions and ideas in English and the teacher is monitoring the conversation.

S1 : People should think more before buying things to avoid making too much trash.

S2 : Everyone should tries to reduce their carbon footprint.

S3 : Yes, using public transportation can helps a lot.

T : May I quickly jump in? I've noticed a few verb form errors. Remember, after "should", and "can", we use the base form like "should try" and "can help". Keep up the good discussion!

T=teacher, S=student

Among the options A1, A2, B1, and B2 in <A>, identify the option of focus on form used in each example in <B>, respectively. Then, explain your answers with evidence from <B>.

Your Answer

2 How to Teach Writing Skills

01 Read the teacher's beliefs in <A> and the part of the lesson plan in <B>, and follow the directions.

A

To enhance the effectiveness of writing, I emphasize certain key guidelines for students during writing lessons:

Key Guidelines for Effective Writing

#1. Identify the Main Idea: Good writing starts with a clear goal or main idea. This central theme guides the direction of the writing.

#2. Plan Before Writing: Effective writers invest time in planning. This includes brainstorming and outlining the main points to be covered.

#3. Allow Ideas to Flow Freely: Initially, writers should let their ideas flow without restraint. This phase is more about getting thoughts on paper through freewriting, before writing the first draft without worrying over details.

#4. Follow an Organizational Structure: As they write, students should adhere to a general organizational plan, which helps in maintaining a logical flow.

#5. Revise Willingly and Efficiently: Good writing often requires revision. Students should be encouraged to revise their work, making necessary changes and improvements.

#6. Be Patient with Revisions: Patience is key in the revision process. Effective writers revisit and refine their work multiple times.

By focusing on these guidelines, students can develop their writing skills and produce well-structured, coherent, and engaging pieces.

B

Stages	Teaching & Learning Activities
Introduction	• Introduce the concept of blog writing. • Discuss its purpose and importance in digital communication. • Show examples of successful blog posts. • Analyze these examples to highlight their main ideas and organizational structure.
Development #1	• Guide students in brainstorming ideas for their blog posts. • Ask Ss to identify a central theme or main idea on their blog posts. • Students create an outline for their blog post. • Emphasize the importance of a logical structure they should adhere to in writing. • Students begin writing their blog posts based on their outlines. • Encourage them to focus on clarity, and coherence among detailed information.
Development #2	• In pairs, students exchange drafts and provide feedback on the organization and clarity of the main idea and detailed information. • Teach specific strategies for revising their work, focusing on enhancing the argument and readability. • Ask students to revise their drafts using the feedback from peers and make the final revisions.
Consolidation	End with a reflection session where students discuss what they learned about writing a blog post and how they can apply these skills in the future.

Guideline for Pre-service Teachers

Based on <A>, choose the TWO guidelines that the teacher does not follow in the lesson plan from <B>. Then, explain your answers with evidence from <A> and <B>.

Your Answer

02 Read the passages in <A> and <B>, and follow the directions.

A

In the process of writing, students employ various strategies to enhance the effectiveness of their compositions. When students employ various strategies throughout the phases of pre-writing, while-writing, and post-writing, several advantages emerge. Encouraging students to utilize these strategies in their writing classes can lead to improved writing skills, enhanced clarity, and more effective communication. Teachers play a crucial role in motivating and guiding students to harness these techniques, ultimately empowering them to become proficient and confident writers. Below are some of the writing strategies that students can use during the writing process.

Writing Strategies

- In Pre-writing Stage
  - Assessing the audience's needs and expectations
  - Using pre-writing devices

- In While-writing Stage
  - Writing with fluency in the first drafts
  - Using paraphrases and synonyms
  - Using feedback for revising and editing

- In Post-writing Stage
  - Reflecting on your writing
  - Having conferences with the teacher

B

After having a writing lesson, Ms. Park, a middle school English teacher, wanted to identify the strategies that her students found the most useful. Thus, she had a conference with two of her students. Below is an excerpt from the conference with two students, Jongmin and Mina.

Ms. Park : I've noticed significant improvement in your writing skills. Can you share what aspect of our writing lessons helped you the most?

Jongmin : For me, watching a short video and then brainstorming about a related topic really made a difference. The video provided us with a wealth of new information relevant to the topic. After watching the video, working in groups to brainstorm helped us explore a variety of ideas that we wouldn't have thought of on our own. This process significantly aided my writing. When it was time to write, I could select the most relevant ideas from the video and our brainstorming sessions.

Mina : In my case, the feedback I received from my peers after my first and second drafts was crucial for both revising and editing my writing. In the first round of feedback, they provided comments on how to improve the content of my writing. Then, in the second round of feedback, they suggested corrections for grammatical and punctuation errors, which was very helpful in the editing process. Revising and editing my work based on their feedback significantly enhanced the overall quality of my writing.

Identify the ONE specific writing strategy from <A> that Jongmin and Mina have each described as the most useful in <B>, respectively. Then, support your answers with concrete evidence from <B>.

Your Answer

Guideline for Pre-service Teachers

03 Read the passages in <A> and <B>, and follow the directions.

A

The writing course places a strong emphasis on teaching diverse categories of classroom writing performance, equipping students for success in education and the professional world. Below are five major categories of classroom writing performance.

Categories of Classroom Writing Performance

Imitative or Mechanical writing	In this type of writing, students will simply 'write down' English letters, words, and possibly sentences in order to learn the conventions of the orthographic code. Some forms of dictation fall into this category, although dictations can serve to teach and test higher order processing as well.
Intensive or Controlled writing	Writing is sometimes used as a production mode for learning, reinforcing, or testing grammatical concepts. This intensive writing typically appears in controlled, written grammar exercises. This type of writing does not allow much, if any, creativity on the part of the writer.
Self-writing	When people write for themselves, they have the freedom to express their own thoughts, ideas, and experiences without worrying about what others will think. This type of writing can be incredibly therapeutic, allowing students to reflect on their own lives, and process their emotions.
Display writing	Academically bound ESL students need to master a range of display writing techniques, where they demonstrate information or knowledge they have learned.
Real writing	Real writing refers to writing tasks that mimic authentic, real-world communication scenarios. The primary focus of real writing is on the purpose, audience, and context of the writing, aiming to engage students in meaningful communication rather than simply practicing grammar or writing structures in isolation.

B

Below are two students' reflections after taking a writing class that focus on one of the categories of classroom writing performance.

Eunmi's Reflection

Engaging in the journaling activity has been an incredibly valuable experience for me. This practice consistently gives me the opportunity to reflect on my thoughts and feelings. What makes it even more meaningful is that even though my teacher reads my journals, she doesn't judge whether my entries are right or wrong. This allows me to express myself freely without worrying about her opinions.

Haesol's Reflection

Today in my writing class, I completed my research paper on water pollution. This assignment required me to demonstrate what I had learned through my research. Clearly organizing and presenting the information helped solidify my understanding of the topic, and it was rewarding to see how much I had learned.

Referring to <A>, identify the writing performance categories demonstrated by Eunmi and Haesol in <B>, respectively. Then, explain your answers with evidence from <A> and <B>.

Your Answer

Guideline for Pre-service Teachers

04 Read the teachers logs in <A> and the writing activities in <B>, and follow the directions.

A

Mr. Park's Planning Log

As I prepare for the next English class, I am focused on selecting a writing activity that matches my students' proficiency level. My low-intermediate students could benefit from a method that emphasizes producing well-structured, polished texts. The plan is to engage them in an activity where they copy exemplary writing pieces. I believe that by immersing them in high-quality examples, their understanding of proper grammar and effective writing will improve.

Ms. Oh's Planning Log

In preparation for our upcoming English session, I am seeking an personalized writing activity that emphasizes the process rather than just the final product. My aim is to introduce an exercise that emphasizes the journey of writing itself, particularly for my students who are still developing their linguistic skills. The essence of this approach is to encourage students to draft texts, receive and share feedback, and revise their work. I believe that through repeated practice and constructive feedback, students will improve their ability to express themselves more effectively in English.

B

Activity 1

※ Directions: Write the passage again by changing past tense to the past perfect tense. Retain the original meaning of each sentence.

[Original Text]
   Last semester, I **enrolled** in a challenging calculus course. Throughout the term, I **encountered** difficult concepts that **challenged** my understanding. I **sought** out additional resources to improve my comprehension. By the final exams, I **mastered** the material and **achieved** a high grade.

[Rewriting]
_____
_____
_____

Activity 2
"My Favorite Memory"

(1) List your happy or significant memories:
   _____

(2) Pick one memory that stands out to you:
   _____

(3) Write about your chosen memory. Include:
   • Who was there? _____
   • What happened? _____
   • Why is this memory important to you? _____

[Your writing]
_____
_____
_____

> Guideline for Pre-service Teachers

(4) Share your writing with your partner, who will provide feedback based on these questions:
- Did the writing explain why this memory is special?
- Can you clearly understand and feel your partner's experience? If not, why?

(5) Improve your story by:
- Referring to your partner's feedback.
- Adding details to show your feelings.
- Making sure the events are clear.
- Fixing any spelling or grammar mistakes.

[Your revised writing]
_____
_____
_____

(6) Share Your Story
- If you're comfortable, share your story with a classmate.
- Listen to their story and share kind thoughts.

Based on the information provided in <A>, recommend the most suitable writing activity from <B> for each teacher. Then, write the reasons of your recommendations with evidence from <A> and <B>.

Your Answer _____
_____
_____
_____
_____

05 Read the passage and follow the directions.

> Below is part of the conversation between two English teachers, Ms. Park and Ms. Yoo, talking about the results of diagnostic test.

T1 : Hi, Ms. Yoo. What are you working on?
T2 : I'm reviewing the results of last week's diagnostic test.
T1 : How did it go? Were the results good?
T2 : The students' overall proficiency is at an intermediate level, but their writing scores are significantly lower than their other skills.
T1 : Is that so? Do you know the reason for that?
T2 : One of the major reasons comes from the lack of their grammatical knowledge. They seem to understand the rules but not to apply these in context appropriately.
T1 : And the other reason?
T2 : I haven't been able to identify it yet, despite reviewing the test results several times.
T1 : Can I take a look and see if I can help you identify the issue?
T2 : Sure, here are the test sheet and its results.
 (T2 shows T1 the test sheet that her students took and some sample answers from her students.)
T1 : (Upon examination briefly) They seem to struggle to write in a discourse level. I mean, all the sentences are separated and unrelated in their writing contexts.
T2 : Yes, you're right! They're not just making grammatical errors but also struggling with writing in paragraphs.
T1 : I have an activity that can fix both of these problems. First, you prepare a model text containing target rules and then read the texts three times. Also, you do not forget giving some keywords or an outline of the story. Finally, you ask students to reproduce the model text just as they are told.
T2 : I got it. Through well-structured paragraphs of the given model text, students can learn how to write contextualized sentences and appropriately use target grammar, can't they?

Guideline for Pre-service Teachers

> T1 : Yes, you got the point!
> T2 : Thanks a lot, Ms. Park. That's exactly what I need! Can you send me an example of the activity?
> T1 : Of course, I'll email it to you this afternoon.
> T2 : Thank you, Ms. Park!
>
> T=teacher

Based on the conversation above, identify the type of the writing activity Ms. Park recommends for Ms. Yoo and explain how the identified writing activity can improve students' writing weaknesses in Ms. Yoo's class.

Your Answer

06 Read <A> and <B>, and follow the directions.

A

Writing Activity Procedure

Step 1: Preparation
　T chooses a text that is suitable for their students' language proficiency level. The text should be rich in the language feature (grammar, vocabulary, etc.) I want to focus on.

Step 2: 1st Reading
　T reads a short story about a family's vacation to the Eiffel Tower to students at normal speed without interruption. Students listen and try to understand the general meaning of the text.

Step 3: Two times of Reading
　T reads the text two times asking students to listen to the key ideas or events.

Step 4: Writing
　Students write their own version of the text from memory. They should aim to reproduce the original text as closely and accurately as possible, trying to remember the exact words.

Step 5: Comparison
　Each student shares their version of the text. They compare these versions with the original text and find out the differences.

Step 6: Feedback & Discussion
　T collects Ss' written pieces and reviews them, focusing on the content and the use of grammar or vocabulary.
　T returns the compositions to Ss and conducts a group discussion on common mistakes and corrections.

B
Students' Logs

Student 1	In class today, we heard this super cool story about a family's trip to the Eiffel Tower. It was kind of awesome because my family and I have been to Paris too, so it felt like I was reliving my own adventure. But then, we had to remember the whole story and write it down. That was tough! I mean, I got the main stuff down, but there were so many little details that I just couldn't remember. It made me realize how hard it is to memorize a whole story just like that, without any help. Maybe next time, it would be really helpful if our teacher could show us some pictures or something while telling the story. That way, I think I'd be able to remember not just the big parts, but also the small details and how the story goes.
Student 2	So today in class, our teacher told us this story about a family's trip to France. She read it out loud three times and then we had to write it down from what we remembered. It was really hard for me to remember everything that happened and write the whole story exactly as she told it. I tried my best to do it on my own. When I got my paper back with the teacher's comments, I saw that I left out a lot of parts of the story and made a bunch of grammar mistakes. That was kind of a bummer. Looking at what my classmates wrote, I saw that the other kids who are also at the lower level had the same problems. I think next time, it might be easier if I could work with some of the kids who are at a higher level. That way, they could help me remember the story better and write it down more accurately.

Identify the name of the writing activity demonstrated in <A>. Based on the information in <B>, also, write about one common problem that both students encounter and then provide the solution suggested by Student 1 and Student 2, respectively.

Your Answer _____
_____
_____
_____
_____

Guideline for Pre-service Teachers

07 Read the passage in <A> and the activity procedures in <B>, and follow the directions.

A

Display writing refers to writing that is primarily intended for the teacher, who already possesses knowledge about the content the student is writing. In this form of writing, students showcase their proficiency in grammar, vocabulary, and sentence formation, essentially displaying what they already know. On the other hand, real writing involves writing where the teacher or reader is unaware of the specific content the student is conveying. Consequently, real writing prompts students to engage in genuine communication with the reader, striving for authentic and meaningful interactions.

B

Activity Procedure 1

1. After completing a writing lesson, instruct students to reflect on their experience of the lesson with a reflective journal entry.
2. Guide students to begin their journal entry with a brief introduction, mentioning the purpose of the entry and the specific writing lesson they participated in.
3. Encourage students to express their thoughts, feelings, and insights about the writing lesson.
4. Instruct students to conclude their journal entry by summarizing their overall experience and reflecting on the importance of the writing skills they acquired.

Activity Procedure 2

1. Provide students with a printed copy of a paragraph about 'Future Cities' that uses present tense verbs.
2. Explain the concept of verb tenses, specifically focusing on the future tense and its purpose in describing actions that will happen in the future.
3. Instruct students to rewrite the paragraph by changing the present tense verbs to the future tense.
4. Have students share their rewritten paragraphs with the class, discussing the tense changes made and the impact of using the future tense on the paragraph's tone and meaning.

Based on <A>, identify the type of writing that each Activity Procedure in <B> exemplifies. Then, explain each reason of your answers with evidence from <A> and <B>. Do NOT copy more than FOUR consecutive words from the passages.

Your Answer

Guideline for Pre-service Teachers

08 Read the passages and follow the directions.

A

Ms. Park's Teaching Log

I recently started using a new feedback tool for my students' written assignments due to its numerous benefits. One of the most notable advantages is the precision that this tool brings to my feedback. Standardized codes provided by this tool offer a clear roadmap for students, allowing them to pinpoint the exact areas that need correction without feeling overwhelmed by extensive comments. Additionally, this tool can provide an opportunity for my students to self-correct their errors and actively engage with their own learning. After decoding the codes, they are required to make corresponding corrections, essentially undertaking a process of self-editing. This process empowers them to become active participants in their own learning journey.

Symbol	Meaning	Incorrect	Correct
P	Punctuation	I live⌄work, and go to school in Walnut. [P]	I live, work, and go to school in Walnut.
=	Capitalization Needed	The dodgers play in los angeles.	The Dodgers play in Los Angeles.
VT	Verb Tense	I never work as a cashier until I got a job there. [VT]	I never worked as a cashier until I got a job there.
SV	Subject-verb Agreement	The manager work hard. [SV]	The manager works* hard. * This is just one correct tense that can be used. Depending on the time of the action, conjugate accordingly.
TS	Tense Shift	After I went to the store, I eat the ice cream I bought. [TS]	After I went to the store, I ate the ice cream I bought.
⌒	Close Space	Every one works hard.	Everyone works hard.
#	Space Needed	Going⌄to class is awesome. [#]	Going to class is awesome.
SP	Spelling	The maneger is a woman. [SP]	The manager is a woman.

318

B

Student's Reflective Log

　I would like to share my thoughts on the recent feedback I received for my writing assignments. The correction codes provided were helpful in easily identifying and self-correcting specific errors in grammar, spelling, and punctuation. However, there are a couple of areas to be improved. Firstly, while the codes are concise and standardized, they do not provide enough information on why I made those mistakes or how to avoid them in the future. Understanding the reasons behind our errors is crucial for truly learning and growing as writers. Without such deeper insight, I might continue to make the same mistakes repeatedly. Secondly, these codes focus solely on grammar, neglecting the overall picture of my written work. They concentrate on grammatical accuracy while ignoring content, organization, and overall structure. In my opinion, feedback should consider these aspects more than grammatical accuracy for a better version of my drafts. Therefore, I hope that in the future, my teacher will provide more comprehensive feedback that will help us become well-rounded writers.

Identify the feedback tool that Ms. Park recently uses for her students. Then, based on <A> and <B>, write TWO strengths and TWO weaknesses of this tool.

Your Answer

09 Read the passages and follow the directions.

--- A ---

Below is the evaluation results for Ms. Park's writing course.

Criteria	Questions	3	2	1
Course Objectives	• Are the course objectives clearly defined and aligned with the desired outcomes? • Do the goals of the course match the needs and expectations of the students?		V	
Curriculum Design	• Is there a well-structured curriculum with clear lesson plans and a logical progression of topics? • Are the writing assignments and activities relevant to the course objectives?		V	
Instructional Materials	• Are the textbooks, materials, and resources closely related to students' real lives? • Are supplementary materials, such as writing prompts or online resources, given based on student interest?	V		
Feedback	• Is feedback provided in a sufficient and constructive manner? • Are grading criteria transparent and consistently applied?			V
Assessment	• Are there clear criteria for evaluating student writing assignments? • Is there a balanced mix of analytic and holistic scoring methods?			V

3=Good, 2=Okay, 1=Poor

B

Below are the students' reflections on Ms. Park's writing course.

Student 1's Reflection

This semester, I took a writing course prepared by Ms. Park. The best thing about the class was that we could choose our own writing topics which are closely related to our daily lives. However, concerning the evaluation part, I have one suggestion. The evaluation for my writing pieces was normally based on specific writing elements. It was great to see my strengths and weaknesses. However, until the course finished, there was no assessment on my overall writing skills. Since I took this course to improve my writing skills, which are relatively low compared to the other skills, it would have been better if I had had a chance to assess my writing skills based on comprehensive evaluation.

Student 2's Reflection

While taking this writing course, I actively participated in writing activities because I could choose my own topics based on my interests. Furthermore, I believe that peer feedback is an essential part of improving my writing skills because the more readers there are, the more feedback I can receive to enhance my writing. However, this writing course only provided me with a couple of chances to receive feedback from my peers. I shared this concern with Ms. Park, but she explained that there was not enough time for peer feedback during lessons due to time constraints. Thus, for the next semester, if I take this writing course again, I'd like to suggest a way to post my writing pieces on our class blog to give and receive more feedback from fellow students.

Guideline for Pre-service Teachers

Based on <A> and <B>, identify the criteria that demonstrate the strength(s) and weakness(es) of Ms. Park's writing course. Then, suggest solution(s) for Ms. Park to address the problems that each student mentions in <B>.

Your Answer

10 Read the passages and follow the directions.

A

Student writing can be evaluated on five features: fluency, content, conventions, syntax, and vocabulary.

- **Fluency**: A simple curriculum-based measure of fluency is the total number of words written during a short writing assignment. When assessing fluency, misspellings, poor word choice, and faulty punctuation are not taken into account. Attention is only directed to the student's facility in translating thoughts into words.
- **Content**: When evaluating content, features including the composition's organization, cohesion & coherence, accuracy (in expository writing), and originality (in creative writing) should be considered.
- **Conventions**: In order to fulfill the communicative function of writing, the product must be readable. Thus, writers are expected to adhere to the standard conventions of written English, including correct spelling, punctuation, capitalization, grammar, and legible handwriting.
- **Syntax**: When assessing syntax, teachers examine the structure and complexity of the sentences students produce, including their ability to vary sentence patterns.
- **Vocabulary**: The words used in a student's composition can be evaluated according to the uniqueness of the words used in the composition. Both quantitative and qualitative methods can be used to evaluate vocabulary.

Guideline for Pre-service Teachers

B

Teacher's Note

In my writing class, I'd like to evaluate the writing skills of my intermediate level students. Thus, I conducted a formative writing assessment last week. They were asked to write an essay about their best memory from the last summer vacation within 1000 words. In this evaluation, I heavily focused on evaluating two critical aspects from students' essays: First, while reading their essays, I evaluated whether they understood the established rules of written English adhering to effective writing. So, I checked if they used proper spelling, accurate punctuation, and correct capitalization. Additionally, I evaluated their legible handwriting which plays a significant role in ensuring that the message is conveyed effectively. As the second aspect, I focused on the organization of the composition. I checked whether there was a clear and logical structure that would guide readers to comprehend the writing. Cohesion and coherence were other key element. I asked myself: Are the sentences connected logically? Do the ideas flow smoothly? By highlighting these aspects in my evaluation, I was able to provide constructive feedback that helped my students enhance the overall quality and effectiveness of their writing.

Based on <A>, identify TWO aspects that the teacher focuses on in evaluating students' writing mentioned in <B>. Then, support your answer with evidence from <B>. Do NOT copy more than FOUR consecutive words from the passages.

Your Answer

11 Read the teacher's and the student's reflections. Then follow the directions.

A

Ms. Yoo's Reflection

When evaluating my students' journals, I provide corrections across all types of errors from grammar to writing conventions. I believed that this comprehensive approach would help them enhance their writing skills. However, after discussing with students, I discovered that my detailed corrections were not always effective. Some students were merely replicating my corrections without understanding why they made those errors or how to avoid them in the future. Reflecting on their own mistakes is actually a critical step in improving their writing skills. Additionally, some expressed frustration at seeing their work marked up with corrections across various error types. To address these issues, I'm considering a new correction technique that uses symbols to highlight only major errors. This approach aims to encourage students to be more actively involved in the revision process.

B

Min-su's Reflection

I'm thankful that my teacher reviews our writing every week. However, when I receive my paper covered in red marks, I feel overwhelmed and frustrated. I recognize that she diligently points out our mistakes. Yet, seeing so many corrections demotivates me. Moreover, my revision process merely involves copying her corrections. To truly enhance my writing skills, I believe it is crucial to reflect on my errors and correct them on my own. Thus, I wish she would simply indicate areas only for specific types of errors, instead of correcting all types of errors. By doing so, I will not feel frustrated and also focus on self-correcting those specific errors.

Guideline for Pre-service Teachers

Based on <A> and <B>, suggest ONE alternative to the current correction method for the teacher and explain how the alternative meets the student's needs. Do NOT copy more than FOUR consecutive words from the passages.

Your Answer

NEW Build Up

Chapter 05

Vocabulary & Grammar

Chapter 05 Vocabulary & Grammar

📖 정답 및 모범 답안 p. 463

1 How to Teach Vocabulary

01 Read the passage in <A> and students' logs in <B>, and follow the directions.

A

  In the field of language education, particularly in the area of vocabulary acquisition, two distinct methodologies play crucial roles: intentional and incidental teaching. Each approach offers unique benefits tailored to different aspects of language learning. Intentional learning involves students in activities specifically designed to focus their attention on acquiring new vocabulary. These activities may include semantic mapping, word association activities, and the study of word formation. On the other hand, incidental learning occurs indirectly, often while the learner's primary focus is on understanding a text or participating in communication. In this approach, the acquisition of new vocabulary is a beneficial byproduct rather than the primary goal.

B

Sunmi's Log

  Today in the library, I grabbed a book perfect for my reading level. As I got absorbed in the story, I also encountered new words that were suitable for my level. It felt like finding treasures without even searching for them. The story made the meanings of these words clear, so I didn't have to pause and look them up. Learning new words this way seemed to stick better. It was more fun than actual studying. By the end of the book, I realized I had picked up many new words almost without effort. It's incredible how much you can learn by just enjoying a story. I'm going to keep reading these books; it's a fun way to improve my vocabulary.

Jihoon's Log

Today's class was really engaging. We chose basic words and then added different suffixes to create a bunch of new words. It was cool to see how adding just a few letters can completely change a word's meaning or how it's used. I never knew how these groups of words were connected and that knowing basic words well could help me learn many more. This method made me see how complex and rich language is. What started as something small ended up expanding my vocabulary a lot. Learning this way felt like solving a puzzle—finding one key piece helped make sense of the whole thing. Now, I feel much more confident in recognizing and using these words.

Based on the terms in <A>, identify the type of vocabulary learning that each student in <B> has described in their log. Then, explain your answers with evidence from <A> and <B>.

Your Answer

Guideline for Pre-service Teachers

02 Read the passage in <A> and the word entries in <B>, and follow the directions.

A

A corpus is a comprehensive collection of written or spoken texts from various sources compiled in digital format. By analyzing corpus data, students can uncover diverse information about language patterns, usage trends, and linguistic structures. Therefore, contemporary online dictionaries, enriched by corpus analysis, offer detailed insights into words, including authentic examples, context, collocations, grammatical information, and word families.

1. Context: By examining concordance lines, students can see how a word is used in various contexts, which helps in understanding its application and connotations in real language use.
2. Collocations: Corpus analysis can reveal common collocations, showing which words frequently occur with the target words.
3. Grammatical Patterns: Through examining concordance lines, students can observe grammatical patterns related to a word, such as its typical position in a sentence.
4. Word Families: A corpus aids in learning word families by providing insights into how base words, their inflected and derived forms, and cognates are used in various contexts.

B

The following two online dictionaries are developed based on corpus data.

Dictionary 1

Innovative [ˈɪnəveɪtɪv]
adjective [more~; most~]
introducing or using new ideas or methods

- Innovative *approach*
- Innovative *technology*
- Innovative *design*
- Innovative *solution*

Dictionary 2

in·no·va·tive /ˈɪnəveɪtɪv/
adjective
(of a product, idea, etc.) featuring new methods; advanced and original

> 1. (mostly appears before a noun)
>   *Innovative* idea
> 2. (often follows a linking verb)
>   The company's approach is *innovative*.

Identify ONE corpus-based feature mainly described in <A> for each Dictionary in <B>, respectively. Then, provide evidence from <A> and <B> for each feature you choose.

Your Answer

03 Read the passage in <A> and the teaching procedures in <B>, and follow the directions.

A

A thorough understanding of vocabulary knowledge is crucial for language acquisition, encompassing not only the basic meaning of words but also a multifaceted grasp of their usage and nuances. Depth of vocabulary knowledge refers to a learner's comprehensive understanding of various aspects of a word, illustrating the extent to which the learner is acquainted with it. This concept emphasizes that for higher-frequency words, learners must possess more than just a rudimentary understanding of their meanings. It encompasses a range of components including pronunciation, spelling, meaning, register, usage frequency, and their morphological, syntactic, and collocational properties. Such a deep understanding enables learners to effectively utilize these words in both spoken and written communication, enriching their language proficiency.

Components of Vocabulary Knowledge

- Pronunciation: The way a word sounds when spoken, including the correct articulation and stress on syllables.
- Spelling: The correct arrangement of letters in a word.
- Meaning: What a word represents, which can vary depending on the context. A word may have multiple meanings.
- Register: The level of formality or informality showing how a word is used appropriately. This also includes the field where a word is commonly used, such as medical, legal, or academic.
- Frequency: The rate at which a word is used in language, distinguishing between high-frequency and low-frequency words.
- Morphological Properties: The structure of words, including the understanding of roots, prefixes, suffixes, and word formation processes.
- Syntactic Properties: The grammatical function of a word in a sentence and its interaction with other words.
- Collocational Properties: The patterns of word co-occurrence in common phrases or combinations, such as "make a decision" vs. "do a decision."

B

Teaching Procedure 1

1. Below are four sentences using the word "charge." Write what you think "charge" means in each context.
   - The battery has lost its charge. _____
   - The general led the charge into battle. _____
   - She faced a charge of theft. _____
   - Can you charge my phone? _____

2. Now, it is your turn to be creative. Write two sentences using "charge" with different meanings. Share your sentences with a partner and discuss.
   - Sentence 1: _____
   - Sentence 2: _____

Teaching Procedure 2

1. Read the following sentences where "consult" is used. Decide if each sentence is formal, or informal, and write your answer next to it.
   - I'll consult my calendar to see if I'm free this weekend.
     _____
   - The engineer will consult with the project manager to review the technical specifications. _____
   - Let's consult the app to find out where we can grab a bite to eat.
     _____

2. Read the following sentences where "consult" is used. Decide the field where each sentence is used. (e.g., legal, academdic, etc.)
   - The physician will consult with the specialist to determine the best course of treatment for the patient.
     Field: _____
   - Before proceeding with the lawsuit, it is advisable to consult with a legal expert to ensure all procedural requirements are met.
     Field: _____
   - Students should consult the academic advisor to discuss their course selections and ensure they meet graduation requirements.
     Field: _____

Guideline for Pre-service Teachers

Identify the ONE component of vocabulary knowledge in <A> that each teaching procedure in <B> focuses on, respectively. Then, explain your answers with evidence from <A> and <B>.

Your Answer

04 Read the passage in <A> and activities in <B>, and follow the directions.

A

The following is a summary of seminal materials prepared by Ms. Lee, a high school English teacher, focusing on the use of concordance programs in teaching. By utilizing these programs, educators can teach students various aspects of vocabulary and language usage.

Aspects	Descriptions
Collocations	These are words that frequently appear together. Concordance programs can highlight common word pairs or combinations, aiding in natural language usage.
Frequency	Students can see how often a word is used within a text or corpus, helping them understand its commonality or rarity.
Connotations	By examining words in varied contexts, students can learn about the positive, negative, or neutral connotations words may carry.
Grammatical Patterns	Students can observe how words fit into grammatical structures, aiding in the understanding of syntax and word order.
Register	Concordance data can reveal in which registers (formal/informal or usage fields like academic, professional, technical, etc.) a word is most commonly found, guiding appropriate usage.

Guideline for Pre-service Teachers

B

Activity 1

- Step 1: In groups of 3-4, you will be given a list of words that have different implied meanings.
- Step 2: Use the concordance program to look up your assigned words. Examine the sentences from the program and discuss the implications of the word in each context.
- Step 3: For each word, choose two sentences that show different implied meanings. Fill in the table below with these sentences and your analysis for each.

Word	Two Sentences from Concordance	Implied Meanings (Positive, Negative, Neutral)	Analysis
...	...	...	...

- Step 4: Be prepared to present your findings, focusing on how the context has influenced the implied meanings of the words.

Activity 2

- Step 1: Form groups of 3-4 and assign each group a list of words.
- Step 2: Use the concordance program to search for your assigned words. Review the sentences provided from the program and discuss the usage context with your group.
- Step 3: For each word, fill in the table below with two sentences from the concordance results and your guess for where it is commonly used.

Word	Two Sentences from Concordance	Formality & Specific Field of Usage
...	...	...

- Step 4: Prepare to share your findings with the class, explaining why you chose the usage field.

Based on the information in <A>, identify the specific aspect that each activity in <B> focuses on, respectively. Then, explain your answers with evidence from <B>.

Your Answer

05 Read the passages and follow the directions.

A

Below is an excerpt from a reading text that Ms. Kim has prepared for her intermediate level students.

Sarah and Mark were exploring an old attic filled with mysterious things. As they searched through the dusty boxes, Sarah accidentally found an old diary. She was excited and quickly opened it.

Sarah : Mark, look! I found this old diary with stories from the past.
Mark : Wow, that's interesting! Can I see it?

Sarah **handed** the diary to Mark. He got the diary for Sarah, and started reading the yellowed pages. Suddenly, something caught his attention. He found a photo hanging from one of the pages.

Mark : Sarah, look at this! There's a photo **dangling** from one of the pages. It seems to be a family picture.
Sarah : Oh, let me see! It's **delicate**, so be careful not to tear it. It looks like it could be easily damaged.

Mark carefully took off the photo and showed it to Sarah. They examined the faces, wondering about the people captured in the picture.

B

Ms. Kim's Note

For the upcoming lesson, my objective is to teach intermediate-level students the underlined words through reading. As students read the conversation between two friends, they will identify the underlined words and determine their meanings using contextual clues from the text or their extratextual knowledge. I believe that the most effective method for teaching vocabulary is to provide example sentences that illustrate when and how to use the vocabulary within a specific context. This approach allows students to gain a more profound understanding of the meaning and usage of the target words.

Based on <A> and <B>, write the idea (principle) that Ms. Kim thinks as the most important in teaching vocabulary and explain the vocabulary strategy that she aims to teach her students. Do NOT copy more than FOUR consecutive words from the passages.

Your Answer

06 Read the passage in <A> and the activity procedure in <B>. Then, follow the directions.

A

The very best language educators can often be identified by their commitment to creative and innovative classroom teaching strategies. They constantly try new language teaching strategies to engage their students, experimenting with new language learning activities and teaching tools to improve learning outcomes. There are several classroom teaching strategies suggested for great language teachers: the natural approach, the lexical approach, and the lexicogrammatical approach. First of all, the natural approach is a language teaching method that simulates child language acquisition by emphasizing communication, comprehensible input, kinesthetic activities, and virtually no grammatical analysis. It emphasizes communication while de-emphasizing conscious grammar study and explicit correction of student errors. Next, the lexical approach in language teaching seeks to develop proposals for syllabus design and language teaching founded on a view of language in which lexis plays the central role. It is based on the belief that the building blocks of language learning and communication are not grammar, function, or notions but lexis, that is words and word combinations. Finally, the lexicogrammatical approach represents a view that lexis and grammar are two inherently connected parts of a single entity and shouldn't be treated separately. From this view, a grammatical structure may be lexically bound and lexical items also have grammatical features. This view has been supported by corpus research, which illustrates a strong connection between contextual patterns.

B
Activity Procedure

Step 1. T presents three key verbs and some related words on the board. Then, T asks Ss to match the verb with the appropriate words and say the meaning of each phrasal verb.

- Take   a decision

             happy
- Make   an effort

             a break
- Have   fun

             a photo

Step 2. T checks the answers with the whole class. Then, T puts Ss in groups of three.

Step 3. T asks Ss to search for five more example phrases of the three verbs in the corpus website.

Step 4. After coming back to the classroom, T asks Ss to present what they have found.

Step 5. T observes Ss' presentations and gives proper feedback about grammatical points such as the structure 'verb + (a/an) noun' or 'verb + adjective.'

T=teacher, Ss=Students

Based on the terms in <A>, identify the appropriate language teaching approach that the activity procedure in <B> exemplifies. Then, support your choice with evidence in <B>.

Your Answer

Guideline for Pre-service Teachers

07 Read the passage in <A> and the test items in <B>, and follow the directions.

A

Vocabulary knowledge is commonly understood to encompass two primary dimensions: breadth of vocabulary knowledge (referring to the number of words a learner has some basic understanding of) and depth of vocabulary knowledge (encompassing all lexical traits, including syntactic, semantic, and collocational characteristics, as well as frequency and register). Over the past few decades, a significant number of research projects has established that L2 vocabulary size is essential for successful L2 reading comprehension. Yet, recent studies have increasingly focused on the role of the quality of L2 vocabulary knowledge, especially in ESL/EFL settings.

B

Test Item 1

※ Match the words to their corresponding primary meanings.

1) apply
2) elect
3) jump
4) manufacture
5) melt
6) threaten

_____ choose by voting
_____ become like water
_____ make

Test Item 2

※ Choose two words from each column, which can be related to the given word. Then, write how the chosen words are related to the given word.

Word: Sudden

Column 1	Column 2
beautiful	change
quick	doctor
surprising	noise
thirsty	school

Referring to terms in <A>, identify the dimension that each test item in <B> aims to evaluate, respectively. Then, explain your answers with evidence from <A> and <B>.

Your Answer

Guideline for Pre-service Teachers

2) How to Teach Grammar

01 Read the passages in <A> and <B>, and follow the directions.

A

Ms. Kang's Belief

As an English teacher, I often find that students perceive grammar as a daunting set of rules and terminology rather than a valuable tool for improving the clarity and impact of their writing. Unfortunately, this misunderstanding often stems from traditional teaching methods, including the use of sentence diagrams and excessive red marking. However, by making grammar both relevant and practical, I believe I can create a more conducive learning environment in my classrooms. The following are some research-supported practices for teachers on designing grammar lessons more relevant and useful to students.

1. Conduct unplanned grammar teaching in the process of authentic writing.
2. Focus on usage over terminology.
3. Teach and assess one skill at a time.
4. Scaffold learning first through practice and then application.
5. Model grammar concepts by demonstrating grammar rules and nuances.
6. Refrain from marking every single error you come across.

B

The following two learning logs are written by students after attending Ms. Kang's grammar lessons.

Student 1's Learning Log

Before taking Ms. Kang's class, I found grammar to be the most challenging subject due to its complex and seemingly unimportant rules. However, Ms. Kang's approach to teaching grammar goes beyond mere memorization. She involves us in practical activities that make learning engaging and relevant. Even for students who are not very familiar with English grammar, like me, she provides support starting with the basics of constructing sentences, allowing us to build our skills gradually. For instance, after we learned how to use the present perfect tense, we began by completing sentences using the correct verb forms. As our confidence increased, Ms. Kang encouraged us to write short essays about events from the past year, using the present perfect tense wherever applicable. Initially, practicing grammar was unfamiliar and challenging, but through gradual and structured learning, I now feel confident enough to apply these skills directly in my writing.

Student 2's Learning Log

Among the English classes I've taken, Ms. Kang's class stands out as the best because it focuses on practical grammar. In previous classes, merely memorizing numerous rules and taking tests didn't effectively enhance my ability to apply grammar. However, Ms. Kang tailors her teaching to address grammar that is relevant to our immediate needs, making the lessons both more engaging and practical. For example, during a recent writing session, she asked us to write and share our favorite recipe with friends. Throughout the editing process, Ms. Kang observed our work and introduced adverb clauses as a useful tool for writing recipes. She explained how to use adverb clauses to provide additional information such as time or temperature, with examples like, 'When the water is boiling, put the pasta in the pot.' After learning this valuable skill, we revised our recipes, and everyone enjoyed applying and using the new grammar rule.

Identify the ONE specific grammar teaching practice in <A> that Student 1 and Student 2 have described in their logs from <B>, respectively. Then, explain your answers with evidence from <A> and <B>.

Your Answer

02 Read the passages in <A> and <B>, and follow the directions.

A

High school English teacher, Mr. Yoo, conducted a survey among 50 fellow English teachers to explore the most effective methods for teaching grammar to low-intermediate students. Mr. Yoo intends to incorporate the two most effective techniques revealed in the survey into his upcoming grammar lessons. Here are the survey results:

Grammar Techniques	Description	Vote Counts
Charts, Objects, Maps, and Drawings	Utilize visual aids such as charts, objects, maps, and drawings to help students make focus on grammatical forms somewhat concrete.	4
Dialogues and Conversations	Teach grammar through real dialogues and conversations, allowing students to learn language form and meaning in context.	3
Input Enhancement	Highlight specific grammar forms within sentences to help students easily recognize them.	17
Input Flood	Provide texts that contain a target structure that appears repeatedly, making the structure more salient.	4
Input Processing	Make learners attend to meaning and form in the input at the same time. Help learners make the necessary connection between form and function in authentic contexts of L2 use.	3
Dictogloss	Require students to listen to a short text and then reconstruct it. Through the reconstruction of a text, learners come to notice certain grammatical features.	19

> **B**
>
> After the survey, Mr. Yoo presented following some grammar teaching activities at the weekly teacher workshop.
>
> ### Activity 1
>
> Tell students read a story about Eunji and choose the appropriate adverb of frequency.
>
> | Never | Seldom | Sometimes | Often | Usually | Always |
> |---|---|---|---|---|---|
> | | | | | | |
> | | | | | | |
> | | | | | | |
> | | | | | | |
>
> a. Eunji works hard.
> b. She is on time for work.
> c. She is early for work.
> d. She types letters.
>
> ### Activity 2
>
> (1) Inform students that they will listen to a text about friendship. Have them predict the possible content of the text. Clarify any challenging vocabulary and instruct them to pay special attention to relative clauses.
> (2) Read the text at a normal speed. Ask students to listen carefully and jot down key words or phrases related to the content as they listen.
> (3) Read the text again at a normal speed. Encourage students to expand their notes during the second listening.

(4) Have students form groups of three to reconstruct the text based on their notes. Emphasize the importance of creating a version as close to the original text as possible, with particular attention to relative clauses.
(5) After completing their reconstructions, display the original text. Then, have students check their versions for any grammatical errors, particularly focusing on the relative clauses highlighted in the original text.

> [Original Text]
> We are always looking for good friends. These days it is hard to find true friends **whom we can trust**. Certainly, it is important to be considerate of those **who care for us**. However, a true friend is someone **who is sincere and loyal**, and is with us through tough times.

Activity 3

T provides students with a worksheet where students have the chance to process the target feature in a controlled manner.

※ Instructions: Listen to the following sentences and decide whether they describe an action that was done before or is usually done.

	Usually	Before
1. The teacher corrected the essays.		
2. The man cleaned the table.		
3. I wake up at 5 in the morning.		
4. The train leaves the station at 8 am.		
5. The writer finished writing the book.		
6. The trees go green in the spring.		

Guideline for Pre-service Teachers

Based on <A>, identify the ONE activity in <B> that most teachers may prefer and then, explain your answers with evidence from <A> and <B>.

Your Answer

03 Read the passage in <A> and the lessons in <B>. Then, follow the directions.

A

In grammar teaching, the deductive and inductive approaches are two different methods used to introduce and explain grammatical concepts to students. These approaches differ in how they present and teach grammar rules and structures. In the deductive approach, the teacher first presents a grammar rule or concept to the students, often through explicit explanations and examples. After presenting the rule, students are given example sentences to practice the rules. Whereas, in the inductive approach, students are presented with examples of sentences first. Then, they are encouraged to analyze and discover the underlying grammar rules themselves. The choice between the deductive and inductive approaches often depends on the specific learning objectives, the complexity of the grammar concept, and the preferences of both the teacher and the students.

B

Lesson A

T: Last time, we learned how to describe the difference between two people using '-er'. Today, let's learn how to compare more than two people.
(Writing the rule on the board.)

[On the Board]
Superlatives
: the + adjective + est

Lesson B

(Last class, students learned how to compare between two people and continue to learn how to compare more than two people.)
T: Everyone! Today, you will read through the text and underline the words for comparisons.
- Ss read the text and underline the words used for comparison.

T: As you can see, we put '- est' instead of '-er'. Plus, we need 'the' in front of the adjective. Let's practice it!

(T shows some pictures and describes the pictures by writing down example sentences on the board.)
ex) Jina is the tallest.
　　She lives in the highest building in town.
　　　　　(...)
- T asks Ss to read aloud the example sentences.
- T asks Ss to describe pictures by using the superlatives.

(Students practice making superlatives with other adjectives like 'large, short, cute ...' based on given pictures.)
　　　　(ellipsis)

[Text]
　Most of the performers are human! There is Leopold, the <u>strongest</u> man in the world. His father also worked in the circus, but Leopold was <u>stronger</u> than him. He has the <u>biggest</u> arms and the <u>longest</u> legs in his village, too! His incredible strength allows him to perform even <u>riskier</u> feats than the other circus acts
　　　　(ellipsis)

- T checks the answers with the whole class.
- Ss are asked to re-read the text and think about two ways to make comparisons.
- Ss in groups discuss how to express comparison based on the underlined words (strongest, stronger, biggest, longest, riskier) and figure out each rule of when to use the comparative and superlative forms.

e.g.,
(1) To make a comparison between two things, I would say something is adjective + er than the other.
(2) To make a comparison among more than three things, I would say something is the + adjective + est.
(ellipsis)

Based on the information in <A>, identify the approach to teaching grammar that each lesson in <B> exemplifies and explain the reason for your choice.

Your Answer

04 Read the passages and follow the directions.

A

Following are some techniques for teaching grammar, especially for helping learners notice and pay attention to grammatical features they need for the completion of given tasks.

1. Using charts, tables, or drawings
These are effective devices for calling students' attention to grammatical forms. For example, a chart requires students to notice, check off (√), or check their comprehension on target forms.

2. Using dialogues and conversations
Dialogue and conversations have been successfully used to focus learners on form and meaning simultaneously. For beginners, they provide models for practice, even if all the lexical and grammatical components are not completely understood. For intermediate learners, dialogues and conversations give learners a chance to confidently produce language, and then to vary the models with their own creative additions.

3. Using input enhancement
This is a more recent common technique that involves highlighting (or boldfacing) certain target grammatical forms in a reading text or stressing certain forms when speaking.

4. Using input flood
This technique presents texts that contain a target structure that appears frequently or repeatedly, and is therefore more salient. This may trigger syntactic priming, as learners tend to "produce a previously spoken or heard structure".

5. Using dictogloss
This is a task-based procedure designed to help L2 learners internalize certain grammatical elements that are built into a text. Through the reconstruction of a text, students come to notice certain grammatical features.

B

The following is the lesson procedure to teach grammar in context for middle school students.

Lesson Procedure

Step 1. T displays a picture of a ship and a map of the world on the board.

Step 2. Ss in pairs predict what they are going to read talking about the picture and the map.

Step 3. Ss read the story from the textbook.

Step 4. T checks students' understanding of the story.

Step 5. T shows the following specialized passage onto the screen.

> On 6 July 1931, the Baychimo, the ship, **was left** from Vancouver, Canada, under the command of Captain John Cornwall. Passing through the Bering Straits, the ship entered the Northwest Passage. The captain spent hundreds of thousands of dollars purchasing furs along the Victoria Island coast. On the return journey, the ship **was trapped** in early winter ice and couldn't move. With the ship in danger of **being crushed**, Captain Cornwall and his crew made a camp on safer ice closer to shore and prepared to wait there until the spring.

Step 6. The class pays attention to the words underlined and boldfaced.

Step 7. T writes down two sentences and then asks students to find out the difference between the two sentences.
　　　　Ex: The cat chased the mouse.
　　　　　　The mouse was chased by the cat.

Step 8. T explains how to make passive form.

　　　　Passive: Subject + "be" + past participle of the main verb

> Guideline for Pre-service Teachers

Step 9. Ss do an activity to check their understanding on using passive forms depending on the tenses.

[Activity]
※ Complete the table below with the correct passive forms.

Active	Passive
does	
is watching	
caught	

T=teacher, Ss=Students

Referring to <A>, identify TWO grammar teaching techniques which are utilized in the lesson procedure above. Then, support your choices with the corresponding steps and evidence from <B>.

Your Answer

05 Read the passages in <A> and <B> and follow the directions.

A

In conducting speaking classes, teachers should adhere to several principles, one of which is the need to balance meaning-focused and form-focused activities to foster both fluency and accuracy. Particularly, form-focused activities must meet two requirements. Firstly, contextualized practice is essential, where the target structure is practiced within situations where it is commonly used. Secondly, students should be able to personalize the language while using the target structure. In other words, students should be provided with opportunities to express their own ideas, feelings, experiences, and opinions using the target form in real-life situations.

B

Activity 1

Teacher : Today, we're going to review some historical events in Korean history that we learned last week while practicing the present perfect tense. Respond to the questions using the appropriate subject and the present perfect tense. Sarah, when did King Sejong invent Hangul?

Student 1 : King Sejong has invented Hangul in 1433.

Teacher : That's not quite right. Remember, we use the present perfect for actions that don't reference a specific time. The correct sentence is: "King Sejong has invented Hangul," but only if we're not mentioning in the year 1433. Since we are referring to a specific date, we should use the past simple: "King Sejong invented Hangul in 1433." Eunji, when did Seoul become the capital?

Student 2 : Seoul became the capital in 1948.

Teacher : Excellent! Sungjoon, when was Gyeongbokgung Palace constructed?

Student 3 : Gyeongbokgung Palace was constructed in 1395.

Guideline for Pre-service Teachers

Activity 2

Teacher : Let's start today's lesson with a little conversation. We're going to talk about traveling around the world today. Jisoo, have you ever traveled abroad?
Student 1 : Yes, I have visited France with my family.
Teacher : Fantastic! Hoyoung, what about you? Have you ever traveled abroad?
Student 2 : Yes, I have traveled to Japan. I enjoyed sushi there.
Teacher : Sushi! Sounds yummy! Sooji, have you ever traveled abroad?
Student 3 : Yes, I have visited Vietnam! They have very good pho!
Teacher : Nice! Sunghee, have you traveled abroad?
Student 4 : I have visited New York. I have cousins there.

Activity 3

Teacher : Alright class, let's practice forming sentences in the present perfect tense. I'll give you the subject and the base form of the verb. You'll respond with a sentence using the subject and the verb in the present perfect tense. Respond in the order of seating, starting from the first row. Sarah, **arrive**.
Student 1 : Sarah has arrived.
Teacher : Correct! Then, David, **swim**.
Student 2 : David has swum.
Teacher : Excellent! Next, Emily, **walk**.
Student 3 : Emily has walked.
Teacher : Very good. Alex, **run**.
Student 4 : Alex has run.

Based on the information provided in <A>, choose the most suitable form-focused activity from the three options listed in <B> to enhance students' speaking skills. Then, explain your choice with evidence from <A> and <B>.

Your Answer

06 Read <A> and <B> and follow the directions.

A

Ms. Park, a high school English teacher, prepared an activity for her low-intermediate level students. The target form is past tense. Below is part of the activity she designed.

Activity Procedure

1. Introduce a story of two friends making onion curry together and let Ss listen to the story.
2. Have Ss listen to the teacher's instruction on the activity.
3. Distribute the activity slip.
4. Ask Ss to do Task A after listening to the story again.

Task A

※ Write the number for the following sentences in the order that they presented from the story.

- They gathered all the ingredients—onions, tomatoes, spices, and oil. ____
- Once the ingredients were ready, they heated oil in a pan. ____
- Aram didn't know how to cook curry, so Sujin explained the recipe to her. ____
- Two friends, Sujin and Aram, decided to make onion curry together. ____
- They started by slicing the onions and chopping the tomatoes. ____
- Sujin sautéed the onions until they turned golden, while Aram prepared the ginger and garlic paste. ____

---

5. Make Ss check the answers in pairs talking about what they have listened to and then give the answers in a whole class.
6. Explain how a past tense is constructed in English.

Guideline for Pre-service Teachers

7. After listening to the story again, Ss do the Task B in pairs.

Task B

※ Decide whether the following sentences refer to an action (or a state) that was done in the past or is done currently (exists).

	Present	Past
1. Two friends, Sujin and Aram, decided to make onion curry together.	☐	☐
2. They gather all the ingredients—onions, tomatoes, spices, and oil.	☐	☐
3. Aram didn't know how to cook curry, so Sujin explained the recipe to her.	☐	☐
4. They start by slicing the onions and chopping the tomatoes.	☐	☐
5. Once the ingredients were ready, they heated oil in a pan.	☐	☐
6. Sujin sautéed the onions until they turned golden, while Aram prepared the ginger and garlic paste.	☐	☐

---

8. Check the answers with Ss and review the form with usages.

B
Ms. Park's Teaching Note

Today, I arranged a special focus-on-form activity, unlike the traditional grammar activity. Usually, I have thought that students should be equipped with the grammatical accuracy needed for communication. Through this activity, I wanted students to make necessary connections between form and function(meaning) in a more structured manner. That is, students gave priority to meaning and then focused on the target form. As can seen in Activity Procedure from <A>, firstly I asked students to listen to a story of two friends making onion curry and then complete Task A by identifying cooking order by numbers. In Task B, then, I encouraged students to pay close attention to the past tense in order to grasp clear meaning. In this way, this special grammar activity was carefully structured for form-meaning relationships. Another intention behind choosing this activity is that students can improve their input processing skills without feeling stressed about producing language. In simpler terms, this grammar activity doesn't require students to produce any language forms; instead, it leads them to understand necessary input more accurately based on its structured manner. Thus, this activity can reduce the pressure on students to produce language while still enhancing their comprehension skills.

Based on <A> and <B>, identify the type of activity exemplified in <A> using THREE separate words from <B> and write TWO reasons why Ms. Park chooses the identified activity.

Your Answer

Guideline for Pre-service Teachers

07 Read the passages and follow the directions.

A
Activity Procedure

Step 1
- T distributes a worksheet to Ss.

  [Worksheet]
  a) The plane had experienced a mechanical malfunction. _____
  b) The pilot had gotten out to restart the plane. _____
  c) The pilot waited for clearance for take-off. _____
  d) The plane started to move along. _____
  e) The pilot landed. _____

- T reads a story to the class and asks Ss to number the events in the worksheet in the order they happened, 1-5 (a-e) in order to help Ss' comprehension.
- T checks the answers together with Ss.

Step 2
- T gives the written story to Ss and tells them to underline every word in past tense or past perfect form. In groups, Ss share the words they underlined. Then, T introduces the past perfect form on the board.
- T asks a question to Ss. Ss in groups discuss the answers.
  Q: "Why is the past simple used for one event in the text and the past perfect used for another?"
- T asks each group to present their own answers.

Step 3
- T asks Ss in groups to categorize those underlined words and to complete the given table.

  ```
  Past      Simple
  Perfect   Past
    X         X
  ─────────────────────►
   Past     Present
  ```

Past perfect	Simple past

- T checks the answers together with Ss.

Step 4	• T gives the questions again and asks Ss in groups to write down the rule they have discovered. 1. When do we use simple past tense? _____ _____ 2. Then, when do we use past perfect? _____ _____ • T checks the answers of each group. T explains the general rules of the target structure precisely.

B

Teacher's Note

I am an English teacher for second-grade middle school students who are generally at an intermediate level of language proficiency. However, their writing skills are not as strong as their other language abilities, and they often make numerous grammatical errors. To address this, I have decided to focus more on teaching grammar rules explicitly. Thus, I have designed a special grammar activity that allows students to learn the target rules directly. Instead of providing lengthy explanations on grammar rules, I encouraged students to deduce these rules from given examples. This approach promotes active participation and fosters autonomy in the learning process. Moreover, this activity encourages active interaction among students, similar to other communication activities. For instance, while discussing the usage of past and past perfect tense in groups, students can offer mutual support and assistance. Considering these benefits, I believe this form-focused activity will effectively enable my intermediate-level students to acquire the necessary grammar rules.

Identify the form-focused activity exemplified in <A>. Then, write TWO benefits the teacher mentions about the identified activity, adding some evidence from <B>.

Your Answer

08 Read the passages in <A> and <B>, and follow the directions.

A

Ms. Park's Teaching Note

I believe that to help my students use language accurately, meaningfully, and appropriately, it is essential to teach the three interconnected and non-hierarchical dimensions of grammar: *form*, *meaning*, and *use*. With this in mind, I will prepare a lesson plan that explicitly addresses these dimensions. I will include relevant examples and provide practice opportunities for my students. During the learning process, I plan to incorporate input processing techniques to enhance their understanding. Finally, I will conduct an informal assessment to gauge their comprehension of the grammar dimensions.

B

Step 1: Introduction (5 minutes)
- Begin the lesson by discussing the importance of grammar in language use.
- Introduce three dimensions of grammar briefly.

Step 2: Explicit Instruction (15 minutes)
- Clearly explain the three dimensions of grammar.

> - Form dimension refers to observable structural components such as phonemes, graphemes, inflectional morphemes, and syntactic patterns.
> - Meaning refers to the semantic level of the structural items including lexical and grammatical meaning.
> - Use dimension accounts for meanings of utterances across different contexts and cohesion in discourse.

- Provide examples that illustrate the distinctions between form, meaning, and use.

> [Worksheet]
> Example: Modal Verb "Can"
>
> Form: "Can" is a modal verb.
> Meaning: It expresses the ability or possibility to do something.
> Use: It is used to indicate one's capacity or permission to perform an action.
> - I can swim. (ability)
> - Can I go to the restroom? (request for permission)

- Engage students in a brief discussion to ensure they grasp the concept of these dimensions.

Step 3: Practice and Application (20 minutes)
- Distribute the authentic reading text to students.

> [Text] Title: A Busy Day
>
> Today was an ordinary day in the bustling city of Metropolis. People **were walking** along the streets, cars **were honking** in traffic, and life **was buzzing** with activity. As the sun **was setting** in the west, Mary **was sitting** at a café, sipping her favorite cappuccino.
> (...)

- Ask students to identify examples of form, meaning, and use within the text. Discuss their findings in groups and fill in the blanks from the worksheet.

[Worksheet continued]

Form	be + ing
Meaning	...
Use	...

- Circulate the classroom to provide guidance and clarification as needed.

Step 4 : Assessment (10 minutes)
- Review the key points of the lesson and emphasize the importance of considering all three dimensions when analyzing language.
- Conduct an informal assessment by giving students a text and asking them to identify the form, meaning, and use of the expression, 'That is enough'.

Let's Check Your Understanding

[A short story]
　On a sunny Saturday afternoon, Tom and his daughter Lily were at the park. Lily's endless chatter started to wear on Tom. "That is enough, Lily," he said. Lily, understanding, sat beside him and drew in the sand. Later, they went to a café for lunch. When the waiter poured water into Tom's glass, Tom said, "That is enough."

※ Fill in each blank with *form*, *meaning*, or *use* of "That is enough" from the story.

- (ⓐ): When Tom said to Lily, "That is enough", it was a command for her to be quiet. However, when Tom said to the waiter, "That is enough", it indicated that Tom had a sufficient amount of water to drink.
- (ⓑ): The utterance consists of three single morphemes, where the verb *be* is inflected for the third person singular form *is*.
- (ⓒ): The demonstrative pronoun that refers to a preceding context, the copula *is* indicates "having a particular state or quality", and shows the relationship between *that* and *enough*. Finally, *enough* signifies sufficiency or adequacy.

- Provide feedback and address any misconceptions.
- Summarize the lesson, emphasizing the interconnected nature of form, meaning, and use in grammar.

Guideline for Pre-service Teachers

Fill in each blank ⓐ, ⓑ, and ⓒ in <B> with the most appropriate word. Then, identify the ONE Step in <B> that does NOT align with the teacher's beliefs in <A>, and explain how she actually instructs the target form in the identified Step with evidence from <A> and <B>.

Your Answer

NEW Build Up

Chapter 06

Assessment

Chapter 06 · Assessment

📖 정답 및 모범 답안 p. 465

1 Testing Principles

01 Read the passages in <A> and <B>, and follow the directions.

─────── A ───────

Ms. Kim, a high school English teacher, designed the following speaking test as a final exam before finishing the semester.

Test Descriptions

This speaking activity is framed as a conference where 50 students are invited to present innovative solutions to contemporary issues. The theme of the conference will be "Innovative Solutions for a Sustainable Future," allowing students to choose topics that interest them within the realms of technology, environment, education, healthcare, etc. This format has not been previously attempted in class, offering a novel experience for all students; however, it carries the risk of not accurately measuring what needs to be assessed.

Test Procedure

1. Preparation Phase (before the conference)
   - Students are briefed on the conference theme and are asked to select a topic for their presentation. They are encouraged to conduct extensive research on their chosen topic.
   - Guidelines for creating the PowerPoint (PPT) presentation are provided, including instructions on the structure, content, and design of the slides.

374

2. Presentation
- The presentation room is arranged to mimic a conference setting, with a podium for the speaker and seating arranged for the audience and evaluators.
- The "conference" is held, with each student allocated a 10-minute slot for their presentation, followed by a 10-minute Q&A session.

Evaluation

- Two teachers will evaluate each presentation based on a set of predetermined criteria, such as clarity of speech, audience engagement, content accuracy and relevance, and the effectiveness of the Q&A session.
- To ensure a common understanding of the criteria, the evaluators will discuss them prior to scoring.
- Presentations will be recorded, allowing evaluators to review the performances and discuss the criteria before finalizing the scores.
- In cases of significant discrepancies between evaluators' scores, a median value will be used.

Pilot Testing:

   The speaking task will be pilot-tested with a small group of students who have previously scored at an intermediate level on a validated speaking test. This ensures that the format and difficulty level of the assessment task are appropriate for the target intermediate-level students.

Potential Washback Effect:

   The immediate washback effect might be limited because students do not receive feedback immediately after the speaking test.

B

Ms. Kim asked five English teachers to review the speaking test. The following are their comments.

Teacher 1

As a summative assessment, it works well as an achievement test; however, since it is conducted at the end of the course, its washback effect is limited.

Teacher 2

The test can be considered highly reliable because it is evaluated by two teachers who have reached a common understanding of the criteria through discussion.

Teacher 3

Given that the test format—a conference—has not been previously conducted in class, the test is fair to all students; however, its reliability may be relatively low.

Teacher 4

Having 50 students each present for 10 minutes, followed by a 10-minute Q&A session is inefficient, in terms of both test duration and evaluation time. It is simply not practical.

Teacher 5

The speaking task will be trialed with a small group of students who have previously achieved an intermediate level on another validated speaking test. This will help ensure that the task's item discrimination is appropriate.

Identify the TWO teachers in <B> whose comments are NOT correct. Then support your answers with evidence from <A> and <B>.

Your Answer

02 Read the passage and follow the directions.

A

Tests can serve as valuable teaching tools. Teachers should possess the skill to create well-designed tests for their students. A well-structured test can positively impact learning, leading to improved study habits. Such tests should be designed to identify specific areas of difficulty experienced by the entire class or individual students, allowing for targeted support through additional practice and corrective exercises. Therefore, when designing assessments, teachers should consider aspects such as practicality, validity (content, construct, concurrent, predictive), reliability (inter-rater, intra-rater), authenticity, and washback.

B

Mr. Park's Teaching Log

Last week, I conducted a formative assessment for my third-grade middle school students. After the assessment, I held individual conferences with each student. During these discussions, I identified issues with the assessment design in relation to assessment principles. The assessment was primarily designed to test both speaking and writing skills. However, the majority of the evaluation criteria within the grading rubric were mainly based on speaking skills such as pronunciation, fluency, and vocabulary. As a result, students who were proficient in speaking tended to receive better grades. Regrettably, the components to evaluate writing skills were not sufficiently included in the scoring rubric. Additionally, I faced a significant difficulty in listening to 30 students who individually speak for 5 minutes and then evaluating their written work all by myself until the next day. The process was quite exhausting. To complete the evaluation quickly, I gave higher scores to students who are usually fluent in class and relatively lower scores to the other students. However, according to the evaluation results, my subjective judgements heavily seemed to influence the assessment, leading to entirely unfair scoring. For future test preparation, I will be more careful in planning the assessment to avoid such mistakes.

Based on <A>, identify all testing principles violated in <B>. Then, support your answers with evidence from <B>.

Your Answer

03 Read the passages in <A> and <B> and follow the directions.

A

Ms. Jung, a middle school English teacher, designed a writing test to assess writing abilities of intermediate-level students. She believes it is essential for students to write a summaries based on their note-taking skills, particularly for academic or occupational contexts. This test will be assessed based on the clarity of the content, logical organization, variety of academic vocabulary, correct use of grammar and adherence to mechanics. In total, 15 students will take the test, which will last for 20 minutes.

Below is part of a writing test designed by Ms. Jung for her middle school students, who attended the reading lesson about 'The importance of recycling'.

[Writing test]

Listen to a 200-words lecture about the importance of recycling. You will listen to the lecture three times. While listening, take notes and revise them as needed. Afterwards, using the notes, write a 70-word summary of the lecture. You will be given 10 minutes to complete your summary, and it should be no longer than 10 sentences. The entire activity will take approximately 20 minutes.

...

After the test...

Two teachers will evaluate each student, spending 10-15 minutes per student. This will total approximately 150-225 minutes (2.5 to 3.75 hours) to evaluate 15 students. The following is the rubric and part of the evaluation results by the two teachers.

Scores of Examinees' Performances

Students	Criteria	Teacher A	Teacher B
Kim, Jungmin	Content	2	5
	Vocabulary	5	1
	Organization	4	2
Lee, Yongjoo	Content	1	4
	Vocabulary	4	2
	Organization	5	2

1=lowest 5=highest

B

Five colleague teachers of Ms. Jung have reviewed the writing test. Here are their feedback:

Teacher 1

The evaluation rubric is carefully designed to reflect all essential sub-components of writing, providing a comprehensive assessment of students' writing abilities.

Teacher 2

The test requires integrated skills such as listening and writing, based on a lecture about recycling—a topic the students have previously studied.

Guideline for Pre-service Teachers

Teacher 3

This assessment is designed to be completed within a 20-minute period by 15 students, ensuring that it is practical for the students to complete and teachers to evaluate.

Teacher 4

According to the test results, the grading is fully objective and consistent across different evaluators, demonstrating high reliability through uniform evaluation.

Teacher 5

The test requires students to listen to a lecture, take notes, and then write a summary—a task that simulates real-life academic or professional situations. This process demonstrates the test's authenticity.

Identify the TWO teachers in <B> whose feedback is NOT correct. Then support your answers with evidence from <A> and <B>.

Your Answer

04 Read the conversation below, and follow the directions.

  Mr. Park, a new English teacher, has visited the office of Ms. Lee, a senior teacher, to ask for advice about the speaking test that he has prepared for 2nd-grade students. Below is an excerpt from the conversation between two English teachers.

Mr. Park : Hi, Ms. Lee. Do you have a minute?
Ms. Lee : Mr. Park. Come on in. How's your speaking test going?
Mr. Park : It's almost done. But I want you to check the test before finalizing it.
Ms. Lee : No problem. Can you show me the test?
  (Mr. Park shows Ms. Lee the test he has designed. Below is the part of the test specification.)

[Test Specification]

No.	Types	# of students	Time	Score
1	Interview	1	5 mins	20
2	Picture description I	1	5 mins	20
3	Picture description II	1	5 mins	20
4	Role-play	3	10 mins	20
5	Discussion	3	10 mins	20

Ms. Lee : How many students do you have?
Mr. Park : 40. All intermediate level.
Ms. Lee : I have a question. Did you calculate the time you need to test all of your students?

Mr. Park : No.... Not yet.
Ms. Lee : Let me do it just for the first one. For the interview, you need 200 minutes without considering the intervals. That's more than 3 hours! Also, you have four more speaking tests!
Mr. Park : You mean, there are too many different types of tests?
Ms. Lee : Exactly! It does not seem practical. How about choosing only 2 types of tests?
Mr. Park : That's better. Then, I will arrange the picture description and discussion only.
Ms. Lee : Okay. So, how will you evaluate your students?
Mr. Park : I will ask Mr. Kim to be another evaluator. First, while recording students' performances, I will evaluate them on a real-time basis. After the test, Mr. Kim will watch the recording and evaluate them once again. The average between the two scores will become my student's final score.
Ms. Lee : One more thing. Did you conduct a pilot test?
Mr. Park : Yes, I did. Here are the test results. Three students from Mr. Kim's class have taken the tests.
(Below is the part of the test results.)

[Test results]

No.	Types	Student	Score from Mr. Park	Score from Mr. Kim
1	Interview	A	18	10
		B	9	17
		C	11	20
2	Picture description	A	7	16
		B	18	10
		C	12	19

...

Ms. Lee : Hmm... The test results seem to have another problem.
Mr. Park : Can you clarify the problem?
Ms. Lee : The test results are inconsistent. There must be some misunderstanding about the scoring criteria between you and Mr. Kim.
Mr. Park : Well... Could be. Then, I should ask another person for the evaluation?
Ms. Lee : It's not the problem of Mr. Kim. When there are two or more scorers, it is better to have a training session about the scoring criteria before evaluation. It will help you to avoid such a huge gap between scores.
Mr. Park : You're right. We had not talked about the criteria yet. I need to take some time to deeply talk about the scoring criteria with Mr. Kim. Thank you, Ms. Lee.

Identify TWO problematic principles of assessment that Ms. Lee points out about Mr. Park's speaking test. Then, write the reasons for your choice with evidence.

Your Answer

Guideline for Pre-service Teachers

05 Read the passages and follow the directions.

A

Mr. Park attended a workshop for English teachers where he could get useful information about how to make a test as authentic as possible. Based on the information below, Mr. Park decided to use Test 1 for his students rather than Test 2.

> ※ Evaluate the extent to which the given test task has the _____ based on the following criteria:
>
> Criterion 1 The language in the test is as natural as possible.
> Criterion 2 The items are as contextualized as possible rather than isolated.
> Criterion 3 Topics and situations are interesting, enjoyable, and humorous.
> Criterion 4 The test task represents or closely approximates tasks that might occur in the real world.

B

Test 1	Test 2

"Going to"
 1. What _____ this weekend?
   a. you are going to do
   b. are you going to do
   c. your gonna do
	1. There are three countries I would like to visit. One is Italy.
	   a. The other is New Zealand and the other is Nepal.
	   b. The others are New Zealand and Nepal.
	   c. Others are New Zealand and Nepal.

2. I am not sure. _____ anything special?
   a. Are you going to do
   b. You are going to do
   c. Is going to do
	2. When I was twelve years old, I used _____ every day.
	   a. swimming
	   b. to swimming
	   c. to swim

3. My friend Jieun and I _____ a party. Would you like to come?
   a. am going to
   b. are going to go to
   c. go to
	3. When Mr. Brown designs a website, he always creates it _____.
	   a. artistically
	   b. artistic
	   c. artist

4. I'd love to! _____.
   a. What's it going to be?
   b. Who's going to be?
   c. Where's going to be?
	4. Since the beginning of the year, I _____ at Millennium Industries.
	   a. am working
	   b. had been working
	   c. have been working

5. It is _____ to be at Ruth's house.
   a. go
   b. going
   c. gonna
	5. When Mona broke her leg, she asked her husband _____ her to work.
	   a. to drive
	   b. driving
	   c. drive

Guideline for Pre-service Teachers

Fill in the blank in <A> with ONE word. Then, from <A>, identify the ONE most appropriate criterion that makes Mr. Park decide to choose Test 1 instead of Test 2 and provide the reason of your choice based on its characteristic from <B>.

Your Answer

06 Read the passages and follow the directions.

A

Below is part of a speaking test that 2nd-graders in a middle school took yesterday.

Directions: Traditions are the beliefs and ways of doing things that are passed down from parents to children. Some traditions have been around for a long time, but sometimes people decide to start new traditions! Talk about one tradition of your family using the questions below. You will have 5 minutes for preparation. Answer each question for 30 seconds to 1 minute. Use the expression box, if needed.

Questions
1. What are some traditions your family celebrates in the fall?
2. Who is/are included?
3. What do you wear?
4. What do you eat?

[Expression Box]
- Eat dinner as a family.
- Do the dishes together.
- Have the same meal on the same day each week.
- Have a family movie night.
- My family celebrates ~.
- My family tradition is ~.
- Usually, (list of family members) gathered in (place) at/on (time).
- My mother/father/sister/brother/family likes/dislikes to ~.

[Scoring rubric]

Criteria	Poor	Okay	Good	Very good
Pronunciation				
Content				
Grammar				

B
Minsu's Learning Log

Yesterday, I took a speaking test and my test result was not good. What a disappointing result! I thought my speaking skills are pretty good but, in a conference after the test, my teacher commented that my speaking skills are lower than the other students. Thus, she recommends practicing speaking skills a lot. I could not accept that my speaking skills are lower than those of other students, so I checked the test result once again. Then, I found that the scoring rubric includes only three criteria to evaluate my speaking skills. That's why my speaking skills are evaluated as not good. Before the test, my teacher talked about how to improve speaking skills and emphasized various aspects of speaking skills such as fluency, appropriateness, diversity of vocabulary, etc. However, such aspects were not reflected in the scoring rubric, which ought to be included. Moreover, I found another problem. Since this test could not measure my speaking skills accurately, it did not provide me with sufficient diagnostic information, either. Actually, the test results we got consisted of only a scoring rubric without any comments. Then, how could I improve my speaking skills? My teacher gave 'poor' in my pronunciation. If she evaluated so, at least she should have given me some comments on what the problems are and how to solve them.

[Minsu's Speaking Test Result]

Criteria	Poor	Okay	Good	Very good
Pronunciation	✓			
Content			✓	
Grammar		✓		

Based on <A> and <B>, write TWO testing principles that are poorly applied in the given speaking test. Then, explain your answers with evidence from <B>.

Your Answer

Guideline for Pre-service Teachers

2 Testing Purpose, Types, and Methods

01 Read the conversation in <A> and the draft of the test specifications in <B>, and follow the directions.

A

Two English teachers, T1 and T2, are discussing the test specifications for the upcoming English exam.

T1 : Mr. Kim! I've been working on the test specification for the upcoming English exam. Let's go over them and make sure everything looks good.

T2 : Of course, Ms. Choi. I'd be happy to review them. Where should we start?

T1 : Let's start with the purpose of the exam. It's essential to have a clear objective. We've mentioned that this is to assess students' speaking proficiency and facilitate their speaking skill development. What are your thoughts on this?

T2 : I agree. It's crucial for the purpose to be well-defined. Our primary objectives are to diagnose their speaking abilities and help them improve their weaknesses.

T1 : Cool. About the task type, we've chosen a Picture Description activity. It's a practical way to assess their speaking skills. What's your take on this?

T2 : I think it's a suitable choice. It aligns well with our language learning objectives.

T1 : Great. Now, let's talk about time allocation. I've allotted 10 minutes for the Picture Description activity within the 10-minute exam. Does that seem reasonable to you?

T2 : Sounds good. But, Ms. Choi, can you share more about how those 10 minutes will be structured? Any specific guidelines for students during that time?

T1 : Absolutely, Mr. Kim. During the 10 minutes, I plan to have students use the first 7 minutes for preparation. They will be given a picture to observe, gather their thoughts, and plan their description. Then, the remaining 3 minutes will be dedicated to the actual description time, where they will verbally present their observations and thoughts about the picture.

T2 : In that case, 7 minutes of preparation must provide students with enough time to describe the picture adequately without feeling rushed during the exam.

T1 : Now, let's discuss the scoring method. We've decided to use an analytic scoring rubric. It allows us to evaluate different language aspects comprehensively. Is this scoring method acceptable to you?

T2 : Absolutely. Incorporating analytic scoring, we can assess various elements such as vocabulary, grammar, pronunciation, and delivery.

T1 : Lastly, for the scoring procedure, we have two examiners who will evaluate each student's exam. If there's a significant discrepancy, they'll reach a consensus. What do you think of this approach?

T2 : I think it's fair. Having two examiners and a consensus process ensures that our scoring is consistent and reliable. But, what if the examiners still cannot agree?

T1 : In such cases, we can request the third examiner to assess and calculate the average score based on the evaluations of all three teachers. However, typically, two evaluators are able to reach a consensus, so there's not much to worry about.

T2 : Excellent, Ms. Choi. With these clear guidelines, we can conduct a fair and effective assessment of our students' English skills.

Guideline for Pre-service Teachers

B

This is the draft of the test specifications T1 and T2 wrote.

Categories	Description
Purpose	To determine students' current speaking levels and place them into the most appropriate speaking courses
Task Type	Picture Description activity
Time Allocation	• The exam will last a total of 10 minutes. • 7 minutes for preparation and 3 minutes for picture description
Scoring Method	• An analytic scoring rubric will be used. • Various aspects of students' vocabulary, grammar, pronunciation, and delivery will be assessed.
Scoring Procedure	• Two examiners will evaluate each student's exam. • In case there is a difference of 2 or more points between the two examiners, they will reach a consensus and determine the final score. • If the two examiners still cannot agree, the average score from the two examiners will be used.

Based on <A>, choose the TWO categories in <B> that do NOT correspond to the teachers' ideas about their test. Then, explain your answers with evidence from <A> and <B>.

Your Answer

02 Read the passages and follow the directions.

A

English Speaking Test Plan

This test is designed to diagnose the current strengths and weaknesses of 3rd-grade middle school students in various aspects of speaking skills. Based on the results, the teacher will design subsequent speaking lessons to address specific needs and improve the overall proficiency of the students.

Test Design

1. Format:
   - The test will be an oral examination.
   - Approximately 10 minutes per student.

2. Content:
   A. Self-Introduction (2 minutes)
   Students will introduce themselves, talking about their hobbies, family, and favorite subjects in school.

   B. Picture Description (3 minutes)
   Students will describe a picture provided to them, focusing on details and storytelling.

   C. Role Play (5 minutes)
   Students will engage in a role-play scenario with the teacher, simulating a real-life situation (e.g., ordering food in a restaurant, or asking for directions).

3. Evaluation Criteria:
   - Each criterion will be scored out of 10 points.
   - Criteria include: (1) Content & Preparation, (2) Organization, (3) Language, (4) Delivery

4. Test Administration:
   - Tests will be conducted individually.
   - The teacher will record each student's performance for detailed assessment and feedback.

5. Post-Test Analysis:
   - Feedback will be provided to each student, highlighting areas of strength and areas for improvement.
   - Results will guide the planning of future speaking lessons, focusing on addressing the identified weak areas.

B

Below is the conversation between two English teachers talking about the speaking test.

Ms. Yoo : Hi, Ms. Park! (1) <u>I'm setting up a placement test for our 3rd graders</u>.
Ms. Park : Oh, that's interesting. Can you tell me more about it?
Ms. Yoo : Sure! (2) <u>It's a 10-minute test for each student</u>. (3) <u>They start by talking about themselves for two minutes</u>. (4) <u>Then, they describe a picture for three minutes</u>, which helps us see how well they use words and tell stories.
Ms. Park : What about the last part?
Ms. Yoo : (5) <u>The last five minutes are for role play, like pretending to order food or ask for directions</u>. This shows us how well they can talk in real-life situations.
Ms. Park : How will you grade them?
Ms. Yoo : (6) <u>I will use a holistic scoring system</u>.
Ms. Park : Sounds like you've got it all planned out!
Ms. Yoo : Yeah, I'm excited! (7) <u>It'll help us teach better and show the students how they can improve their speaking</u>.
Ms. Park : Great idea, Ms. Yoo. Can't wait to hear how it goes!

Based on the test plan in <A>, choose TWO incorrect statements among (1) to (7) in <B>, and rewrite each of them by correcting the incorrect part of the statement.

Your Answer

Guideline for Pre-service Teachers

03 Read the passages and follow the directions.

A

Below are two types of scoring rubrics to evaluate students' speaking skills. Each rubric presents the exam results of a student in a different manner.

Rubric A

	Criteria	Score
Nam, Eunjin	Fluency	5/5
	Pronunciation	2/5
	Grammar	1/5
	Vocabulary	4/5

1=lowest ↔ 5=highest

Rubric B

Test taker's name: Nam, Eunjin

Excellent (100-90)	Excellent use of English. Quite clear oral production. Experiences little or no difficulty in understanding. Almost no errors of pronunciation, grammar, or vocabulary.
Very good (89-80)	Satisfactory verbal communication. Limited number of errors of pronunciation, grammar, or vocabulary. Occasional self-corrections. Little difficulty in understanding.
Good (79-70)	Verbal communication usually fairly satisfactory. Repetition and rephrasing sometimes necessary. Experiences some difficulties in communicating. Some errors of pronunciation, grammar, or vocabulary.
Fair (69-60)	Understanding very limited, although communication on everyday topics is possible. Many errors of pronunciation, grammar, or vocabulary.
Unsatisfactory (59 or fewer)	Extreme difficulty in communication in any subject. Failure to understand adequately and to make him/herself understood.

B
Eunjin's Log

Today, I reviewed the results of my speaking test, which were evaluated using a/an _____ scoring rubric. This method of scoring provides detailed feedback about separate components of the speaking test, which is beneficial for strategically planning my future learning. For example, the feedback highlights my strength in fluency and the areas for improvement, particularly in grammar, where my scores were notably lower. Such tailored feedback is crucial as it helps me understand exactly where I need to improve and continuously track my advancement over time.

Fill in the blank in <B> with the ONE most appropriate word that best describes the scoring rubric used. Then, identify the ONE scoring rubric in <A> that Eunjin has been assessed with for her speaking test and explain how it is beneficial for Eunjin with evidence from <A> and <B>.

04 Read the passages in <A> and <B>, and follow the directions.

A

Regarding classroom assessment, middle school English teachers participated in a workshop on writing performance assessment and received a sample evaluation sheet as a reference. This evaluation sheet is intended for assessing individual student writing assignments.

Performance Evaluation Rubrics

Test taker: Kim Jinsuk

Non-essay part	Multiple choice, etc	\multicolumn{5}{l	}{The non-esssay part of the test will consist of multiple-choice and other similar question types that will be graded with the automated computer grading system (test reader) used by the school for midterm and final examinations. The grading system will analyze students' work using algorithms that detect grammar and spelling errors, sentence structure, vocabulary usage, and more. Points for individual questions may not vary on the basis of difficulty.}	7/10

		Excellent	Good	Acceptable	Developing	Total
		10-9	8-7	6-5	4-3	
Essay Part	Body and Main Points	• Main points are clear and well explained. • Paragraphs are ordered logically. • Ideas are very well developed.	• Main points are clear. • Paragraphs are ordered logically. • Ideas show good development.	• Main points are unorganized. • Paragraphs are not in a logical order. • Ideas show little development.	• Main points cannot be found, or are illogical. • Paragraphs are not organized or unclear. • Ideas are not developed.	9/10
	Errors	The essay has between 0-5 grammatical or spelling errors.	The essay has between 6-10 grammatical or spelling errors.	The essay has between 11-15 grammatical or spelling errors.	The essay has over 16 grammatical or spelling errors.	6/10

Compo-sition	• All points of the essay are very well explained with insightful background information given. • All points are relevant and fit with the topic question very well. • Tone is natural and appropriate for the audience of the essay.	• Points are explained well with clear background information. • Points are relevant to the essay topic. • Tone is natural and suitable for the audience of the essay.	• Some points are hard to follow because there is little background information given. • The points made are mostly relevant to the essay topic. • Tone is somewhat unnatural, or is not suitable for the audience.	• All points are hard to follow because no background information is given. • Points do not seem relevant to the essay topic. • Tone is unnatural and unsuitable for the audience.		7/10

※ Students who do not take the test or who perform below minimum requirements or expectations will receive a grade of 30 on the test.

B

Using the reference test results, six teacher share their interpretations on the results.

Teacher 1

In some tests with multiple-choice items, difficult questions might be worth more points. However, in this test, all questions are worth the same number of points regardless of their difficulty level.

Teacher 2

The essay writing test is evaluated based on rater's impressions of the overall quality of writing.

Teacher 3

In the non-essay part, the automated computer grading system will use algorithms to analyze the text and content of the student's work. These algorithms would identify grammar and spelling errors, sentence structure, vocabulary usage, and more.

Teacher 4

Based on the test results, the test taker's essay had approximately 11-15 grammatical or spelling errors, which is the area that the test taker needs to improve.

Teacher 5

According to the evaluation results, the test taker received a poor evaluation in the composition section because he did not provide explicit background information and had an unnatural tone.

Teacher 6

According to the evaluation results, the test taker's strength lies in paragraph organization, where the main ideas are exceptionally well revealed, and ideas are logically well-developed.

Identify the TWO teachers in \<B\> whose interpretations are NOT correct. Then support your answers with evidence from \<A\> and \<B\>.

Your Answer

05 Read the passages in <A> and <B>, and follow the directions.

A

※ Test Directions: Welcome to your English proficiency assessment. This test evaluates your overall language proficiency level across key areas such as listening, reading, speaking, writing, vocabulary, and grammar. Read the instructions for each section carefully.

- Listening: Listen to audio recordings (conversations, lectures) and answer questions to demonstrate understanding.
- Reading: Read texts (articles, essays) and answer questions to assess comprehension and analysis.
- Speaking: Participate in tasks requiring spontaneous speech, judged on fluency, coherence, and clarity.
- Writing: Respond to prompts with well-organized essays or reports, assessed on grammar, vocabulary, and communication effectiveness.
- Vocabulary and Grammar: Complete exercises to demonstrate knowledge of vocabulary and grammar rules.

Proficiency Test Results
Name: Nam Eun suk

	L	R	S	W	V	G
Score	4/(5)	2/(5)	2/(5)	4.5/(5)	3/(5)	2/(5)

L=listening, R=reading, S=speaking, W=writing, V=vocabulary, G=grammar

Comments on Your Strengths & Weaknesses

- Listening: Your listening skills are notably strong.
- Vocabulary: You demonstrate a good understanding and show a moderate vocabulary, enabling you to comprehend and use words in various contexts.
- Reading: Due to limited reading comprehension skills, you encounter difficulties with more complex texts, leading to an incomplete understanding
- Speaking: Despite your confidence in speaking, you may find it challenging to engage in spontaneous conversations with an examiner.
- Writing: Your essay and report composition skills are remarkable, reflecting a strong proficiency in writing.
- Grammar: There is room for improvement in your grammar skills, especially in sentence structure and verb forms.

B

Five teachers discuss the proficiency test and its results. The following are their interpretations and suggestions.

Teacher 1 : The student demonstrates outstanding writing skills as well as good vocabulary knowledge, which positively contributes to his language proficiency.

Teacher 2 : The student's command of vocabulary is good. He demonstrates an ability to comprehend and use a wide range of words.

Teacher 3 : The student excels in reading and speaking skills in all aspects but need to work on grammar.

Teacher 4 : The student's grammar skills, particularly in sentence structure and verb forms, could benefit from further improvement.

Teacher 5 : This test neither covers key language areas nor provides detailed insights into a student's overall language proficiency.

Identify the TWO teachers in <B> whose interpretation is NOT correct. Then, support your answers with concrete evidence from <A>.

Your Answer

Guideline for Pre-service Teachers

06 Read the teaching log in <A> and examine the description of two types of test in <B> and follow the directions.

A

Mr. Kim's Teaching Log

I'm a big believer in the idea that testing is super important in the language learning process. It's a key part of the curriculum. So, when I'm planning my lessons, I try to pick the best type of test that fits perfectly with both the lesson and assessment objectives. The main goal of the test is to check if students have hit the course objectives. So, I'm planning to give the _____ test to my students in the second to last lesson of this semester. Also, I plan to grade each student's performance based on the pre-set criterion which indicates the overall level of achievement. For students who don't quite hit the mark, I'm thinking of giving out extra worksheets for them to catch up after each class. But, I'm still thinking of how to set up the testing format and which type of test to choose that would best show what I'm aiming for. When I asked Ms. Park, our school's head English teacher, for some advice, she suggested two types of tests that she used before for final exams.

B

Test A

Sections	Target Skills	Types of Questions	Test Score	Total Score	Standard for Pass/Fail
Section 1	Listening/Reading	Multiple-choice Items	100	200	Top 50% of students
Section 2	Speaking/Writing	Open-ended Questions	100		

Test B

Sections	Target Skills	Types of Questions	Test Score	Total Score	Standard for Pass/Fail
Section 1	Listening/Reading	True/False Questions	20	50	Score over 25
Section 2	Speaking/Writing	Open-ended Questions	30		

Fill in the blank in <A> with the ONE most appropriate word. In <B>, choose the test type that Mr. Kim needs and then write how the chosen test corresponds with Mr. Kim's testing purposes with evidence from <A> and <B>.

Your Answer

07 Read the passages and follow the directions.

A

Below are the example of test results based on two different types of testing.

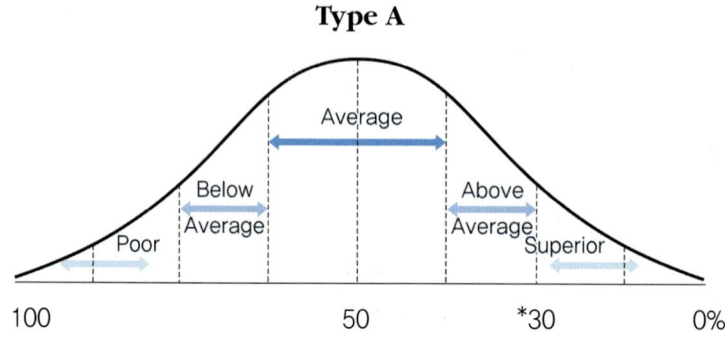

Type A

*Your score: 30%

Type B

Components of Writing	Score	Level	Indicators
Conetent (C)	4	Excellent	Present the information well chosen details across the paragraph
	3	Good	Present the information with details in parts of the paragraph
	2	Fair	Present the information with some details
	1	Poor	Present no clear information
Vocabulary (V)	4	Excellent	Good in vocabulary choice
	3	Good	Error in vocabulary choice are few and do not interfere with understanding
	2	Fair	Error in vocabulary choice are and sometimes they interfere with understanding
	1	Poor	Many error in vocabulary choice that severally interfere with understanding

	4	Excellent	Good in grammar
Grammar (G)	3	Good	Error in grammar choice are few and do not interfere with understanding
	2	Fair	Error in grammar choice are and sometimes they interfere with understanding
	1	Poor	Many error in grammar choice that severally interfere with understanding
Mechanics (M)	4	Excellent	Good in spelling, punctuation and capitalization
	3	Good	Error in spelling, punctuation and capitalization are few
	2	Fair	Error in spelling, punctuation and capitalization and sometimes interfere with understanding
	1	Poor	Error in spelling, punctuation and capitalization and severely interfere with understanding

(The rest of the rubric is omitted.)

※ *If a score is equal to or greater than 70, it is considered a passing score, and if the score is less than 70, it is considered a failing score.*

- Your total score: 75/100 (pass)
- Teacher's Comments:

Guideline for Pre-service Teachers

B

Ms. Park's Reflection

This semester, I had a writing course for 1st-year middle school students at an intermediate level. As the semester is ending, I want to prepare a test to assess the students' learning progress. There are two important things I'm focusing on: Instead of making students compare their results with each other, I want to evaluate each student's writing skills they have achieved this semester by comparing their own performance to specific criteria. To do this, I plan to set a standard and assess their results based on that preset standards, not by comparing them to each other. Furthermore, this assessment isn't just about the test itself; it's also about providing appropriate feedback. So, based on the assessment results, I want to give individual students feedback tailored to their needs. This way, I can help them understand which areas they need to focus on for their studies in the next semester. Following these two requirements, I conducted the test and obtained the results in the way I intended.

Based on <A>, choose ONE type of testing that Ms. Park should use and identify the name of the testing. Then, referring to <B>, write TWO reasons of your choice.

(Your Answer)

08 Read the passages and follow the directions.

A

Mr. Jung's Teaching Note

Anticipating the upcoming class, I realized that the current reading materials might be too challenging and could potentially demotivate most students. To maintain their motivation, I needed to select new reading texts that were better suited to their proficiency level. Therefore, I examined several reading materials, primarily focusing on _____ which refers to the ease with which my students can understand and enjoy the text. In other words, by limiting the number of unknown words and lengthy sentences, I aimed to choose the most appropriate text corresponding to students' current level. Meanwhile, Ms. Park, a head teacher, advised me to arrange a reading proficiency test, which can serve as a diagnostic tool. She suggested planning gap-filling tests based on the chosen reading materials. In each blank, students are expected to write down an appropriate word that they deduce from multiple contextual clues while reading the gap-filling texts. According to her, the test results can provide information related to students' vocabulary knowledge, calculated guesses, linguistic expectations and background knowledge about the selected texts. Besides, she advised caution, saying that I should not give too many clues to measure reading proficiency. The following are test samples I will provide to my students.

Guideline for Pre-service Teachers

B

Test Type A	Test Type B
What is Artificial Intelligence?	What is Artificial Intelligence?
Artificial Intelligence often abbreviated as _____, is a fascinating field of _____. It's all about creating _____ that can think and learn like _____. Imagine if your computer or phone could _____ and solve problems on its own!	Artifi_____ Intelli_____ oft__ abbre_____ as AI, i_ a fasci_____ fie____ of tech_____. It_ al_ ab__ cre_____ com_____ pro_____ that can th__ and lea__ li_ hu_____. Ima____ if yo_ com__ or ph____ co__ under_____ an_ so__ prob____ on it_ ow_!

Fill in the blank in <A> with ONE word. Then, choose the ONE test type in <B> that Ms. Park recommends for Mr. Jung and provide the reasons of your choice. Do NOT copy more than FOUR consecutive words from the passages.

Your Answer _____

_____

_____

_____

_____

3 Alternative Assessment

01 Read the passages and follow the directions.

A

Below is part of a speaking lesson procedure prepared by Ms. Kim, a middle school English teacher.

Topic: Talking About Your Favorite Food
Procedure:
- Introduce the Topic: Display images of various foods to engage students and spark discussion.
- Presentation Explanation: Teach the format for a short spoken presentation, including stating an opinion, providing supporting reasons, and concluding effectively.
- Brainstorming Session: Have students select their favorite food and brainstorm reasons for their choice. Guide them in creating a brief outline to use during their presentation.
- Presentation and Recording: Set up a recording area in the classroom for students to present their favorite food. Each student will record their presentation using a camera or tablet. Encourage practice before recording to minimize anxiety and enhance performance.

Assessment:
- Provide students with clear instructions for evaluating their presentations using a checklist.
- Have students watch their recorded presentations and assess their performance based on the checklist.

Checklist	YES	NO
Does your presentation clearly state your opinion about your favorite food?		
Does your presentation include supporting reasons? (At least two reasons - Yes, fewer than two - No)		
Is your speech clear and understandable? (Yes, if it's mostly clear; No, if there are many unclear parts)		
Do you maintain eye contact with the audience (or camera) throughout the presentation?		
Are your voice tone and pace appropriate for the presentation?		

- After evaluation, have students reflect on their performance and identify areas for improvement. Encourage them to consider ways to enhance their speaking skills for future presentations.

Feedback and Further Learning:

Students should upload their video presentations and reflections on areas for improvement to the class digital platform for teacher feedback.

B
Sunjin's Reflection

Today, in my speaking lesson, I presented on sushi, my favorite food. After the presentation, my teacher provided us with a special checklist containing five criteria to assess our speaking performances based on our video recordings. This was an unusual but insightful task for me.

I marked 'YES' for having a clear statement of opinion, as I began my presentation with a strong declaration of my love for sushi. For the second criterion, I gave myself a 'YES,' believing I provided sufficient reasons to support my preference. I also checked 'YES' for grammar, confident in my pronunciation and sentence structure. Although I only sometimes maintained eye contact, I still marked 'YES,' Finally, I marked 'YES' for the appropriate tone and pace, believing I spoke clearly and engagingly. Overall, I was very satisfied with my presentation and thought I demonstrated a great performance.

However, after my teacher's evaluation, it became clear that my assessment did not fully align with her observations. My teacher noted that while my content was good, my eye contact was inconsistent, and my pace was sometimes too rapid—issues I hadn't fully realized. Despite my initial confidence, the feedback indicated that there were noticeable gaps in the performance I thought I had delivered, which left me a bit confused. Given these insights, I want to request a one-on-one review session with my teacher to better understand the specific aspects of my speaking that were weaker than I had initially assessed.

Identify the type of alternative assessment exemplified in <A>. Then, explain the problem with the identified assessment that is evident in <B> and the solution to this problem from Sunjin's perspective.

02 Read the passages and follow the directions.

A

Bulletin Board

Q: How did you feel about the English test last week? Please provide your feedback freely.

Student 1 : I felt that the test included too many questions asking about new grammar rules that I had never learned before. In my opinion, a good test should closely relate to the content learned during lessons, but this test did not cover the materials covered in class.

Student 2 : I do not believe that this kind of multiple choice item testing measured the progress of our language skills appropriately. I believe that for evaluating the progress and achievement of my English proficiency, my teacher should conduct periodic evaluations instead of using one-time multiple-choice questions.

Student 3 : In spite of differentiated instruction, every student took the same test. I think it does not make sense. The test should be tailored to different proficiency levels in the same way we have lessons.

B

Ms. Lee's Teaching Note

Last week, I administered a formative test to monitor my students' progress in English. However, after the test, some students provided negative feedback, stating that the test didn't closely align with the content covered in class, and the results didn't reflect their progress or achievements. They also complained that the test didn't consider their diverse proficiency levels. Taking this feedback into consideration, I decided to implement a new type of assessment from the upcoming semester. First of all, students will be instructed to collect the works they have done in class throughout the semester including compositions in draft and final forms, project reports, and recordings of their presentations. During the semester, they will regularly have my feedback on their works and conferences with me to reflect on their progress over a certain period of time. In addition, with the regular feedback and conferences, students will be able to set their own learning goals based on their proficiency levels. I am confident that implementing this new assessment will address the complaints raised by my students and help them showcase their progress more accurately.

Identify the type of assessment Ms. Lee plans to newly implement from the upcoming semester. Then, explain how the identified assessment can resolve all students' complaints.

Your Answer

Guideline for Pre-service Teachers

03 Read the passages and follow the directions.

A

There are three alternative testing activities that teachers can utilize for students. The first is Portfolios, which are the carefully accumulated collection of students' work that demonstrates their efforts, progress, and accomplishments in a particular area. A portfolio can include a variety of students' outcomes such as essays, reports, poems, prose, artwork, or audio/video recordings of presentations. The second option is Journals, which serve as a record of one's thoughts, feelings, reactions, ideas, or progress toward goals. Journals are often written without strict adherence to structure or correctness. For instance, dialogue journals facilitate ongoing conversation with a reader. The third activity is Self- and Peer Assessment. This form of assessment is beneficial for both students and teachers. To be specific, it reduces teachers' workload while enhancing engagement and comprehension between students. Additionally, it places value on students' insights and observations, playing a crucial role in fostering their self-awareness and enhancing their understanding of the learning process.

B

Teacher's Note

I've been thinking about how I can better gauge my students' progress, and I believe I've come across an excellent strategy. I will compile a meaningful collection of my students' work that demonstrates their growth in a particular subject. This method seems to be a game-changer, as it enables me to witness their accomplishments more vividly. This collection can include a variety of classroom tasks, not just from listening exercises, but also from reading, speaking, and writing activities. This way, I can observe various aspects of their current learning and achievement as I wish. Also, through this testing approach, I can have the opportunity to evaluate students' work, providing timely feedback and encouragement on an ongoing basis. With these two purposes in mind, I am thinking of implementing this alternative testing approach next semester. I can't wait to see the positive impact this approach will have on my students' learning experiences.

Based on the information in <A> and <B>, identify the alternative testing activity that the teacher in <B> is discussing. Then, provide TWO intentions for why the teacher uses the identified activity. Do NOT copy more than FOUR consecutive words from the passages.

Your Answer

Guideline for Pre-service Teachers

04 Read the passages in <A> and <B>, and follow the directions.

A

Lesson Procedure

1. Pre-stage (10 minutes):
   - Introduce the topic of 'healthy habits' to the students.
   - Display pictures or examples of healthy habits on the board or using visual aids.
   - Engage students in a whole class discussion about the importance of maintaining good health.

2. While-stage (40 minutes):
   - Explain a speaking activity where students will discuss and present their own healthy habits. Divide students into groups of four and assign roles: *leader, timekeeper, writer,* and *presenter.*
   - Provide each group with a list of suggested healthy habits.
     (e.g., exercising regularly, eating nutritious food, getting enough sleep, drinking plenty of water, etc.)
   - In groups, students discuss their own healthy habits, rank them in order of importance, and create a PowerPoint presentation with up to 5 habits.
   - Encourage students to engage in active discussion and collaborative decision-making.
   - Allocate 30 minutes for group discussions and PowerPoint preparation.
   - Before starting the presentation, give the groups 10 minutes for _____ time to prepare a more successful and impactful presentation.
   - Students use the time to refine their presentation skills, improve their delivery, and increase their confidence.

3. Post-stage (30 minutes):
- Ask each group to present their PowerPoint presentation to the class.
- Distribute evaluation sheets with a checklist for evaluating group presentations to each group.
- Instruct the students to listen attentively to each group's presentation and evaluate their performance based on the checklist.
- After each presentation, allocate a few minutes for students to briefly write feedback and suggestions to the presenting group.
- Collect the evaluation results from each group and return them to the respective groups.

4. Wrap-up (10 minutes):
- Ask each group to revise their presentation based on the evaluation results and feedback they received from other groups and post it to the class blog until tonight.
- Recap the main points discussed during the presentations.
- Summarize the importance of developing and maintaining healthy habits.

B

Mr. Kim's Teaching Note

In today's lesson, while listening to the group presentations on 'healthy habits', I asked my students to evaluate each other's presentations using a checklist. Since they are not accustomed to evaluating each other, I provided guidelines for this type of assessment and explained how to assess each other using the checklist. The major reasons that I used this assessment were because of the two benefits. First, it empowered students to take ownership of their own learning. By participating in the process of assessment, they could develop a sense of ownership and accountability on learning speaking skills. Moreover, it promoted collaborative learning. That is, by sharing some feedback and suggestions with each other, they could create a peer learning environment. Overall, this type of assessment was an effective way to foster responsibility and promote learning from each other.

Guideline for Pre-service Teachers

Fill in the blank in <A> with the ONE most appropriate word. Then, identify the assessment type that Mr. Kim uses in Post-stage with TWO words from <B> and explain the reasons he chooses the identified assessment with evidence from <B>. Do NOT copy more than FOUR consecutive words from <A> and <B>.

Your Answer

05 Read the passage and follow the directions.

Ms. Park's Reflection

Throughout this semester, I provided students with a rubric to evaluate each other's presentations. The rubric I provided encompasses a variety of criteria related to speaking skills.

Criteria	Indicators	E	VG	G	S	P
Content & Organization	• The speech is clearly organized, and logical. • The speech deals with interesting topics.					
_____	The presenter speaks fluently with only rare repetition, self-correction, fillers, and pauses.					
Grammar	The speech incldues complex sentence use and minor grammatical occurrence.					
Vocabulary	The speech uses diverse vocabulary appropriately.					
Pronunciation	(ellipsis)					

E=excellent, VG=very good, G=good, S=satisfactory, P=poor

Guideline for Pre-service Teachers

At the start of the semester, I believed that the rubric I provided would be effective for assessing students' presentations. However, after a round of presentation evaluations and discussions with my students, I recognized some issues with using the presentation rubric. The first issue was a discrepancy in students' interpretations of the criteria. For instance, when evaluating pronunciation, some students considered good pronunciation to be dependent on natural intonation, while others thought that clear individual sounds like 'r,' 'l,' 'p,' and 'f' constituted good pronunciation. To address this, I conducted a training session before students evaluated each other's presentations. In this session, I clarified the meaning of each indicator and provided guidance on how to apply them effectively. After learning about the indicators, students practiced the assessment process using a sample speech. Additionally, feedback from the discussions revealed that elements assessing speaking activities were not adequately considered in the rubric. Students suggested that evaluation criteria should include aspects related to presentation skills beyond just structuring the speech. As a result, I added a new criterion, "delivery," which assesses aspects such as the presenter's voice volume, eye contact with the audience. In the future speaking assessments, I hope that students can use this revised rubric to conduct peer assessments more effectively and accurately.

Fill in the blank with the ONE most appropriate word. Then, explain how Ms. Park addresses the issues that arose when students used the speaking skill rubric.

Your Answer

4 Multiple-choice Item Testing

01 Read the passages in <A> and <B> and follow the directions.

A

  Creating effective multiple-choice questions (MCQs) is an art that requires careful consideration to ensure they accurately assess students' knowledge and reasoning skills. The following five rules are essential guidelines for constructing high-quality MCQs. Adhering to these rules will enhance the reliability (the consistency and stability of the assessment over time) and validity (the extent to which an assessment measures what it is supposed to measure) of multiple-choice assessments.

Five Rules for Writing Multiple-Choice Questions

- Use believable incorrect options to challenge the students.
- Keep the part of speech for all options consistently.
- Do not include hints that could lead to the correct answer.
- Offer only one option as the correct answer.
- Do not use options like "All of the Above" or "None of the Above."

B

Below are four sample questions that Ms. Kim has designed.

Question 1
Which of the following words is semantically correct to complete the sentence?

The company's new marketing campaign aims to _____ brand awareness.

A) enhance
B) decrease
C) diminish
D) increase

Question 2
Which of the following terms correctly completes the sentence based on its definition?

A/an _____ is a word that describes a noun.

A) adverb
B) adjective
C) conjunction
D) preposition

Question 3
Read the following sentence, and choose the best option.

The boat sank when it hits a _____ that was hidden under the water.

A) ice
B) atoll
C) rock
D) ocean animal

Question 4
Read the following sentence, and choose the meaningfully most appropriate word:

She was feeling very _____ after receiving the good news.

A) sad
B) angry
C) joyful
D) tired

Identify the TWO questions from <B> that each violate one of the principles in <A>. Then, explain the reasons for your choices with evidence from both <A> and <B>.

Your Answer

Guideline for Pre-service Teachers

02 Read the passages and follow the directions.

A

At a classroom assessment workshop, a teacher trainer taught how to interpret a table showing response frequency distribution. The trainer used data from an English reading test with 20 multiple-choice questions. Below are the basic concepts of multiple-choice items that the trainer explained:

- **Item Discrimination (ID)**: Item Discrimination is assessed by calculating the difference between the proportion of high-scoring students who answered the item correctly and the proportion of low-scoring students who answered the item correctly. An ID of ≥ 0.35 is considered excellent, an ID around 0.3 is acceptable, and an ID of ≤ 0.2 is considered poor. Therefore, items with an ID of ≤ 0.2 should typically be revised to better differentiate between different levels of test-taker abilities. ($-1 \leq \text{ID} \leq 1$)

$$\text{ID} = \frac{\text{Items correct in high group } (n) - \text{Items correct in low group } (n)}{.5 \times \text{Students in the two comparison groups } (n)}$$

- **Item Facility (IF)**: Item facility can be measured by calculating the proportion of test-takers who answer an item correctly. A higher proportion indicates that an item is easier. A well-constructed test should include a mix of easy, moderate, and difficult questions to accurately assess a range of abilities and mastery levels. Therefore, whether to revise difficult questions should be determined based on the purpose of the test, its statistical properties, and how the questions align with the broader educational goals of the assessment. ($0 \leq \text{IF} \leq 1$)

$$\text{IF} = \frac{\text{Students answering the item correctly } (n)}{\text{Students responding to the item } (N)}$$

- **Functional Distractors**: All distractors should serve a function. They should be designed to be plausible enough to be selected by students who do not have a firm understanding of the material.

B

Below is part of the response frequency distribution of the multiple-choice items.

Response Frequency Distribution

- Number of students: 20
- * is the answer.

	Groups	A	B	C	D
Item 1	High-ability students (n=10)	2	1	2	5*
	Low-ability students (n=10)	3	2	2	3*
Item 2	High-ability students (n=10)	3	0	7*	0
	Low-ability students (n=10)	1	5	4*	0
Item 3	High-ability students (n=10)	0	9*	0	1
	Low-ability students (n=10)	2	4*	3	1

...

Based on the information in <A>, identify the TWO test items should be considered for revision in <B>. Then, explain your answers with evidence from <A> and <B>.

Your Answer

Guideline for Pre-service Teachers

03 Read the passages and follow the directions.

A

Below are some examples of multiple-choice items that are intended to measure students' knowledge of language.

※ Choose the one that best fits in each blank.

1. After spending 5 years in Sydney, I now _____ in New York.
   ① lived   ② am living   ③ live
   ④ lives   ⑤ have lived

2. While the Eiffel Tower is located in France, the Statue of Liberty is in _____.
   ① Korea   ② U.S.A.   ③ Germany
   ④ Canada   ⑤ Australia

3. For buying a new cellphone, ____ costs $1000.
   ① it   ② they   ③ he
   ④ I   ⑤ was

B

Response Frequency Distribution on the Multiple Choices

	Groups	①	②	③	④	⑤
Item 1	High Group (n=10)	1	2	5*	1	1
	Low Group (n=10)	2	2	2*	2	2
Item 2	High Group (n=10)	2	2*	3	2	1
	Low Group (n=10)	0	4*	3	2	1
Item 3	High Group (n=10)	7*	1	1	1	0
	Low Group (n=10)	2*	2	4	2	0

* : Key Answers

Based on <A> and <B>, identify TWO poorly designed testing items and explain why each identified item is problematic in terms of the construction of multiple-choice items and test results.

Your Answer

Guideline for Pre-service Teachers

04 Read <A> and <B>, and follow the directions.

A

The quality of a question can be assessed through three key indexes: Item Facility, Item Discrimination, and Distractor Analysis.

1. **Item Facility (I.F.):** This index measures the proportion of students who have answered a question correctly, represented as a value between 0 and 1. Appropriate test items generally have IFs that range between 0.15 and 0.85.

2. **Item Discrimination:** This index helps determine whether high-performing students outperform, underperform, or perform similarly to low-performing students on a given question.

3. **Distractor Analysis:** This index evaluates how effectively distractors function in distracting test-takers away from the correct answer. This analysis is particularly crucial when using a multiple-choice format test. A test with ineffective distractors may not accurately measure a student's knowledge or understanding.

In summary, these three indexes provide valuable insights into the quality and effectiveness of test questions.

B

Ms. Kim, a high school English teacher, is reviewing the analysis of the final term exam questions taken by 80 students. The table presented here is a portion of the complete analysis.

Items	Proportion of correct answers	Option analysis			
		A	B	C	D
3	0.5	40*	20	0	20
4	0.312	25*	14	24	17
5	0.1	3	65	8*	4
6	0.625	7	8	50*	15
7	0.437	14	16	35*	15

* means the correct answer.

Referring to the terms in <A>, identify TWO indexes that the table in <B> reflects. Then, choose the problematic items in <B> and write the reasons for your choices with evidence from <B>.

Your Answer

05 Read the passages and follow the directions.

A

Analyzing the reliability, difficulty level, and discrimination of your multiple-choice questions requires only a few simple calculations and can help you determine the effectiveness of your assessment, whether it is a quiz, exam, or in-class question.

- Reliability: coefficient alpha—a measure of the internal consistency of the exam. This statistic ranges from 0 to 1.00, and the higher the value the better.

- Item difficulty: the percentage of students answering the question correctly. It can range between 0.0 and 1.0, with a higher value indicating that a greater proportion of examinees have responded to the item correctly, and it is, thus, an easier item.

- Item discrimination: the ability of an item to differentiate among students based on how well they know the material being tested. The possible range of the discrimination index is - 1.0 to 1.0; however, if an item has discrimination below 0.2, it suggests a problem.

B

Below is part of the results of the multiple-choice test taken by 2nd graders in a middle school.

Option Item	Upper Group (%)				Lower Group (%)			
	a	b	c	d	a	b	c	d
1	21	26	23	30*	22	25	24	30*
2	13	10	70*	7	25	27	28*	20

* denotes the answer.

Between Item 1 and Item 2 in <B>, choose ONE problematic item and identify the major cause of problem in <A>. Then, explain why it is problematic with evidence from <B>.

Your Answer

06 Read the passages and follow the directions.

A

Teacher's Note

Last week, I attended a teacher training on how to design a multiple-choice item. A multiple-choice question consists of a problem, known as the stem and a list of suggested solutions, known as (1) _____. They include one correct answer and the other incorrect options, known as (2) _____. Below are the principles from the workshop.

Designing an Effective Stem

Rule 1
The stem should be meaningful by itself and should present a definite problem.

Rule 2
The stem should not include irrelevant information in the stem, which can decrease the reliability and the validity of the test scores.

Rule 3
The stem should be negatively stated only when significant learning outcomes require it.

Rule 4
The stem should be a question or a partial sentence, instead of being constructed with an interior blank.

B

The following are some of the multiple-choice items that Ms. Jung designed to assess her students' comprehension after reading a text about a hedgehog, Henri.

※ Choose the best answer for the following questions.

Q1. Which of the following is a true statement?
(a) Henri likes to eat fish and chips.
(b) Henri likes to eat sandwiches and crisps.
(c) Henri likes to eat beetles and earthworms.
(d) Henri likes to eat peas and carrots.

Q2. Hedgehogs have a really short _____ period: it's only around 35 days from conception to birth.
(a) juvenile
(b) gestation
(c) marriage
(d) hibernation

Fill in each blank in <A> using ONE word. Write the answers in order. Then, referring to the rules from <A>, explain each reason why the two testing items in <B> are problematic.

Your Answer

Build Up

정답 및 모범 답안

정답 및 모범 답안

Chapter 01   Second Language Acquisition   본문 p. 006

1   Language Learning Approach

01   Min-ji and Chan-ho make errors due to 'interlingual transfer' and 'communication strategy', respectively. For example, Min-ji omits the '-s' from English plural words like 'buses' and 'trains' because Korean lacks plural forms for non-living things. Similarly, Chan-ho creates the word like 'cleaning-trees' for 'air-purifying plants' due to his limited vocabulary.

02   Jaemin is at developmental stage 6, whereas Sara is at stage 4. Jaemin employs a negative question using the 'do' operator, by asking, 'Doesn't your brother play soccer, too?' to Sara. On the other hand, Sara's questions, 'Will you play soccer with us someday?' and 'What is yours?' demonstrate the use of inversion in yes/no questions with modal and inversion in 'wh-' questions with the copula, 'be', respectively.

03   Eunji, who has procedural knowledge, applies the past tense of regular verbs correctly in her speech, by saying "I danced". In contrast, Jaeho does not possess procedural knowledge of irregular verbs, thereby using the incorrect past tense, as in "I eated".

04   comprehensible input.
Dialogue 1 exemplifies the classroom dialogue of meaning negotiation. When the student does not understand the word 'appetizer', she uses a 'clarification request' by asking "can you say that again?" and a 'confirmation check' by asking "You mean, like soup or salad?" as meaning negotiation strategies.

05   Ms. Kim adopted the natural approach to maximize students' exposure to a natural and comprehensible level of the target language without forcing them to produce any language. Thus, in Step 1, she introduces Total Physical Response where students engage in physical actions based on their comprehension without producing spoken or written language.

06 Ms. Yoo recommends a task-based lesson for Mr. Kim based on its two advantages: first, it fosters student talking time (STT) in class by making students collaborate in authentic group tasks. Next, it encourages students' active participation by assigning them individual roles. Plus, she suggests the approximation strategy for Mr. Kim's students when there is a communication breakdown in group activities.

07 Stage 1. Pre-task and Stage 2. Task cycle of the lesson plan deviate from those in the TBI model. During the Pre-task, the teacher does not present useful words and phrases, instead focusing solely on activating students' schematic knowledge through the pictures and given questions. In the Task cycle's planning stage, the teacher provides only affective support without offering language-related advice.

08 Lesson A is a meaning-focused instruction, whereas Lesson B is a form-focused instruction. In Lesson A, the teacher introduces the topic 'Planning for weekends' with pictures and then students share their weekend plans and top 3 plans using level-appropriate language. In Lesson B, however, the teacher intends to direct students' attention to the target form, "have p.p", through a clear explanation and then leads them to discuss their own experiences on global warming using the present perfect.

09 Eunji is engaged in the immersion model, where all academic subjects are conducted entirely in English, integrating language learning with content instruction. Conversely, Sungho participates in the adjunct model which combines academic and language coursework. In this model, a subject teacher and a language teacher collaborate in a team-teaching approach.

10 In the given conversation, "Do you have any plans this weekend?" as Step 2 and "See you on Saturday then!" as Step 8 are used. Also, saying "So, I can come to your house at any time?" Jisoo uses a confirmation check as a negotiation strategy to check her understanding of Sam's statement.

11 In the conversation, Verbal Ellipsis is used in 'Yes, I can,' because the verbal phrase 'finish the assignment by tomorrow' is omitted. Additionally, Nominal Ellipsis occurs in 'I haven't even started yet.' because the noun, 'the assignment', is omitted. Lastly, the last sentence employs Clausal Substitution with 'I think so, too,' because 'so' substitutes for the entire preceding clause 'she might give us some information about the extension later.'

12 Version 1

S1 uses reference, specifically the pronoun 'it', to refer to 'writing stories'. Meanwhile, S2 employs reference, substitution, conjunction and ellipsis by using 'they' for 'teachers', 'In the same way' for 'making a lasting impression', 'Just like', and omitting the phrase 'My dream job is' before 'a teacher'.

Version 2

S1 uses reference, specifically the pronoun "it", to refer to the specific phrase "writing stories". Meanwhile, S2 employs reference, conjunction, and substitution. With "they", "just like" and "in the same way", respectively, S2 refers back to "teachers", establishes comparative sentences, and avoid repetition by substituting 'making a lasting impression'. Also. S2 uses ellipsis by omitting the phrase 'My dream job is' before 'a teacher'

13 sociolinguistic.

Activity 1 aims to develop discourse competence. In this activity, students rearrange sentences to create a coherent narrative and then complete the cohesive story using appropriate references and conjunctions. Activity 2, on the other hand, focuses on strategic competence. In this task, students are required to describe or explain the unknown word, 'a needle', to overcome the communication challenge.

14

Case A exemplifies the interpersonal communication, whereas Case B belongs to the interpretive communication. In Case A, the conversation shows the process of meaning negotiation through the spontaneous two-way communication. On the other hand, Case B represents message interpretation that the student as a receiver writes after reading a book, and thus there is no meaning negotiation involved.

15

To actualize student-centered instruction, Ms. Kim utilizes peer feedback, whereas Ms. Yoo encourages peer scaffolding. Each way has its benefit. The former enables students to take responsibility for their own learning as active learners. The latter can provide more customized support based on students' current proficiency level compared to guidance solely provided by the teacher.

16 experiential learning.

Minsoo is currently in the stage of reflective observation, while Eunji is in the stage of active experimentation. To be specific, Minsoo carefully reflects on his entire farming experience after visiting an animal farm. On the other hand, Eunji is inspired by her time at an elderly center and plans a painting session as a new group activity.

17 inquiry-based.
Inquiry-based instruction, a form of active learning, offers two key advantages. Unlike rote learning, it fosters higher-order thinking skills like critical thinking. In this lesson, students can analyze and evaluate data and necessary evidence before drawing their own conclusions. Additionally, it enhances students' engagement and motivation by not merely transmitting information one-way but by linking their learning to real-world problems.

18 The lesson in <B> exemplifies project-based learning for two main reasons. First, it features a long-term approach as shown by the activity's duration of around three months. Second, the lesson's objective is to produce a meaningful product, as reflected in the final assessment focusing on the students' promotional video.

19 culture shock.
Ms. Yoo utilizes an artifact study to teach foreign students the Korean culture. By reading a story about Norigae and discussing its cultural significance, they can develop a deeper understanding of Korean culture and gain confidence in acculturating to it.

2 Learning Phenomenon

01 Suji goes through the first developmental stage, the declarative knowledge stage, in that she knows the rule of the third-person singular '-s' but is not able to use it correctly. Then, Ms. Kim gives direct correction to prevent Suji from permanently internalizing (fossilizing) the incorrect forms.

02 Ms. Park suggests that the errors are due to overgeneralization, whereas Ms. Kim thinks her students' errors are caused by interference (negative/interlingual transfer of L1). In the case of Ms. Kim, based on the contrastive analysis hypothesis, she believes if she teaches students all grammatical differences between English and Korean preemptively, their errors can be prevented.

03 ergative.
A certain phase underlined in <A> indicates backsliding where students go through in the learning process. For example, in the beginning, they use the verb "broke" in transitive and ergative context. However, at the next step, they recognize the ergative construction, "The vase broke" as an error.

04 In <B>, Juwan goes through 'fossilization' in that he keeps mispronouncing 'island' ['aɪlənd] into 'island' [áislənd], even following the teacher's repeated correct pronunciation of 'island' ['aɪlənd]. Also, Minju shows 'hypercorrection' in that she mispronounces even /l/ sound into /r/ sound caring too much for /r/ sound after the teacher's explicit correction on confusing sounds, /r/ and /l/.

Chapter 02 Classroom Context

1 Teaching Principles

01 Principle No. 4 is applied in Lesson B, where students choose the topic, *Mistery*, from the *available options* and select one activity such as discussion, creative writing, or a presentation. Principle No. 8 is exemplified in Lesson A, where the teacher offers two different writing tasks—a full paragraph and a 3-line reflection—catering to both higher and lower levels of ability.

02 Principle No. 2 is applied in Activity 1 where students do a schema building activity by predicting the positive and negative aspects of using a mobile phone in class before listening. Conversely, Principle No. 7 is utilized in Activity 4, which encourages students to think creatively by imagining the conclusion of the given story.

03 Design Principles, 'Focusing on listening strategies' and 'Providing interactive activities', are applied in Steps 2 and 3, respectively. In Step 2, students use listening strategies while individually writing down the main idea and key information about the accident, such as when, where, and why. In Step 3, they participate in interactive activities, including a group discussion and a Q&A session related to the presentations delivered by each group.

04 In Lesson 3, Ms. Yoo aims 'to provide students with real-life examples of the topic being studied' by showing a video documentary that introduces concrete instances of environmental challenges. Then, in Lesson 5, she intends 'to promote cultural awareness' about the civil rights movement by using the authentic material, the transcript of Martin Luther King, Jr.'s speech.

05 Both teachers want to apply Principle 4 for English only classroom. To achieve their goal, Ms. Park plans to provide students with more instructions in English and more group discussions. As for Ms. Yoo, she will use a reward system to incentivize students to speak more English in class.

06 Ms. Park applies two teaching principles: 'Focus on meaningful and authentic communication' and 'Encourage active listening for dynamic interaction'. First, by organizing a pair work and a group work, she asks students to share their memorable travel experience and their ideas, thoughts, and experiences for the best summer vacation plan. Besides, she teaches necessary interaction(al) strategies like how to ask for clarification and respond appropriately.

07 Ms. Park incorporates Suggestions (1) and (3) in her lesson. First, she presents authentic reading material about Word Festivals from a magazine, aiming to enhance both language acquisition and cultural awareness of the students. Also, she introduces essential learning strategies such as metacognitive strategies, so that students can be autonomous and independent learners.(autonomy)

08 Mr. Kim does not follow Strategies 3 and 4. Firstly, he uses advanced vocabulary instead of language accessible to all students in the whole-class activity of activating their schematic knowledge. Additionally, during the reading activity, he provides uniform feedback on content and language to students of all proficiency levels, rather than tailoring it to meet the specific needs of each group.

09 Ms. Park does not apply two principles: Principles (5) and (6). In Step 5, instead of giving students opportunities for self-correction, she provides correct language forms immediately. Besides, in Step 6, she assesses the target function, *prediction*, using a multiple-choice item test, not based on a communicative activity.

10 Suggestions (1) and (5) are not implemented in the lesson. Ms. Kim selects a culturally related topic after asking questions but does not identify students' cultural interests and needs through surveys or interviews. Additionally, she asks students to write reflections on their performances without providing feedback to support their learning.

Guideline for Pre-service Teachers

2 Textbook Evaluation or Modification

01 The most appropriate textbook for the teachers is Textbook B. Firstly, it offers a variety of activities suitable for students with different proficiency levels. Additionally, the textbook incorporates both focus on form and focus on forms instructions.

02 Textbook B is a suitable choice for the student for the following three reasons. Firstly, in relation to language proficiency, the vocabulary and grammar utilized in this textbook align with the student's desired intermediate level. Secondly, the textbook aids the student in developing all four language skills in a balanced manner. Finally, it offers a variety of activities that promote genuine interaction among students, including discussions and survey activities.

03 For Ms. Yoo, Textbook A is more suitable because it provides cultural guidance, various speech styles, and additional vocabulary and grammar learning. On the other hand, Textbook B is better suited for Ms. Park as it is designed for students with diverse proficiency levels and provides opportunities to use multimedia in lessons, along with the chance to learn various learning strategies.

04 Textbook A is a better choice for a new textbook. It improves upon the current book's presentation issues such as inappropriate font size, spacing and the lack of visual aids. Also, it offers comprehensive exercises and activities that cover not only listening and reading but also speaking and writing. Lastly, it includes content relevant to students' real lives, making up for the current textbooks' lack of motivation due to unfamiliar topics.

05 The underlying hypothesis of Ms. Park's primary criterion for text selection is the episode hypothesis. According to both teachers, episodic stories can be more engaging and relatable for students of all proficiency levels, as they closely mirror real-life experiences. Consequently, these stories are easier for students to understand and remember.

06 According to the teacher's note, News script A is preferred as it uses authentic spoken language. It naturally progresses information with appropriate transitions like 'Let's go live', and 'Well, now'. It also includes conversational elements such as fillers ('well', 'you know') and colloquial language ('go live', 'cool stuff').

07 Mr. Kim and Ms. Park choose Textbook B, which lacks advanced grammar exercises and sufficient opportunities for speaking practice. To compensate for these shortcomings, they plan to supplement the textbook with online grammar exercises and hold speaking workshops every two weeks.

08 Mr. Park applies 'adding' for textbook adaptation. To compensate for the lack of speaking activities, he expands some new types of speaking activities such as role-plays and discussions. Whereas, Ms. Yoo employs 'simplifying' techniques to make the textbook more accessible to her students. Specifically, she rewords the reading text with easier vocabulary and grammar and breaks down the complex writing activities into several achievable steps.

09 Ms. Yoo has implemented 'simplifying' and 'adding' strategies for her students. First of all, she rewords 'Biodiversity' into 'The variety of plants and animals' to make the phrase more understandable for her students. Besides, she additionally provides supplementary materials such as a video clip and an infographic.

10 Ms. Park uses Replacement by changing the overly easy texts into the article with the same topic extracted from The New York Times, which is more authentic, appropriate and challenging for her advanced students. On the other hand, Mr. Jung employs Reordering in that he rearranges reading chapters, Chapter 7. K-pop culture, first, Chapter 5. Future jobs, second and lastly, Chapter 1. Social Media, to accelerate students' motivation.

11 Ms. Kim asks Mr. Choi for advice on supplementary materials and text modifications to match students' current level. First, he suggests adding multimedia resources such as podcasts, videos, and interactive games related to the textbook themes. Then, he advises simplifying more difficult vocabulary or complex grammatical structures to align with students' proficiency level.

12 First, pre-listening videos and websites related to the topic are requested to give students background information and activate their schematic knowledge. Next, more group activities, such as problem-solving tasks and discussions are needed to promote meaningful communication among students. Finally, freer writing exercises will be prepared to diversify the current types of writing activities.

> Guideline for Pre-service Teachers

13 Ms. Lee wants to adapt the classroom material by individualizing it based on her students' learning style and proficiency levels. First, she adds a video watching activity when introducing the topic in the modified version. In terms of language, she simplifies the original text 'Storytelling Tips' using simpler vocabulary such as 'Interesting' and 'Start', instead of 'Engaging' and 'Opening'.

14 The teachers consider two factors—'Task' and 'Learner'—to adjust the difficulty of the task. First, they help students build confidence for the actual presentation by providing a 30-minute rehearsal period. Additionally, they aim to bridge the students' knowledge gap and increase engagement by showing an additional video clip followed by a Q&A session.

15 Ms. Lee lowers the difficulty of the original task based on factors (1) and (5). First, she adds two sub-steps to the original task: Topic-related vocabulary, and Planning and rehearsal. Second, she provides students with various forms of assistance such as pre-teaching vocabulary, guiding questions, and a writing template.

3 Classroom Observation or Course Evaluation

01 First, students will be able to describe what to buy using target vocabulary related to colors, fabrics and clothing items. Next, students will be able to use appropriate sentence stress to convey their exact meaning (or to solve miscommunication).

02 The two lesson objectives, 'listen to a dialogue and take notes on details,' and 'revise a writing based on grammatical feedback', are realized in Stage 3 and Stage 4, respectively. In Stage 3, students jot down as much additional information as possible during the final listening session. In Stage 4, they refine their group summary by correcting errors in the original text based on grammatical feedback from another group.

03 For receptive skills, students can "identify the main idea and details from a written text" in Step 3. They skim the text to find the gist and answer five comprehension questions about the details. For productive skills, students "organize ideas logically and coherently in writing tasks" in Steps 5 and 6. In groups, they write a clear and logical paragraph about environmental protection ideas, then refine it with peer feedback to ensure clarity and coherence.

04 The lesson excels in the Affective aspects, with the teacher effectively building strong rapport with students through active class interactions. However, Lesson preparation should be improved as some speaking activities are overly complex for the students' current level of proficiency.

05 The student participates in Teacher B's lesson. First, Teacher B directly demonstrates the example activity while circling or crossing out dream jobs with students. Next, she confirms students' understanding of the activity procedure by saying "What do you circle?" and "What do you cross out?".

4 Instructional Techniques(classroom activities) or Syllabus

01 Syllabus A is a functional syllabus, whereas Syllabus B is a structural one. According to the e-mail, the teachers should use Syllabus A. First, it introduces specific language functions such as 'greeting people' and 'asking for/giving personal information'. Besides, it provides students with communicative activities like role-play, and simulation, so that they can use the functions in real-life contexts.

02 Skills and activities in <B> do not align with the teachers' ideas. The syllabus focuses solely on listening and speaking skills and does not include reading skills. Additionally, it only covers structured role-play and dialogue practice, rather than group discussions and survey.

03 Syllabus B is suitable for Ms. Kim in that it consists of lessons centered on predetermined rules and patterns to give students a strong foundation for grammar and sentence structure. Conversely, for Mr. Choi, Syllabus A is more appropriate. It introduces lessons based on real-world tasks and specific pedagogical tasks aiming to develop students' communication skills.

04 Teacher A plays the role of 'Teacher as Director,' guiding the smooth and efficient flow of the debate by providing directions regarding specific roles (for and against), time management, and rules. On the other hand, Teacher B acts as a 'Teacher as Facilitator,' allowing students to choose the topic, like 'movies' and providing them with helpful words such as *'genres,' 'funny,' 'laugh,' and 'joke.'*

05 For Minsoo, the most suitable activity is Blindfolding. This activity aligns with his preference for learning through physical movement, making him act based on verbal directions as the 'follower.' For Jisoo, Reported Interview is ideal. It involves pair interviews, and collaborative writing, which suits Jisoo's strengths in interaction and collaboration.

06 Task 2 is appropriate for Mr. Park while Task 3, for Ms. Yoo. In Task 2, low intermediate students can describe Minji's daily routines based on the given pictures only using the simple present tense as Mr. Park desires. In Task 3, high intermediate students can complete the initial draft of the summary by answering a series of questions after reading a short story as Ms. Yoo plans.

07 The "Culture capsule" is utilized in this activity. Students view a brief video clip that outlines the distinctions between Chuseok and Thanksgiving Day, which are holidays celebrated in Korea and America, respectively. They discuss the similarities and differences between these two holidays. After creating a group script, they engage in a role-play activity that allows them to apply integrated skills, specifically writing and speaking.

08 Student A participates in a jigsaw activity with the following characteristics: required interaction, a convergent goal orientation, and a closed outcome. Conversely, Student B is involved in a decision-making task with the following characteristics: optional interaction, a convergent goal orientation, and an open-ended outcome.

09 In this lesson, two main problems have emerged: the inappropriateness of the activity (being overly demanding) and difficulties in communication and collaboration within groups. To address these issues, Ms. Park plans to introduce a 'reasoning gap activity' as an alternative, and implement mixed-level grouping where low level students are paired with high level students.

10 In Classroom 1, the teacher demonstrates semantic modification by paraphrasing a difficult word like 'protagonist' into a simpler term as 'main character'. In contrast, in Classroom 2, the teacher employs syntactic modification by decomposing a complex question into two simpler ones, "what do trees need to be healthy and strong?" and "how can we help them grow?".

11 Ms. Park applies two categories, 'modifications of interaction' and 'modifications of information choice' to her teacher talk for her students. First, she uses pauses between words for 1.0 or 1.5 seconds. Besides, she explicitly develops the logic of the narrative by adding extra information such as 'this tin is to collect money', and 'he was begging people'.

12 In conversation 1, the teacher poses an application question by encouraging students to apply the information they read about renewable energy to the new situation: their school environment. On the other hand, the teacher's question in Conversation 2 is a knowledge question, designed to immediately test recall and recognition of learned information, 'evaporation'.

13 App 1 Bookopolis, is recommended for Sarah because it offers personalized book recommendations and online discussions that align with her needs. On the other hand, App3 LitPick, is ideal for Jaewon, as it provides a platform for sharing his critiques with young readers in a global community.

14 Tool 4 is a perfect fit for Teacher 1, as it enables him/her to assess students' vocabulary and grammar knowledge and fosters healthy rivalry among students while providing instant results. Meanwhile, Tool 3 is ideal for Teacher 2, allowing students to upload their speaking presentations on a given topic and share peer feedback.

15 Tool B is best for Ms. Jang due to three key characteristics. First, it is equipped with supportive features, such as subtitles and text-to-speech technology, which are beneficial for low-level students. Second, it offers real-time feedback to help students self-correct. Lastly, it provides detailed analytics on students' performance and learning progress, which is valuable for educators.

16 App 2 is well-suited for Teacher 1 as it facilitates explicit vocabulary lessons, adjusting the content to each student's proficiency level through adaptive learning algorithms. In contrast, App 5 enables Teacher 2 to provide listening exercises targeting various listening strategies, such as focusing on identifying specific information and key details, along with real-time application of these strategies.

17 App 2 can assist Jaejoon in practicing natural conversations, similar to interactions with native speakers, while providing feedback on his pronunciation. In contrast, App 3 is ideal for Sunghee as it offers a vocabulary learning game tailored to her language proficiency level and allows her to track the learning progress.

5 Learner Variables

01 Yongwoo demonstrates reflectivity and introversion, needing time or writing to organize his thoughts, which can delay his responses. He prefers working independently on research or writing projects, where he feels fulfilled and recharges. In contrast, Dahae displays impulsivity and extroversion, enjoying spontaneous situations where she can express herself. She, also, prefers taking on the role of group leader in collaborative group projects or activities.

02 Activity 1 requires students to use both 'cognitive' and 'interpersonal' strategies by first predicting the content of a telephone message based on a bicycle shop advertisement and then cooperating with each other while comparing their predictions. On the other hand, Activity 2 emphasizes a 'linguistic' strategy, where students engage in selective listening to identify specific numbers mentioned in the story.

03 Version 1
Ms. Kim wants to teach her students one of the indirect strategies, metacognitive strategies to help them be skilled readers. To achieve this, she applies a think-aloud technique by verbalizing her thoughts as she reads a story.

Version 2
Ms. Kim wants to teach her students metacognitive strategies which belong to the indirect strategies so that they can plan and monitor their reading process. To facilitate students' metacognitive strategies, she demonstrates a think-aloud technique by verbalizing her thoughts as she reads a story.

04 Student A employs Strategy 2, whereas Student B uses Strategy 4. Specifically, while silently reading a text, Student A can enhance his reading speed, thereby improving his fluency. Conversely, through semantic mapping, Student B can organize a complex story structure, facilitating better comprehension without being overwhelmed by the lengthy narrative.

05 Minsoo uses two communication strategies: prefabricated patterns and keeping the floor. First, he uses memorized expressions for asking the price or for trying the sneakers on by saying "How much?" and "Can I try these?". Next, when he cannot recall what he memorized, he uses fillers such as "well", "I mean" and "like" to fill the pauses and gain time to think.

06 In this dialogue, S1 and S2 show uptake in their utterances. After the teacher's feedback, by saying "It's an animal hops around the ponds and swims.", S1 uses circumlocution to describe the animal he refers to. Whereas, saying "They have...sort of... Never mind.", S2 displays message abandonment as he doesn't complete his message, likely due to language difficulty.

07 Ms. Kim plans to teach 'circumlocution' to the higher-level students and 'clarification request' to the lower-level students. With circumlocution strategy, the higher-level can easily describe or exemplify unknown words that the lower-level do not understand. Additionally, the clarification request strategy enables the lower-level to ask for clarification on the preceding utterance while expressing their lack of understanding to the higher-level.

08 In the presentations, Min-ho employs a syntactic avoidance strategy by choosing 'future technology' as his topic to avoid using the past tense. On the other hand, when Ji-hyun forgets a fact, she uses an appeal to authority by indirectly seeking help from her teacher, indicated by her rising intonation (changing in pitch) and a confused expression (facial cue).

Chapter 03 Receptive Skills

1 How to Teach Listening Skills

01 The comments from Teachers 2 and 4 are misguided. First, the lesson is designed to engage students in attention to not only content but also language form during text reconstruction, meaning the lesson objective is about both content and structure. Moreover, the teacher acts as a facilitator, providing essential support to help students reconstruct the text, rather than controlling students in the process of text reconstruction.

02 To solve the problems of the listening lesson, the teacher should provide pre-listening activities before listening. As pre-listening activities, the pre-set questions should be provided so that students can get a clear purpose (authentic reason) for listening. Also, personal questions or photos related to the topic should be offered to activate students' schematic knowledge.

Guideline for Pre-service Teachers

03 Mr. Choi's listening procedure presents two challenges: the unfamiliarity of the topic and the demanding nature of the task. To address these issues, pre-listening activities can activate students' schematic knowledge and provide necessary information on unfamiliar topics. Additionally, a partial dictation activity can help students focus on listening itself and reduce their cognitive load by requiring them to dictate only keywords during the listening process.

04 Ms. Choi activates socio-cultural knowledge before listening by explaining the cultural context of 'tip culture'. On the other hand, Ms. Kim encourages students to draw upon their extratextual knowledge to connect with the reading topic. During the brainstorming session, she asks students to share their own experiences and ideas about future technology, the reading topic.

05 Ms. Yoo will teach Jaebum the concept of redundancy so that he can get additional information or processing time to clarify his misunderstanding. Also, she will teach Mina a scanning strategy which helps her selectively listen for specific information based on some pre-set questions.

06 In Steps 3 and 4, the teacher employs the information transfer technique that prompts students to convert auditory information into visual one by making them draw a picture or simply write down short phrases, respectively. This approach allows students to hone their listening skills by concentrating solely on auditory content, without the added burden of reading or writing tasks.

07 Activity A is a responsive type which requires only limited interaction. For instance, it facilitates meaningful language use while students shortly answer referential questions about their own ideas or experiences. However, Activity B is an extensive one which involves a story-telling activity about six pictures. Also, there is a lack of oral interaction from listeners including essential elements like the teacher's questions or feedback.

08 Ms. Park conducts extensive listening, where students can feel motivated and enjoy their listening based on their own chosen materials without any listening tasks to be completed. On the other hand, Mr. Kim adopts intensive listening, which helps accurate listening but covers a limited amount of content in time due to repeated listening (frequent stops).

2 How to Teach Reading Skills

01 Mr. Jung incorporates factors (2) and (3) into his lesson. He activates students' schemata by asking questions and provides background knowledge through a pre-reading video. He also teaches reading strategies such as predicting, skimming, scanning, and summarizing. However, he violates Principle C by using an authentic text with advanced vocabulary and grammar, which makes it difficult to balance authenticity with readability.

02 The two steps, While-reading and Assessment, does not align with the teacher's discussions. Specifically, the lesson focuses on predicting, skimming and scanning techniques during the reading but does not incorporate inferencing strategies. Additionally, the plan emphasizes a voting process for selecting the best script but lacks opportunities for students to provide peer feedback / specific feedback to one another.

03 Activity 1 focuses on Reading Comprehension, requiring students to engage in high-level thinking through on analysis questions about the story's mood, future events, and character traits. Activity 2 involves Book Talks, where students in pairs summarize the story and discuss character analysis, personal opinion, and recommendations in depth using a structured outline. Both activities promote a deeper understanding of the text.

04 Jihae's strong reading strategy is skimming, while her weak reading strategy is inferencing. To improve her inferencing skills, Ms. Park advises Jihae to read between the lines. That is, after asking herself questions such as "What does this line imply?" and "What details support that implication?" she should search for answers using personal experiences and textual clues from the passage.

05 Mr. Kim wants to teach predicting and inferencing strategies for his students. First, before listening, he provides students with the news title, 'Top 3 K-Movies', related photos, and 10 preset questions to help them predict what the news clip is about. Next, by giving two inferential level questions, he leads the students to infer the implied meaning and hidden intention based on some clues.

> Guideline for Pre-service Teachers

06 To enhance reading comprehension, Minjae utilizes the strategy, 'recognizing story structure'. Specifically, he attempts to understand the main idea better by analyzing the plot of the story and the relationships between characters. On the other hand, Eunhee's strategy focuses on 'answering questions'. She responds to comprehension questions that request explicit information, hidden meanings, and critical thinking.

3 How to Improve the Receptive Skills

01 For the development of listening skills, students can 'associate the topic with their prior knowledge and opinions' as they share their ideas on the topic with their partners during Step 4. When it comes to enhancing their reading skills, students can 'engage in a group activity using textual and extratextual information' in Step 8 where they have a group discussion using given information and personal experiences.

02 Questions (1) and (2) are evaluative and inferential level, respectively. First off, Question (2) can help Jihye think beyond the surface level of a text and predict the outcome using her personal experiences. Whereas, Question (1) can provide an opportunity for Jungho to make judgements about the writer's opinions based on his own knowledge related to the topic.

03 Questions with literal comprehension are easy for Sungjin because the answers are explicitly stated in the passage. However, questions with critical comprehension are overwhelming for him to answer as they require him to critically analyze the writer's intention, drawing on his personal experience and knowledge.

04 The original comprehension question given by T2 requires an inferential level in that students need to infer the implied information in the text. However, inferencing is too demanding for low intermediate students in T1's class. Accordingly, T1 suggests the literal comprehension questions (level) in that they can easily find the answers in the text.

05 In Stage 1 and Stage 3, students are expected to use both levels of processing. In Stage 1, they elicit their prior knowledge and new information about the metaverse through a video clip. Also, they preview some words and phrases extracted from the text before reading. Also, in Stage 3, they should answer some questions of literal and inferential levels. That is, they find out information stated in the text and beyond the text.

06 Activity 1 focuses on literal comprehension and Activity 2 requires interpretive comprehension. In Activity 1, the answers to whether the sentences indicate facts or opinions are explicitly written in the text. As for Activity 2, the two why questions make students infer the answers which are not directly stated in the story.

Chapter 04 Productive Skills

본문 p. 250

1 How to Teach Speaking Skills

01 Activity 2 is best for Student 1 because it allows students in smaller, supportive groups to engage in discussions that focus on fluency over accuracy, while receiving private feedback and personalized encouragement from the teacher. Additionally, weekly reflection sessions help track their progress. Activity 4 is ideal for Student 2 as it allows students to explore word meanings and practice usage through group activities, weekly reviews, and role-playing.

02 Eunha has applied Microskills (1), whereas Sungjin has used Macroskill (3). For example, Eunha produces reduced forms of words and phrases, such as saying "comin'" and "gettin'". On the other hand, Sungin uses constrastive markers like "but", and "nevertheless" in conversation.

03 Tip No. 2 is applied in Activity 3, where students collaboratively decide among three options for the theme of the upcoming class party. Next, Tip No. 6 is demonstrated in Activity 1, which provides differentiated support for students of varying proficiency levels: more fluent students are asked to choose Card A based on lengthy directions without support, while less fluent students select Card B with the aid of a table and useful expressions.

04 Ms. Yoo incorporates 'Genre Structure' into her teaching by providing the basic framework for debates and conventional expressions associated with each structure. However, she does not allow students to choose the topic, instead providing the predetermined one, which goes against Principle (4).

05 Ms. Kim emphasizes Colloquial Expressions and Reduced Forms in each listening activity. First, she wants her students to enhance their understanding of spoken English phrases, such as "Catch some Z's" and "hustle", commonly used in daily life. Next, she aims to improve their comprehension of the fast and natural flow of speech, focusing on contractions like "gimme" and "lemme".

06 Student A learns colloquial language, while Student B focuses on performance variables. By mastering idioms such as "break a leg", Student A is able to converse fluently and comprehend the informal language usage of native speakers with ease. On the other hand, Student B uses fillers like "I mean" and "You know" to bridge pauses and hesitations, thereby having a smoother flow of speech.

07 The speaking activity is an information gap activity, promoting a transactional dialogue. While performing this activity, students in pairs communicate to convey specific information and also negotiate to confirm the information for taking the order of some items including the customer's name and address, item number, quantity, etc.

08 Kyuhee practices Vowel and Consonant Combination Drills, repeating words including "at" and "ba" sounds in chorus. Meanwhile, Wonji engages in Role-play Practice mimicking a restaurant setting, focusing on appropriate intonation patterns based on different contexts such as rising for questions and falling for expressions of gratitude/politeness.

09 Teaching Procedure 1 targets articulation, focusing on the formation and the production of specific sounds, /p/ and /f/, or words accurately, while Teaching Procedure 2 centers around intonation, encouraging students to practice the rise and fall of pitch and different melodic patterns in the phrase "you're going" to show meaning differences about different intentions.

10 Teacher A takes a bottom-up approach, while Teacher B, a top-down approach. To be specific, Teacher A asks students to distinguish confusing sounds, [b] and [v], by providing minimal pairs. Teacher B makes students discern the implied meanings of 'I didn't say he stole your money' based on stress modulation of a sentence in discourse context.

11 Intelligibility.

To address the pronunciation issues that Mr. Jin's students are experiencing with individual sounds, Ms. Kim suggests the use of meaningful/contextualized minimal pairs. This approach enables students to distinguish confusing sounds within a meaningful context (sentence), thereby naturally comprehending the distinctions in meaning.

12 The lesson's strength lies in the topic relevant to students' real lives. However, a notable challenge is students' lack of abilities to articulate their arguments effectively. To solve this problem, in Step 3, the teacher should provide a list of key expressions to construct their opinions fluently. Additionally, in Step 4, the teacher should allocate time for preparation (rehearsal) before the actual debate.

13 Classroom 1 employs strategies (2) and (5), where the teacher poses questions about students' dream vacation destinations and delays error correction until the end of the activity, taking notes on common errors during the activity. Classroom 2 implements strategies (3) and (4), where students corrects the pronunciation error from [fam] to [pɑːm] following the meaning negotiation prompt 'Can you say that again?' and engage in peer evaluation, offering feedback on each other's description.

14 In response to the student's error, the teacher uses feedback No 2, No 4, and finally No 5. When the student does not recognize the errors through the teacher's implicit feedback, the teacher progressively provides more explicit feedback, leading the student to eventually self-correct the error.

15 In Conversation 1, the teacher conducts an accuracy-based activity where he/she interrupts the conversation to provide feedback. This includes pinpointing and metalinguistic feedback, aiming to immediately address the mistake related to past perfect tense. In Conversation 2, a teacher conducts a fluency-based activity by giving feedback through recast after the activity to maintain the flow of the students' conversation about last weekend.

16 Excessive error correction and frequent interruptions during a speaking activity by Ms. Choi demotivate her students and raise their affective filter. As a solution, Ms. Park will suggest that Ms. Choi allow her students to engage in the speaking activity without interruption first, and then address any errors later in a follow-up treatment.

> Guideline for Pre-service Teachers

17 The teacher provides implicit feedback, recast without overtly indicating the student's error, saying "She bought a car!" Immediately reacting to the teacher's feedback, also, the student successfully repairs the error, saying, "Yes, she bought a car."

18 The teacher provides negative feedback for Junho by asking 'Your favorite hobby is…?, while he only gives Minji positive feedback by saying 'That's impressive' and 'Great'. Accordingly, Junho can correct his error by changing 'paint' into 'painting' but Minji can not. Giving no negative feedback on Minji's error can lead to fossilization of her incorrect use of 'either'.

19 Firstly, the teacher gives a recast as a form of implicit feedback, stating "He is planting a tree! However, due to Seojoon's repeated errors, the teacher adopts metalinguistic feedback, an explicit type of feedback, asking 'Do you remember how to use the present progressive?'. Finally, the teacher uses elicitation, saying 'Three children are?' in an attempt to prompt the correct form from Seojoon.

20 pushed output.
In the conversation, the teacher uses repetition that repeats the ill-formed part of the student's utterance such as "watches?". Besides, she uses elicitation saying "how do we say it already happened?" to prompt/elicit the student to self-correct.

21 Example 1 exemplifies Option A2 in that students practice using the predetermined target form—past simple tense—such as 'played' and 'went' while talking about their favorite childhood memories. Meanwhile, Example 2 represents Option B2 since the teacher reactively corrects the students' errors observed during discussion by providing the correct forms, 'should try' and 'can help'.

2 How to Teach Writing Skills

01 The teacher does not adhere to Guidelines #3 and #6. Instead of allowing ideas to flow freely through freewriting, she/he asks students to directly write the first drafts. Additionally, she/he requires students to make only one-time revision based on peer feedback, rather than encouraging multiple revisions to refine their writing.

02 Jongmin describes 'Using pre-writing devices' such as watching a short video and brainstorming about the topic as the most helpful strategy. On the other hand, Mina considers 'Using feedback for revising and editing' to be the most important. Thanks to two rounds of peer feedback, she first revised the content of her writing, and then corrected its grammatical and punctuation errors.

03 Eunmi engages in Self-writing through journaling, where she reflects on and expresses her thoughts and emotions without worrying about her teacher's opinions. In contrast, Haesol focuses on Display writing, showcasing the knowledge he gained from his research on water pollution in his paper.

04 For Mr. Park, Activity 1 is the best fit, as it involves students changing past tense to past perfect, using/copying well-structured texts to reinforce good grammar and effective writing. For Ms. Oh, Activity 2 is more suitable, where students draft their writing about 'My Favorite Memory' and then revise it based on peer feedback, enhancing their expressive ability.

05 Ms. Park recommends a dictocomp as a writing activity for Ms. Yoo to address her students' writing weaknesses. Within this activity, students can learn how to use the target grammar appropriately and contextualize sentences properly in paragraphs by rewriting the model text.

06 The writing activity presented in <A> is a dicto-composition(dictocomp). However, both students encounter difficulties in recalling and accurately rewriting the text independently. Thus, as a solution, Student 1 hopes to have visual aids, such as pictures related to the story, while Student 2 wishes to engage in group activities with students of a higher level.

07 Activity Procedure 1 represents real writing, where students express personal experiences in reflective journal entries related to the lesson. The teacher remains unaware of the content. In Activity Procedure 2, display writing is showcased. Here, students rewrite the paragraph, changing verb tenses from present to future, while the teacher already knows the correct answer.

> Guideline for Pre-service Teachers

08 **Version 1**

Ms. Park identifies the two advantages of the Error Correction Code (ECC) system: the precision of the feedback and the opportunity for students to self-correct their errors. However, the student points out a couple of weaknesses with this tool. Firstly, it does not provide enough information on the source of errors or how to avoid them in the future. Secondly, it focuses solely on grammar, neglecting the overall picture of the written work such as content and organization.

Version 2

While Ms. Park identifies the two advantages of the Error Correction Code (ECC) system, the student points out a couple of weaknesses. It can bring the precision of the feedback and provide the opportunity for students to self-correct their errors. However, it does not provide enough information on the source of errors or how to avoid them in the future. Also, it focuses solely on grammar, neglecting the overall picture of the written work such as content and organization.

09 Ms. Park's writing course excels in the criteria of instructional materials, but it faces weaknesses in the areas of feedback and assessment. To strengthen weaknesses, Ms. Park needs to utilize the untimed online class blog so that students can get more opportunities for feedback. Also, she should add holistic assessments(rubric/evaluation) to comprehensively evaluate students' overall writing skills.

10 The teacher focuses on conventions and content in writing evaluation. First, the teacher evaluates students' adherence to established rules in writing English, including spelling, punctuation, capitalization, and legible handwriting. Next, he/she assesses the organization of the writing based on its logical structure as well as cohesion and coherence, by examining the connection between sentences and the smooth flow of ideas.

11 As an alternative, Ms. Yoo can utilize the Error Correction Code (ECC). By indicating only major errors instead of providing corrections for all kinds of errors, she would enable Minsu to reduce the potential frustration and also self-correct his mistakes as he wishes.

Chapter 05 Vocabulary & Grammar

본문 p. 330

1 How to Teach Vocabulary

01 Sunmi engages in incidental learning, picking up new words as a beneficial byproduct while her primary focus is on reading a story (or a book). In contrast, Jihoon demonstrates intentional learning by actively creating new words through the process of adding suffixes to basic words, as a form of word formation.

02 Dictionary 1 highlights the collocations by showing which words frequently occur with 'innovative' like 'innovative approach' and 'innovative technology.' In contrast, Dictionary 2 focuses on grammatical patterns, such as the typical positions of 'innovative' in a sentence: appearing before a noun, as in 'innovative idea' and following a linking verb as in 'is innovative.'

03 Teaching Procedure 1 focuses on 'Meaning,' by helping students explore the different (multiple) meanings of the word "charge" depending on the context. In contrast, Teaching Procedure 2 emphasizes "Register" by helping students determine the level of formality or informality at which the word "consult" is used. This approach also guides students in using the word commonly in fields like legal or academic context.

04 Activity 1 and Activity 2 focus on connotations and register, respectively. In Activity 1, students explore assigned words, analyzing their different implied meanings—positive, negative, or neutral—based on two different sentences from the concordance. Conversely, in Activity 2, students examine the formality and usage field of words by reviewing two concordance sentences.

05 Ms. Kim emphasizes the importance of teaching vocabulary within context. In this lesson, thus, she encourages students to use a guessing strategy, which is to deduce the meaning of the underlined words by utilizing contextual clues within the text or their existing knowledge beyond the text.

06 The activity procedure in <B> is based on the lexicogrammatical approach: first, students examine collocations of key verbs, 'take, make, and have' from corpus data. Next, they have the opportunity to focus on grammatical structure of each phrasal (lexical) verb such as 'verb +(a/an) noun' or 'verb + adjective'.

> Guideline for Pre-service Teachers

07 Test item 1 assesses students' breadth of vocabulary knowledge by requiring them to match words with their primary meanings, thereby gauging their basic understanding of words. On the other hand, Test item 2 measures the depth of students' vocabulary knowledge by asking them to select words that match the semantic and collocational characteristics of the given word.

2 How to Teach Grammar

01 Based on Practice 4, Student 1 learns the present perfect tense through practice and application by first completing sentences and then writing short essays about events from the past year. On the other hand, Student 2 learns about adverb clauses to provide additional information while editing a recipe, showcasing the unplanned grammar teaching of Practice 1.

02 Most teachers prefer Activity 2, which includes Dictogloss and Input enhancement. First, the activity requires students to listen to a short text on friendship and then reconstruct it, focusing on grammar, specifically relative clauses. Second, the original text is provided with the relative clauses (target forms), highlighted in bold for emphasis, making them easily noticeable to students.

03 Lesson A takes a deductive approach where the teacher explicitly teaches the target form, superlatives, and then later provides example sentences for practice. On the other hand, Lesson B uses an inductive approach in that the teacher gives examples of the comparisons in context and asks students to discover when to use comparative and superlative forms by themselves.

04 In the activity procedure, two grammar techniques are used: 'Using input enhancement' and 'Using charts, tables, or drawings'. In Step 5, the target forms—passive voice—like 'was left', 'was trapped' and 'being crushed', are highlighted by underlining and boldfacing. Later, in Step 9, the table activity is utilized to assess the students' comprehension on the target forms.

05 Activity 2 is the most suitable form-focused activity for improving students' speaking skills for two reasons. First, it offers contextualized practice by integrating the present perfect tense within the theme of traveling abroad. Additionally, it encourages students to personalize the language by allowing them to share their own experiences of traveling to different places like Japan, Vietnam and New York.

06 Ms. Park arranges the structured input activity for two specific reasons. First, she wants students to make form-meaning connections in the input so that they can give priority to meaning and then focus on form. Also, she wants to improve students' input processing skills without the pressure of language production.

07 The teacher introduces a consciousness-raising task to the students, citing the two benefits. Firstly, this task fosters active learning (participation) and autonomy among students by encouraging them to deduce the target rule from the provided examples. Secondly, it promotes peer interaction by providing mutual support and assistance on the usage of past and past perfect tense in groups.

08 ⓐ: use, ⓑ: form, ⓒ: meaning
Step 3 does not align with the teacher's belief in <A>. In Step 3, the teacher uses the input enhancement technique by highlighting the target form, 'be+~ing' in bold, instead of using the input processing technique.

Chapter 06 Assessment

1 Testing Principles

01 Teachers 3 and 5 provide incorrect interpretations regarding aspects of the test. First, the fact that the assessment task has never been implemented in the classroom suggests concerns over its content validity—whether it accurately measures what needs to be assessed—rather than its reliablity. Moreover, the use of a pilot test aims to ensure the appropriate format and difficulty of the assessment task, not item discrimination of the test.

02 Ms. Park's testing method lacks construct validity, practicality, and intra-rater reliability. Firstly, she uses a rubric that mainly grades speaking skills, but neglects writing criteria. Secondly, she struggles to assess 30 students' oral and written works for a single day. Lastly, she unfairly gives scores based on in-class fluency regardless of test performance.

03 Teachers 1 and 4 provide incorrect feedback on the writing test. The rubric does not reflect all the essential sub-components of writing, as it focuses only on content, vocabulary, and organization, excluding grammar and mechanics. Additionally, scoring between evaluators is inconsistent, as seen with Jungmin's content receiving a 2 from Teacher A and a 5 from Teacher B, indicating unreliability.

04 Ms. Lee points out that Mr. Park's speaking test has some problems with practicality and (inter-)rater reliability. First, conducting five types of speaking tests which take 5 or 10 minutes per test for 40 students does not seem practical timewise. Also, the evaluation results from two scorers are inconsistent. For example, in the interview, Student A gets score of 18 from Mr. Park but 10 from Mr. Kim.

05 authenticity.
Mr. Park chooses Test 1 based on Criterion 2, whose all items are contextualized.

06 Construct validity and washback are poorly applied in the speaking test. First, the scoring rubric only consists of three criteria, pronunciation, content, and grammar, minus fluency and appropriateness, which should be included. Also, the test result does not give students any diagnostic information on what problems are and how to solve them.

2 Testing Purpose, Types, and Methods

01 The Purpose and Scoring Procedure in <B> do not align with the teachers' ideas. The purpose outlined in the test specifications suggests a placement test, not a diagnostic test for assessing students' speaking abilities as the teachers plan. Additionally, the specifications indicate that if two examiners disagree, they will average their scores, without provision for involving a third examiner.

02 According to the test plan, statements (1) and (6) are incorrect. The first one should be "I'm setting up a diagnostic test for our 3rd graders". The second one should be "I will use an analytic scoring system"

03 analytic.
Eunjin has been assessed using Rubric A, which evaluates four components of speaking ability and provides detailed feedback. This allows her to strategically plan her future learning. Based on her excellence in fluency, scoring 5 out of 5, and her weakness in grammar, scoring only 1, she will focus her future learning efforts.

04 Teachers 2 and 5 misinterpret the test results. The essay section evaluates three specific elements rather than overall writing quality. Additionally, the test taker provides clear background information and a natural tone, earning a good evaluation in the composition section, not a poor one.

05 Teachers 3 and 5 misinterpret the proficiency test and its results. The student struggles with reading complex texts and spontaneous conversation, scoring 2 out of 5 in both areas. These issues highlight significant challenges in both reading and speaking skills. The test assesses overall language proficiency, covering listening, speaking, reading, writing, vocabulary, and grammar and provides detailed insights, supported by specific feedback.

06 achievement.
Mr. Kim should take Test B, a criterion-referenced test. This test measures each student's performance as a pass or a fail based on the predetermined achievement standard of 'score over 25', which allows him to identify who needs additional work or does not.

07 Type B, known as Criterion-referenced testing, is ideal for Ms. Park. It allows her to measure student achievement against set standards instead of relative to other students. Additionally, it facilitates personalized feedback for students, directing them to improve their identified weak areas.

08 readability.
In Test type A, students deduce an appropriate word from multi-contextual clues while reading a gap-filling text and thereby utilizing calculated guesses based on their linguistic expectations and background information.

3. Alternative Assessment

01 The alternative assessment used in <A> is self-assessment. In Sunjin's reflection, she evaluates her performance subjectively, leading to discrepancies between her self-assessment and the teacher's evaluation. To address this issue, Sunjin suggests that the teacher hold one-on-one conferences (review session) to offer specific feedback on the areas where her speaking performance needs improvement.

02 The assessment type is a portfolio, which can address the students' complaints. First, it evaluates the works that students have done in class, as S1 desires. Next, through regular feedback and conferences with the teacher, it allows students like S2 to track their progress or achievement over a specific period. Finally, as S3 believes, it can be tailored to different proficiency levels by having students set their own learning goals.

03 The teacher intends to implement portfolios as an alternative assessment for the students. By collecting a variety of student works, the teacher can more effectively gauge the students' progress and proficiency (achievement) in different skills. Also, this method allows the teacher to provide students with continuous evaluation and timely feedback.

04 rehearsal.
Mr. Kim utilizes peer assessment to evaluate students' group presentations for two reasons. Firstly, he aims to engage students in the assessment process, enabling them to take ownership and responsibility for their learning. Additionally, he seeks to foster collaborative learning by encouraging students to share feedback and suggestions on each other's presentations.

05 Fluency.
As solutions, Ms. Park first organizes a training session to prevent inconsistent interpretations of criteria. This allows students to understand the meaning of each criterion and practice its effective application using a sample speech. Additionally, she introduces a new criterion, 'delivery', to supplement presentation skills such as maintaining eye contact with the audience and controlling voice volume.

4 Multiple-choice Item Testing

01 There are issues with Questions 1 and 3 for the following reasons. In Question 1, two options, A) enhance and D) increase, could both be considered correct, which presents a problem because only one answer should be provided. In Question 3, the presence of the article "a" within the question inadvertently hints that Option C) rock is the correct answer.

02 Item 1 should be revised due to its poor item discrimination, which has a value of 0.2. Additionally, Item 2 should be modified because it includes a non-functional distractor, Distractor D, which does not fool anyone.

03 Items 2 and 3 are problematic. First, Item 2 measures students' knowledge of the world, resulting in negative item discrimination in which the low group chooses correct answers more than the high group does. Next, in Item 3, the lexical category of Distractor ⑤ is different from the other options, and thus, no one selects it.

04 The table in <B> presents the results of item facility and distractor analysis for each item. Item 3 appears problematic as it contains a non-functional option, Option C, which was not selected by any test-takers. Additionally, Item 5 exhibits a notably low item facility, 0.1, with only 8 students choosing the correct answer, Option C, but 65 students choosing Distractor B.

05 Item 1 is problematic because the same percentage of students in each group choose option d, the correct answer. Thus, since it shows zero item discrimination between the upper and the lower groups. it should be revised.

06 (1) alternatives, (2) distractors.
The two items, Q1 and Q2, violate Rule 1 and Rule 4, respectively. First, the stem in Q1 is not meaningful in that it does not give a concrete problem. Next, in Q2, the stem is constructed with an interior blank, instead of a question or a partial sentence format.

Build Up
박현수 영어교육론 Ⅳ-2 문제은행 [서술형]
Guideline for Pre-service Teachers

초판인쇄	2025. 7. 10.	**초판발행**	2025. 7. 15.	**편저자**	박현수
발행인	박 용	**발행처**	(주)박문각출판	**표지디자인**	박문각 디자인팀

등록 | 2015년 4월 29일 제2019-000137호
주소 | 06654 서울시 서초구 효령로 283 서경빌딩　**팩스** | (02)584-2927
전화 | 교재주문·학습문의 (02)6466-7202

저자와의
협의하에
인지생략

이 책의 무단 전재 또는 복제 행위는 저작권법 제136조에 의거, 5년 이하의 징역 또는 5,000만 원 이하의 벌금에 처하거나 이를 병과할 수 있습니다.

정가 45,000원(1, 2권 포함)
ISBN 979-11-7262-948-9　|　ISBN 979-11-7262-946-5(세트)